The Story of
ASIA'S ELEPHANTS

The Story of
ASIA'S ELEPHANTS

Raman Sukumar

Marg

General Editor PRATAPADITYA PAL
Text Editor RIVKA ISRAEL
Senior Executive Editor SAVITA CHANDIRAMANI
Senior Editorial Executive ARNAVAZ K. BHANSALI
Editorial Executive RAHUL D'SOUZA
Designer NAJU HIRANI
Senior Production Executive GAUTAM V. JADHAV
The design concept of this book is based on *The Story of Asia's Lions*, the first title in the series

November 2011
Price: ₹ 3500.00 / US$ 82.00
ISBN: 978-93-80581-10-1
Library of Congress Catalog Card Number: 2011-312023

The Asian Nature Conservation Foundation will receive 5% of the net sales value of each copy sold

Marg is a registered trademark of The Marg Foundation
© The Marg Foundation and Raman Sukumar, 2011
All rights reserved

Published by Radhika Sabavala for The Marg Foundation at
Army & Navy Building (3rd Floor), 148, M.G. Road, Mumbai 400 001, India.
Printed at Spenta Multimedia, Mumbai and Processed at The Marg Foundation, Mumbai.

Unless otherwise credited, all photographs are from the author's collection.
In case of images from other sources, every attempt has been made to contact copyright holders.
Pages 2–3: A young tusked bull in association with an older tuskless bull elephant at Kaziranga.
Photograph by Karpagam Chelliah.
Page 5: An elephant family socializing along the backwaters on Kabini reservoir in Karnataka.
Pages 6–7: An elephant family feeding at Kaziranga, Assam.
Pages 8–9: A female elephant feeding on bark at Nagarahole, Karnataka.
Page 9: Elephant motif on a haveli in Farrukhnagar, Haryana.
Photograph by Tanmay Tathagat.
Page 12: A young tusked bull cautiously approaching at Kaziranga, Assam.

**Marg wishes to thank Mr N. Srinivasan and The India Cements Ltd, Chennai
for generous support towards the purchase of images for this book**

To the Fond Memory
of
My Parents
and
My Grandparents

The Marg Foundation acknowledges the generous support of
The Corbett Foundation, a non-profit and non-governmental
organization established by Shri Dilip Khatau in 1994,
dedicated towards wildlife conservation, environmental
awareness, community health, tribal welfare, habitat
restoration, veterinary interventions, and sustainable
development in and around Corbett, Kanha, Bandhavgarh,
and Kaziranga tiger reserves and the Greater Rann of Kutch.

The Corbett Foundation is happy to partner
with The Marg Foundation for this publication which is
an excellent resource on the Asian elephant and will help
in the conservation of this magnificent species.

Contents

acknowledgements

IN SEPTEMBER 1986 I travelled by road from Bangalore to the hill-station Udhagamandalam (Ooty) along with Professors D.K. Lahiri-Choudhury and Madhav Gadgil. We could not take the more direct and interesting route through Mysore and the forests of Bandipur and Mudumalai, where we would have undoubtedly encountered wild elephants, because farmers had set up road blocks at places to make political demands from the government. We thus undertook the day-long journey through the more circuitous southern route along the cultivated plains of Tamil Nadu. Early in the drive, the conversation inevitably drifted towards the elephant, a creature that Professor Lahiri-Choudhury was fiercely passionate about, and that was the subject of my recently concluded doctoral thesis under the supervision of Professor Gadgil. The two professors entered into an animated discourse on the elephant-human relationship, a conversation that ended only when we reached our destination after sunset. Although I had been investigating the negative aspects of the elephant-human interaction, or the conflict between the two species, and was dimly aware of the significance of elephant symbolism in Indian culture, this discourse was fascinating stuff. I tucked away at the back of my mind the possibility of a book on the subject, an idea that I was able to work upon only two decades later.

In the course of several years of researching and travel for this book, a large number of people have helped me through discussions, clarifying doubts, hosting me and transporting me to historical monuments, and procuring references and images. They include, in no particular order, V. Nanjundaiah, Razi Aquil, Nayanjot Lahiri, R. Nagaswamy, S. Balasubramanian, M.R.N. Murthy, S.T. Baskaran, A. Raman, Mukundan Chittiappa, Prajna Chowta, Jayant Kulkarni, R.K. Dixit, Ashok Kumar, Vivek Menon, Shanti Pappu, Sadasiba Pradan, Chanchal Sar, P.K. Singh, Vijaya and Murthy, P.C. Bhattacharjee, Vijay Sathe, Shyamala and Srikumar, Manmohan Kapshe, Rajashree and Srinivas, T.S. Suryanarayanan, Charles Santiapillai, S. Wijeyamohan, Sunel Rambukpotha, Selvakumar Ramakrishnan and Beverly Bryant, Jonathan Mark Kenoyer, Feza Günergun, Nirmal Ghosh, L. Jeyakumar, Dami Buchori, Shiro Kohshima, Tatsuo Sweda, and Aster Li Zhang.

Several museums opened their doors and collections, or provided photographs for this book. Among the museums in India I would like to especially thank the Government Museum (Chennai), Orissa State Museum (Bhubaneswar), Archaeological Museum (Konarak), Chhatrapati Shivaji Maharaj Vastu Sangrahalaya (Mumbai), Government Museum (Mathura), Indian Museum (Kolkata), National Museum (New Delhi), and Jaganmohan Palace (Mysore) for their help. The Archaeological Survey of India also provided images and permitted photography of murals at the Dariya Daulat, Srirangapatana. Among the museums abroad, the British Museum and Victoria and Albert Museum (London) have done a great service by not only placing their entire photographic collection online but permitting its free use by researchers in academic publications. Musée Guimet (Paris) welcomed me to photograph their magnificent Asian sculptures as well as a rare Tibetan painting in their collections; I am especially thankful to the President, Jacques Giès, and his staff for their immense help. Likewise, the Freer Gallery of Art at Washington DC permitted me to view elephant-related pieces not on exhibit and provided me photographs. Desrika at the National Museum, Jakarta, kindly permitted me to photograph their impressive collection of ancient Ganeshas from Java.

Other institutions that provided me images, allowed me to reproduce published images, or take photographs that have been used in this book are: Publication Board (Guwahati), Topkapi Museum (Istanbul), British Library (London), National Library of France (Paris), Field Museum of Natural History (Chicago), Art Resources (New York), Metropolitan Museum of Art (New York), Milwaukee Public Museum (Milwaukee), and Yale University Press (New Haven).

I would also like to thank many individuals for their help with providing me their own photographs, figures, and maps, or sourcing them elsewhere for me; these include chapterwise: Chapter 1: Adrian Lister, Shanti Pappu, Dilip Padhe, Omar Khan; Chapter 2: Biswajit Kar; Chapter 3: Andrew Chugg, M. Harikrishnan, Thomas Trautmann; Chapter 4: Luigi Boitani, Francesca Boitani; Chapter 5: Rev. Innamaluwe Sri Sumangala Maha Nayake Thera of the Siyampolai Maha Nikaya, Dambulla; Chapter 6: S. Balasubramanian, S.P. Goyal, Jacob Cheeran, P.K. Singh, Soonoo Taraporewala; Chapter 7: Ezra Müyesseroglu; Chapter 8: S.V.P. Halakatti, Michael Ludgrove, Lakshmi Sarath, Vikram Nanjappa, Kamakshi and R. Anandakrishna, Jayantha Jayewardene, Anand Kumar, Bruce Read, Uwe Wilkens, Stephan Hering-Hagenbeck; Chapter 9: Shariff Daim, Raymond Alfred, Mattana Srikrachang, Dheeraporn Saenthawee, Prithviraj Fernando, H.R. Janaka, Asad Rahmani, Karpagam Chelliah, Ashish and Shanthi Chandola, Subrata P. Chowdhury, N. Baskaran, Vivek Menon, Balan Madhavan; Chapter 10: Smita Nair, Rohini Balakrishnan.

My work with elephants over the past three decades has been made possible with the support of many institutions and individuals most of whom I have acknowledged in my previous books – however, I must again acknowledge the Indian Institute of Science that has given me the freedom to pursue my research interests, the Ministry of Environment and Forests (New Delhi) for long-term support in much of my work, the forest departments of several Indian states where I have observed and studied elephants, and the Wildlife Trust (now the EcoHealth Alliance, New York) for its consistent support.

Dr Divyabhanusinh Chavda and Dr Pratapaditya Pal have expertly guided the overall structure of this book. Mahesh Rangarajan read through the entire manuscript and pointed out an important omission that I subsequently added in Chapter 7; however, I am responsible for all mistakes and other inadequacies in the book.

At The Marg Foundation, Gayatri Ugra patiently urged me at regular intervals to get on with the task of writing and helped me put the book together. Rivka Israel's skills in editing the manuscript with thoroughness and finesse have considerably enhanced the quality of the book. Savita Chandiramani, Arnavaz Bhansali, and Rahul D'souza carried out the final checks and saw this volume through to publication, while Naju Hirani and Gautam Jadhav looked after its design and production, respectively.

A. Maheswari and S. Nirmala laboured on the computer with my draft handwritten chapters. My daughters Gitanjali and Hamsini provided some of the artwork and photographs for the book, while my wife Sudha accompanied me to many historical monuments and endured my long bouts of writing. As I complete this acknowledgement, by coincidence on the festival of Ganesha: September 1, 2011, I fervently hope that I have not forgotten anyone who has contributed to this book.

Raman Sukumar
Bengaluru

introduction

INDIAN MYTHOLOGY TRACES THE ORIGIN of elephants to a cosmic event related to the formation of the sun. Sage Palakapya, the most ancient of elephantologists, explains it thus. After the sun was created from a golden egg, Brahma solemnly held the two halves of the cosmic eggshell in his two hands and chanted seven Vedic mantras. From the half shell in his right hand sprang Airavata followed by seven other noble male elephants. Soon the half shell in Brahma's left hand gave birth to eight female elephants, the consorts of the eight noble bulls. These 16 elephants and their succeeding generations went on to occupy the forests, rivers, and mountains of the whole world. The venerable sage emphasizes that Brahma created elephants for the profit of offering sacrifice to the gods, and *especially for the welfare of kings*.

Even though the elephant had already been tamed in the Indian subcontinent by the time this creation myth arose, and had possibly reached an advanced stage of deployment in the armies of kings, this myth provides the theoretical underpinnings for the complex relationship between elephants and people in Asia over thousands of years, a unique relationship that is unlikely to arise between animal and man in the future. The more you research the elephant in history, the more you realize that this great beast has played a pivotal role in the rise of Asian civilizations. This relationship has not always been a compatible one; *Elephas maximus* and *Homo sapiens* have at the same time been close, mutually supportive companions, as well as competitors for space and resources, eliminating each other in brutal fashion.

The elephant is omnipresent in southern Asia. From India to Indonesia, across one of the most densely populated regions in the world, the elephant stares at you from the most unexpected places. In the nondescript northern Indian town of Kalsi along the banks of the Yamuna in Uttarakhand, a small figure of a musth elephant, etched on a rock alongside one of Emperor Ashoka's famous edicts of the 3rd century BCE, triumphantly announces its elevation to supreme status with the label "Gajatame". At Bhimbetka in central India, small bands of people inhabiting rock shelters many centuries earlier expressed their artistic awakenings by sketching elephants and other animals inside their shelters. Deep south in the coastal town of Mamallapuram, the Pallavas of the late 7th or early 8th century created the Descent of the Ganga, described as the largest open-air bas-relief anywhere, portraying the most lifelike sculptures of the elephant you would ever see, amidst a potpourri of gods, humans, and other animals. Through the vast region in between, also arose scores of temples and other monuments, adorned with sculpted elephants seemingly supporting entire massive structures; decorating walls, pillars, and architraves; or standing guard at the entrance to these shrines.

By no means does India have a monopoly on grand sculptural depictions of elephants. In the ancient Sri Lankan city of Anuradhapura, an impressive array of sculpted tusked elephants flanked the great basal platforms of the colossal *dagabas* (Buddhist relic shrines or stupas) that arose about 2,000 years ago. Across the ocean eastward into Cambodia, the Terrace of the Elephants that came up in the Angkor complex a millennium later is equally impressive in its scale. A thousand kilometres to the south, sculpted royal elephants with their riders, and free-ranging elephants along with other denizens of the jungle, adorn the bas-reliefs of central Java's monument Borobudur that pre-dates Angkor Wat by several hundred years.

If you had been a traveller in ancient southern Asia, you would have encountered not only some of these elephants in stone but also multitudes of real elephants wherever you went – wild herds as you trekked through the jungles that still covered vast areas, and tamed ones as you entered river valleys under human settlement. Today you may fortunately still encounter them, but unfortunately with a much diminished chance. As people captured elephants and entered into a special relationship with them, the tamed elephant gradually replaced the wild elephant, the sculpted elephant replaced the tamed elephant and, eventually, a transmogrified elephant divinity raced across Asia as far as Japan, replacing even the sculpted elephant. Thus, in the Indian state of Maharashtra, where the cult of Ganesha has reached its pinnacle of glory, the entry of a handful of wild elephants from neighbouring Karnataka is today viewed with dismay and hostility.

I have been privileged to travel across this land in search of wild and tamed elephants, and of the human expression in art of their age-old association with these creatures. Growing up in Chennai as a young boy, I had often seen the magnificent *koomeriah* (royal elephant) that seems to walk straight out of the great bas-relief at Mamallapuram, during weekend family excursions in the 1960s and '70s. Since 1980 I have had a different professional engagement with the elephant. From the dense forests of Buxa and the grasslands along the Brahmaputra in northeastern India to their strongholds in the mixed forests of the Western Ghats in the south, and from the island of Sri Lanka to the war-ravaged jungles of Vietnam, I have been a privileged researcher and an observer of the life of wild elephants in their remnant habitats, and of captive ones in temples, timber camps, and tourist centres. Since 1990 I have been invited to many Western zoos to see how they are managing this exotic creature, and have travelled many times to Africa to see the Asian elephant's closest living relative. Over the past decade I have also increasingly been attracted to the amazingly rich and varied artistic representation of the elephant. This has taken me to the famous Asian monuments – Ajanta, Ellora, Sanchi, Konarak, Hampi, Belur, Halebid, Mamallapuram, Thanjavur, Anuradhapura, Polonnaruwa, the Angkor complex of temples, Prambanan, and Borobudur to name the main ones – as well as to less-visited historical sites such as Kalsi (near Dehra Dun), Bhaja (near Pune), Udayagiri and Khandagiri (at Bhubaneswar), Bhimbetka and Udaygiri (near Bhopal), and Somnathpur and Hoshaholalu (near Mysore). My research on the cultural history of the Asian elephant has also taken me to museums in New Delhi, Mathura, Kolkata, Mumbai, Chennai, Colombo, Phnom Penh, Bandung, Jakarta, and Tokyo, as well as temples at Kyoto and Matsuyama. I have used opportunities to travel outside Asia to visit the famous museums of culture and natural history at Paris, London, Edinburgh, New York, Washington DC, Chicago, and Milwaukee. In the course of writing this account of the elephant-human relationship from the Stone Age to the present, I have delved into literary sources from the Vedas and the two great Indian epics, through the remarkable *Gajashastra, Arthashastra, Mahavamsa,* and the ancient Greek and Roman accounts, to the *Akbarnama* and *Ain-i Akbari.* This historical journey has been a great learning experience and a very enjoyable one, only a shade less so than my trips to the jungle to watch elephants in their natural habitat. My passion for photography was also fulfilled at the monuments and museums I visited; I have thus used my own pictures of not only wild elephants but also their depiction in art, wherever possible.

I begin this story of the Asian elephant with a brief account of the ancient origins of this creature and its possible relationship with early humans leading eventually to the taming of the animal between 4,500 and 5,000 years ago in the Harappan period (Chapter 1). From then on I take the reader through successive periods in Asian history, examining in each chapter the ecological and cultural history of the elephant broadly under the major religious establishments – Vedic (Chapter 2), Buddhist and Jain (Chapter 5), post-1st century Hindu (Chapter 6), and Islamic (Chapter 7) – of the Indian subcontinent and beyond. Two chapters in between (Chapters 3 and 4) also cover the Mauryan period when an interesting adventurer came to the subcontinent from Macedonia, and the fate of the elephants that he and his successors took with them to the Mediterranean region for use in battle. Chapter 8 looks at the fate of the elephant under colonial rulers in Asia, followed by an account (Chapter 9) of the post-independence history of the elephant in 13 range countries. Needless to state, there is a certain degree of chronological overlap in these chapters. Finally, Chapter 10 provides a summary of the latest scientific knowledge of the elephant's ecology and behaviour, and of how we can perhaps plan for the conservation of the species.

In this account of the relationship between elephants and people through the ages, I have focused on India because of the much greater significance of the elephant in this ancient Asian civilization as well as the profusion of material, both artistic and literary, available from the Stone Age to the present – thus India has the earliest known depiction of the elephant in art, the first monograph on the species was composed in this land, the elephant was almost certainly first tamed here, and the country presently has the distinction of holding the largest global population of *Elephas maximus*. At the same time, I have taken care not to neglect a discussion of the elephant-human relationship across the Asian continent, from the Tigris-Euphrates basin in the west to the Mekong in the east. I must also emphasize that this book is neither an art history of the Asian elephant nor of ivory, but rather an ecological and cultural history of the species accompanied by illustrations of the elephant in art through the ages.

A short distance south of Bangalore (Bengaluru), a city that leads the information technology revolution of India, if not of Asia, a towering multicoloured Ganesha, by the side of a highway to the town of Kanakapura, virtually oversees the shrinking habitat of the wild elephant close by. The transformation of the real elephant to a virtual elephant seems almost complete. The nature of the elephant-human relationship will surely change further in the coming decades as societies across Asia transform in tune with a globalized world. Yet there is hope. The elephant is not only a highly intelligent and sensitive animal possessing superior cognition, it is also a remarkably resilient creature that can survive with only a little help from us. All that it needs is some space and safety from wanton hunting. We in Asia surely owe this creature a deep debt of gratitude for the immeasurable contribution it has made to our civilizations.

CHAPTER 1

The Asian Elephant in Prehistory and Proto-History

THE STORY OF ASIA'S ELEPHANTS, known to zoologists as *Elephas maximus*, begins in Africa about 6 million or 60 million years ago, depending on how far back we wish to trace the origins and evolution of this remarkable group of creatures.[1] While the elephant family, Elephantidae, emerged only 6 million years ago, the order in the animal kingdom known as Proboscidea – with a long snout – had its origins in northern Africa over 60 million years ago, when Earth was warm and moist during the geological epoch termed as the Palaeocene. Along the shallow waters of the ancient Tethys Sea, in the region of the present-day Mediterranean coast of northern Africa, small, pig-sized animals with barely extended snouts began to differentiate from their closest relatives, the sea cows (order Sirenia) whose descendants such as manatees and dugongs continued an aquatic existence.[2]

Earth's climate changed as a consequence of natural processes, first warming during the Early Eocene epoch (55–35 million years ago), but then cooling into the Oligocene (35–24 million years ago) and the Miocene (24–6 million years ago). The resulting drier vegetation hastened evolutionary changes in the ancient proboscideans. These creatures were forced to consume more forage of lesser quality and became larger in size. Examples of these are *Barytherium* that had reached the size of a modern elephant as early as Late Eocene, and a strange 4-metre-tall creature from the Miocene, *Deinotherium*, with a pair of recurving tusks in its lower jaw. Their teeth also developed more complex surfaces and high crowns in order to effectively chew the coarse plants that were their food. Some very impressive elephant-like creatures, the stegodontids, evolved in Asia during the Miocene. The best known of these is *Stegodon ganesa* from South and Southeast Asia, a proboscidean that stood 3.5 metres at its shoulder and sported from its upper jaw a formidable pair of tusks that almost reached the ground. The stegodontids mainly ate the leaves of trees and bamboos. They eventually died out several million years after their sister group, the true elephants, had emerged. The tree of elephant evolution (figure 1.1) shows the major geological epochs and some of the well known proboscidean genera referred to here.

For our purposes, the most important proboscidean that lived during the Miocene was *Gomphotherium*, with tusks in both upper and lower jaws. This is accepted as the direct ancestor of modern elephants. By the Late Miocene, 8 to 6 million years ago, the stage was set for the emergence of the true elephants. Zoologists now believe that an advanced gomphothere in Africa gave rise to a little-known group of the subfamily Stegotetrabelodontinae which evolved into *Primelephas gomphotheroides*, the immediate ancestor of the true elephants (family Elephantidae) that emerged by the end of the Miocene epoch.

Palaeontologist Vincent Maglio concluded on the basis of the fossil record that *Primelephas* gave rise to three elephant genera, *Loxodonta*, *Elephas*, and *Mammuthus*, about 5.5 million years ago in the African continent.[3] More recently, other biologists have estimated on the basis of the molecular genetic clock that this split may have occurred even earlier, about 7.6 million years ago.[4] Whatever the actual period for the origin of the true elephants, we now recognize *Loxodonta* as the African elephant, *Elephas* as the Asian elephant, and *Mammuthus* as the mammoth. *Loxodonta* never left the African continent, while *Mammuthus* emigrated to Eurasia and on to North America across the Bering Strait, but eventually became extinct as recently as 4,000 years BP on Wrangel Island north of Siberia.[5] We need to follow in the evolutionary footsteps of *Elephas* that became extinct in Africa, but not before it had emigrated to Eurasia, where it has continued to survive until the present time.

About 6 million years ago the world simultaneously supported an amazing 22 of the 39 recognized genera of proboscideans that ranged over all continents with the exception of Australia and Antarctica. These included the giant but primitive deinotheres, the nipple-toothed mammutids, the four-tusked gomphotheres, the formidably-adorned stegodontids, and the true elephants. This may have been possible because the incredibly diverse mosaic of vegetation types allowed the giant herbivores to occupy different niches.

When *Elephas* emerged in sub-Saharan Africa at the beginning of the relatively cool and dry Pliocene epoch (6–2 million years ago) it shared the same habitat as the early mammoths. The earliest species *Elephas ekorensis* soon gave rise to *E. recki* that dominated the African continent for over two million years with its teeth becoming more complex to adapt to the increasingly coarser vegetation. At this time South and Southeast Asia was still a stegodon kingdom, but this was soon to be challenged by the elephant. A late form of *E. ekorensis* or an early form of *E. recki* emigrated from Africa to Asia about 4 million years ago to serve as the ancestor of the modern *E. maximus*.

There are several twists and turns in the story of the final emergence of the elephant we are familiar with, and it is not easy to be certain of the precise evolutionary path that it followed. T.N.C. Vidya, Don Melnick, and I carried out comprehensive genetic analyses of elephant populations across Asia, and used the fossil record meticulously assembled by Vincent Maglio to infer the most plausible evolutionary route taken by *Elephas* after its migration out of Africa (figure 1.2).[6] Fossils of a derivative of the *E. ekorensis–E. recki* group, known as *E. planifrons*, are common in Asia from Bethlehem in the west to Java in the east. Some of the earliest fossils of *E. planifrons* are found in 3.6-million-year-old deposits in the Siwalik hills of the northwestern Indian subcontinent.[7] Not long after, about 2.7 million years ago, there appeared another species named *E. hysudricus* in the same hill range, which spread east to the Irrawaddy basin of Myanmar. The distinguishing feature of *E. hysudricus*, which was larger than the modern elephant, was its very prominent pair of domes (or bumps) at the top of the skull; this can also be seen though less prominently on the head of the Asian elephant, especially older male elephants (figure 1.3).

Beginning about 2 million years ago, the world transited into the so-called Ice Age (the Pleistocene epoch) when average global temperatures were 5°C below present-day values. Ice sheets crept southward from the North Pole; the Tibetan plateau in Asia was completely frozen. Needless to say, the moist tropical forests virtually disappeared, giving way to dry and arid landscapes, with the exception of small pockets (termed by ecologists as "Pleistocene refugia") closer to the Equator. Long periods of intense cold (glacial periods) were punctuated by only short warm spells (interglacial periods); about 20 such glacial-interglacial cycles have been recorded during the Pleistocene.

Elephas responded to the Ice Age climate by hastening the rate of change in their teeth characters; the number of plates or lamellae in the molars increased even further, the tooth enamel became thinner, and the crown height increased. At the same time, the grinding component of mastication reduced in favour of the shearing component to enable them to eat the coarse grasses and other dryland plants. The prominent bumps on the head also reduced as *E. hysudricus* evolved into the modern *E. maximus* during the Pleistocene.

Genetic analyses in *E. maximus* of a section of the DNA present in the mitochondria of cells have shown the existence of two distinct groups or clades.[8] One group termed as the alpha-clade (or A-clade) is presently distributed along the Himalayan foothills, Myanmar, and Indochina. The more ancient group or beta-clade (B-clade) is mainly seen in east-central and southern India, Peninsular Malaysia, Sumatra, Borneo, and some regions of Southeast Asia. Sri Lanka has mostly B-clade but also some A-clade elephants. Each of these clades also has several unique but closely-related matrilines or "haplotypes".[9]

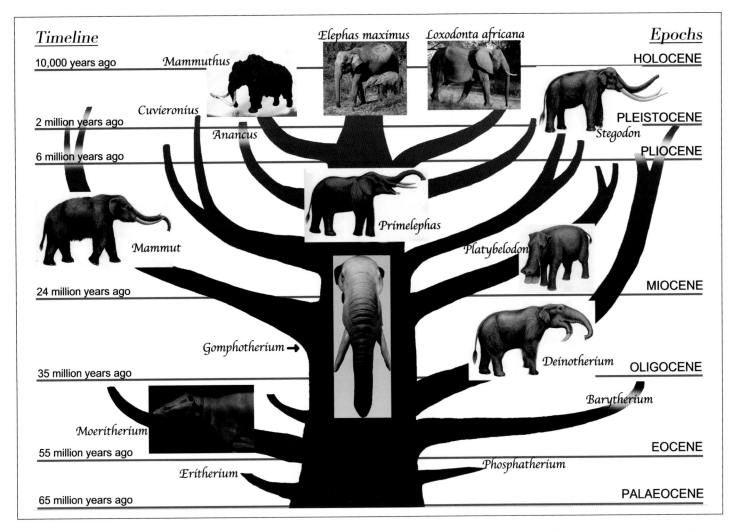

Timeline

10,000 years ago

Mammuthus

Elephas maximus   *Loxodonta africana*

Epochs

HOLOCENE

Cuvieronius

2 million years ago

Anancus

PLEISTOCENE

6 million years ago

Stegodon

PLIOCENE

Mammut

Primelephas

Platybelodon

24 million years ago

MIOCENE

Gomphotherium →

Deinotherium

35 million years ago

OLIGOCENE

Barytherium

Moeritherium

55 million years ago

EOCENE

Eritherium

Phosphatherium

65 million years ago

PALAEOCENE

1.1 Tree of elephant evolution (not drawn to scale).
Although the Palaeocene epoch began about 65 million years ago, the evolution of the earliest proboscideans is only about 60 million years ago. *Elephas maximus* refers to the modern Asian elephant. Recently a strong case has been made out on the basis of genetic studies for two species of African elephants, *Loxodonta africana* or the savannah elephant and *Loxodonta cyclotis* or the forest elephant (not shown in this tree).
Artwork by Gitanjali Sukumar.

Based on the available genetic and fossil evidence, Vidya, Melnick, and I proposed the following revised evolutionary history of the Asian elephant.[10] The divergence between the two clades took place sometime between 2.1 and 1.6 million years ago during the Early Pleistocene; this distinction obviously occurred in *E. hysudricus* much before it transformed into *E. maximus*. The cold snap of the Early Pleistocene would have driven *E. hysudricus* from its northern homes, where the species originally evolved, to more southerly locations whose warmer climate and moister vegetation were more hospitable. We think that the B-clade arose in the Siwalik population of *E. hysudricus* during its sojourn in southern India or Sri Lanka,[11] while the A-clade arose perhaps somewhat later in the Myanmar population. When a long, cold spell of the Ice Age was interrupted by a shorter period of warmth much like the present-day climate, the environment was conducive for elephants (*E. hysudricus*) to migrate northwards. Remember that there were several such cold–warm climatic oscillations; during one such early warm spell the B-clade elephants not only reached Myanmar but were soon squeezed southward into the Sunda shelf (Sumatra, Peninsular Malaysia, and adjoining islands) where they again evolved in isolation and gave rise to the now extinct *E. hysudrindicus* of Java. The B-clade elephants also made contact with their A-clade compatriots in Myanmar at some stage, and bulls of both clades exchanged genes with the females of the opposite clade (but remember that this will not be reflected in the mitochondrial genes inherited only through the mother). At a later time, the B-clade elephants that had by now evolved into

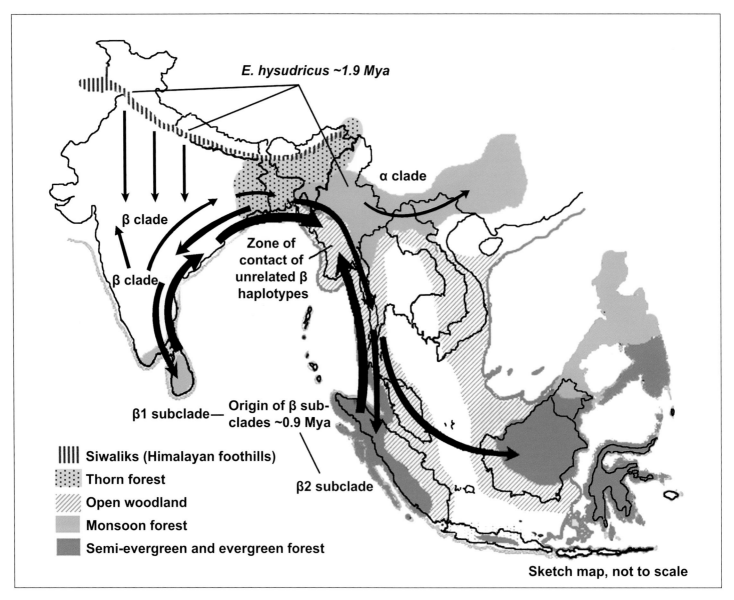

E. hysudricus ~1.9 Mya

α clade

β clade

β clade

Zone of
contact of
unrelated β
haplotypes

β1 subclade—

**Origin of β sub-
clades ~0.9 Mya**

β2 subclade

|||| Siwaliks (Himalayan foothills)

Thorn forest

Open woodland

Monsoon forest

Semi-evergreen and evergreen forest

Sketch map, not to scale

1.2 Map showing a revised evolutionary history of the Asian elephant *Elephas maximus* from its ancestor *Elephas hysudricus* during the Pleistocene epoch (about 2 million to 10,000 years ago), based on the genetic record. The Ice Age cycles resulted in contraction and isolation of *E. hysudricus* populations during cold periods, resulting in the origin of two major clades, termed alpha and beta clades, that subsequently expanded and mixed during a warm spell. Colours show the vegetation types at the peak of the last Ice Age, a very arid period about 18,000 years BP. Arrows of increasing thickness indicate more recent time periods.
Artwork by Gitanjali Sukumar, based on work by Vidya et al. (2009).

independent forms in Sri Lanka and the Sunda region also met with each other, again in Myanmar that has acted as a melting pot of elephant genetic evolution. The intriguing question of how elephants came to inhabit a small region on the island of Borneo is discussed later in this volume (see Chapter 8).

The precise date and the place of emergence of *E. maximus* from *E. hysudricus* are not known because of a paucity of fossils of the modern species, but the most likely date is about 250,000 years ago in the Indian subcontinent, somewhat earlier than the evolution of modern humans, *Homo sapiens*, in Africa. We can now move on to trace the interaction between elephants and humans in Asia.

***

What do we know about the cultural relationship between elephants and prehistoric humans in Asia? In spite of a rich haul of remains of proboscideans (elephants and related creatures) and early humans[12] going back over a million years into the Stone Age, it is not an easy task to reconstruct past events unambiguously. As eminent fossil scientist Gary Haynes puts it, "A lively imagination is needed to visualize the events of the past, and for decades prehistorians have indeed been reconstructing the past based on intuition, unreined imagination, and emotions and feelings about the plausibility of certain actions...unsupported by actualistic studies that could prove or disprove such beliefs."[13]

It is clear that elephant flesh, where available, was a part of the diet of early humans; the opportunity provided by a mountain of meat would have been too good to pass up for bands of hunter-gatherers. What is not clear, however, is the manner in which Stone Age people retrieved elephant meat. To put it more simply, to what extent did they scavenge meat from elephants versus actively hunting the giant beasts? Products other than meat derived from elephants would also have been a bonanza for humans, the most obvious being skin, bone, and ivory for shelter, clothing, tool-making, or creative expression.

The modern Asian elephant *Elephas maximus* is rarely preserved in fossil form. Because the fossil evidence does not say much about the cultural association between *Elephas maximus* and *Homo sapiens* during prehistory, it would be useful for us to first review the nature of the interaction between other elephant forms and early humans. A basic question we can ask is: when did the flesh of elephants first enter the diet of humans in the course of their evolution? Anthropologists who study human evolution assume quite reasonably that acquisition of meat from the larger mammals by early humans is related to manufacture of stone tools, even if these were crude, for butchering, scraping, and preparing the meat for consumption. We should thus look at patterns of human diet from the Early Stone Age, about 2.5 million years ago, during the Late Pliocene in Africa, the cradle of both elephant and human evolution.[14]

The earliest tool-making human *Homo habilis* was a scavenger rather than a hunter in the African savannas during the Late Pliocene and Early Pleistocene. Humans located kills made by carnivores or perhaps waited for an animal to die naturally before retrieving pieces of flesh, bone marrow, and brain matter. The archaeological sites at Gona in Ethiopia are possibly the earliest ones where clear evidence is available that humans butchered large animals.[15] The bones of many mammals recovered here show the characteristic cut marks of primitive stone tools used by hominids. Tools termed as the Oldowan technology (named after the Olduvai Gorge in northern Tanzania, the site of many discoveries by the famous Mary and Louis Leakey), dating to 2–1.5 million years ago, are still primitive stone flakes but effective in splitting tough skin, breaking bones, or scraping flesh off them.

About 1.8 million years ago, an anatomically more advanced human *Homo erectus* evolved in Africa (some anthropologists distinguish an earlier form *Homo ergaster*) and soon moved out into Eurasia. For long *H. erectus* was believed to be the first big-game hunter who developed weapons sufficiently sophisticated to bring down animals as large as an elephant; much of this thinking was based on simplistic interpretation of elephant fossils and heavy-duty tools indicative of the so-called Lower Acheulian technology at sites such as Torralba and Ambrona in central Spain that may be up to 500,000 years old.[16] More critical examination of the patterns of breakage and markings of the elephant bone has shown that this could have occurred by natural processes.[17] Thus, anthropologists have moved away from labelling *H. erectus* as a socially advanced, cooperative hunter capable of actively bringing down animals as large as elephants. Instead, these early humans, too, were mostly scavengers and butchers of large animals that died of other causes, though they might have indulged in some hunting.

Most anthropologists now believe that the advanced abilities – not only in terms of weaponry but also in hominid brain development, agile anatomy, and social group coordination – needed to successfully hunt animals as large as elephants became possible only with the evolution of the modern human *Homo sapiens* sometime between 200,000

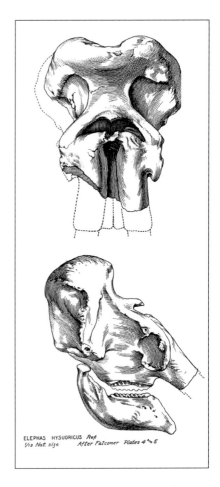

ELEPHAS HYSUDRICUS *Ref*
1/12 Nat. size   After Falconer Plates 4 & 5

1.3 Skull of *Elephas hysudricus*, the immediate ancestor of the modern Asian elephant. Fossils of this species sporting a prominent double-domed skull are found in the Siwaliks.
These drawings, taken from a monograph by Henry Fairfield Osborn (1942), are based on an earlier work by Falconer in 1857.

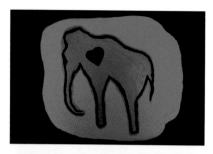

1.4 a Mammoth from the approximately 12,000-year-old rock art site of Pindal in Spain. The depiction of the animal's heart may have been intended to show the best spot for a hunter to aim his spear.
Redrawn by Gitanjali Sukumar from the reconstruction of a poorly preserved picture by Abbé Breuil (1877–1961).

b The crimson elephant with a triangle within its body, from the medieval period at Bhimbetka in central India, may have conveyed a similar message to hunters.

c Clovis hunting points from North America that were hafted on to wooden shafts and used to hunt animals including mammoths about 12,000 years BP.
Photographed at the Field Museum of Natural History, Chicago.

and 100,000 years ago. At Lehringen in Germany there is reasonably clear indication of a prehistoric elephant hunt that may have taken place about 125,000 years ago; a 2-metre-long wooden spear was found between the ribs of a straight-tusked elephant *Palaeoloxodon antiquus*. However, the animal may not have been actively pursued and hunted but merely finished off in the last stages of its natural death. European cave art at places such as Lascaux, Rouffignac, and Chauvet in France and Altamira in Spain, dating to between 31,000 and 11,000 years BP, has numerous depictions of mammoths; some of these clearly hint at the hunting or trapping of these giants. For instance, a mammoth figure in a cave at Font-de-Gaume, France, suggests that the animal had been trapped in a pit, while another famous painting at Pindal, Spain, of a mammoth with a prominent heart (figure 1.4a) suggests that the artist was depicting the correct point at which a hunter should aim his projectile (see also figure 1.4b).

There is also ample evidence that Stone Age peoples, including the Neanderthals, used mammoth bones and hides to construct dwellings during the last Ice Age. Dozens of sites with mammoth-bone huts have been found in the central Russian plain.[18] The bones used in each hut, however, date over several thousand years; thus this does not suggest that mammoths were slaughtered in large numbers to yield bones for construction but rather that these palaeolithic cultures merely gathered the mammoth bones they found in the landscape. They also carved mammoth figures in stone and tusk.

The most controversial discussions about the mammoth-human relationship possibly relate to the North American continent.[19] After the arrival of the Clovis people from northeastern Siberia about 12,000 years BP, the mammoth and the distantly-related mastodon became extinct within a short span of less than 500 years. One popular (and scientific) view is that the Clovis people armed with advanced tools such as wooden shafts fitted with razor-sharp stone points, the so-called Clovis points (figure 1.4c), went on a killing spree (a *blitzkrieg* in the words of palaeontologist Paul Martin) as they swept southwards and wiped out the continent's megafauna.[20] Although there is some definite evidence that Clovis people hunted mammoths, other competing theories for this extinction spasm include climate change, disease brought in by humans, and a combination of various causes.

At the end of the last Ice Age, about 10,000 years BP, the megafauna of the Americas and northern Eurasia had become extinct, with the exception of a small population of woolly mammoth that had been isolated on Wrangel Island north of Siberia because of a rise in sea levels following the melting of ice sheets. The African elephant (*Loxodonta africana*) and Asian elephant (*Elephas maximus*) were the two surviving proboscideans. Their populations would have expanded across Africa and South and Southeast Asia, respectively, in a warmer, moister world. The Sahara that was a desert during the Ice Age now turned greener with shallow lakes and savanna-like vegetation that supported elephants. African tribes in the Saharan region certainly had knowledge of elephants as evidenced by rock engravings in Libya, Chad, and Algeria that go back to the "Age of hunters" during the 7th and 6th millennia BCE. The most convincing evidence that the African people actively hunted elephants during this period comes from rock paintings in southern Africa, particularly Zimbabwe. Stone Age Bushmen used iron oxides, kaolin, and animal fat and blood to paint scenes of elephants being pursued and hunted with spears and, later, bows and arrows. As in other parts of the world, rock engravings (or petroglyphs) and paintings in Africa are not only among the earliest expressions of art by Stone Age people but also symbolize the various animalistic cults that arose with the passing of time.

***

With this background we can now examine the evidence for the nature of the relationship between Stone Age humans and elephants in South and Southeast Asia. Unfortunately, the evidence is scanty, and we have little idea how humans and elephants interacted during the Stone Age. As in parts of Africa and Europe, there are sufficient fossil remains of elephants in South Asia (e.g. in the Siwaliks and the Narmada valley) and rich yields of Stone Age tools across the subcontinent, but a great paucity of hominid fossils or elephant fossils associated with the archaeological sites. In any case there is nothing to directly prove that early humans ever hunted or butchered elephants. A recent global survey by Todd Surovell and colleagues of 41 archaeological sites that show overlap of humans and proboscideans in space and time over the past 1.8 million years does not list a single site in South Asia.[21] If we exclude Russia from consideration, the only two sites in the whole of Asia providing some indication that humans exploited elephants are in Israel and Japan. At Gesher Benot Ya'aqov in the Jordan valley of Israel there is some evidence that *Homo erectus* exploited *Elephas antiquus* about 750,000 years ago during the Middle Palaeolithic. Corresponding to the first arrival of humans in Japan about 30,000 years BP there seems to have been exploitation of *Elephas naumanni* at Lake Nojiri.

While we know that *H. erectus* emigrated from Africa close to 1.8 million years ago, it is unclear as to when they first moved into the Indian subcontinent. These early humans brought with them their typical stone tool culture, the so-called Acheulian technology of fashioning bifacial artefacts such as hand-axes, cleavers, and scrapers out of hard quartz or, less commonly, limestone, granite, and basalt. Indeed, the subcontinent has been the richest source of Acheulian artefacts anywhere in the world, and possibly represents the easternmost limit of this culture.[22] Some archaeologists recognize another class of artefacts, the Soanian (or Sohanian) industry characterized by pebbles chipped to fashion chopping tools. Soanian culture is mostly restricted to Pakistan and northwestern India while Acheulian culture is widespread across India. The Acheulian hunter-gatherers occupied the Siwaliks in the north, the arid deserts of Rajasthan, rock shelters such as at Bhimbetka and Adamgarh in central India, and river valleys such as Chambal, Narmada, Mahanadi, Godavari, Krishna, and Palar in central and peninsular India. These ancient hunter-gatherers seem to have penetrated the entire subcontinent with the exception of Kerala and the northeast, presumably because the dense forest cover here may not have been conducive to human occupation.

In spite of the rich Acheulian and Soanian material across the subcontinent, the dating of these cultures has been problematic. Indeed, many scholars question the Acheulian-Soanian dichotomy. A British Archaeological Mission to Pakistan dated three hand-axes found in the Rawalpindi area of the Siwaliks at between 700,000 and 400,000 years ago but this is much disputed. Typical Acheulian artefacts in peninsular India have been dated at between 400,000 and 150,000 years ago. Most Soanian pebble tools are now believed to be as recent as 10,000 years or less. It is clear that the Lower Palaeolithic culture of *H. erectus* persisted for a very long time, perhaps adapting to local environments through use of various materials and design of appropriate tools. Thus, in the opinion of eminent archaeologist V.N. Misra of the Deccan College at Pune, human occupation of the subcontinent is *at least* half a million years and perhaps much earlier.[23]

Unlike in Africa, fossils of early humans are extremely rare in the Indian subcontinent. The best preserved of these is a cranium, termed "Narmada man", from Acheulian deposits (dated at around 200,000 years ago) along the Narmada river at Hathwora, Madhya Pradesh. Elephant fossils found in the Lower Palaeolithic include *Stegodon insignis-ganesa*,[24] the straight-tusked elephant in the Potwar Plateau in Pakistan, and *Elephas hysudricus*, the immediate ancestor of the modern Asian elephant.

1.5a The Attirampakkam archaeological site near Chennai in Tamil Nadu (2006). This site shows a sequence of at least one million years of occupation by early humans that has been investigated in detail by Shanti Pappu and her associates.
b Acheulian heavy-duty stone tools found at this site.

Although more direct evidence of elephant exploitation by early humans is lacking for the subcontinent we can safely assume that this did occur. Heavy-duty tools such as choppers, hand-axes, and cleavers were obviously fashioned for butchering large animals. If *H. erectus* in Africa scavenged meat, marrow, and brain from elephants that died naturally, there is no reason to believe that their Asian counterparts armed with similar tools desisted from such exploitation. At Attirampakkam in Tamil Nadu, archaeologist Shanti Pappu and her associates have been painstakingly excavating a long and unique chronological sequence of human occupation going back at least one million years (figure 1.5).[25] Typical Acheulian tools have been found here, as have impressions resembling footprints. I have examined these impressions, the smallest of which perfectly fit the feet of a one-year-old elephant while larger ones could be of older animals. Are these really elephant footprints? Could these animals have been trapped in the soft mud along the river? Could they have been butchered by early humans using heavy-duty tools like the ones found in this layer?

The Acheulian culture gradually changed by the Middle Palaeolithic (about 150,000 years ago) through the evolution of new tool types and the discarding of some older ones. While there was a decrease in some heavy-duty tools, others such as scrapers, borers, and points were now fashioned through finer trimming of stone flakes and blades. These could have been used to process animal skin, or manufacture wooden tools and even weapons by hafting stone points on to wooden shafts. Big-game hunting and scavenging were certainly possible but again there is no direct evidence of these in the fossil record. *Elephas maximus* had evolved by this time though fossils are not available; on the other hand, fossils of *Stegodon insignis-ganesa* and *Elephas hysudricus* are found in the Narmada valley. During the Middle Palaeolithic, a period of cold and aridity, settlements were widespread across the subcontinent.

Modern humans *Homo sapiens* emigrated out of Africa about 85,000 years BP and entered the subcontinent within a few thousand years. The great volcanic explosion of Toba on the island of Sumatra about 74,000 years ago spewed out a huge plume of ash that was carried across by winds over the Indian subcontinent.[26] This was the biggest volcanic explosion in the world during the past two million years, and could have potentially devastated the human population along with larger animals such as elephants. There has been much debate over the extent of the impact, with some archaeologists arguing for a relatively mild impact[27] and those studying past climates and vegetation producing evidence for substantial change.[28]

About 30,000 years ago there were again more changes in tool type during the Upper Palaeolithic lasting until 10,000 years BP. The globe was slipping again into an intense cold and dry period that peaked sometime between 20,000 and 16,000 years BP, termed as the Last Glacial Maximum (LGM), when extensive ice sheets covered the northern hemisphere and high altitudes such as the Tibetan plateau. The Indian subcontinent had much drier vegetation; ostriches now seen only in Africa flourished in Rajasthan, Madhya Pradesh, and even Maharashtra! It is certain that elephants (*E. maximus*) would have been squeezed out of a large part of the subcontinent especially the northern and central regions due to the arid conditions. Human settlements were widespread with much regional diversity in tool-making. A variety of materials was now used to make lighter and versatile tools including blades, scrapers, and burins. The smaller, lighter tools would have been useful for nomadic groups moving seasonally in search of scarce game and other resources in very arid environments. Tools made from bone appear at places such as Kurnool in Andhra Pradesh. The first traces of cave art appear in central India towards the end of this Palaeolithic phase but the elephant does not figure as yet in this early creative expression.

***

By about 10,000 years BP, Earth had warmed considerably, the vast ice sheets and glaciers had largely melted, sea levels risen about 130 metres from glacial times to present-day levels, and the vegetation changed to moister types. The Ice Age or Pleistocene had given way to the Holocene, and the Palaeolithic now transformed into the Mesolithic when humans began to master agriculture and lead a more settled life. The monsoon intensified over the Indian subcontinent, arid landscapes turned green, moist forest expanded, and humans quickly extended their settlements. Although farming communities spread gradually, especially from 6000 BCE onwards, the subsistence economy of hunting-gathering was still the main means of existence.

With the changes in environment and human way of life, tools became further refined and smaller. Termed microliths, these tiny tools of 1–5 cm length were used as spearheads and arrowheads or fitted into grooves in bone and wood using adhesives such as gum and resin. Bows and arrows were also used for hunting.

The Mesolithic also witnessed the flowering of rock art in the subcontinent, and we must examine these prehistoric figures for the most ancient depiction of the elephant

1.6 Rock art of central India:
a and b Petroglyphs of elephants at Ambajholkhol in Orissa, dated to 7000–6000 BCE, possibly the earliest known depictions of the Asian elephant in art.
Photographs by Dilip Padhe.
c Elephant (restored) dated as Early Mesolithic or earlier from Adamgarh, Madhya Pradesh
From Brooks and Wakankar 1976, p. 35, with the permission of Yale University Press.
d Shelter E-9 at Bhimbetka that has the oldest elephant painting dating to the Mesolithic or earlier according to Mathpal (1984).
e and f (opposite right-hand corner) Elephant (restored) with geometric design dated as Late Mesolithic; and elephants being hunted dated as Neolithic/Chalcolithic, from Raisen, Madhya Pradesh.
From Brooks and Wakankar 1976, pp. 54 and 71, with the permission of Yale University Press.

by humans. The most famous of the rock art sites, Bhimbetka near Bhopal in Madhya Pradesh, is actually only one among a large number of similar sites in northern, central, and peninsular India featuring engravings, carvings, and paintings in rock shelters and caves in sandstone hillocks.[29] Since its discovery in 1956 by Vishnu S. Wakankar, the rock art of Bhimbetka is perhaps the best studied among similar locations, and thus it would be useful to look here for clues to the elephant-human relationship. Bhimbetka is also noteworthy as it was a shelter for ancient humans from the Lower Palaeolithic to the Mesolithic as seen from tools ranging from hand-axes and cleavers to microliths unearthed by V.N. Misra from a rock shelter (III F-23) here.

After Wakankar's initial study the rock art of Bhimbetka was documented in detail by Yashodar Mathpal of the Deccan College at Pune.[30] As with rock art in other parts of the world, the Bhimbetka shelters and caves mainly feature animals and people, and their interactions. Depictions of a variety of animals – deer, antelopes, monkeys, cats (including tiger, lion, leopard, and even a cheetah), bovids, horses, elephants, and a rhinoceros – adorn the rocks as do scenes of hunting and the social life of people. Twenty-one colours or shades can be discerned, the pigments being derived from minerals such as red hematite. Bhimbetka's rock art was executed over a long period from the Upper Palaeolithic (the engravings, for instance) through the Mesolithic and Neolithic to recent historical times. We thus have to be careful about the date of a particular image before using it to interpret the animal-human relationship. Fortunately, both V.S. Wakankar and Yashodar Mathpal have provided rough chronologies based on style of execution, colour, cultural content, superimposition of paintings over time, and even archaeological associations. According to Mathpal most of the drawings at Bhimbetka can be classified under just two periods – the hunter-gatherers of the Mesolithic, and the soldiers riding elephants and horses of a more recent historical period. There are also a few images older than the Mesolithic while some others belong to a younger transitional period (the Neolithic).

Among the 61 elephant figures that Mathpal recorded, not a single figure can be attributed to the Upper Palaeolithic. Further, only one of these figures – that of a tuskless elephant – belongs to the earliest phase (Phase A in Mathpal's chronology) of the Mesolithic (8000–2500 BCE). In Mathpal's words, "The drawing of an elephant on the western face of the inner wall in this shelter [i.e. E-9] is the oldest elephant drawing at Bhimbetka. The animal, of which only the hindquarters are visible, is decorated with four units of concentric lozenges in crimson."[31] I have examined this cave in some detail but the elephant figure he refers to is barely discernible to the untrained eye (see figure 1.6d). Thus, all that we can say is that this elephant image, if it is an elephant in the first place, was perhaps drawn sometime during the Early Mesolithic. Mathpal also attributes eight other elephant images to later periods during the Mesolithic.

The interesting part of the Mesolithic elephant drawings is that all of them are of tuskless elephants but the significance of this pattern is not known. None of these early images depicts an elephant with rider – thus it is clear that tamed elephants were not known to the Mesolithic people of central India. Mathpal recorded only one elephant drawing from the so-called transitional phase corresponding to the Neolithic/Chalcolithic and Early Iron Age (2500–300 BCE in central India). On the other hand, a Mesolithic elephant image with two humans in the background has been recorded at Kharvai, while an elephant hunt from the Neolithic/Chalcolithic period is known from central India.[32]

The remaining elephant images at Bhimbetka come from the historical period, and most depict scenes of elephants with riders, sometimes carrying weapons, or elephants in royal processions. I should mention one remarkable drawing of a well-proportioned tusked elephant with a triangle inside that immediately reminds us of the unique Pindal image of Spain of a mammoth with a prominent heart (see figures 1.4a and b). This image without a rider has been dated to the medieval period.[33]

At least two more sites vie with Bhimbetka for the earliest depiction of the elephant (figures 1.6a–d). One such site close to Bhimbetka is Adamgarh that features a tuskless elephant in scarlet dated to "Early Mesolithic or earlier".[34] The second site is Ambajholkhol in the Rairakhol forests of Orissa.[35] Sadasiba Pradhan, professor of archaeology at Utkal University, places two rock engravings or petroglyphs of elephants at this site within the Mesolithic. He is of the view that the earliest elephant depictions in Orissa and Madhya Pradesh can be safely dated to 7000–6000 BCE.[36] Depictions at a third site, also in Madhya Pradesh, date to the Late Mesolithic period (figures 1.6e and f).

I must also make a brief reference to rock art sites in Sri Lanka that depict elephants, including tuskers, engraved or painted on rock.[37] This rock art is believed to be the creations of the Veddahs, the indigenous forest-dwellers. Some of the elephant figures have humans associated with them, suggesting a historical period. The dating of the rock art of Sri Lanka is problematic but it seems unlikely that any of the elephant figures are older than those in central India.

The Neolithic period witnessed the spread of agriculture and animal husbandry across the subcontinent but hunting-gathering was still a very common occupation. Farming communities would obviously have spread gradually along river valleys, while pastoralists used semi-permanent settlements in the valleys and plains for penning cattle and other domesticated animals, perhaps using the hill forests too for grazing their livestock. Hunter-gatherer societies still occupied substantial areas of the valleys and plains but would have also been increasingly pushed up into the hill forests. We can only speculate upon the elephant-human relationship during this transitional phase to the historical period. Elephant meat would have been consumed by the hill people, either through scavenging or occasionally hunting. It is also possible that the odd elephant calf that might have accidentally strayed, perhaps along with livestock, into a pastoral settlement, was raised as a pet by Neolithic people.

***

Nearly 2,800 ancient sites or "cities" ranging in size from a few hectares to 500 hectares have been identified across a vast region from the Pamirs in the north through Baluchistan, Sindh, Punjab, Haryana, Rajasthan, Gujarat, and northern Maharashtra – in present-day Pakistan, India, and even Afghanistan.[38] Any account of the origins of agriculture and the rise of civilization in South Asia invariably leads to one of these cities: Mehrgarh, a 200-hectare site located on the bank of the Bolan river in Baluchistan in the northwest of the subcontinent. The beginnings of settled life here have been dated as far back as 7000 BCE followed by an almost continuous sequence of occupation for five millennia. Wheat and barley were the principal cereals cultivated, while cattle, sheep, and goats were the common animals herded. Mehrgarh was a precursor to the spectacular Harappan culture, or the Indus Valley Civilization as it was earlier known, that was to eventually develop and encompass an area of over one million square kilometres. The terms Harappan or Indus Valley Civilization usually refer to the mature phase of the developments in the region between 2600 and 1900 BCE. Hence, the term Indus Valley Tradition has been used by American archaeologist Jonathan Kenoyer to denote the much longer chronology of an urban culture that struck roots at Mehrgarh circa 7000 BCE, grew and flowered over a vast region covering the Indus and Ghaggar-Hakra river basins, and culminated in the rather rapid decline of the flourishing urban conglomerate by 1900–1500 BCE.[39]

This was essentially a civilization of well-planned city-states supplied by abundant agricultural production in the floodplains of the several rivers flowing through the

1.7 The so-called Pashupati seal from the Mature Harappan Phase (2600–1900 BCE) at Mohenjodaro, showing a horned figure surrounded by various animals including the elephant.
Courtesy: National Museum, New Delhi.

region. The urban centres were linked through extensive trade in various commodities including semiprecious stones. A variety of ornaments was crafted; bead-making was especially popular and the materials used included steatite, stone, gold, copper, shell, and ivory. Trade links extended as far west as Mesopotamia. In fact, there are references in ancient Mesopotamia to the products of the Indus cities; among these ivory is specifically mentioned.

Among the material remains of the Indus cities are the rather intriguing seals engraved with animal figures and inscriptions. Typically small and square or rectangular shaped (as opposed to the round seals of Mesopotamia), Harappan steatite seals feature animals such as humped bull, gaur, rhinoceros, buffalo, goat, elephant, tiger, the mythical unicorn or composite animals, along with three to seven engraved pictograms and sometimes an unidentified object or symbol associated with a particular animal. The most accepted explanation is that these seals were used by traders to convey a message of identity by literally stamping a relief image onto a piece of wet clay applied to a pot or bales of merchandise. Some images such as the so-called "Pashupati" or horned figure surrounded by various animals clearly convey religious symbolism of some kind (figure 1.7).

The Harappan culture is the least understood among the major ancient civilizations in the world, in part because its script has not been satisfactorily deciphered. The relationship of the Harappan people to the Vedic ("Aryan") and the Dravidian cultures of the subcontinent is a hotly debated topic today but this need not concern us here. Our interest lies in the elephant-human relationship during Harappan times. For long it has been accepted that this culture provides the earliest evidence for the taming of the elephant not just in Asia but anywhere, and we should examine this in some detail.

With the intensification of the Indian monsoon circa 8000–7000 BCE, the northwestern region of the subcontinent was also moister than it is today. The Indus basin would have been covered with more extensive forests, particularly moist forests along river and stream courses, and drier vegetation in the plains. It is therefore conceivable that the range of the wild elephant extended from the Siwaliks southwest into the Indus basin (as did the range of other large mammals such as rhino, gaur, and tiger). However, it would be wrong to assume that the Mature Harappan culture flourished under a very much wetter climatic regime, because the monsoon had weakened after attaining its peak strength during the very early Holocene. More recent evidence suggests that environmental conditions circa 2500 BCE were rather similar to those prevailing at present.[40] Again, it would be incorrect to assume that elephants would have been abundant in the Indus basin prior to or during the

1.8 Depiction of the elephant on seals and tablets from the Indus civilization provide the earliest evidence for the taming of the animal:
a A broken seal from the Kot Diji Phase (2800–2600 BCE) of the Early Harappan civilization, possibly the oldest seal showing an elephant.
Courtesy: Harappa.com.
b An intact steatite seal from the Mature Harappan Phase (2600–1900 BCE) depicting the elephant with lines on its back suggestive of a cloth draped over it.
Courtesy: Harappa.com.
c Seal of elephant with lines resembling ropes around the neck and cloth on its back, from the Mature Harappan Phase (2600–1900 BCE).
d Copper tablet from the Mature Harappan Phase (2600–1900 BCE) showing a "horned" elephant.
From D.P. Sharma (2000), Harappan seals, sealings, and copper tablets, *National Museum, New Delhi.*

peak phase of the Harappan civilization. The elephant could certainly have been present in reasonable numbers here during the Early Holocene when the monsoon was stronger than at present; but conditions would have changed by the Late Holocene when the monsoon had weakened.[41]

The elephant is not the most common image depicted on the Harappan seals (that distinction being conferred on the mythical unicorn) but there are several depictions that can be examined (figures 1.8a–d). Almost invariably the elephant is shown with a line extending across its body, from behind the shoulder down to behind the front leg, sometimes curving backward to merge with the hind leg. Richard Carrington is of the opinion that "as the natural conformation of the elephant's skin does not show a fold at this place, it is reasonable to assume that the line represents the forward edge of some kind of saddle or drapery".[42] Placing a cloth on an elephant's back before riding it is a practice that is seen even today in southern India among the Jainu Kurubas who are superb mahouts. Some seals also show five concentric rings behind the neck of the elephant; these can be interpreted as ropes to restrain the animal.[43] However, it must also be pointed out that many other creatures depicted on seals, including the mythical unicorn, the rhinoceros, the markhor, the ibex, the water buffalo, the tiger, and even composite animals are shown sometimes with similar concentric rings, and these are not necessarily animals that were tamed, restrained with ropes, and ridden.

Another line of reasoning as to whether or not a Harappan animal was wild or domesticated is based on the presence or absence of an unidentified object, interpreted by some scholars as a shallow trough or bowl, in association with the animal on the seal. In many seals, animals such as gaur, rhinoceros, and buffalo are shown bending over this object as if to drink. Even the tiger is shown on a seal with such an object. To our way of thinking, a creature bending as if to drink from a bowl would be indicative of a domesticated animal, but apparently this was not the case with the Harappan artists! All these animals who are depicted drinking from a bowl are obviously wild ones. In contrast, the humped bull or zebu, clearly a domesticated animal, is depicted without this bowl-like object, and so is the elephant. If this line of reasoning is correct the elephant was a tamed animal during Harappan times. What were the Harappan seal-makers trying to convey through this seemingly illogical symbolism? Was it wishful thinking on their part, their dream being to tame all wild creatures? Or does the bowl-like object in front of these animals convey some other meaning? Actually, another such taller object seen on seals depicting the mythical unicorn is believed to have ritualistic associations. Overall, the evidence of the elephants depicted on the Harappan seals points to these being tamed animals.

One striking aspect of the elephant figures on seals and other Harappan objects such as copper tablets is that they are all tusked elephants (and therefore males). The elephant on the "Pashupati" seal too is clearly a tusker as is the horned elephant on a copper tablet. As in modern times, the tusker could have represented the ideal for the Harappan people, and it is not unexpected that it should be the predominant elephant image. At the same time, not a single elephant figure has a rider; this is rather surprising if the elephant had been tamed and put to some human use. Putting all the evidence together we can cautiously conclude that the elephant had been tamed by Harappan times, but not necessarily that the Harappan people were the first to achieve this feat in the subcontinent.

When was the elephant first tamed by the Harappan people? Our most reasonable estimate would come from dating of seals that have been unearthed at a number of sites including Mohenjodaro, Kalibangan, Jhukar, and Harappa, and have been generally

1.9 Terracotta elephant figure with red and white bands (seen only faintly now) painted on its face suggestive of decorations on a captive animal. This figurine was discovered in 1987 on Mound E at Harappa dating to about 2200–1900 BCE.

Courtesy: Harappa.com.

attributed to the Mature Harappan Phase (2600–1900 BCE), also termed by Jonathan Kenoyer as the Integration Era. Jonathan Kenoyer and Richard Meadow, however, describe a broken, unfinished elephant seal from an older phase – the Kot Diji Phase (2800–2600 BCE) – of the Regionalization Era or Early Harappan Phase. From this seal it is difficult to make out if the elephant is a tamed one (it is clearly a tusker, and the bowl-like object is absent), but there is no reason to believe otherwise. We can thus conclude that the elephant had been tamed by the Harappan people at least 4,600 years ago. Kenoyer also describes an elephant figurine with red and white painted bands across the face suggesting that the animal may have been used to a limited extent by the Harappan people for some ritual/ceremonial purpose (figure 1.9).

Bones of elephant along with those of camel occur only sparingly at Harappan sites though the geographical spread of such finds extends across Sindh, Punjab, Rajasthan, and Gujarat. It is unlikely that the Harappan people consumed elephant meat to a significant degree, though occasional use cannot be ruled out.[44] The bones may have been used to fashion tools and other objects. Elephant tusks and ivory artefacts such as awls,

1.10 Bronze elephant "toy" from Daimabad, a Late Harappan site in Maharashtra. It is now believed that this object on wheels was used in rituals.

Photographed at the National Museum, New Delhi.

PREHISTORY AND PROTO-HISTORY

seals, combs, hooks, jar stoppers, and hairpins are also known from many Harappan sites; indeed, at Lothal in Gujarat a partially cut tusk was found from the "acropolis" area, termed the "ivory worker's shop".[45] Whole elephant tusks are also known from pre-Harappan sites such as Mehrgarh. Excavations at Daimabad, a Late Harappan site in Maharashtra have yielded bronze figures, including an elephant on a platform about a foot long that was drawn on wheels (figure 1.10). Once described as a toy, this is now believed to have ritualistic significance.[46]

It is easy to see how the taming of the elephant and eventually putting it to the service of humans became a reality in the course of history. Once modern humans equipped themselves with tools to exert control over large animals, often dangerous to humans, this activity would have been a challenge to their mental and physical prowess. Thus, Ann Baker and Clyde Manwell proposed the "dare theory of domestication" in which they argued that the taming of cattle, horses, and elephants fulfilled this newfound desire at a particular stage in human evolution.[47] Such creatures were then naturally incorporated into ceremony and religious rituals.

What sparked the idea of keeping a pet elephant may have actually been a rather tame event. An elephant calf separated from its herd wanders into a group of domestic cattle grazing in the jungle. In the evening the cattle are driven back to their pen near a settlement. The curious calf causes great excitement among the villagers who decide that it must remain amidst them. The challenge of rearing a young elephant and training it to be totally under human command as it grew bigger would still remain, but it would not be insurmountable for a people who were already familiar with the control of other large animals. The accoutrements needed to control an elephant are quite basic – stockade, ropes, and spears – and would have been available locally. This creature was also more intelligent than other animals already tamed, and provided the opportunity for a new relationship between man and beast. In fact, the diversity and splendour of this relationship has not been exceeded by any other human-animal relationship since.

CHAPTER 2

Elephants in Vedic and Epic Literature

THE DECLINE OF THE HARAPPAN CIVILIZATION was complete by about 1700 BCE. Now begins a period in Indian history, the entry of the "Aryans", that is one of the most contentious as regards its civilizational continuity. The predominant view for nearly a century, first enunciated by British archaeologist Gordon Childe,[1] was that a group of barbaric nomads from Central Asia migrated through passes in the Hindu Kush range into northwestern India, beginning sometime before the middle of the second millennium BCE. These pastoralist tribes, riding horses, are said to have raided and sacked the towns of the advanced Harappan civilization of the Indus region, causing its dramatic collapse.

Based on a more careful examination of the archaeological and literary evidence, present-day historians have largely rejected the "Aryan invasion hypothesis".[2] There was no single, large-scale incursion of people during the second millennium BCE but, rather, a series of migrations over centuries of many tribes who obviously shared several cultural traits. The view that these Indo-European tribes sacked the Harappan towns is not tenable; it is far more likely that they assimilated gradually into the existing societies. The real debate today, and a very acrimonious one at that in view of its political overtones, is whether the Harappan people were the ancestors of the Dravidians of peninsular India, or were related to the "Aryans" with whom they had a direct civilizational link. However, this debate does not concern us here.

The earliest literary sources for this period of history are the Vedas. Meaning "knowledge", the four extant Vedas – *Rigveda, Yajurveda, Samaveda,* and *Atharvaveda* – are essentially compendiums of hymns, sacrificial rituals, and magical spells. Attached to the Vedas are prose manuals – the Brahmanas whose concluding portions called Aranyakas (forest books) have esoteric commentaries, the Upanishads, appended. The Vedas and their commentaries make only passing references to the elephant, as could be expected of a people more familiar with the horse, still in the process of assimilating the culture of the land they had migrated to. At the same time it could be argued that even the later Vedic texts, the Brahmanas and the Upanishads, composed after a distinct elephant culture had developed in the subcontinent, do not talk much about the animal because their purpose was quite different.[3] In any case, since Vedic literature comprises ritualistic texts, not many firm conclusions may be drawn from the incidental references to elephants.

The *Rigveda*, believed to have been originally composed around 1500 BCE, refers to the elephant variously as *mriga-hasti,*[4] *hastin,*[5] *ibha,*[6] and *varana.*[7] The first reference in the *Rigveda* to the elephant is by the term *mriga-hasti,* literally a beast with a hand (figure 2.1). To the Aryans unfamiliar with any creature possessing a proboscis or trunk this was the most natural description of the elephant. The term *mriga* was later used in Sanskrit texts such as the *Gajashastra* (see Chapter 3) to refer to a particular breed of elephants (though it generally meant animal, and more specifically deer). The word *ibha* in the Vedic texts has been correctly interpreted as elephant; indeed, the Greek word "*elephas*" and the English "elephant" may be derived from this Sanskrit source.[8]

Apart from the strange appearance of this creature with a long nose that functioned as a hand, its size and strength were also striking. Thus, in the *Rigveda* the elephant is mentioned most commonly in the form of a simile to sing the praises of the various gods.[9] A hymn to Agni, the god of fire, compares his actions to an elephant consuming the trees,[10] as does another hymn to the Maruts, the spirits of tempest and thunder ("Like the wild elephants ye eat the forests up when ye assume your strength among the bright red flames").[11] Indra, the king of the gods, is compared in his strength to a mighty wild elephant in musth ("As a wild elephant rushes on this way and that way, mad with heat"),[12] and likewise the Ashvins (twin charioteers) are compared to "two mad elephants

2.1 A female elephant raises its trunk to locate the direction of an intruder. To the immigrant Vedic people unfamiliar with the elephant, a creature with a trunk was appropriately termed *mriga-hasti* in the *Rigveda*.

bending their forequarters and smiting the foe".[13] Soma, the moon god, in contrast, is likened to "a docile king of elephants".[14] There is also mention of hunters following two wild elephants[15] presumably with the intention of capturing or killing them.

These early references to the elephant indicate familiarity with wild elephants, but not necessarily with the use of captive ones, during the latter half of the second millennium BCE. The description of two elephants "smiting the foe"[16] is considered by some as evidence for the use of elephants in war, but is disputable. The immigrant people would certainly have encountered captive elephants if the people of the Harappan civilization had already tamed them, but the *Rigveda* does not present compelling evidence that the former used them in war. This does not rule out the limited use of captive elephants in Rigvedic times. Historian Sarva Daman Singh is of the view that, since captive elephants were invariably derived from the wild, it would be natural for the early Vedic people to describe them as wild animals.[17] He suggests that "the use of the elephant is not impossible during the Rigvedic period.... It would be difficult to explain the supposed Aryan indifference towards the elephant throughout the five hundred years or more of Rigvedic composition, specially if we recall its domestication by the people of the Indus valley. The animal...must have been occasionally used in some engagements – not in large numbers, of course – though its efficacy on the field of battle was yet far from established."[18] Singh also points out that the word *chaturanga* appears in the *Rigveda*[19] with reference to the human body; this term was later commonly applied to the fourfold division of the ancient armies of the subcontinent – foot-soldiers, horse-riders, chariots,

2.2 The concept of the fourfold organization of the army that first came into vogue during late Vedic times, can be traced to the use of the term *chaturanga*, *anga* meaning body, in the *Rigveda*. The elephant as part of the *chaturanga sena* is illustrated here in the 13th-century Hoysala temple at Somnathpur.

and elephants (figure 2.2). The ancient Indian game of *chaturanga*, the forerunner of chess, had corresponding pieces – *raja* (king), *mantri/senapati* (minister or general – the queen in chess), *ratha* (chariot – rook), *gaja* (elephant – bishop), *ashva* (horse – knight), and *padati* (foot-soldier – pawn).

The horse is mentioned far more frequently and accorded greater importance in the *Rigveda,* and in the three later Vedas for that matter, than is the elephant. This is in contrast to the Indus civilization, where the elephant is found on seals but not the horse, and may be taken as an indication of the non-indigenous origins of the Vedic people. Of the sacrificial rituals elaborated in the Vedic literature, the most prestigious was the *ashvamedha yajna* (horse sacrifice) in which a specially chosen horse was let free to roam at will followed by a band of 400 warriors. Any neighbouring ruler who dared to capture the animal in effect challenged the power of the owner and was at risk of being attacked. At the end of one year the horse was brought back to the king's capital and sacrificed along with 600 bulls.

The *Yajurveda, Samaveda,* and *Atharvaveda* are usually dated to the first half of the first millennium BCE. The *Yajurveda* explicitly states that only three animals – man, elephant, and ape – have use of the hand.[20] There is reference to the *hastipa,* a category of people who were elephant-keepers or elephant-owners,[21] and even a mention of sacrifice of elephants.[22] The *Atharvaveda* makes an observation of an elephant tormented by (biting) flies,[23] which is common even today during the monsoon in dense tropical jungle. A hymn composed for the consecration of a newly-built house compares it to a standing she-elephant; presumably it has been built on four posts as solid as an elephant's legs.[24] In the *Atharvaveda* we find a clear reference to the taming of an elephant that was to be the royal mount: an entire hymn, the only such hymn in the Vedic corpus, is devoted to describing the attributes of the elephant, the most pleasant among beasts to ride upon.

> Famed be the Elephant's strength, the lofty glory, which out of
> Aditi's body took existence!
> They all have given me this for my possession, even all the Gods
> and Aditi accordant.
> On this have Mitra, Varuna, Indra, and Rudra fixed their thought.
> May those all-fostering deities anoint and balm me with their strength.
> The strength wherewith the Elephant was dowered, that decks a
> King among the men, in waters,
> O Agni, even with that strength make thou me vigorous to-day.
> The lofty strength which sacrifice brings, Jatavedas! unto thee,
> What strength the Sun possesses, all strength of the royal Elephant – such strength
> vouchsafe to me the pair of Asvins
> lotus-garlanded!
> Far as the heaven's four regions spread, far as the eye's most
> distant ken.
> So wide, so vast let power be mine, this vigour of the Elephant.
> Now hath the Elephant become chief of all pleasant beasts to ride.
> With his high fortune and his strength I grace and consecrate myself.[25]

If the king rode a state elephant it is certainly likely that this animal along with other elephants was also trained for use in battle, though the Vedas do not explicitly mention such deployment. By late Vedic times, around the 6th century BCE, there is incontrovertible evidence that elephants were being used in war.

The prose manuals attached to the Vedas, but composed during later periods, also provide glimpses into the assimilation and elaboration of the elephant culture by the Vedic people. The *Aitareya Brahmana*, a text of the 7th century BCE, mentions an elephant that comes up "when bidden by the voice", a clear reference to a well-trained elephant.[26] The same text also speaks of Bharata Dushyanta, the ruler of Anga, conquering neighbouring lands and performing the horse sacrifice, on which occasion he gifted 10,000 tusked elephants along with 10,000 slave girls to brahmans.[27] Such grossly exaggerated numbers recur in many later accounts of the strength of the elephant corps or other wings of the army in Indian history. Nevertheless, it is significant that large numbers of elephants have been attributed to Anga, a region encompassing present-day Bihar/Jharkhand that supported a sizeable population of wild elephant over the centuries. As we shall see later in this account, Anga was the origin of the ancient elephant lore of India. Whatever the numbers of elephants that exchanged hands following the *ashvamedha yajna* in ancient Anga, it is certain that the practice of gifting elephants was well established by late Vedic times.[28] The *Sama Vidhana Brahmana* clearly mentions the elephant as being part of the fourfold division of the army,[29] while the *Chandogya Upanishad* lists elephants along with a number of other possessions that measure a person's wealth.[30]

The Vedic people arrived as semi-nomadic pastoralists but gradually assimilated the agricultural practices of the local communities as they pushed eastwards, burning the land in the process to facilitate cultivation and settlement. A passage in the *Satapatha Brahmana* relates how Agni moved eastward, setting fire to the land, until he reached the river Sadanira (modern Gandak).[31] Gradual mastery over iron technology by the late Vedic period made it possible to cut forests more easily with iron axes and break the land for cultivation with iron ploughs. The use of iron implements to clear the forest would have been especially more useful in the moister and denser forested tracts of the east. The geographical descriptions in the *Rigveda* refer essentially to the northwest of the subcontinent, the region of the Indus and its tributaries known as *sapta-sindhu*, but the later Vedic literature includes the rivers of the Gangetic basin. Prominent among the few material remains of the period is the clay pottery, the so-called Painted Grey Ware, sometimes found in association with iron objects in western Uttar Pradesh dated to late Vedic times. Over a period of about a thousand years the relationship of the Vedic people to the elephant developed from mere curiosity about this creature with a hand to the matter of its capture, taming, use as a beast of burden and, perhaps, even limited use in skirmishes. The agro-pastoralist culture, nevertheless, remained a horse-based one over this time. As D.K. Lahiri-Choudhury points out, the horse remained the *vahana* or mount of the supreme Vedic god, Indra – it was not yet time for Indra to mount Airavata, the royal white elephant.[32]

***

We may now turn to the two great epics of heroism and moral instruction from India, the *Ramayana* and the *Mahabharata*, for further facets of the interaction between the later Vedic people and the elephant. This is not an easy task given that these accounts began at an indeterminate time in the past as oral traditions that were memorized and handed down the generations with several interpolations over time. Thus, references to the elephant in the epics cannot be dated within a sufficiently narrow window for reconstructing historical trends. There have been debates over which of the two epics is older. Scholarship suggests the 8th or 9th century BCE for the origin of the *Mahabharata*, with later additions up to the 4th century CE;[33] for the archetype Valmiki *Ramayana*, the probable date of composition is between 750 and 500 BCE with the present version dated to the late 2nd century CE.[34]

2.3 A scene at the Ramachandra temple (early 15th century), Hampi, showing Rama and Sita, and possibly Lakshmana and his consort, riding elephants. Although the elephant as a royal mount is mentioned, such a description of the prince of Ayodhya actually riding an elephant is absent in the archetype *Ramayana*.

The stories central to the epics may, of course, have their roots in historical events from a much earlier period. Set in the northern plains around Kurukshetra, the *Mahabharata*, the world's single longest poem, relates the struggle of the Pandavas and the Kauravas, the sons of two brothers descended from King Bharata. The *Ramayana*, set in the kingdom of Kosala to the east of the Ganga-Yamuna confluence, is the tale of Rama's life in exile as a forest-dweller, his search for his abducted wife Sita, and his eventual victory over her kidnapper, the demon king Ravana. The *Ramayana* "can be seen as the expression of a certain historical consciousness"[35] that profoundly influenced the cultural life not only of India but of Southeast Asia as well.

I begin with the *Ramayana* that gives a more sober account of the use of elephants and more graphic descriptions of the forests and the denizens of the region.[36] Indeed, as we shall see below, the entire story of the epic can be related through episodes which all have references to the elephant. The description of Ayodhya, the capital of Kosala, begins with a powerful statement that it is full of gigantic bull elephants in rut.[37] Three breeds of elephants – *bhadramandra*, *bhadramriga*, and *mrigamandra* (*bhadra* meaning excellent/auspicious and *mandra* meaning pleasant) – descended from the cosmic elephant are mentioned. This classification of elephants, common in Indian tradition through the centuries, corresponds to the *koomeriah*, *dwasala*, and *mriga* of later Sanskrit texts. Further, the *Ramayana* states that these elephants were born in the Vindhya and the Himalaya, clearly indicating knowledge of the occurrence of wild elephants both to the north and to the south of the Gangetic plains.

For Rama's consecration as prince regent, a rutting bull elephant fit for a king to ride is made ready, in addition to a white bull and a white horse (figure 2.3).[38] Upon receiving a message that his father Dasharatha and his step-mother Kaikeyi wish to see him, Rama rides a chariot to the palace along a road lined with adoring people, and teeming with trumpeting elephants and neighing horses.[39] Kaikeyi breaks the news to him that it is not Rama, but her son Bharata, who should rule the land of Kosala with all its treasures including its horses and elephants.[40] Rama calmly agrees to lead a life of an exile in the forest for 14 years and, sighing like an elephant, goes to his mother Kaushalya's chambers to break the news.[41] His brother Lakshmana angrily shakes his hand as an elephant would shake its trunk, from side to side or up and down, as he tries to persuade him not to yield to this unreasonable demand,[42] and asserts that he will turn back this fate that is running wild like a rutting bull elephant.[43] He swears to slaughter the enemy including their elephants and horses with his sword and his arrows.[44] Rama's calm arguments finally prevail and, as he departs, Kaushalya prays that the huge wild elephants and other

2.4 An elephant herd drinks at a river deep inside a forest. When Rama in exile reached the forests of the Chitrakuta mountains he expressed his desire to live by a river where elephant herds would come to drink and stir up the waters.

beasts in the forest will not harm him.[45] Back at his palace, his wife Sita laments that the royal elephant which was to lead the procession for his consecration is nowhere to be seen[46] and, upon hearing the news of Rama's banishment, vows to accompany him to the forbidding forest teeming with elephants and other creatures.[47] Before Rama departs for the Dandaka forest along with Sita and Lakshmana, he gives away all his wealth to brahmans and his dependants; his prized elephant Shatrumjaya, worth more than a thousand others, is gifted to the priest Suyajna, a master of the Vedas.[48]

Upon Rama's departure, the animals and the people of Ayodhya go into a state of shock. The elephants become unruly[49] and stop feeding.[50] The cries of the women resemble those of cow elephants when their bull is captured.[51] The words of their husbands pierce the wives as would the goad of an elephant.[52] King Dasharatha, grief-stricken at Rama's banishment, broods over the curse pronounced upon him by the blind parents of a young boy he had killed with his arrow a long time ago on the banks of the Sarayu, mistaking the sound of the boy's pitcher filling water from the river for that of an elephant drinking.[53] Dasharatha dies of sorrow the same night. This story perhaps indicates that the hunting of elephants was a royal sport during that period.

Wandering through the forest, Rama, Sita, and Lakshmana reach the hermitage of the sage Bharadvaja at the confluence of the Ganga with the Yamuna. When they depart after an overnight stay, the illustrious sage urges them to go to the Chitrakuta mountain which has a dense forest safe from fires, where herds of elephants are to be found, and the sounds of birds, rutting deer, and many elephants would make it a pleasant spot to establish their ashram.[54] Rama obviously relishes the beauty of this forested landscape as

2.5 In this Pahari painting (Chamba style, 18th century), Rama accompanied by Lakshmana and Hanuman rides an elephant in the assault on Lanka. The *Ramayana* itself describes Rama and his antagonist Ravana riding chariots in the climactic battle.

he describes to his wife its enchanting trees, animals, rocks, and streams, concluding that no human can fail to find contentment and happiness in a place where herds of elephants come to drink in the river and stir up the waters (figure 2.4).[55]

Bharata in the meantime, enraged to hear that his mother Kaikeyi is responsible for Rama's exile, enters the forest with a retinue that includes many elephants, to locate his brother and persuade him to take his rightful place at Ayodhya.[56] The wild elephants of Chitrakuta flee upon seeing the approaching retinue.[57] The brothers have an emotional reunion, but Bharata fails in his mission and returns to Ayodhya with Rama's footwear placed on the head of "a splendid elephant",[58] as an emblem of his brother's supreme position. Lahiri-Choudhury points out that the action of placing the sandals on the elephant's head, and not its back, recalls a bas-relief at Bharhut depicting the Buddha's relics being similarly transported.[59]

In the course of their wanderings, Rama, Sita, and Lakshmana observe beautiful landscapes and the wild denizens of the forest, including elephants pushing over trees or playing in ponds covered with lotuses and lilies.[60] The main danger to them comes from the *rakshasas* whom they have to fight on several occasions; some of these demon-like people are powerful enough to kill lions, tigers, and elephants with their iron spears.[61] As their 14-year exile nears its end, Ravana, the king of the *rakshasas*, kidnaps Sita and carries her away to his kingdom on the island of Lanka. He woos the fair Sita by praising her beauty, describing her thighs to be "as smooth as an elephant's trunk",[62] but the virtuous lady spurns his advances. Ravana then orders his monstrous *rakshasa* women to not only guard Sita but also use "terrible threats and gentle coaxing" to break her will "as one does with a cow elephant".[63]

Rama enters into a pact with the monkey-king Sugriva who assembles his hordes of monkeys, strong as elephants, to search for Sita in Lanka.[64] Hanuman, a noble and wise monkey given the task of crossing the ocean to Lanka, increases enormously in size and, as he presses his foot on Mount Mahendra to take a gigantic leap, the mountain pours out its waters as a bull elephant in musth would secrete from its temples.[65] Hanuman locates

2.6 According to the *Ramayana*, in the battle for Lanka, the monkey warrior Angada fighting on the side of Rama wrenched off the tusk of Ravana's brother Mahodara's elephant. In this painting Angada strikes down Devantaka with the tusk torn from Mahodara's elephant. Folio from the *Ramayana of Valmiki*, Mughal, late 16th century, artist Shyam Sundar.
© *Freer Gallery of Art, Smithsonian Institution, Washington DC: Gift of Charles Lang Freer.*

2.7 Indra riding the elephant Airavata, as depicted at the Hoysaleshvara temple, Halebid, Karnataka, Hoysala period, early 12th century. Indra's change of mount from the horse to the elephant during late Vedic times indicates a transition from a horse-based to an elephant-based culture during the early first millennium BCE.

Sita in the Ashoka grove within Ravana's palace, and he is captured, bound, and his tail set on fire, but he manages to use that to his advantage by setting the grounds on fire.

After Hanuman returns with the news that Sita is alive in Lanka, Rama and the monkey army prepare for the climactic battle with Ravana whose forces are organized in the conventional fourfold manner that includes elephants.[66] When news of the approaching army reaches Lanka, Ravana's generals boast that their forces are capable of crushing these monkeys, but his brother Vibhishana advises him to rightfully return Sita to Rama before the latter lays waste to Lanka along with its elephants and other precious things.[67] When Ravana refuses to heed his advice, Vibhishana defects to Rama's side and provides him a description of Lanka's forces comprising 1,000 elephants, 10,000 chariots, 20,000 horses, and 10 million *rakshasa* soldiers;[68] even if exaggerated this is certainly a more sober estimate of elephants in a subcontinental army as compared to the hyperbole that is common in the *Mahabharata*. Rama's combined force is now ready to begin the assault on Lanka (figure 2.5). Elephants and other wild creatures of Lanka flee in terror from the approaching monkey force that fills the air with deafening roars as it sweeps across the land.[69] These are no mere monkeys; some of them are as powerful as ten elephants, others as powerful as one hundred, and still others as one thousand elephants as they lay siege to Ravana's palace.[70] The slaughter on both sides is immense but the monkey force holds the upper hand. Lanka's giant Kumbhakarna, notorious for his long bouts of sleep, is woken up by marching elephants over his body so that he may join the battle.[71] Ravana's brother Mahodhara rides the elephant Sudarshana against the monkeys but an agile Angada fells the beast, wrenches off its tusks, and boldly sallies into the battlefield (figure 2.6).[72] Ravana's valiant son Indrajit heads a force that includes powerful warriors riding elephants.[73] In spite of his large elephant army, Ravana rides a chariot in the final encounter with Rama who does likewise. Rama uses a special arrow gifted to him by Brahma to kill Ravana, whereupon the latter's consorts wail like female elephants.[74] When Rama does not accept the rescued Sita, suspecting her chastity, she wilts like a creeper that has been pulled down by an elephant's trunk,[75] but undergoes a fire-ordeal to prove her innocence, and the united couple return to Ayodhya for Rama's consecration. Interestingly, it is not Rama but Sugriva (on the excellent Shatrumjaya) and his monkey force who ride elephants during the triumphant procession at Ayodhya.[76]

What can we glean from the *Ramayana* about the elephant and its cultural relationships with people during the first half of the first millennium BCE? It is clear that wild elephants were plentiful in their natural habitat, the forests and mountains of the north, including the Vindhya and the Himalaya. At the same time, captive elephants were now common in the towns and armies of the local republics. The concept of a mighty bull elephant, a *bhadramandra*, as the royal mount was firmly established, and riding an elephant was a desirable skill for a prince. However, the ownership of elephants was not a royal monopoly; nobles and other wealthy citizens too possessed elephants and had the privilege of riding them (as they did when accompanying Bharata in search of Rama as well as when the prince returned from exile). A prosperous town was one that possessed many elephants in addition to horses and chariots; thus, the concept of the *chaturanga sena* or army with four divisions is well established. Elephant-hunting was an accepted royal sport (thus, Dasharatha indulges in it though he makes a bad mistake on one occasion). The indigenous forest-dwellers, too, probably hunted elephants, perhaps even more commonly. Elephants were also caught in snares[77] or perhaps using nooses from the back of captive elephants.[78] Musth in elephants was clearly recognized, as was their habit of feeding by pushing over trees and their peeling or rubbing off bark with their tusks.

2.8 Two young bulls lock tusks in a friendly duel at Kabini in Karnataka. The fight between two bull elephants is often used as a simile in the *Mahabharata* to describe the clash between two warriors.

The specific mention in the *Ramayana* of the king of the gods (Indra) riding the rutting (i.e. in musth) elephant Airavata,[79] in contrast to Indra's horse *vahana* in the Vedas, may be taken to imply a society in an early phase of transition from a horse culture to an elephant culture (figure 2.7). Interestingly, war elephants are mentioned more frequently and explicitly as a part of Ravana's forces, perhaps indicating their more common use south of the Vindhyas. However, as emphasized by Lahiri-Choudhury, the kings and the heroes ride horse-drawn chariots and not elephants in battle.[80] Further, the role of the elephant is not defined in any of the skirmishes or the climactic battle of Lanka, unlike in the other great epic, the *Mahabharata*.

The *Mahabharata* describes the struggle of the Pandavas and the Kauravas for the kingdom of Hastinapura, literally "town of elephants". The might of the elephant attracts the usual comparisons in the *Mahabharata* with the strength of its heroes (or villains as the case may be).[81] Thus, the might of Bhima, the strongman of the Pandava brothers, is compared to that of 10,000 elephants. His clashes with Duryodhana, the eldest of the Kaurava brothers, and later with Jarasandha are described as contests between roaring elephants. A particularly pithy simile, in the words of Lahiri-Choudhury, is the description of Bhima's engagement with Duhshasana, another Kaurava prince, as a clash between two rutting bulls over a cow elephant (figure 2.8), as its original cause was Duhshasana's molestation of Draupadi, wife to the Pandava brothers. Other heroes of the *Mahabharata*, including Arjuna, the valorous Pandava brother, and his equally brave son Abhimanyu, are also likened to elephants, the father to the master bull of a herd and

2.9 The elephant is more integral to the descriptions of war in the *Mahabharata* as compared to the *Ramayana*. A contest between the Pandavas and the Kauravas is depicted in this painting from a *Razamnama*, the Persian translation of the *Mahabharata*, circa 1800 CE, Murshidabad. *Courtesy: National Museum, New Delhi.*

the son to a furious elephant. The old, blind king Dhritarashtra, on the other hand, aptly moves like an "age-afflicted King Elephant".[82]

The *Mahabharata* also mentions trade in elephants, the gifting of elephants, and even elephants as wager (Yudhishthira, the righteous and eldest Pandava brother, loses 100 fine elephants among other possessions to the Kauravas' cunning uncle Shakuni in the legendary game of dice).

Where the *Mahabharata* differs distinctly from the *Ramayana* is in its descriptions of the use of elephants in war (figure 2.9). The most famous elephant-related incident in the *Mahabharata* is that of Ashwatthama, the name of an elephant as also of the son of the veteran guru Drona who fought on the side of the Kauravas. On the fifteenth day of the great war at Kurukshetra, the Pandavas are wilting under the relentless assault of the great teacher's weapons. Krishna, the master strategist of the Pandavas, comes up with a game plan to dishearten Drona by deceiving him into believing that his son Ashwatthama is dead. The Pandavas are aware that Drona will not believe this story unless he hears it from the mouth of Yudhishthira who is known for his adherence to truth. Seeing Yudhishthira's initial hesitation, his brother Bhima picks up a mace, kills the elephant named Ashwatthama and announces in his stentorian voice that Ashwatthama is dead (figure 2.10). Drona turns in disbelief to Yudhishthira for confirmation, whereupon the latter pronounces *"Ashwatthama hathaha kunjaraha"* ("Ashwatthama is dead, the elephant"), the last part spoken softly and drowned by the sound of Krishna beating his drums. Drona instantly collapses, giving victory to the Pandavas that day. Lahiri-Choudhury feels that this episode is too central to the main story of the epic for it to be a latter-day interpolation.[83] The episode could therefore indicate the use of the elephant as an instrument of war in early *Mahabharata* times.

Most of the elaborate accounts in the *Mahabharata* of the deployment of elephants in the army are clearly later interpolations. Military strategist Brigadier G.D. Bakshi has termed the *Mahabharata* the "Indian *Weltanschauung*" that enunciates a paradigm of war based on attrition and annihilation of the enemy.[84] The *chaturanga bala* or *chaturanga sena*, the fourfold army is a recurring feature in Indian history and literature. This ponderous four-armed force comprising infantry, chariotry, cavalry, and elephants was designed for major battles in the flat terrain of northern India. Each *akshauhini* or unit of the field army is described as comprising 21,870 chariots (each with five men), 21,870 elephants (each with six men), 65,610 cavalry, and 109,350 infantry. It is claimed that 18 such *akshauhini*s, 11 of the Kauravas and seven of the Pandavas, fought at Kurukshetra, clearly a case of extreme hyperbole. Lahiri-Choudhury observes that the concept of the *chaturanga sena* is again too central to the *Mahabharata* war for it to be a later addition. Yet, as he also points out, the great heroes of the battle ride chariots and not elephants. The few warriors who ride on elephants, including Bhagadatta on the side of the Kauravas, and Ghatotkacha along with his demon hosts on the side of the Pandavas, are not the principal characters of the epic.

It would thus seem that the *Mahabharata* represents the entire period of transition in ancient Indian warfare during the first millennium BCE, from the predominance of horses and chariots, through the development of the four-armed field army, to the decline in chariotry with strengthening of the elephant corps. This could also represent a change in military strategy along a geographical gradient from the dry plains of the north to the moist forests of the east; Lahiri-Choudhury also quotes the advice provided by the venerable Bhishma to Yudhishthira – use a force predominantly of horses and chariots during the dry season, but shift to infantry supported by elephants during the monsoon.

At this stage we must pause to ask a fundamental question: when was the elephant first decisively used as an instrument of war in the subcontinent? If the elephant had been tamed and put to human use during pre-Vedic times it is obvious that the animal could always have been used to intimidate an enemy. This is however not the use of the elephant in organized warfare. In early Vedic literature there is only a hint of the use of the elephant in battle. By the 6th century BCE elephants were not only being used by Indian rulers in local wars but they were also being sent to rulers in the West for

2.10 Bhima armed with a mace fights an elephant in this sculptural depiction at the Chennakeshava temple, Hoysala period, early 12th century, at Belur, Karnataka. The scene could represent Bhima either killing the elephant Ashwatthama or fighting Bhagadatta's elephant.

2.11 The *Gajashastra* alludes to crop raiding by wild elephants in the ancient kingdom of Anga. In this photograph a herd of elephants tramps across a harvested crop field in southern West Bengal. These elephants from Jharkhand have since the 1980s begun to move deeply into West Bengal to raid agricultural crops.
Photograph by Biswajit Kar.

use in their battles (see Chapters 3 and 4). It is obvious that the export of elephants trained in battle points to a much earlier cultural development of the war elephant in the subcontinent. Considering all evidences, including those of the epics, I would date the origin of the war elephant to the very early part of the first millennium BCE. It would take a few hundred years more for elephants to be deployed on a much larger scale in subcontinental battles.

***

Since Anga is mentioned in the *Mahabharata* as an important source of elephants, it is interesting to note that ancient elephant lore in India is generally traced to the mythical sage Palakapya who is reputed to have lived in the region of Anga during the 6th or 5th century BCE. Three Sanskrit texts attributed to Palakapya's exposition of the science of the elephant are known today. Of these, the *Hastyayurveda* and the *Gajashastra*, the former from the Anandashram Series at Pune, and the latter from Sarasvati Mahal Library at Thanjavur, are considered as older.[85] While the two texts have much in common, they also have differences, with the *Hastyayurveda* providing more details of anatomy and physiology, and the *Gajashastra* an account of elephant distribution. It is not possible

to date the archetypes of these texts, but they have some material in common with the *Arthashastra* (circa 300 BCE – 300 CE, see Chapter 3). The third text, *Matangalila* of Nilakantha, is a succinct treatise that may be about a thousand years old or perhaps earlier.[86] In all, the elephant lore covers a range of subjects – from the creation of elephants, their morphology, and growth with age, to methods of capture, psychology, physiology, treatment of diseases, diet, and distribution in the *gajavana*s or elephant forests. I shall use the term *gajashastra* to generally refer to the ancient science of the elephant.[87]

Elephant lore as we know it today has undoubtedly been compiled over a long period of time but seems to have its beginnings in Anga during the reign of King Romapada. The people of Anga approach the king with an anguished plea to catch the wild elephants that have been ravaging their crop fields (figure 2.11). Romapada obliges them (after obtaining a boon from various distinguished sages) and the elephants are rounded up and brought to the palace grounds. Sage Palakapya, who has wandered among the elephants and studied them, then appears before the king and pleads with him to release the elephants. The venerable Palakapya then goes on to relate his knowledge of the biology of elephants

2.12 Musth, a physiological and behavioural state in male elephants, has been described in amazing detail in ancient elephant lore such as the *Gajashastra*. In this close-up shot of a tusked bull elephant the secretion of the musth gland behind the eye is clearly seen.

and their management. His *Gajashastra* is an impressive narration of ancient scientific knowledge of elephants, even assuming that the present version is possibly quite different from the sage's exposition (if such a sage did indeed live in Anga). Its descriptions of musth in bull elephants are especially notable for their scientific precision, a remarkable achievement for its times considering that biologists have had only a rather hazy knowledge of this phenomenon until very recently (figure 2.12).[88]

There are two observations I would make on the *Gajashastra*. It seems to have grown out of an animal rights' perspective – the sage's plea to the king to release the marauding elephants back into their natural habitat has obvious parallels in today's animal rights and even conservation movements. The second point to note is that the conflict between wild elephants and people over the destruction of crops, a major modern-day concern, was also an ancient one. As the Vedic people spread into the Gangetic basin, establishing small settlements and cultivating a variety of crops in the lowlands, amidst jungle, the elephants would have been gradually pushed into higher ground or land less suited to agriculture. At the same time the crop fields would have attracted the elephants, resulting in serious elephant-human conflict. Eventually as the size of settlements and extent of cultivation increased and then merged into even larger human-dominated landscapes, the lowland forests would have been cleared across the Gangetic plains, and the conflict would have reduced or disappeared locally. The capture of elephants to reduce conflict would have also provided the opportunity for the republics, kingdoms, and empires to build up their elephant forces.

***

At the time that the *Rigveda* was being composed around 1500 BCE, an isolated population of the elephant, generally believed to be the Asian species, was still found over an extensive area from Syria to the Tigris-Euphrates valley, the region of the Mesopotamian civilization. Evidence from ivory objects, stone vessels, and steatite seals for the presence of elephants has to be interpreted cautiously because some of these objects may have come from outside the region.[89] We know that Mesopotamia traded with the Indus cities and, thus, some of the ivory objects found in Mesopotamia may have come from the Indus[90] or perhaps Africa.[91] Mesopotamian cylinder seals depicting elephants are not of the Harappan style, but could have been fashioned in a region intermediary to Mesopotamia and the Indus.[92]

The pharaohs of the other major ancient civilization, spread along the Nile river in Egypt, exploited the elephants of this region. Kings Thutmose I (1525–1512 BCE) and Thutmose III (1504–1450 BCE) both hunted elephants in northern Syria.[93] Amenemhab, an officer of Thutmose III, records an elephant hunt at Niy in the following fragmentary inscription: "Again [I beheld] another excellent deed which the Lord of the Two Lands did in Niy. He hunted 120 elephants, for the sake of their tusks and [-----]. I engaged the largest which was among them, which fought against his majesty; I cut off his hand [i.e. trunk] while he was alive [before] his majesty, while I stood in the water between two rocks. Then my lord rewarded me with gold...."[94] The tomb of Thutmose's vizier Rekhmire is lavishly illustrated with various scenes including that of Nubians carrying tusks as tribute, and a retinue from Syria leading a small elephant with tusks, commonly interpreted as the Asian species.[95]

An inscription of the late 12th century Assyrian king Tigleth-Pileser refers to the hunting and capture of elephants along the river Habur as follows: "Ten powerful male-elephants in the land of Harran (Karrani) and (on) the bank of the Khabur I slew. Four elephants alive I captured. Their hides (and) their teeth along with the live elephants I brought to my city Asur."[96] That elephants continued to survive in this region into the early centuries of the first millennium BCE is also seen from an inscription (circa 879 BCE) of Ashurnasirpal II on the occasion of a grand banquet organized at the inauguration of the palace of Calah.[97] This records that the king caught 30 elephants in pits, in addition to killing 450 lions, 390 bulls, and 200 ostriches as befitted a ruler of his stature. Further, he received five live elephants as tribute from the governor of Suhu and Lubda. Elephants were among the animals he maintained at a menagerie within the city of Calah.

2.13 The Black Obelisk of Shalmaneser III (858–824 BCE), a black limestone bas-relief erected around 841 BCE at Nimrud in northern Iraq, glorifies the achievements of the Assyrian king after a successful campaign in Syria. Among the figures depicted on the five bands of relief on one side of the obelisk is an elephant brought as tribute from Musri in present-day northern Iraqi Kurdistan; the small ears of the elephant suggest that it was the Asian species.
Photographed at the British Museum, London.
© *Trustees of the British Museum, London.*

2.14 Among the archaeological remains of the Shang dynasty (16th–11th century BCE) in China are elephant-shaped, wine-serving bronze vessels (*zun*), as shown in this image.
Photographed at the Musée Guimet, Paris.

Ashurnasirpal's son Shalmaneser III (859–824 BCE) also exacted tributes of elephants from Syria and other places in the Persian Gulf, as depicted in the famous "Black Obelisk", though some of these may have originated in India (figure 2.13).[98] The "Syrian elephant" seems to have gone extinct by the early 8th century BCE as a result of capture and hunting for ivory.

***

Finally, we turn to the other major Asian civilization, namely ancient China, and very briefly review its relationship to the elephant at this time. During the second millennium BCE elephants were found in the north of China as far as the region of present-day Beijing.[99] Archaeological remains of the Shang dynasty (circa 16th to 11th century BCE) of the north, the earliest Chinese dynasty with a written history,[100] clearly point to the incorporation of the elephant into the material culture of the period. Inscriptions of the Shang period are found on the animal bones or shells known as oracle bones that represent the beginnings of the Chinese writing system. A feature of this early writing system is the use of "rebus writing" in which the sign or pictogram for one word is also used for another word with a similar sound. A stylized elephant is used in the oracles to mean the "elephant" itself, as well as "image" that has a similar pronunciation.[101] An oracle bone inscription also refers to elephants being sacrificed to the ancestors.[102] The Shang archaeological sites have yielded a rich haul of bronze castings that include, in the southern sites of a late period, an elephant-shaped *zun* (wine-serving vessel), and a *nao* (cymbal or bell-type percussion instrument) decorated with a pair of elephants (figure 2.14).[103]

Elephant-related objects also appear among the remarkable material finds of Sanxingdui in the southwestern province of Sichuan, discovered as late as the 1980s.[104] This site of a "lost civilization" of China, located in the Chengdu plains on the south bank of the Yazi river, is a fortified city covering over 12 square kilometres that is believed to have flourished during 1500–1100 BCE. More than a tonne of artefacts of bronze, jade, gold, and stone, along with animal bone and a large haul of elephant tusks, recovered from two "sacrificial" pits have dramatically transformed our knowledge of the Chinese Bronze Age. Along with the amazing bronze heads and masks of Sanxingdui is a larger-than-life sculpture of a human, possibly a shaman or king, standing barefoot on an elongated base supported by four elephant-like heads.[105] The pit containing the remarkable bronze figures, sometimes broken, also yielded 60 charred elephant tusks strewn on the top layer.[106] The significance of this find is not clear – the deliberate burning and breaking of many items perhaps indicates symbolic "killing" in ceremonial rituals.[107] In this respect, Sanxingdui, though contemporary with the Shang dynasty, was clearly different culturally from the latter whose sites have yielded evidence of real sacrifices.

The Zhou dynasty replaced the Shang dynasty in the mid-11th century BCE. The philosopher Mencius (4th century BCE) recorded that the king of Zhou "drove far away also the tigers, leopards, rhinoceroses, and elephants" to the great delight of all the people of the middle and lower valley of the Yellow River, clearly implying the nuisance value of these animals to the peasants.[108] It is almost certain that elephants had been tamed to a limited extent and even used in war in ancient China; there is a brief record that during the 6th century BCE the ruler of Chu lashed torches to elephants and set them against the army of the state of Wu.[109] The Chinese relationship to the elephant thus shows some similarities but also many differences with that of India; the elephant was used to a limited extent and incorporated into the expression of art, but it was also considered an agricultural pest that had to be eliminated as civilization spread southward in the centuries before the dawn of the Common Era.

CHAPTER 3

Elephant Armies
and the Rise of Empire

THE RISE OF LARGE ELEPHANT ARMIES in the subcontinent is inextricably linked to the establishment of kingdoms in the 6th century BCE and the eventual emergence of empire under the Mauryas. A sovereign king could now establish laws sanctifying coercion as a means of absolute control over and loyalty from the citizens. A large standing army was needed to protect the kingdom from surrounding rivals. Among the kingdoms that arose in the Gangetic plains were Kashi, Kosala, and Magadha, the last-mentioned located in southern Bihar being the most important for our purposes.[1]

Located strategically across several nodal points along the Ganga river system, Magadha was able to control trade through this region. It also had access to rich natural resources both to the north and to the south, including forests with abundant elephant populations. The rich iron-ore deposits in the region helped in making weapons and agricultural implements to clear the forests and bring more land under the plough. Around 542 BCE Bimbisara ascended the throne of Magadha. He organized an efficient system of administration, conquered neighbouring Anga, and gained part control of Kashi.

By this time, not only were the chiefdoms and republics in the north capturing and maintaining small elephant armies, they were also supplying these to rulers further west. Cyrus the Great (559–530 BCE) who established the Achaemenid empire encompassing Mesopotamia and Persia was killed fighting the Derbikes (Scythians) when at a crucial stage in the battle they suddenly brought in some elephants that had been kept in hiding. According to the Greek historian Ctesias of Cnidus (circa 400 BCE), the elephants were supplied by Indians who also controlled the animals.[2] These elephants most likely came from a satrapy in the northwest of the subcontinent. Cyrus fell from his horse when his cavalry fled upon seeing the elephants, and an Indian wounded him grievously with a javelin. Before he died, however, Cyrus received help from the Sacans (Shakas) who, together with the Persians, defeated the Derbikes at great loss of men to both sides.

Darius I, the third of the Achaemenid emperors, continued to expand the greatest empire then known to the world until it encompassed 5 million square kilometres. An Achaemenid inscription dated circa 519 BCE claims possession of Gandhara, while in a later inscription Darius I also claimed "Hindush" (India). The Greek historian Herodotus (484–circa 425 BCE), who wrote extensively of the conflict between Greece and Persia, even lists India as one of the 20 satrapies of the Persians, an obvious exaggeration. The extent of Persian hold over the northwest of the subcontinent is not clear but it may have been considerable and included the region up to the Punjab.

Besides the threats from rival kingdoms, the events in the northwest may have spurred the Magadhans to secure their kingdom and strengthen their army. Takshashila (Taxila) in the northwest was an important centre of learning, and young men from Magadha travelled here to complete their education. Bimbisara was also in contact with the king of Gandhara whose kingdom may have included Takshashila. The imperial ambitions of the Achaemenids would certainly have alarmed the rulers of the northwest, and Magadha would not have been unaware of the events taking place here. According to Buddhist sources, king Bimbisara maintained a large and well-trained elephant corps. We have no idea of the number of elephants in the army, but this is likely to have been of the order of a few hundred; much larger elephant armies were to be raised later in Magadhan history. The organization of the army into the four-armed division – chariotry, infantry, cavalry, and elephants – possibly began to be elaborated by this time.

While Bimbisara was largely a man of peace, and an efficient and just administrator, his six successors beginning with son Ajatashatru were ruthless perverts. Finally, the weary Magadhans deposed the last of these kings and established the Shishunaga dynasty that lasted for half a century, before being overthrown by Mahapadma Nanda in about 343 BCE. Although the Nanda dynasty lasted for only a brief period, it was the beginning of imperial ambitions in the subcontinent, and important from the viewpoint of the military history of the elephant. The Nandas expanded the already large kingdom of Magadha, primarily through control of Kalinga (Orissa) and other parts of the Deccan, but also defeated a number of kshatriya kings and chieftains to the west as far as Kuru near present-day Delhi. An even larger army was obviously needed for these conquests as well as to secure the external borders. According to Greek sources (which vary in their estimates), the last Nanda king maintained an army of 200,000 foot-soldiers, 20,000 cavalry, 2,000 chariots, and anywhere between 3,000 and 6,000 elephants. These figures are now considered exaggerations, but we shall examine the size of Magadha's elephant force later in this chapter.

At this time a threat more ominous than the one posed earlier by the Persians was looming in the northwest. A young general in his 20s, Alexander III of Macedon, was on an invincible blitzkrieg across West Asia and would be soon knocking at the northwestern doors of India. Alexander's famous battle of the Hydaspes against Porus (Puru) who fielded an elephant force is among the most celebrated accounts in Western history of Alexander's campaigns.[3] Strangely, there is no mention of Alexander, much less the battle of the Hydaspes, in any of the ancient Indian sources. Romila Thapar concludes that the Greek intrusion made little lasting impression historically or politically on India. According to her the most significant outcome of Alexander's jab at India "was that he had with him literate Greeks who recorded their impressions of India".[4] The most important of the original Greek accounts of Alexander's campaign were of Admiral Nearchus, and of Alexander's own captain Onesicritus. These accounts do not survive but fragments are known from the writings of later historians such as Arrian. Another important Greek source of this period of Indian history is Megasthenes who was sent by Alexander's successor Seleucus Nikator as ambassador to the court of the Mauryan emperor Chandragupta. Again, only fragments of Megasthenes' account survive in later works by historians such as Arrian and Strabo (60 BCE–19 CE); in fact, Strabo dismisses much of Megasthenes, Onesicritus, and Nearchus in that order! This is not surprising given that ancient Greek accounts of India are an obvious mixture of fact and fiction. Nevertheless, quite credible details of elephants can be gleaned from these classical sources.

By the end of the summer of 326 BCE, Alexander's forces had swept across the Persian empire, encircled Egypt, thrust northwards into the Hindu Kush, crossed the main Indus and, after a much written about tactical victory over an elephant force at the Hydaspes (Jhelum), reached the Hyphasis (Beas), the easternmost tributary of the Indus. The popular perception that Alexander first encountered elephants at the famous battle on the banks of the Jhelum is incorrect. Not only had he seen elephants in Persia, his own forces included a sizeable number of elephants by the time he reached the Jhelum. Before he reached northwestern India, Alexander's main battles were against Darius III, ruler of the Persian Empire. In late September 331 BCE, Alexander's army of 40,000 infantry and 7,000 cavalry descended the hills of Jebel Maqlub to confront the much larger force of Darius (greatly exaggerated accounts of one million infantry and 40,000 cavalry are given by Arrian) at the decisive battle of Gaugamela (near present-day Mosul in Iraq). Unlike during earlier encounters between the two foes, Darius fielded two strange units, a force of 200 scythe-bearing chariots and 15 elephants brought in by his Indian supporters to astonish and terrify the Greeks.[5] On the day of battle the elephants along with 50 chariots were to be placed at the centre of the frontline to closely support the king's cavalry (according to battle plans that fell into Greek hands later). Alexander dealt effectively with the scythed chariots but, unfortunately, we have no accounts of how he handled the elephants. It is possible that the elephants did not effectively participate in the battle, as the Persians were inexperienced in deploying the beasts. All that we know is that one of Alexander's generals "Parmenio seized the Persian camp with their baggage, elephants, and camels".[6] In spite of a decisive though hard-fought victory at Gaugamela, Darius escaped, and Alexander continued his pursuit to establish complete control over the Persian empire. After a month's sojourn at Babylon, Alexander marched to Susa (Khuzistan) whose satrap Abulites greeted him with gifts of swift camels and 12 elephants that Darius had originally obtained from India.[7]

In the spring of 327 BCE Alexander gazed eastwards from the slopes of the Hindu Kush mountains perhaps expecting to see not just fabled India but also the ends of the earth as conjectured by his teacher Aristotle. He probably realized from these heights that Aristotle's geography was not correct after all, and that it would be a long march across India. When he descended from the Hindu Kush he was greeted by Taxiles, the ruler of Takshashila, escorted by his chiefs and 25 elephants; Taxiles promised him these beasts when he eventually reached their kingdom.[8] Before Alexander reached the Indus he had to overcome resistance from the Assacenians of the lower Swat valley whose forces included 30 elephants.[9] When he captured the town of Ora several elephants left there presumably by the Assacenians seem to have fallen into his hands.[10] According to Arrian, Alexander was "especially anxious to find out all about the elephants" because he sent a force to locate the brother of Assacenus who had fled into the hills along with the beasts.[11] Alexander had also received news that Abisares, a hill tribe leader from present-day Kashmir, had left his elephants to graze in the Indus valley. With the help of his informers who clearly were local tribesmen skilled at capturing elephants, Alexander set out to "hunt" these elephants, driving two of them over a precipice unfortunately, but successfully rounding up the rest.[12] These elephant catchers then mounted the elephants and brought them into Alexander's army. When Alexander reached the Indus he was greeted by Taxiles as promised with many gifts including 30 elephants. Taxiles also surrendered his kingdom to Alexander. More gifts were to follow when Alexander reached the capital of Takshashila: Taxiles' son Mophis gave him another 56 elephants.[13]

Thus, Alexander was quite familiar with elephants and possessed 100–150 animals when he reached the west bank of the Jhelum in May 326 BCE for his famous encounter with King Puru.[14] The ensuing confrontation is among the most written about battles in Western historical accounts; probably the sheer novelty of a Greek army meeting up with an elephant force and defeating it was too attractive a tale to pass by. The Greek sources in particular are sufficiently detailed for a graphic reconstruction of the tactical victory achieved by Alexander under difficult conditions.

Pre-monsoon showers and snow melt in the mountains had already swelled the Jhelum as Alexander and Puru's forces faced each other near present-day Haranpur. Alexander knew that attempting to cross at this point would be virtually suicidal because Puru's "elephants...would render it impossible for the horses to land".[15] Thus he decided to ford the river about 25 kilometres upstream, with an elite force of 5,000 cavalry and an equal number of infantry, under cover of darkness amidst a heavy downpour. At dawn a surprised Puru rushed his son with a small force of cavalry and chariots upstream but it was too late to stop Alexander. Puru now reorganized his main army to face Alexander. Leaving a small number of elephants to deter Alexander's general Craterus from crossing the Jhelum at Haranpur, he advanced with his remaining force of 30,000 men, 4,000 cavalry, 300 chariots, and anywhere between 80 and 200 elephants.[16] The elephants were

3.1 "The Phalanx Attacking the Centre on the Hydaspes", a painting of the battle at the Jhelum between Alexander and Puru's elephant army, by A. Castaigne, 1899.
Courtesy: Andrew Chugg.

placed in front with the infantry behind and on the wings in the expectation that "none of the enemy would have the audacity to push themselves into the spaces between the elephants", and in order to "produce terror everywhere among Alexander's cavalry".[17] The experienced Alexander however launched his elite cavalry on the left wing of Puru's army. Puru's forces were pushed back towards their own elephants for protection, but the elephants were advancing against the enemy in the meantime. In the heat of battle the elephants did not recognize friend or foe and trampled them all alike. Alexander's horse-mounted archers selectively picked off the mahouts, while the infantry armed with long pikes and machetes blinded the elephants, hacked their trunks, and grievously wounded them. As the trumpeting elephants retreated in confusion, Alexander surrounded them with his cavalry and advanced upon Puru's disarrayed force with his infantry in phalanx formation (figure 3.1).[18] Although comprehensively defeated, the mighty Puru seated on his elephant "did not depart as Darius the Great [had done], setting an example... to his men".[19] It was only after he was wounded on his right shoulder that Puru gave up the fight. As he fell from his elephant, the story goes that his elephant, the faithful and sagacious Ajax, guarded him from the enemy and even pulled out the spears from his body.[20] When Alexander reached the fallen king and asked him what treatment he would like to receive, Puru's dignified reply was "*basilikos moi chresai*" ("treat me like a king"). Realizing that the tall Indian ruler was his equal in every way, Alexander not only restored his kingdom to him, but added more territory to it.[21]

What was the eventual role of the elephant in Alexander's fortune? The first point to note is that Alexander did not deploy any of his elephants against Puru, even though the two forces had roughly similar numbers of elephants. What could be the reason for this? Historian H.H. Scullard speculates that Alexander may not have had the time to coordinate the elephants he had obtained from various sources into a cohesive force or to train his cavalry to work with them,[22] and therefore perhaps did not wish to experiment with using his elephants in battle.

The second and more important issue relates to the role of the elephant in Alexander's unexpected retreat not long after his victory at the Hydaspes when his heart seemed set on the conquest of the whole of India and beyond, to the ends of the earth. With the help of his Indian allies, including King Puru, Alexander pushed further east, crossing the Acesines (Chenab) and the Hydraotes (Ravi) overcoming the towns of the Glausae tribe (that he handed over to Puru) and sacking Sangala in the process. This advance was not easy as the monsoon had broken and the rivers were in spate, but the battle-hardened Macedonians nevertheless made it to the west bank of the Hyphasis (Beas) in two months' time.

At the Beas the Greeks did a curious volte-face. Alexander's soldiers refused to go any further. Alexander made spirited attempts to rally his troops but failed upon which he sulked for the next three days and then announced his decision to turn back; conquest of the whole of Asia would have to wait for a more opportune moment.

Alexander's journey down the Indus on a large fleet of galleys and boats (with his general Hephaestion marching along the left bank with 200 elephants), his savage attacks on several towns in the Punjab, his disastrous march westwards through the desolate Makran desert, and his eventual entry into Babylon have been described in various accounts. Many of the surviving elephants from his Indian campaign, including those he received as tribute after his decision to turn back from the Beas, seem to have reached Babylon. Although Alexander strangely never used his elephants in an offensive role, he undoubtedly used them as beasts of burden to maintain supplies for his army, as well as in ceremony. Phylarchus, for instance, describes the splendour of Alexander's pavilion at Babylon and states that "round the tent, was [stationed] a troop of elephants regularly equipped, and a thousand Macedonians" in addition to 10,000 Persians.[23] That his encounter with Puru's elephants made a lasting impression on Alexander can be seen from the commemorative silver coins (decadrachms) that were minted at Babylon. One of these special coin types, only three of which have been found, shows Alexander on his favourite horse Bucephalus charging with his lance at the great elephant carrying Puru

3.2 Decadrachm or silver coin (obverse) of Alexander riding his horse Bucephalus, charging with his lance at the great elephant (supposedly called Ajax) carrying Puru and his mahout.
© Trustees of the British Museum, London.

and his mahout (figure 3.2). (On the reverse of the coin Alexander is depicted god-like, with the thunderbolt of Zeus, the Greek king of the gods, and the god of the sky and thunder, in his right hand, and Nike, the goddess of victory, flying to crown him with a wreath.) After Alexander's death at the age of 33 at Babylon, his embalmed body was taken in a vehicle whose rich decorations included a painting of war elephants led by their Indian mahouts and followed by armed Macedonians.

We now go back to examine what really broke the will of the Greeks at the Beas. Though these soldiers had fought some tough battles in Persia, the hot and muggy weather in the Indus basin during the summer monsoon was a very different experience. The encounter with Puru's elephants had shaken them in spite of their tactical victory. Then, the advance from the Jhelum to the Beas took 70 hot days under almost continuous rains, accompanied no doubt by disease, snake-bites, and death. If the India beyond were to be no better, it is not surprising that the Greeks chose to go back, as Commander Coenus put it, "to see their parents, if they are still alive, their wives and children, and their homeland".[24]

When Alexander reached the Beas, he was informed by the local ruler Phegeus that it was a 12-day march across arid land to the mighty river Ganga, beyond which was the real India, a vast and fertile land ruled by powerful kings possessing armies that included much larger numbers of elephants. Alexander doubted these reports but Puru confirmed this was indeed true.[25] The Greek sources differ on the number of kings and the size of their armies. Plutarch mentions that the kings of the Gangaridai (lower Bengal) and the Praesii (Magadhans under the Nandas) awaited Alexander with their force of 80,000 cavalry, 200,000 foot soldiers, 8,000 chariots, and 6,000 fighting elephants.[26] Megasthenes, on the other hand, states that to the east of the Ganga the king of the Gangaridai possessed "a vast force of the largest-sized elephants", estimated at 4,000 animals, and this was a deterrent to any enemy.[27] Diodorus similarly gives a figure of 4,000 elephants.[28]

Some historians consider the reported numbers of elephants in the Indian armies as exaggerated, perhaps made up by Greek historians to justify the retreat of their army. I would argue that a few thousand captive elephants in the Magadhan kingdom was certainly not impossible, considering the intense exploitation of elephants that must have taken place during the 4th century BCE; after all, Puru and other tribes in the northwest, outside the range of wild elephant distribution, had between them 350 to 400 elephants.

Referring to the kingdom beyond the Ganga, Megasthenes stated that "all other nations dread the overwhelming number and strength of these animals [i.e. elephants]. Thus Alexander the Macedonian, after conquering all Asia, did not make war upon the Gangaridai, as he did on all others; for when he arrived with all his troops at the river Ganges, and had subdued all other Indians, he abandoned as hopeless an invasion of the Gangaridai when he learned that they possessed four thousand elephants well trained and equipped for war."[29] Obviously there are some inaccuracies here; Alexander never reached the Ganga itself but only the Beas. Nevertheless, the role of the elephant in the revolt of Alexander's soldiers cannot be denied. H.H. Scullard, an authority on the elephant in ancient Europe, agrees with this opinion that the Greek soldiers were most alarmed by the prospect of facing yet another and much larger elephant army, and thus "One not inconsiderable factor which forced Alexander to break off his incredible march of conquest was the elephant."[30]

***

We now move on to the Mauryans who, it is commonly acknowledged, established the first empire in India (figure 3.3). Chandragupta Maurya, the protégé of the brahman

Kautilya, according to tradition, overthrew the last of the Nanda kings circa 321 BCE to ascend the Magadhan throne. He then went on, through a series of military campaigns, to lay the foundations of a vast empire whose territories extended from the northwest across the Indo-Gangetic plains and into the southern peninsula up to the region of Mysore.

In 305 BCE, Chandragupta launched a campaign against Seleucus Nikator, one of Alexander's generals, who had succeeded the latter in the northwest. Seleucus made peace with Chandragupta by ceding his Indian territories; in exchange Chandragupta gifted him a considerable number of elephants – reported variously as 130 or 500 animals. The two continued to maintain friendly relations, and Seleucus' envoy Megasthenes spent time at Chandragupta's court at his capital Pataliputra (present-day Patna).

The Greek sources point to an interesting aspect of the control of elephants in the subcontinent during this period.[31] Nearchus, the admiral of Alexander's fleet during their retreat from the northwest, alludes to the private ownership of elephants, though mainly by the wealthy, in towns along the Indus. The position seems to have been quite the contrary in the Gangetic plains where the kingdoms and empires established a royal monopoly over elephants. Megasthenes' description of the Mauryan army implies a professional fighting force and an imperial monopoly of horses and elephants, animals that were essential to a formidable war machine. A reading of the *Arthashastra*, that brilliant manual of statecraft, strongly reinforces the Greek observations.

The *Arthashastra* is originally attributed to Kautilya, also known as Chanakya or Vishnugupta, who is reputed to have strategized the defeat of the Nandas and the ascension of Chandragupta to the Magadhan throne. The present-day version of the *Arthashastra* undoubtedly has many additions variously dated up to 150–300 CE by scholars.[32] However, the numerous references to elephants in this text seem to essentially relate to their role in the Mauryan war machine and the administration of its forests for the purpose of exploiting these animals.

The Mauryans went on an expansionist mode not only through conquest of neighbouring lands but also through opening up of new land for settlement and cultivation. The *Arthashastra* advises the ruler to actively clear the jungle and river valleys (and by implication, eliminate its wild animals including elephants) for new

3.3 Silver coin (obverse) of the the Mauryan period, 3rd century BCE, with five punches depicting elephant, bull, chakra, tree on hill (or crescent moon), and sun.
© *Trustees of the British Museum, London.*

3.4 The Kautilya *Arthashastra* (circa 300 BCE) exhorts the king to set up sanctuaries for the protection of elephants because they were useful for capture and use in the army, and also mentions several *gajavana*s or elephant forests in the country. This photograph (1987) shows the forests of the Anamalais (or elephant hills) along the border of Tamil Nadu and Kerala in southern India, recently constituted as an Elephant Reserve.

settlements[33] and, at the same time, establish sanctuaries for the protection of elephants along the periphery of the kingdom (figure 3.4).[34] These elephant sanctuaries, arguably the first such recorded preserves for the protection of a species, were to be patrolled by guards under the direction of a *nagavanadhyaksha* or "Superintendent of the Elephant Forests",[35] and the death penalty imposed on anyone killing an elephant here.[36] Other passages in the *Arthashastra* are explicit as to why elephants must be protected in sanctuaries. To quote from one translation: "some teachers say that land with productive forests is preferable to land with elephant forests, because a productive forest is the source of a variety of materials for many undertakings while the elephant forests supply only elephants. Kautilya disagrees. One can create productive forests on many types of land but not elephant forests. *For one depends on elephants for the destruction of an enemy's forces* [emphasis mine]."[37] Elephant sanctuaries were needed to ensure a steady supply of elephants for the king's army, a no-nonsense, utilitarian view. That these forests were to be subject to the least disturbance is also clear from another passage that prescribes the width of roads to be laid in different land forms. A road or a path within an elephant forest could not exceed thirteen and a half feet (about 4.5 metres) in width, or only a fourth of that suggested for towns and the countryside.[38] One cannot help but draw parallels between these contrary views over land use in ancient times and the modern conservation debates within India and elsewhere.

The *Arthashastra* also gives specific instructions about the type of elephant to be captured. A well-rounded elephant with a curving backbone and patches of red (presumably on the trunk or ears) was the best;[39] this corresponds to the physical descriptions of the *koomeriah* or royal elephant in ancient Sanskrit texts (figure 3.5). Summer was the best time of the year to capture elephants.[40] The capture of a calf (*vikka*), an elephant with small tusks (*modha*), a tuskless male or *makhna* (*makkana*), a diseased elephant (*vyadhita*), and a pregnant or a suckling female (*garbini, dhenuka*

3.5 A perfect *koomeriah* or royal elephant in the forests of Periyar in southern India (1960).

Photograph by M. Krishnan, courtesy: Estate of M. Krishnan.

3.6 The *Arthashastra* proscribed the capture of pregnant or suckling cow elephants as well as a tuskless bull or *makhna* (**a**), while prescribing that a 20-year-old elephant, meaning a tusked male (**b**) (following pages) should be captured, presumably because this was the most suited as a war machine.

hastini) was prohibited.[41] On the other hand, a 20-year-old elephant had to be caught for training. Considering that one could not catch a juvenile elephant or a tuskless bull, and that a mature cow was likely to have a calf at heel or a suckling offspring practically throughout her reproductive lifespan, it becomes clear that the *Arthashastra* was recommending the selective capture of male tuskers that had just attained adulthood (figure 3.6). The capture of young adult tuskers best served the needs of an elephant force in the king's army. Whatever the actual fighting qualities of a *makhna* as compared to a tusker, the latter was clearly the most sought after for its psychological effect on the enemy. It would not be out of place to mention here that, in spite of Megasthenes' observations that the elephants of Lanka (Taprobane to the Greeks) were larger than those of India – quite possible when you consider the robust build of the former's predominantly *makhna* population as compared to the tuskers of neighbouring southern India – the island's rulers had always sought tuskers from the mainland for use in battle and in ceremony.

There is no hint of sentiment in the Mauryan desire for elephants. These creatures were invaluable in the army and had to be protected (figure 3.7). The only exception to this is when the *Arthashastra* concedes that a calf may be caught to play with![42] The *Arthashastra* also does not provide any insights into the biology of elephants as given in the *Gajashastra*, granted that this was the latter's main purpose.

Elephants were not easy to capture and tame. This was no indiscriminate capture but selective acquisition based on the trainers' judgement of individual behaviour and physique after tracking the animals in the jungle. Trained cows were used as decoys to lure and trap the young adult bulls considered to be excellent. Those in the royal stables were classified into four types – elephants under training, riding elephants, war elephants, and untrainable elephants.[43] Instructions are given in the *Arthashastra* for the initial training of captured elephants, and for their eventual use for riding or in war. That elephants are highly intelligent is clearly recognized: those not amenable to training are recorded as being mischievous, vicious, genuinely mad, or clever enough to feign madness.

The upkeep of elephants in captivity was a serious matter that engaged the attention of the Mauryan administration. Elephants were to be kept in stables whose design and dimensions were spelt out. The *hastyadhyaksha* or Chief Commander of the Elephant Corps was in overall charge of the elephants and the elephant forests.[44] To look after the elephants at least 11 posts – from veterinary doctors and mahouts to cooks and guards – were prescribed in addition to the superintendent and the chief commander;[45] only four or five of these exist at any captive elephant facility in Asia today. Rations were prescribed in units on the basis of the animal's height.[46] A bull that had come out of musth had to be provided with a larger quantity of rations, presumably to enable it to regain body condition it had lost while in musth. The tusks of a bull that came from the plains had to be trimmed every two and a half years while those that came from the hills every five years (figure 3.8).[47] There was obviously a difference in the growth rate of tusks between elephants inhabiting the plains and those from the hills; the former would have been the larger elephants, as seen even today in both Asia and Africa.

The *Arthashastra*'s seeming obsession with tusked elephants for use in the army is at variance with Megasthenes' account of elephant capture by

3.7 Terracotta figure of an elephant with rider from Mathura, Uttar Pradesh, Mauryan period, 3rd century BCE. The elephant's uplifted head, to protect the rider behind, clearly indicates this to be a representation of a war elephant. *Photographed at the National Museum, New Delhi.*

3.8 The tusks of the bull elephant Inder at Mudumalai (southern India) being trimmed to lessen the risks of the animal causing injury to people or other elephants (1994). This practice may go back to Mauryan times as seen from such a prescription in the *Arthashastra*.

3.9 Although this elephant possesses an impressive pair of tusks, its lean build suggests this would have been considered a *mriga* body type that is inferior and not suited for use in war. The *Arthashastra* makes a pointed reference to inferior elephants found in Saurashtra; this could perhaps reflect the ecological status of the habitat that is generally not well suited for elephants.

the Mauryans using the stockade method,[48] arguably the "first datable report" of the use of this method according to Lahiri-Choudhury.[49] Interestingly, three or four female elephants were kept within the enclosure, presumably to lure the wild elephants, as they could help attract bulls or win the confidence of female-led herds. The taming of the captured elephants by breaking their spirit through hunger and thirst, as well as inflicting pain by deliberately cutting the skin around their necks before fitting a noose, are not very different from some of the less desirable methods followed in parts of Asia today. Once the elephants were subdued, the Mauryans seemed to treat the captives more kindly through soothing words and even music. Elephants that were too old or too young were released back into the jungle.

Through the selective capture of tusked bulls and individuals from family herds the Mauryans built up their stocks of elephants. These were undoubtedly supplemented by elephants received as tribute from the lands, especially of forest tribes, they subdued. The best elephants were trained for use in battle in gradual steps, first by making them stand still, then by movement drills that included lying down, supposedly jumping over obstacles (anatomically impossible in elephants), marching ahead trampling horses, chariots, and people before them, confronting other elephants, and assaulting forts. The last stage of training was learning to fight alongside horses, chariots, and foot-soldiers.[50] Although the *chaturanga sena* or four-armed fighting force is already integral to the description of war in the *Mahabharata*, it is perhaps in the *Arthashastra* that the most detailed instructions are available on its actual deployment in battle.[51] The basic unit of the army was a horse with rider supported by six foot-soldiers. There were five such units for each chariot and each elephant deployed. These basic units were then used to form various battle arrays and formations, details of which would be of interest only to military historians. While mixed arrays and formations seem to have been the favoured strategy, when a pure elephant array was to be deployed the war elephants were placed at the centre, riding elephants at the rear, and aggressive elephants along the flanks. Megasthenes adds that the war elephant carried a mahout plus three soldiers for shooting arrows.[52] Lahiri-Choudhury points out that a strong infantry, elephants, and horses were considered the most important in the Mauryan army; chariots are not specifically mentioned, perhaps indicating their declining importance in warfare.

The crafty Kautilya even thought of an ingenious means of breaking an enemy's ranks of horses and elephants – letting loose buffaloes, cattle, and camels with noise-making devices tied to their backs! Several centuries later Timur, the dreaded Central Asian Turk is reputed to have used buffaloes and camels set alight (see Chapter 7) to break the charge of the Delhi Sultanate's elephants, but Kautilya, the master theoretician, had clearly preceded the brilliant warrior in devising a counter-strategy to elephants.

The *Arthashastra* provides perhaps the first geographical account of the distribution of wild elephants in the forests (the *nagavanas* or *gajavanas*) of the subcontinent.[53] While this text merely names the eight *gajavanas* as sources of elephants, historian Thomas Trautmann provides a more detailed description of the geographical boundaries of these forests from a reading of several later Sanskrit texts.[54] It is worth listing these *gajavanas* and their probable locations (see figure 3.10):

– *Prachya Vana* refers to the forests of the Himalayan foothills and the plains along the eastern Gangetic and Brahmaputra basins south to the delta.

– *Kalinga Vana* is clearly the region of Orissa extending into south-central India.

– *Chedikarusa Vana*, *Dasarna Vana*, and *Angareya Vana* are located adjoining each other in north-central India.

3.10 Map showing the approximate locations and extent of the eight *gajavana*s or elephant forests mentioned in the *Arthashastra*, as reconstructed by Thomas Trautmann based on ancient Sanskrit texts. Note: 6000+ amsl = approximately 2000 metres above sea level.
Redrawn by Gitanjali Sukumar from Trautmann (1982).
Key:
1 – Prachya Vana
2 – Kalinga Vana
3 – Chedikarusa Vana
4 – Dasarna Vana
5 – Angareya Vana
6 – Aparanta Vana
7 – Saurashtra Vana
8 – Panchanada Vana

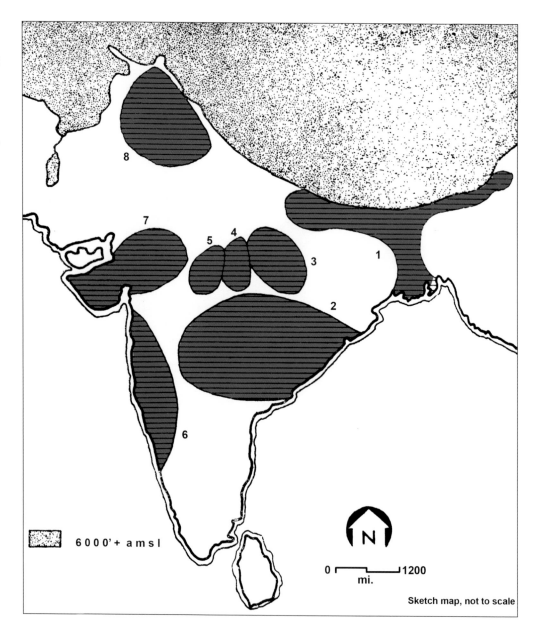

– *Aparanta Vana* is the region of the west coast and the Sahyadris from northern Maharashtra until at least Goa or perhaps further south into Karnataka.

– *Saurashtra Vana* as its name implies is clearly the region of Gujarat.

– *Panchanada Vana* is placed in the northwestern region of the subcontinent between the Himalaya, the Indus, and Kurukshetra to the north of Delhi.

The *Arthashastra* makes no mention of the elephant forests in the south of the peninsula but this is not surprising given that the influence of the Mauryan empire did not extend to the region of present-day Kerala and Tamil Nadu.

The best quality elephants are stated to hail from Kalinga Vana and Angareya Vana, while those of middling quality come from Prachya Vana, Chedikarusa Vana, Dasarna Vana and Aparanta Vana. The *Arthashastra* and other ancient texts are unequivocal in considering the elephants of Saurashtra Vana and Panchanada Vana as being the most inferior. This is again not surprising, considering that these two western regions are located in comparatively arid zones where elephant numbers could have been naturally low, and the animals of a physique (for instance, the lanky *mriga* type) not suited for use in war (figure 3.9). Differences in the build and stature of elephants can be clearly discerned even today in populations inhabiting the diverse eco-regions of Asia and Africa.

The map (figure 3.10) depicting boundaries of the eight *gajavana*s, reconstructed by Thomas Trautmann from ancient Sanskrit texts, shows that large parts of the north including the region between the lower Indus and the western Gangetic plain, as well as possibly in the east where the Mauryan empire was expanding its settlements and cultivation, was already devoid of wild elephants. The northwestern population of elephants in the upper Indus region was possibly already sparse as were the elephants of Saurashtra in the west. Reconstructions of the past climate of India reveal that the monsoon was weak and fluctuating from about the middle of the third millennium BCE to the dawn of the Common Era.[55] It is thus unlikely that the upper Indus or the Saurashtra regions could have sustained healthy or abundant elephant populations. From central India to the southern tip of the peninsula, as well as the entire Himalayan foothills extending east to the Brahmaputra valley and its surrounds, the wild elephant must have been of common occurrence in the plains and the hills. About 2,000 years ago the climate began to ameliorate with the strengthening of the monsoon. These large tracts of *gajavana*s must have ensured a steady supply of elephants to the rulers of the subcontinent whose passion for these beasts of war largely remained undiminished over the next 18 centuries, even if their use in battle seems to have declined for some centuries in the early period of the Common Era.

Before we close this account of the elephant in India during early Mauryan times, it would be useful to mention the status of the elephant elsewhere in Asia. The elephant was widespread on the island of Lanka that had already developed an elephant culture of taming and using the animal (see Chapter 5). We have little knowledge of Southeast Asia before the beginning of the Common Era but the extensive forest cover of this region would also have meant that wild elephants were distributed practically everywhere from Burma to Vietnam, Peninsular Malaysia, Sumatra, and perhaps Java. In East Asia the elephant had disappeared from a large part of China, including the basins of the Huang Ho (Yellow River) in the north and the Huai river in the east-central region, concurrent with the spread of the Shang and Zhou dynasties, and its range was now largely restricted to the region south of the Yangtze river.[56]

CHAPTER 4

The Elephant Goes West

THE WILD ELEPHANT IN THE REGION of the Tigris-Euphrates basin in West Asia, sometimes referred to as the "Syrian elephant" but almost certainly *Elephas maximus*, had died out during the first half of the first millennium BCE. Along with this any European contact with and knowledge of the Asian elephant would have been virtually extinguished. The early classical writings of European historians or travellers to the East provide us some glimpses of Western knowledge of the Asian elephant.[1] Most of these accounts have reached us in the form of extracts, summaries, or quotations from later European sources and, thus, we have to keep in mind that the original observations, quite fanciful at times, could have been distorted.

Ctesias of Cnidus (about 400 BCE) in Asia Minor provided the earliest surviving Greek account of India. He also spent a considerable period of time in the Persian empire as the court physician and, thus, had the opportunity to observe elephants first-hand. His original *Persica* (a 24-volume treatise on Persia) as well as his *Indica* are lost, but fragments are available from the later classical accounts.[2] Ctesias gave the Greeks two accounts of the use of Indian elephants in war. One such story relates to the campaign of the semi-mythical Semiramis, queen of Assyria, against an unidentified Indian ruler.[3] (Some historians identify Semiramis with the historical figure of Sammuramat, an Assyrian queen who ascended the throne around 810–805 BCE after her husband's demise.) The shrewd queen ordered her men to make dummy figures of elephants, using ox-hide stuffed with straw, when she heard that her opponent's forces deployed several of these giant beasts. The ploy did not work because the Indian king's real elephants, though confused at first by the strange smell of these dummies, eventually became wise to the ruse and made short work of them by trampling some underfoot, ripping up others with their tusks, and tossing many of the dummies into the air with their trunks. As mentioned in Chapter 3, Ctesias also related how Cyrus the Great of Persia was defeated in 530 BCE by the Scythians who used Indian elephants possibly commanded by Indian mahouts.[4] This may have been the first time that the Greeks came to know of the use of elephants in war. Ctesias' works were widely read and would have undoubtedly been the original source for the later Greek works on natural history.

The venerable philosopher-scientist Aristotle (384–322 BCE), a contemporary and tutor of Alexander the Macedonian, gave some of the most detailed and accurate accounts of the elephant in his zoological tomes such as *De Partibus Animalium* and *Historia Animalium*.[5] He recognized the existence of two varieties of elephants, the African and the Indian, and emphasized the similarities rather than differences between the elephants of the two continents. Aristotle seems to have been familiar with Ctesias' tomes as he directly quotes the Cnidian in his own writings on the elephant.

***

Alexander's death in 323 BCE triggered an intense struggle among his generals, governors, and soldiers for control of his vast territorial legacy. The main dramatis personae in the Mediterranean war theatre included Perdiccas, Alexander's second-in-command; Ptolemy, his Egyptian general; Lysimachus, one of his bodyguards; Seleucus, his eastern general; Eumenes, the head of the imperial chancery; Antipater, the governor of Macedon; Craterus, an outstanding soldier from Cilicia; and Antigonus, the one-eyed general from Phrygia. A motley group of lesser figures also joined the scramble for power and territory. Strangely, Alexander's successors (the "Diadochoi") seemed to have greater faith in the military role of the elephant. Their reliance on the giant beast was undoubtedly due to the shock and awe they could evoke in an enemy unfamiliar with the creature outside its natural range. At the same time, the elephant still had its utility in terrain where the horse had limitations.

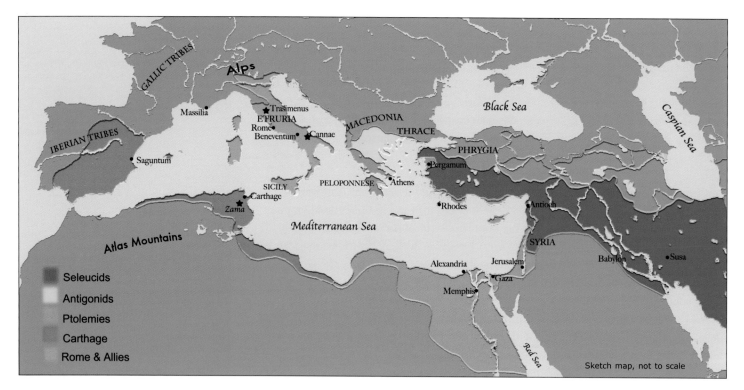

4.1 Map of the Mediterranean region during the late 3rd century BCE, showing the territorial extent of the principal powers that used elephants as war machines in their battles. Several important locations mentioned in the text are also marked here.

Map drawn by Gitanjali Sukumar.

The elephants brought by Alexander from India now began to play an offensive role for the first time in the Mediterranean war theatre. They were deployed not only in the complex internecine struggles of the Diadochoi but also against neighbouring powers (figure 4.1). In these battles, major and minor, the elephants from Asia were sometimes pitted against their African cousins, while at other times they were deployed along with the Africans in mixed formation. Two excellent volumes, one academic[6] and the other popular,[7] have dealt in considerable detail with the early history of the elephant in the Mediterranean. I therefore provide here only a summary of this 300-year history that culminated in the demise of the elephant as a war machine in this region by the time the Christian faith began to spread out from the Holy Land.

We begin with Perdiccas who was in the best position to control the imperial army at Babylon and moved first to elevate himself as supreme commander. He had to contend with Meleager, the commander of the infantry. Perdiccas began his manoeuvres by withdrawing outside Babylon along with the cavalry and the elephants. He then lured Meleager and his infantry out of Babylon under the ruse of conducting a traditional purification ritual for the army. In the process he separated 30 leaders of Meleager's force and suddenly turned his elephants upon them. All the men "were trampled to death beneath the feet of the beasts".[8] The elephants that Alexander had brought back to Babylon had obviously been trained in the art of war, even though they had probably never been used in an offensive role until now. Meleager fled but was pursued and killed.

Perdiccas now turned his attention to Egypt. Ptolemy had not only augmented his forces but also enhanced his prestige by snatching Alexander's corpse from Babylon with the stated intention of burying it in Egypt. Perdiccas and his Grand Army advanced up to the Nile without any opposition. The *hypaspists*, an elite infantry regiment, mounted an assault on Camels' Fort, a fortified post across the river, but Ptolemy managed to stave off the attack. Using his *sarissa*, a long iron spear with a wooden shaft, Ptolemy himself blinded the leading elephant in both eyes and injured its mahout, while his men killed the second elephant's mahout, forcing Perdiccas to retire for the day.[9]

Perdiccas then tried to cross the Nile near Memphis. Owing to the strong current he placed his elephants upstream of his men to break the force of the water – in a novel use of the large beasts. Unfortunately, the elephants and horses placed downstream stirred up the sand on the riverbed and made it deeper for the crossing men many of whom drowned. Fed up with their leader's reckless adventure, the *hypaspists* murdered Perdiccas. Ptolemy thus won without any serious engagement with the Grand Army. Although offered the supreme post he decided wisely to stay in Egypt. So far Ptolemy did not have any elephants but some of his opponent's beasts would have surely fallen into his hands.

The remains of the Grand Army withdrew to Syria where they decided to accept Antipater's supremacy. The former governor of Macedon now divided his forces, leaving 70 elephants – half the number he possessed – with Antigonus whom he appointed as commander of the Grand Army before withdrawing to Europe.[10] Thus, the approximately 200 elephants that Alexander had taken back from his eastern campaign had now dropped to 140 animals, the rest having perished or fallen into Ptolemy's hands. Antigonus now deployed 30 of the 70 elephants he possessed to neutralize Eumenes' superior infantry and cavalry. Eumenes fled to the safety of a hill fort. His next target was Perdiccas' brother Alcetas whom he battled at Pisidia. At the crucial stage of the battle Antigonus, who was holding the high ground, charged downhill with his elephants and his entire force to rout an inferior Alcetas.

Antipater died in 319 BCE leaving his army and his elephants not to his son Cassander, but in the hands of the marshal Polyperchon. With the support of Antigonus and Ptolemy, Cassander challenged Polyperchon. The battle was joined at Megalopolis in the region of the Peloponnese in Greece. Polyperchon attacked through a breach in the city's defence with 65 elephants (five of the original 70 seemed to have disappeared). However, measures had been taken to counter the huge beasts. A man called Damis in the city had accompanied Alexander to Asia and knew how to deal with elephants. He had arranged for a number of frames with sharp projecting nails to be buried along the path of the elephants. The poor, unsuspecting animals were injured by the metal spikes, while the Megalopolitan forces picked off the mahouts with their javelins, arrows, and catapults. Diodorus records that "Finally the most valiant and formidable elephant collapsed; of the rest some became completely useless, and others brought death to many of their own side."[11] The suffering elephants had obviously run amok. Leaving some of his men behind outside the city, Polyperchon withdrew to Macedon.

Many of the Greek cities now switched allegiance to Cassander who eventually drove Polyperchon out of Macedon and captured some of his surviving elephants. A desperate Polyperchon managed to enlist the support of Alexander's mother Olympias but Cassander isolated her at Pydna. In the terrible siege that followed some of the men turned to cannibalism while the remaining elephants subsisting on sawdust died of malnourishment. The city surrendered and Olympias was put to death.

The already complex Greek scenario now became even more so. Cassander transported his elephants in barges to Epidaurus to deal with Polyperchon's son who still held on in the Peloponnese. He then entered into a pact with Ptolemy and with Lysimachus to counter the growing power of Antigonus who was still involved in hostilities with Eumenes. After being ousted from Phoenicia, Eumenes crossed the Euphrates and reached Susa where he built up his force. Eudamus came over to Eumenes' side from India along with a force of 120 elephants; he had apparently obtained these from Takshashila after treacherously murdering Puru.[12]

The first major battle between Antigonus and Eumenes took place in 317 BCE at Paraetacene near present-day Ispahan, a "set-piece [battle] between two large Hellenistic armies and the first in which a very considerable number of elephants was used on both sides" according to Scullard.[13] Antigonus had 64 elephants left of his original 70, as against 125 elephants fielded by Eumenes. Scullard describes the battle formation of elephants, cavalry, and infantry in detail; this is reminiscent of the famous Indian battle scenes involving the four-armed forces but minus the chariots. Eumenes emerged victorious, his 125 war elephants prevailing over the 64 of Antigonus, but this was an incomplete victory as the latter held his ground in spite of heavy casualties to the infantry. A notable observation about this battle is that the cavalry and the elephants of both sides had been well trained to cooperate. In December 317 BCE Antigonus attempted to surprise Eumenes in the dry, salty plains of the Gabiene, fielding 65 elephants against Eumenes' 114 elephants. As the elephants clashed amongst themselves, Eumenes' lead elephant fell and he was forced to retreat. Eventually, Eumenes was captured and killed by Antigonus; the former's larger elephant force did not save him but perhaps prevented a complete rout during the battle. Unlike at Paraetacene, a considerable number of elephants, estimated by Scullard at anywhere between 32 and 77 animals, died at Gabiene.

Antigonus now nursed ambitions of uniting Alexander's empire but he had to contend with Cassander in Macedon.[14] Anticipating an attack from Egypt, Antigonus placed his son Demetrius along with 43 elephants in Syria. In 312 BCE Ptolemy along with Seleucus joined battle with Demetrius at Gaza.[15] Ptolemy had no elephants or very few of them, but effectively used *charax*, a chain of iron spikes along the elephant's path much like what the Megalopolitans had done to Polyperchon's elephants. After the javelin throwers and archers killed the mahouts, all the elephants fell into Ptolemy's hands.

So far we have been tracing the fortunes of the approximately 200 elephants that Alexander had taken back to Babylon from his India campaign. Alexander's satrap in India, Seleucus Nikator, too, acquired a considerable number of elephants, variously estimated by the Greek sources as between 130 and 500.[16] Now these elephants were also thrown into the Greek war arena (figure 4.2).

After a brief lull, in 310–309 BCE a furious Antigonus attacked Seleucus who controlled the eastern source of elephants, then attempted to invade Egypt in 306 BCE with a force of 83 elephants but was thwarted by a swollen Nile and, finally, opposed Cassander in 304–303 BCE at Macedon. The three now joined forces to confront Antigonus in 301 BCE at the battle of Ipsus in Phrygia. As opposed to the 75 elephants that Antigonus fielded, Seleucus launched a numerically much superior elephant corps that may have already experienced battle conditions in India. At a critical juncture at Ipsus, Seleucus' elephants prevented Demetrius, who had routed Seleucus' cavalry, from coming to the aid of his father. Antigonus fought bravely but was killed, and with him died the prospects of a reunited Greek empire.

Seleucus now had the largest elephant force in the region and even his opponents called him "Master of the Elephants". With the passage of time, some of the older rulers died and their sons took their place. Among the many battles fought in their internecine struggles, elephants were surely deployed, but this phase of history is not well recorded. We know that in a confrontation between Seleucus and Demetrius in 287 BCE the former used eight elephants to overawe Demetrius' mercenaries and win the battle. Seleucus also invaded Asia Minor and defeated Lysimachus at Coropedium in a major battle in which his elephants would have come in handy. What happened to the elephants subsequently is not known; Scullard states that "the greatest of all the Hellenistic elephant corps mysteriously disappears from history".[17] Seleucus was murdered by Ptolemy's half-brother Ceraunus in 280 BCE.

4.2 Two drachmas, one silver and the other gold, minted by Seleucus I Nikator at Seleucia circa 300 BCE, showing elephants. According to ancient Greek sources, Seleucus had taken with him anywhere between 130 and 500 elephants he received from Chandragupta Maurya who ruled from Pataliputra in northern India.
Courtesy: Bibliotheque Nationale de France, Paris.

4.3 Painted dish from Capena, Italy, depicting an (Indian?) cow elephant and her calf; 3rd century BCE. This almost certainly represents one of Pyrrhus' elephants.

Courtesy: Museum Villa Giulia, Rome.

We now come to a military general whose name is synonymous with recklessness in war: Pyrrhus of Epicurus who won battles at great cost to his own forces – thus the term "Pyrrhic victory".[18] In the spring of 280 BCE Pyrrhus came to the help of Tarentum, the largest Greek city in southern Italy, against Rome, taking his infantry and 20 elephants across the straits of Otranto.[19] A storm overcame the fleet during this difficult sea journey for the elephants. The fleet sank but Pyrrhus with 2,000 men, some horses, and two elephants managed to reach the shore. Eventually his forces reunited at Tarentum – in gratitude the Tarentines issued coins depicting Pyrrhus and a small Indian elephant below their own symbol of a dolphin rider.[20] Pyrrhus pressed ahead to Heraclea to await the Roman forces there. After a seesaw battle between Pyrrhus' infantry and the Roman cavalry in which several thousand men perished, Pyrrhus launched his elephants at the cavalry. The elephants (or "Lucanian oxen" as the Romans termed them) with towers on their backs holding men inside, crushed the Romans underfoot, flung them aside with their trunks, or gored them with their tusks. Unable to confront the strange beasts, the horses fled with their riders leaving Pyrrhus victorious. One interesting observation emerges from the description of this battle. It may have been the first time that a Hellenistic elephant force used towers on the animals' backs, possibly an invention of Pyrrhus or one of his men. A painted dish of the 3rd century BCE from Capena in Italy, showing an Indian elephant and a calf, almost certainly refers to Pyrrhus' elephants (figure 4.3).[21]

Pyrrhus now aimed at the heart of Rome but the Italian confederacy was not easy to dislodge. He then tried negotiation and bribery but these too failed. The historian Plutarch mentions that Fabricius, a man of integrity, negotiating on behalf of the confederacy was neither lured by gold nor frightened by elephants. After bribery had failed, Pyrrhus arranged for one of his elephants to be dramatically revealed to Fabricius from behind a curtain during the talks. Raising its trunk above Fabricius' head the large beast let out a blood-curdling sound. Fabricius, however, calmly retorted, "You could not move me by your gold yesterday, nor can you with your beast today."[22]

At Ausculum in 279 BCE Pyrrhus' 19 elephants were again used effectively against the Roman ranks, though one elephant may have lost its trunk.[23] Two ancient historians record a curious invention of the Romans, a four-wheeled wagon drawn by oxen and fitted with projecting iron spikes; the men standing on the wagons could fire a variety of missiles at the great beasts.[24] Dionysius states that 3,000 such wagons were fabricated. The veracity of this was doubted by later commentators but Scullard is of the opinion that there could be some truth in these accounts.

Pyrrhus was not so fortunate in his third battle against the Romans near Beneventum, by which time he had only 17 elephants. A calf elephant in distress, hit by a missile, caused its mother to create confusion in its own ranks.[25] (The presence of the elephant calf is interesting in that it indicates some breeding among the captives.) There is a curious anecdote of the Romans letting loose squealing pigs on the elephants to gain victory.[26] Scullard feels there may be some basis to this story; an account of a later battle between the Megarians and Antigonus Gonatus (son of Demetrius) mentions that the former launched pigs, smeared with fat and set alight, on the latter's elephants. Pliny the Elder also mentions that "the very least sound, however, of the grunting of the hog terrifies them [the elephants]".[27] A large stamped bronze brick or *aes signatum*, from central Italy, depicts an Indian elephant on one side and a pig on the other, a possible reference to the battle of Beneventum (figure 4.4).[28] Eight of Pyrrhus' elephants were captured and two killed. In 275 BCE, Manius Curius, one of the two Roman consuls pitted against the Greeks, displayed some of these elephants to the Roman people who had probably never before seen such giant beasts.

Pyrrhus was not yet finished. He pursued Antigonus Gonatus in Macedon but was driven back. He then tried to seize Argos but the city gate would not admit his elephants fitted with towers; these had to be taken off and then remounted after the force passed through. The largest of the elephants fell across the gateway while another elephant named Nicon began to aggressively retrieve its driver who was wounded. Pyrrhus was injured by a tile thrown at his head and then beheaded by an opponent soldier.

The surviving elephants were taken over by Gonatus who used them against the Megarians, only to be repulsed by squealing pigs set on fire, a potent European biological weapon against the large beasts. As we saw in Chapter 3, Kautilya in Mauryan India had already perfected the use of buffaloes, cattle, and camels against invading elephants, while many centuries later Amir Timur the Central Asian warlord was to imitate the Roman strategy of setting alight domestic animals and letting them loose on the war elephants of the Delhi Sultanate.

The elephant war theatre in the West had meantime shifted to the northern frontiers of the Balkan region.[29] Bands of Celtic or Gallic tribes from northwestern Europe had been harassing the Romans and the Greeks. When three such hordes invaded Macedon and Thrace in 279 BCE, Ptolemy Ceraunus rushed to meet them without mobilizing his entire force. Ceraunus' elephant was wounded and threw him down, whereupon he was

captured and decapitated. When one such tribe swept into Asia Minor, Seleucus' son Antiochus I hastily summoned 20 elephants from Babylon to help him beat back the invaders. These elephants may have been a remnant of Seleucus' large force but no one knows for sure. Four of them seem to have disappeared on the way because Antiochus I only had 16 elephants by the time he crossed the Taurus to confront the Gallic tribe. The Gauls apparently had a large force of chariots, including 80 scythed-vehicles. Antiochus' elephants were deployed in three groups, eight in the centre to face the Gallic chariots and four on each wing to face the cavalry. The actual deployment probably did not matter. Neither the Gallic infantry nor their horses had ever seen elephants before. They fled in terror as the few elephants trampled, gored, or flung them aside. As the Macedonians hailed Antiochus for leading them to victory, the leader himself is reputed to have wept in modesty, "My men, we have more reason for shame; saved by those sixteen brutes! If their strangeness had not produced the panic, where should we have been?"[30] The battle could obviously have gone either way, but for the elephants evoking fear by their strange appearance.

The Gallic tribes were only a temporary diversion from the struggles in the Mediterranean lands. Ptolemy II Philadelphus inherited the elephants his father had captured from Demetrius at Gaza in 312 BCE. There are indications that Philadelphus maintained trade contacts with the Indian emperor Ashoka but obtaining more elephants by marching them overland would not have been easy – there would have been too many hostile forces between India and Egypt. (The Seleucids controlled the trade routes to India, the main supply of elephants so far to the warring Greeks.) Philadelphus displayed his elephants in a grand procession at Alexandria. Four elephants drew a chariot carrying a gold statue of Alexander; an elephant each also possibly drew 24 other chariots.[31] As the Ptolemies set about building up their elephant stocks, Philadelphus organized expeditions during circa 270–255 BCE along the African coast of the Red Sea in search of elephants to capture. The story of how the Ptolemies acquired African elephants for use in their army is beyond the scope of this volume but suffice it to state that they built up a mixed force of the two species. They also brought over mahouts from India to help in the training of the African animals. Ptolemy III Euergetes used these elephants in an offensive against the Seleucids, now led by Antiochus' son Seleucus II, sometime after 246 BCE.[32]

We now move to an important battle in 217 BCE between the Ptolemies and the Seleucids, this time led by two very young rulers, Ptolemy IV Philopator and Antiochus III (younger son of Seleucus II). The Seleucids had obtained a fresh group of elephants from India,[33] and in June 217 BCE Antiochus with a force of 62,000 infantry, 6,000 cavalry, and 102 Indian elephants joined battle with Ptolemy IV who mobilized 50,000 infantry, 5,000 cavalry, and 73 elephants of both species at Raphia in Gaza. The historian Polybius gives a detailed account of the battle.[34] Ptolemy's African elephants placed in the left wing were apparently alarmed at the sight of Antiochus' "larger" Indian elephants and had to be withdrawn from the battle. Ptolemy's Indian elephants in the right wing however stood their ground, and helped him to repel Antiochus. Although the precise role of these elephants in the battle is not clear, Scullard speculates that Ptolemy's Indian elephants facing their equals may have helped.[35]

We should examine a curious but consistent belief among ancient European historians that the Indian elephant was larger and stronger than the African elephant.[36] Describing the battle at Raphia, Polybius states, "Most of Ptolemy's elephants, however, declined the combat, as is the habit of African elephants; for unable to stand the smell and the trumpeting of the Indian elephants, and terrified, I suppose, also by their great size and strength, they at once turn tail and take to flight before they get near them. This is what happened on the present occasion; and when Ptolemy's elephants were thus thrown into confusion and driven back on their own lines."[37] Pliny the Elder makes a similar statement when describing elephants: "The African elephant is afraid of the Indian, and does not dare so much as look at it, for the latter is of much greater bulk."[38] Modern historians have considered two possibilities; the African elephant used in the Mediterranean wars may have been the smaller forest elephant,[39] or else the African elephants were younger animals that could be more easily caught and trained. The African animals came from the region of the Atlas mountains in the north where they persisted until they were captured to the point of extinction around the dawn of the Common Era.

Antiochus III's ambitions did not end at Raphia. He reasserted his authority in Asia Minor and the eastern provinces. Polybius records that he also renewed his ties with the Indian king Sophagasenus[40] through whom he procured more elephants.[41] Clearly there was active trade in war elephants between India and the West. Antiochus now had an even larger elephant force with 150 animals, and depicted them in the Seleucid coins he minted. After Ptolemy IV's mysterious death (circa 204 BCE) Antiochus III saw his chance to wrest back the region of Coele-Syria from the young Ptolemy V Epiphanes. Only fragmentary and contradictory accounts of the use of elephants by both sides are available of this showdown at Panium in 202–201 BCE, but it can be safely assumed that the Seleucid elephants were put to effective use.[42] By now a new front for the use of elephants had opened up in the Mediterranean war theatre, namely, the Roman arena.

***

An elephant culture incorporating the African species had independently developed in northern Africa since the 5th century BCE.[43] Sculptures and reliefs from about 400 BCE at Meroe in the upper Nile region depict captive African elephants. The people of Carthage too were familiar since the early 5th century BCE with the presence of wild African elephants in this region between the Atlas mountains and the Mediterranean sea. They captured and trained these animals, believed to be a smaller variety of *Loxodonta africana*, for use in war. The earliest recorded use of their deployment in war was in 264 BCE when the Carthaginians fought the Romans on the island of Sicily; obviously the Carthaginians had the means to transport the elephants across the sea.

We now jump ahead to the remarkable adventure of the celebrated Carthaginian general, Hannibal, against the Romans. After attacking the Roman allies in Spain, he planned an audacious campaign in 219 BCE that involved marching 37 elephants (mostly African) across the Alps under difficult conditions.[44] The elephants had to first get across the Rhone river; for this purpose Hannibal made special rafts but the elephants panicked during the crossing, drowning their Indian mahouts, according to Polybius, though "the elephants were saved, for owing to the power and length of their trunks they kept them above the water and breathed through them, at the same time spouting out any water that got into their mouths".[45]

The crossing of the Alps just as early snowfall began in 218 BCE came at great cost to Hannibal's army but surprisingly all the 37 elephants were alive when they reached the plains of northern Italy. Hannibal notched up some significant victories against the Roman confederation, including at Trebia, Trasimene, and Cannae, but failed to win Rome. Most of Hannibal's elephants died soon after the victory at Trebia as a result of exposure to cold. Polybius is not clear as to how many elephants died but the Roman historian Livy[46] states that "the rain mixed with snow, and the intolerable severity of the cold, destroyed many men and beasts of burden, *and almost all the elephants* [emphasis mine]".[47] Livy's later descriptions of Hannibal's crossing of the Apennines in frigid conditions mention that he lost seven of the elephants that had survived at Trebia,[48] leaving behind only one: the elephant that Hannibal himself rode.[49] There is a curious aspect to this sole surviving elephant that is relevant to our account.

Most historians, or biologists for that matter, have not paid attention to the identity of Hannibal's elephants; they assume that all were African. On the other hand, some historians (notably Gavin de Beer, H.H. Scullard, and W.B. Chandler) have looked more closely at the evidence which shows that Hannibal possibly had some Indian elephants, or at least one – the sole survivor that he rode after the crossing of the Apennines.[50]

One indication that Hannibal may have had some Indian elephants comes from coins issued by certain towns in Campania after his emphatic victory at Cannae in a bloody, pitched battle in 216 BCE, his third major battle against the Romans. Small silver coins of three denominations show the heads of Hermes, Artemis, and Hercules, respectively, on one side, and of an elephant on the reverse. In two of the denominations the elephant

4.5 Coins minted in Etruria in 217 BCE showing an African's head on the obverse and an Asian elephant with a bell on the reverse. It is now believed that the man may be Hannibal and not an African mahout as earlier assumed.

carries a tower while in the third tinier coin this has been discarded possibly for lack of space. Scullard provides a full description of these elephants to conclude that "there can be little doubt that they are Indian".[51] In contrast, the Barcid silver coins clearly show an African elephant as do two specimens of a bronze coin minted outside Campania, possibly in the hill country, and another coin series termed as Aes Grave. More intriguing are earlier bronze coins found in the Chiana valley near Lake Trasimene in Etruria, where Hannibal scored his second major victory against the Romans (figure 4.5). Minted in 217 BCE, around the same time as Hannibal's victory, the coins show an African's head on one side and an elephant with a bell on the other. Gavin de Beer seems to have been the first to point out that the elephant on this coin type clearly is of the Asian species. It is entirely possible, as Scullard mentions, that Hannibal had trained native Africans in the handling of elephants, including the Asian species he possessed, even if he also had Indian mahouts – remember that Polybius mentions Indian mahouts who drowned during the crossing of the Rhone. A more forceful argument, made by W.B. Chandler, is that the black man is Hannibal himself – why would Hannibal consider depicting someone else on the obverse of a coin featuring his favourite mount, and that too after a notable victory? It was also rare for the Carthaginians to depict anyone but gods and the aristocracy in their coins, statues, and stelae; in this instance Hannibal may even have identified himself with the Greek/Roman god Apollo. Also, if Hannibal hailed from northern Africa there was no reason to assume that he was not black.

I must add here that a piece of 3rd century BCE black-glazeware pottery from Etruria, now at the British Museum, shaped like an elephant, can be indisputably identified as the Asian species because of its two-domed head, thus adding to the evidence for the presence of Indian elephants in Hannibal's army (figure 4.6). This identity seems to have escaped the notice of historians, and indicates that Asian elephants were well known in this region during the 3rd century BCE.

4.6 Black-glazeware pottery (pourer) from Etruria (300–200 BCE), shaped like an elephant. The two-domed head clearly identifies this as an Asian elephant and could add to evidence for Indian elephants in Hannibal's army.
© *Trustees of the British Museum, London.*

The second piece of evidence pertains to the name of the Carthaginian elephant that fought with the greatest valour. Pliny the Elder records the name of this elephant as Surus and mentions that it had lost one of its tusks.[52] Scullard argues that "Surus" almost certainly means "the Syrian", thus indicating it was an Indian elephant. Hannibal had lost one of his eyes in the campaign, thus inspiring a rather romantic image of a one-eyed leader riding a one-tusked elephant against the enemy.[53] The question then arises as to how Hannibal of Carthage procured his Indian elephants. Scullard believes that the Ptolemies of Egypt were his most obvious source even if there is no written record of such transfer.

Hannibal's luck eventually ran out. A brilliant counter-offensive in 204 BCE by the Roman general Publius Cornelius Scipio in northern Africa resulted in the defeat of the Carthaginians who fielded 80 elephants (presumably almost all African) at Zama. The elephants, less 11 that were killed in the battle, fell into Roman hands. This abruptly brought to an end any Carthaginian ambitions of conquest through consolidation of their elephant force. More than a decade later, Hannibal was forced into exile, first in the Seleucid court of Antiochus III, then in the Armenian court of Artaxias I and, finally, with Prusias I of Bithynia. Pursued by the Romans, he died circa 183 BCE by consuming poison.

***

The Roman relationship with the elephant was quite different from that of the Greeks and the Carthaginians.[54] It is true that the Romans did sometimes use in war the elephants that fell into their hands. However, their use of the elephant was overwhelmingly as a public spectacle in entertainment (circuses and amphitheatres) and displays of strength (ceremonial processions). The Romans obtained both African and Asian elephants from their opponents and allies. It is difficult to trace their identities in the course of Roman history except when there is visual representation; even this cannot always be relied on as many of the artists did not themselves see the creatures.

The first elephants that the Roman people saw were possibly the Asian elephants that Curius had captured from Pyrrhus and displayed to the public in 275 BCE. The Romans had also seen the use of elephants in battle during the First Punic War (264–241 BCE) against the Carthaginians, and had even captured some of them, but were reluctant to form an elephant corps for nearly half a century. After the victory at Zama, however, there seemed to be some change in thinking on the use of elephants. The Romans began using elephants intermittently in their struggles against the Greeks; the animals included those captured from the Carthaginians or obtained from their ally Masinissa of Numidia (now part of Algeria). These elephants were all clearly African ones.

The Roman armies with their smaller African elephants had to sometimes face opponents who fielded the larger Indian elephants. One such encounter took place in 190 BCE when a Roman army with 16 African elephants led by Publius Scipio crossed over into Asia for the first time. Facing them at Magnesia was Antiochus III with his superior force of men plus 54 Indian elephants, their heads protected with armour and carrying towers with four soldiers each. By now accustomed from their African experience to avoid the direct charge of the elephants, the Roman soldiers effectively used their long *pila* or javelins to strike at the elephants, or their swords to cut their hamstrings. Fifteen of Antiochus' Indian elephants were captured during the battle and, later, the rest of the beasts were surrendered to the Romans. The ten Roman commissioners who took charge of the elephants apparently gave them to Eumenes of Pergamum in gratitude for his help. Once again a sizeable elephant force had been defeated by superior tactics. Scipio did not display any elephants in his victory procession at Rome but instead carried a huge haul of elephant tusks, numbering over 1,231 pieces, obtained from Antiochus' treasure stores.

4.7a The Colosseum at Rome (1989) that was used to stage bloodthirsty spectator sports in ancient times.
b A medallion showing (obverse) a bust of Gordian III, draped and armed with spear and shield, and (reverse) a view of the Colosseum with three rows of spectators watching a fight between a bull and an elephant with rider. Minted under the authority of Gordian III during 238–244 CE, Rome.
© *Trustees of the British Museum, London.*

The Seleucids in the meantime quarrelled with the Jews in Syria. Antiochus III had left a part of his forces including all the elephants with his regent Lysias who was also in charge of his younger son Antiochus V Eupator. In 162 BCE Lysias and Eupator along with either 22 or 32 elephants clashed with the Jewish force led by Judas Maccabaeus near Palestine. The Seleucid elephants had been aroused for battle by making them drink "the juice of grapes and mulberries".[55] (The elephant's fondness for alcohol is well known and this was surely neither the first nor the last occasion that these animals were deliberately stimulated in this fashion.) Judas' brother Eleazar, however, nullified the elephant force by running underneath the lead elephant and spearing it to death, in the process getting trapped beneath the huge beast.

Some of the Indian elephants obtained from Antiochus III may have played a useful part along with their African cousins in the Roman victory over Perseus of Macedon at Thessaly in 171 BCE and again at Pydna three years later. Nevertheless, the Romans did not rely on elephants to the extent they possibly could have done, either using the elephants they had captured from their opponents or the African animals their allies in Numidia were always willing to supply. Scullard is rather puzzled at this lack of enthusiasm on the part of the Romans to use the elephant as a war machine, as all their neighbouring Mediterranean powers had done, even though the opportunity presented itself.[56] I offer a somewhat different view on the seeming Roman reluctance to deploy the elephant in war.

It is indisputable that the Romans used the elephant as an object of public entertainment. When Curius first displayed a few captured elephants at Rome in 275 BCE, or Publius Scipio likewise did on a grander scale two years after the victory at Zama, the intentions were merely to reassure the Roman public that their army had prevailed over dangerous beasts and saved them from subjugation.[57] Rome had the power to transport these large animals over long distances, including across the seas, so that its people could have the pleasure of seeing the exotic beasts. Elephants were symbolic of their militarily strong opponents; yet Rome now had the power "to bend the world to its will".[58] During these public displays the elephant may also have become an object of torment; for instance, the 140 elephants that were paraded in 250 BCE were prodded or perhaps even killed with javelins.[59] This may have been an aberration for the mid-3rd century BCE but became commonplace two centuries later.

Pliny the Elder reports that elephants first fought in the Circus Maximus (as the Romans termed their stadium) in 99 BCE.[60] In 55 BCE the Roman general Pompey organized the infamous Games, a lavish and bloodthirsty spectacle in which man was pitted against beast, and carnivore against herbivore. Designed to provide pleasure to the

4.8 Copper alloy coin showing the Roman emperor Augustus, holding a laurel-wreath in his right hand and a long sceptre in his left hand, seated on a throne placed on a car drawn by four Indian elephants, each with a rider. Minted under the authority of the ruler Tiberius, circa 35–36 CE, Rome.
© *Trustees of the British Museum, London.*

spectator, commoner and noble alike, from the infliction of pain on animals or men alien or hostile to the Romans, it featured the massacre of hundreds of lions and pitted 20 elephants (Seneca mentions only 18) against black African prisoners in a javelin fight on the last day, a "most astonishing spectacle" in the words of Plutarch.[61] The elephants were all presumably African ones but the following incident is worth relating here. The Roman crowd that had been inured to the cruel bloodshed of the past four days unexpectedly had a change of heart upon seeing the plight of the injured and dying elephants. Pliny records: "When, however, the elephants in the exhibition given by Pompey had lost all hopes of escaping, they implored the compassion of the multitude by attitudes which surpass all description, and with a kind of lamentation bewailed their unhappy fate. So greatly were the people affected by the scene, that forgetting the general altogether, and the munificence which had been at such pains to do them honour, the whole assembly rose up in tears, and showered curses on Pompey."[62] Marcus Tullius Cicero, the Roman statesman and philosopher, who was present at these Games, wrote to a friend that "the last day was that of the elephants, on which there was a great deal of astonishment on the part of the vulgar crowd, but no pleasure whatsoever. Nay, there was even a certain feeling of compassion aroused that *that animal has something common with mankind* [emphasis mine]."[63]

The other great Roman general Julius Caesar had taken along an elephant during his second invasion of Britain in 54 BCE; this animal was clearly African. In 48 BCE Caesar defeated Pompey at Pharsalus to wrest supreme control over Rome. During his subsequent African campaign Caesar acquired many war elephants. Forty of these elephants accompanied him, holding torches in their trunks, during his victory celebrations at Rome in 46 BCE. Caesar too displayed his elephants in the "Games" that was mercifully not as bloodthirsty as the one Pompey had organized. Nevertheless, the show featured a fight between men riding these elephants. Caesar himself does not seem to have shown any interest in using elephants directly in his battles. While the other Mediterranean powers had trained elephants for battle, the Romans trained them to fight and perform in the public arena in order to provide thrills to the plebeians thirsty for entertainment (figure 4.7). The Roman emperor rode to the Games in a god-like pose in a state carriage drawn by four elephants instead of horses, as seen in commemorative medallions (figure 4.8). Elephants were taught to kneel down, sit on couches, play cymbals, perform various tricks and even walk on tightropes. Such training schedules and displays of elephants were the precursors of the modern circus ring featuring animals, that was revived in Europe at the beginning of the 19th century.

By the dawn of the Common Era the elephant had virtually disappeared as an instrument of war in the Mediterranean. Elephants did appear in some battles but their deployment was nowhere near the scale witnessed earlier. On the other hand, the elephant became an object of imperial favour; thus the Persians presented an unusually large elephant, undoubtedly an Indian animal, to Aurelian sometime before he became the emperor of Rome in 270 CE. Aurelian apparently presented the animal to the then emperor Valerian, as possessing an elephant was an imperial prerogative, but was allowed by the emperor to keep it – becoming the only commoner at that time to enjoy this privilege.[64]

What could be the reason or reasons that imperial Rome lacked the passion of their Mediterranean competitors for using the elephant in war? One reason could be the relatively late contact the Romans made with the elephant. By this time a number of weapons and tactics to counter an elephant-corps were already in vogue. The Roman commanders could also have realized that elephants were most effective to an unfamiliar opponent, and that this was certainly not the case with their rival Mediterranean powers. Unlike the Carthaginians who could have had a sense of identity with the elephant in their native land, to the Romans the elephant symbolized the enemy. Capture and public humiliation of the elephant was a surrogate for conquest of the enemy himself.

Finally, an important consideration that has been largely overlooked is the issue of uninterrupted supply of elephants. The Carthaginians were well placed to exploit the elephants of northern Africa. The Macedonians inherited a large stock from Alexander's eastern campaign. The Seleucids had ensured through diplomacy a regular overland supply from the large stocks held in India. The Ptolemies sourced some of their elephants from Carthage, in addition to those they acquired from their victories over their eastern opponents. Many of these African and Indian elephants changed hands regularly. During the early period of contact with the elephant, it would have been easier for the Romans to acquire the animal, and the accounts certainly suggest that this was indeed the case. Supply from northern Africa would have soon dwindled with the overexploitation and eventual extinction of this population of the African elephant, believed to be a smaller variety of the species.

The Romans had no real means of acquiring elephants directly from India; the few Indian animals they possessed were captured from their opponents. They could also have been reluctant to pitch their smaller African elephants against opponents who deployed the larger Indian elephant. By the time Rome became the imperial power of the Mediterranean the culture of the war elephant had distinctly faded in the region. The Roman relationship with the elephant is best summed up by Jo-Ann Shelton as follows: "The torment of elephants in Roman arenas represented a victory over the defeated enemy, and it enabled the spectators to participate in the process of imposing Roman justice on a barbarian world...their enormous size and strength made them appear menacing, but their lumbering gait and strange appearance meant that they could be easily ridiculed."[65]

***

During the early centuries of the Common Era, the Asian elephant once again appeared in significant numbers in the Persian armies.[66] The Parthian empire had been replaced by the dynasty of Sassan, whose grandson Ardashir (Artaxerxes) had wrested control over a large area from Mesopotamia in the west to Baluchistan and Afghanistan in the east. The ambitious Ardashir challenged Rome by marching his forces west and laying siege in 230 CE to Nisibis where he clashed with the Roman emperor Severus Alexander. The *Historia Augusta* gives a rather colourful account of this battle in which it claims that

4.9 A Sassanian elephant figure in stone, circa 6th or 7th century CE. This clearly depicts an Asian elephant as seen from its two-domed skull and the ear folded forward at the top.
Courtesy: Metropolitan Museum of Art, New York.

Severus defeated the powerful Ardashir "who had come to the war with seven hundred elephants..." provided with turrets and archers; of these Severus was supposed to have captured 30 elephants, slain 200 in the field and "led eighteen in triumph" to Rome where four elephants supposedly drew the emperor's triumphal chariot.[67]

Although a more sober account of the battle by the historian Herodian[68] does not mention elephants, it is almost certain that the Sassanids possessed some at this time. In 242 CE, the Roman general Gordian III captured 12 (or 22) elephants from Ardashir's son Shapur at Rasaina and sent the animals to Rome, where the emperor Philip celebrated the Games in 248 CE by killing a large number of animals including 32 elephants that may have included those captured by Gordian. Nearly a century later Shapur II used elephants in phalanx formation during his siege of Nisibis but the Romans beat them back with fire and many animals even sank into a bog and died. The Persians, however, eventually prevailed over the Romans. The struggles between the two powers continued with the Sassanids deploying elephants and even using them to trample prisoners to death. It is clear that the Persians maintained trade relations with India, thus ensuring a regular supply of elephants for their armies. A miniature elephant figure, possibly a chess piece, from the 6th or 7th century Sassanid period, clearly bears resemblance to an Asian elephant (figure 4.9).[69] The Sassanids were obviously familiar with the species and may even have possessed several of them.

Indisputable evidence that the Sassanids possessed elephants comes from their impressive visual representation on bas-reliefs that the ruler Khusro II (590–628 CE) had

4.10 Illustration from a medieval manuscript depicting the elephant as a bizarre creature with the body of a horse, the ears of a dog, a stumpy tail, a trunk like a musical trumpet, and the tusks of a wild boar. The serpent in this illustration may be a reference to the temptation of Adam and Eve in the Genesis account of Creation.

© Trustees of the British Library, London.

carved in a grotto at Taq-i-Bistan in Iran. These depict tusked Asian elephants being ridden to hunt wild boar. In one of the scenes the ruler himself is shown standing on a boat and shooting an arrow at the boar. Panels also show the dead boar being loaded onto elephants to transport them to the palace. These reliefs are comparable in artistic quality to similar depictions of the elephant in the Indian subcontinent.

The Persians fell to the Islamic Arab onslaught in 642 CE. The Roman empire too had collapsed by the 5th century, primarily due to the so-called barbarian invasions from the west. By this time, Christianity had spread widely across the erstwhile lands of the Roman empire. Unlike in Eastern religions, the elephant did not, however, have any significance for this major religious movement during the early centuries. With the decline of Rome the use of the elephant completely died out in Europe, as also its depiction in art for several centuries. Knowledge of the elephant, by now considered practically a semi-mythical creature, was confined to stories passed down the generations.

For more than a thousand years European knowledge of a number of creatures from faraway lands, including the elephant, derived from a didactic text, the *Physiologus*, that originated in Alexandria between the late 2nd and 3rd centuries CE. A compendium of early Christian symbolism of mammals, birds, mythical creatures, plants, and even stories, the accounts were infused with moral content. The *Physiologus*, originally in Greek, was eventually translated into a number of European and West Asian languages and was the original source for the "Bestiaries" (compendiums of beasts) that appeared in the Middle Ages.[70]

The elephant is incorporated into the creation legend of the Old Testament as this account in a Latin Bestiary illustrates: "Now if the elephant wishes to beget children it goes to the East to paradise, and there is a tree there which is called Mandragora, and it goes with its female, who first takes of the fruit of the tree and gives it to her male. And she beguiles him until he eats, and immediately she conceives; and when the time for bringing forth has come, she goes into a pool so deep that the water comes up to the udders of the mother. But the [male] elephant guards her while giving birth because of the dragon which is the enemy of the elephant. Now if it should find a serpent it kills it, trampling it underfoot until it is dead."[71]

The parallels with the Genesis account of Adam and Eve in the Garden of Eden, and their partaking of the forbidden fruit, are clear. Not everything stated about the elephant is in the realm of fantasy, however: the Bestiary also says that elephants "are possessed of a vigorous intelligence and memory. They move in herds [and]...bring forth [young] after two years [gestation]". After these accurate observations it relapses into inaccuracy when it states that elephants do not produce young more than once and live to 300 years. These lapses can perhaps be excused since elephants in captivity rarely breed; in fact biologists recorded their longevity correctly only during the 20th century. By the turn of the second millennium CE increasing trade contacts between Europe and the East brought descriptions of strange, giant beasts, but medieval artists still had to depend on secondary sources to represent them in paintings, sculpture, and craft. Their imagination turned the elephant into a bizarre creature with the body of a horse, the ears of a dog, a stumpy tail, a trunk like a musical trumpet, and the tusks of a wild boar (figure 4.10).

The earliest symbolic representations of the elephant in Christian Europe can be seen in Italian and French churches from the 11th century onwards (figure 4.11). The Archbishop of Canosa di Puglia, Italy, sat on a Byzantine-style throne supported by a pair of elephants.[72] The huge Gothic-style cathedrals of France, built during the 12th and 13th centuries, have elephants adorning the capitals, supporting baptismal stone receptacles, majestically overlooking the lofty exteriors, or even worked into the filigree of buttresses.

God be merciful unto me And blesse me And shew the
light of his Countynance vpon me Amen

cum dr̄. q̄cq̄d labrꝭ dū tenet̄. ut pꝭcꝭt serpenſ. Serpenſ aū
nom̄ accipit q̄a occultꝭ accessib; serpit. ñ apꝭtꝭ passib; s; squa
mag; minutissimꝭ nisib; repit. Illa aū q̄ q̄tuoꝛ pedib; m
uūtur. sic̄ lacerte. & stilliones. ñ serpentes s; reptilia nomi
nant̄. Serpentes aūt̄ reptilia s̄t q̄ uentre & pectoꝛe
reptant. Quoꝛū tot uenena; q̄t genera. tot pnicies. tot
doloꝛes. q̄t coloꝛes habentur.   Draco.

Draco maioꝛ cunctoꝛum serpentium siue omnium
animantium s̄t t̄ram. Hunc greci draconta uocant.
Unde & diriuatū e̅ in latinū. ut draco diceretur.
Qui sepe ab speluncꝭ abstract̄ fert̄ in aere. concitatq̄;

4.11 Elephant stone sculpture at the Notre Dame at Paris.
Photograph by Delphine Desoutter.

The elephant in Christian symbolism represented the virtues of wisdom, level-headedness, strength, chasteness, and dependability.

The few live elephants that reached Europe during medieval times came as imperial gifts. The first elephant to have reached north of the Alps since Roman times was a gift from Haroun al-Rashid, the caliph of Baghdad, to the European emperor Charlemagne in 802 CE.[73] The emperor took the elephant along with him on state occasions to impress his people as well as his rivals, but the animal drowned in the Rhine during a military campaign two years later. Four centuries on, the sultan Al-Kamil of Cairo gifted an elephant to the Holy Roman emperor Frederick II in 1229 CE. The king cherished the elephant and used it on state occasions such as his victory procession. This animal survived for several decades and made a lasting impression upon the people. The identity of these elephants is not known but the former was almost certainly an Asian animal. The elephant gifted to Frederick II originated in the Holy Land and, thus, was also most likely from Asia. In fact, Frederick II was on a crusade (under orders from the pope) to free Jerusalem from Muslim rule but he maintained friendly relations with Al-Kamil; this suggests that the elephant gift had its desired purpose as an ambassador of peace.

Soon after, King Louis IX of France brought back an elephant from the disastrous sixth crusade. This was clearly an African animal as seen in a realistic contemporary watercolour drawing.[74] Louis presented the animal to Henry III of England in 1255 CE. This was probably the first elephant seen in England after the time of Julius Caesar. The animal was kept at the Tower of London but died three years later.

The late medieval period witnessed a bitter conflict between France and England, known as the Hundred Years' War (1337–1453 CE), in which gunpowder and heavy artillery were introduced. In between, bubonic plague swept through Europe killing up to one-third of the population during 1348–50 CE. In 1453 CE the Turks captured Constantinople (Istanbul) and threatened European civilization. Strangely, amidst this chaos sprung an amazing renaissance of scholarship and artistry in Europe. The 15th and 16th centuries also witnessed the unprecedented territorial expansion of the European powers. As the Portuguese, Dutch, French, and British colonized South and Southeast Asia there began a new engagement between the Europeans and the elephant. This story is told later (see Chapter 8).

***

Before we close this account we must take a glimpse at an Indian elephant named Hanno (originally Annone, possibly from the Malayalam word *aana* for elephant) that reached the Vatican, the heart and soul of Christendom, in the early years of the 16th century.[75] On July 8, 1497, an intrepid Portuguese explorer Vasco da Gama had set sail from Lisbon with a fleet of ships, and circumventing the African continent had reached the settlement of Calicut (presently Kozhikode) on the southwestern coast of India on May 20, 1498. This sea route around the Cape of Good Hope opened a new European passage to the riches of India, Ceylon, and lands further east. During the first two decades of the 16th century several elephants from Africa and India were taken to Portugal where King Manuel I kept these in special stables constructed adjacent to his palace at Estâos. When Leo X succeeded to the papal throne in 1513 CE, Manuel was keen to impress the pontiff of Portugal's power and reach with gifts from exotic lands. He chose the elephant as one among several animals that had been unfamiliar to Rome for a long time. The elephant selected to be presented to the pope was one of four animals that had been brought along with their Indian mahouts to Lisbon by expeditions led by Afonso de Albuquerque.[76] These elephants had been shipped from Cochin (Kochi) in southwestern India between

1510 and 1514 CE. They had apparently been sent on the condition that they would be well cared for and not carry any burden other than people.

Hanno, the four-year old elephant gifted to the pope, has been described as a "white elephant" by contemporary writers.[77] He is unlikely to have been a true albino but an animal with a lighter coloured skin that is occasionally seen among elephants. It is notable that a white elephant was chosen as it implies that the Portuguese may have been aware of its significance in Asian cultures.

On March 12, 1515, Hanno and the Portuguese entourage led by Tristan da Cunha reached Rome. Rapturous crowds had greeted the ship's royal guest en route; at Rome itself the reception could only be described as delirious. If the pope was amazed at the richness of Manuel's other gifts (including a papal mitre so richly adorned with precious stones that it was described as more valuable than anything seen in Rome), he was absolutely captivated by Hanno the elephant. The animal faithfully paid homage to the pope by kneeling before him. He was rewarded with magnificent quarters in the Vatican garden where the pope visited him regularly. The people of Rome thronged to catch a glimpse of Hanno on every possible occasion. Manuel gained tremendous influence with the Vatican. The gift of an elephant was again a triumph of diplomacy.

Sadly, Hanno lived for only two more years. The story is that the poor animal suffocated from a gold covering used during a ceremonial occasion.[78] After its death Leo X commissioned the court painter, the famous Raphael, to create a life-size painting of Hanno. This great mural no longer exists. Several drawings of Hanno, however, survive; many of these have been attributed to Raphael in their concept though they may have been executed by other artists, in particular Guilio Romano. They generally show very realistically a stocky Indian elephant with small tusks (figure 4.12).

Poets and writers of the period eulogized Hanno as perhaps no other elephant has been celebrated. Aurelio Sereno in his *Theatrum Capitolium* extolled, "How great is the power of the Creator which shows to us today this beast, in which are contained so many virtues, that can live for three centuries, that progenitates one time in its life, that respects religion, that salutes our Holy Father, that understands human speech. Such a portent is seen only once...."[79] The resemblance to the description of the elephant in the Bestiary is clear.

Pope Leo X himself penned an epitaph thus for Hanno:
A beast not seen for a long time,
And in my brutish breast they perceived human feelings.
Fate envied me my residence in the blessed Latium
And had not the patience to let me serve my master a full three years.
But I wish, oh gods, that the time which Nature would have assigned to me, and
Destiny stole away,
You will add to the life of the great Leo.[80]

4.12 This 16th-century sketch of the pope's elephant Hanno is believed to have been conceptualized by the famous Renaissance artist Raphael but executed by another illustrator. The original mural of Hanno by Raphael no longer survives.

CHAPTER 5

The Elephant in the Buddhist and Jain World

DURING THE 6TH CENTURY BCE two great thinkers of the subcontinent, Vardhamana and Gautama, began to preach philosophies of non-violence that challenged the ideology of Vedic Brahmanism and eventually matured as the major religions Jainism and Buddhism, respectively. Both Vardhamana and Gautama were born into martial kshatriya clans in the northern Gangetic basin and, after a life of comfort in their youth, renounced their families in their quest for enlightenment. The elephant is an integral part of Buddhist tradition and precept, and much has been written about this, but the role of the elephant in Jain thinking is less known and appreciated.

The origin of the well-known story of the blind men and the elephant is obscure, but perhaps can be traced to both Jain and Buddhist teachings. In the Jain version six blind men each touch a different part of an elephant and compare it to completely distinct objects – the leg to a pillar, tail to a rope, trunk to a tree branch, ear to a hand fan, belly to a wall, and tusk to a solid pipe. A wise man resolves the conflict among them by explaining that they are all correct. This tale is interpreted as illustrating one of the cardinal principles of Jainism, namely, *anekantavada,* or that truth can be perceived in different ways and no single point of view expresses the complete truth.

The Buddhist version of this story is similar, and is attributed to the Buddha himself.[1] There were many wandering hermits and scholars at Savatthi (Shravasti) who had acrimonious arguments about the nature of the world and of life. When the Buddha's disciples brought this to his notice and sought his views on the matter, he related the story of a raja who assembled a number of blind men from Savatthi and presented them with an elephant. Depending on which part of the elephant they were allowed to feel, each of them came up with a different interpretation of the animal – pot (head), winnowing basket (ear), ploughshare (tusk), plough (trunk), granary (body), pillar (leg), mortar (back), pestle (tail), broom (tuft of the tail). The Buddha compared their dispute to that of blind folk who do not know the *dhamma* (universal law or righteousness), and ended his discourse with an inspirational verse:

O how they cling and wrangle, some who claim
Of brahman and recluse the honoured name!
For, quarrelling, each to his view they cling.
Such folk see only one side of a thing.[2]

This compelling story continued to inspire poets and theologians through the ages. The 13th-century Persian poet Rumi related his own version that he attributed to the Hindu tradition, while the 19th-century American poet John Godfrey Saxe made the tale famous in the Western world.

***

The elephant is central to the Buddhist legend of the birth of Siddhartha Gautama as narrated in the canonical texts.[3] Shuddhodhana, the ruler of the Shakya clan, had his capital at Kapilavastu in the Himalayan foothills. On the seventh day of celebrations of the summer moon festival, his queen Maya rose early, bathed in scented water, adorned herself, gave alms to her subjects, and after taking the *upostha* vows, lay down in the decorated state bedchamber. As she slept she dreamt that four great kings carried her bed to the Himalaya where their queens bathed her, attired her in heavenly clothing, and laid her upon a divine bed with its head to the east. From a nearby mountain the Bodhisatva (Buddha in an earlier birth) in the form of a six-tusked white elephant, holding a lotus in its trunk, descended to the heavenly mansion and entered Mayadevi's womb from her right side (figure 5.1). The next morning the queen related her dream to the king who summoned his priests for an interpretation. After receiving due honour, the 64 brahmans explained to the king that Mayadevi had conceived a son who would become a universal

5.1 The conception story of the Buddha, in which Queen Maya Devi dreams that a sacred white elephant descends from heaven to enter her womb, is illustrated on:
a A Bharhut railing medallion, 2nd century BCE.
Photographed at the Indian Museum, Kolkata.
b The eastern gateway pillar of the Great Stupa at Sanchi, circa 1st century CE.

monarch if he chose to stay within the royal household; if he decided to go forth into the world he would become a Buddha (Enlightened One).

The course Prince Gautama chose is well known. After renouncing his life of comfort at the age of 30, and spending six years as an ascetic in a hermitage, Gautama meditated for 49 days under a Pipal tree (the sacred Bodhi tree, *Ficus religiosa*). In the course of meditation he had to fight a terrible battle against Mara, the personification of evil, before he attained complete enlightenment ("the Awakening").

The Buddha preached his first sermon to a group of five faithful companions at a deer park in Sarnath near Benaras/Varanasi, thus setting in motion the Wheel of Dharma. The six of them formed the first Buddhist *sangha* which then spread the dharma among the people. Buddhism first spread over the Gangetic plains, then to other parts of the subcontinent, and eventually to East and Southeast Asia. The Buddha is believed to have died at the age of 80 under a Sal tree near the town of Kushinagara (there are widely varying views on the period of the Buddha's life; among the more commonly accepted is circa 566–486 BCE).

The sermons preached by the Buddha are contained in the *Sutta Pitaka*, originally recited by his disciple Ananda, and the *Vinaya Pitaka* recited by Upali. The *Jataka* tales of the former births of the Buddha are derived largely from these scriptures as well as oral Brahmanical traditions.[4] Animals including the elephant are an integral part of these parables that illustrate the path of virtuous living preached by the Buddha. Although the existing prose versions of the *Jataka*s are dated to the 5th century CE, the inclusion of these tales in Buddhist canonical literature going back to the 4th century BCE indicate that these were integral to the faith of that period. The rich artistic representations of the *Jataka*s in the reliefs of early Buddhist shrines at Sanchi, Amaravati, and Bharhut, along with the paintings at Ajanta, provide us with unmatched visuals of this ancient folklore.

The elephant finds mention in several dozen of the 537 such tales in the ancient Pali *Jataka*. These provide us with vivid glimpses of not only the social life and customs of early Buddhist times but also the status of elephants and the elephant-human relationship. Among the various forms assumed by the Bodhisatva are those of a beautiful white elephant,[5] a leader of a herd of 80,000 wild elephants,[6] an elephant great and mighty like "a purple mountain of collyrium",[7] and even the son of an elephant trainer.[8] When the Bodhisatva appears as a monkey he is said to be as strong as an elephant,[9] an obvious parallel to the elephant-like strength of Sugriva's monkey troops in the *Ramayana*.

Captive elephants are commonly mentioned in the *Jataka*s. Elephants were trained by tying them to posts and breaking their spirit, much like in present times.[10] In the *Jataka* story, the state elephant was unable to bear the agony of such training and broke down its post to escape to the Himalaya. Its cruel experience of humans made it live in constant fear and the slightest whiff of human scent was sufficient to cause it to flee instantly. The Bodhisatva who was a tree spirit in that region finally cured it of its fear, exhorting it with this verse:

Fear'st thou the wind ceaselessly,
The rotten boughs doth send alway?
Such fear will waste thee quite away!

The king rode a richly caparisoned state elephant, sometimes a white elephant, in procession around his capital city. Elephant training was a noble profession – the Bodhisatva came into this world more than once as an elephant trainer's son and took to the family profession with high perfection. Elephant festivals (*hastimangala*) were conducted each year with pomp and splendour by a hereditary master of ceremonies.[11]

As many as "five score black elephants" participated in such festivals, reminiscent of the present-day Pooram festival at Thrissur in Kerala. The master of ceremonies was obviously a learned man as he was expected to recite the three Vedas and the elephant lore (interestingly only three Vedas, not four, are mentioned, and the elephant lore was considered on par with the Vedas). The Bodhisatva was once born as the son of such a master, but his father died before the season of the elephant festival. As much wealth was at stake, the brahmans planned to usurp the master's role by claiming that the 16-year-old son was too young to recite the scriptures. The young lad, however, undertook a journey to Takshashila, where he learnt the four scriptures overnight from a teacher, and returned in three days in time for the festival. On the day of the festival, the young Bodhisatva openly challenged the brahmans to recite even a portion of the Vedas or the elephant lore. As no one took up this challenge the king was forced to concede the hereditary right of the Bodhisatva to conduct the elephant festival.

That knowledge of elephants and the elephant lore was of great importance is also emphasized when the Bodhisatva laments in another *Jataka* story that "in the days to come kings shall arise who shall know nothing about elephants or other arts, and shall be cowards in the field."[12] The use of elephants in war is clearly established though battle descriptions in the *Jataka*s do not indicate their large-scale deployment as Lahiri-Choudhury rightly points out. In any case, this may be a more truthful account of the extent to which elephants were used in war in pre-Mauryan times as compared to, say, the exaggerated descriptions in the *Mahabharata* that are clearly latter-day interpolations. The war elephant was provided with protective armour, and was a part of the familiar four wings of the army, the others being horse-mounted cavalry, chariotry, and foot-soldiers.[13] Elephants in musth were used to charge the enemy ranks[14] as well as to batter down the gates of an enemy city. The elephant was also an agent of execution.[15]

The *Jataka*s recognize the peculiar temperaments of individual elephants; thus one elephant is virtuous and patient while another is wicked and aggressive.[16] An elephant could form a special bond not just with humans but with a dog as well – when the dog went missing the elephant refused to eat any food.[17] The creature had a keen sense of smell.[18]

Elephants were also associated with the rains and rain clouds – a persistent belief in the subcontinent from ancient times. Eight brahmans from the kingdom of Kalinga that was experiencing a prolonged drought were once sent to Indapatta (Indraprastha) in the Kuru kingdom to fetch the state elephant.[19] The Bodhisatva was the reigning king of the Kurus. When the brahmans reached the gates of Indapatta they saw the Bodhisatva, washed and anointed, riding a richly caparisoned elephant. Hearing the plight of the Kalingas, the Bodhisatva comforted them thus:

This elephant to you for gift I bring:
'Tis a king's portion, worthy of a king!
Take him, with all his trappings, golden chain,
Driver and all, and go your ways again.

The brahmans rode the generous gift back to Dantapura in Kalinga but, sadly, the rains failed the kingdom. They took the elephant back to the Bodhisatva and pleaded instead for knowledge of Kuru righteousness that perhaps held the key to saving their land from the wrath of the rain gods. After learning the true and complex nature of righteousness, the brahmans took this knowledge on an inscribed golden plate back to Dantapura. When the king of Kalinga put into practice the Kuru righteousness so inscribed, the rains finally blessed his kingdom.

We can now take a look at the rich visual representations of the elephant in some of the more famous depictions of scenes from the *Jatakas* and other Buddhist scriptures. The birth legend of the Buddha has obviously been a favourite among artists. Every early Buddhist monument depicts the descent of the Buddha in the form of the elephant from "Tushita Heaven" into the womb of Mayadevi. The earliest and best known of these depictions is on a railing medallion at the Bharhut stupa of the 2nd century BCE (see figure 5.1a). (Although this was the period of the Shunga rulers who essentially promoted Hinduism, new Buddhist monuments were raised at places such as Bhaja, Karli, and Bharhut during their reign.) Queen Maya is shown lying in a bed with her lady attendants by her side. A lamp flickers at the foot of the bed. A large but gentle white elephant wearing a decorated cap hovers above her before it descends into her body. A similar medallion from Stupa II at Sanchi (whose railing is believed to have been built during the 2nd century BCE) was described by John Marshall, who restored the monuments at this site.[20] On the eastern gateway pillar of the Great Stupa at Sanchi, the queen is shown sleeping on the third floor of the palace with a frontal view of the sacred elephant above her feet (see figure 5.1b). The Great Stupa was possibly erected during Ashokan times (3rd century BCE) but the elaborately sculptured gateways were erected during the 1st century CE under the Satavahanas; the fine sculptures are attributed to ivory carvers from nearby Vidisha.[21] Incidentally, the Bharhut and Sanchi sculptures also feature a frieze of a female figure (seated or standing) being bathed by two elephants (figures 5.2a and b). The figure is identified as Mayadevi, the mother of the Buddha.

At Amaravati (again built in Ashokan times and further adorned under the Satavahanas in the 1st–2nd century CE) the elephant is much reduced in size in relation to the queen lying elegantly on a couch. The Gandharan artist of this period, perhaps less familiar with central Indian tradition, reversed the importance of the queen and the elephant. Perhaps the most elaborate depiction of the conception scene is the one at Nagarjunakonda (originally built by the Satavahanas, but renovated by an Ikshvaku princess in the 3rd century CE) in which the *devas* carry the white elephant in a *vimana* (flying chariot).[22] The conception scene also features in one of the more than 1,000 panels narrating the life of the Buddha at the 9th century CE monument of Borobudur in central Java, Indonesia.

Mayadevi has also been identified with Gajalakshmi-like figures in a different representation of the nativity scene in ancient Buddhist structures. A stone carving of the 2nd century BCE from the Buddhist caves of Pitalkhora near Aurangabad in Maharashtra shows her seated on a lotus flower as two gigantic elephants empty their pitchers over her. The stupa at Bharhut as well as the gateways of Stupas 1 and 2 at Sanchi also show such a female divinity, seated or standing on a lotus, and being lustrated by a pair of elephants.

The next scene in the Buddha's life that involves an elephant is that of the ferocious physical and mental assault of the demon king Mara on the ascetic prince as he sits in meditation under the Bodhi tree. Ironically, Mara rides a huge elephant as he and his demon forces mount an assault on this reincarnation of a sacred white elephant. Mara tries every trick from physical intimidation to sending his seductive daughters to distract the meditating prince, but does not succeed. At the end, the motionless Gautama merely raises his right hand and then touches the ground, signalling Mara's comprehensive defeat and his own complete awakening as the Buddha. Mara's assault is depicted on several gateways at Sanchi but the most graphic of these is that on the western gateway. Here, Mara rides a huge, tusked elephant, possibly in musth as seen from the thin vertical line between the eye and the ear, amidst his companions riding other elephants or chariots, all of them armed and full of vigour (figures 5.3a and b).

5.2 Maya Devi lustrated by a pair of elephants may illustrate the nativity story:
a Standing on a lotus, in a Bharhut railing medallion, 2nd century BCE.
Photographed at the Indian Museum, Kolkata.
b Seated on a lotus with left leg pendant, on the northern gateway of the Great Stupa at Sanchi, circa 1st century CE.

5.3 Mara riding an elephant during his ferocious assault on the Buddha is depicted:
a On the western gateway of the Great Stupa at Sanchi, circa 1st century CE.
b In a sculpture from Nagarjunakonda, 3rd century CE.
Photographed at the Metropolitan Museum of Art, New York.

5.4 The Buddha subduing the elephant Nalagiri, painting at Ajanta Cave 17, 5th century CE. The first scene is of Nalagiri charging down the street as people watch from their houses in horror, and the next scene shows the mad elephant kneeling before the Buddha.

As he went around preaching the *dhamma*, the Buddha's jealous cousin Devadatta conspired to kill him on several occasions. At the third such attempt, Devadatta learnt that the Buddha was visiting the city of Rajagraha, and arranged for a ferocious elephant Nalagiri to become intoxicated and to be let loose on the Enlightened One. The huge beast thundered down the street towards an unflappable Buddha who merely raised his hand. Recognizing the Buddha's loving kindness, the elephant miraculously knelt before the Enlightened One in obeisance. A partly faded painting on the verandah of Cave 17 at Ajanta, dating to the late 5th century CE, shows people scattering or watching in fear from their houses as the intoxicated Nalagiri charges down the street and then amazingly kneels before the Buddha who strokes it lovingly (figure 5.4). The sculptural depiction of this scene in marble at Amaravati is similar, with successive carvings of a charging and kneeling elephant as people on the street watch in fear or stand in reverence to the Buddha.

Among the elephant-related *Jataka*s, the favourite of the artists has undoubtedly been the *Chhaddanta Jataka* in which the Bodhisatva appears on earth as a six-tusked white elephant, Chhaddanta. The leader of a herd of 8,000 elephants that roam the forests of the Himalaya, Chhaddanta along with his two consorts, Mahasubhadda and Cullasubhadda, is in the habit of dwelling in a golden cave during the rainy season, and under a banyan tree by the side of a lake during the summer (a possible recognition of the seasonal migration of elephants?). For a long time Cullasubhadda nurses a grudge against her husband because she perceives his preferential treatment of the senior queen Mahasubhadda. Matters come to head one day when Chhaddanta innocently presents a lotus to his senior queen. The junior elephant queen prays to be reborn as the consort of

the king of Benaras in order to take revenge on Chhaddanta. Her wish is soon fulfilled. As the queen of Benaras she influences her husband to provide her with the most skilled hunters in the kingdom for an undisclosed mission. Selecting a well-built, toughened hunter named Sonuttara, she equips him with arms and orders him to kill Chhaddanta and bring her his tusks. After a long and treacherous journey through the jungles and across the mountains, Sonuttara reaches the dwelling place of Chhaddanta and his followers. He digs a pit along the elephants' path, covers the top with wood, grass, and mud, and hides inside dressed in yellow robes, with a plan to kill the elephant when it passes over. Using a poisoned arrow, the hunter wounds the Bodhisatva elephant in its belly.

The story now takes a poignant turn. Although mad with pain, Chhaddanta enquires of the hunter, "Why do you want me? Was it for your own advantage or were you sent by someone else?" Hearing Sonuttara's reply, Chhaddanta realizes his former junior queen is responsible. He offers to let the hunter cut out his six tusks so that he may fulfil the queen's command. Sonuttara climbs onto the kneeling elephant's forehead and thrusts his saw into its mouth but is unable to cut off the tusks. In spite of the excruciating pain the Great Being takes the saw from Sonuttara and cuts off his own tusks, handing them over with the words, "I do not give you these, friend hunter, because I do not value them, nor because I desire the position of Sakka, Mara, or Brahma, but the tusks of omniscience are a hundred thousand times dearer to me than these are, and may this meritorious act be to me the cause of attaining Omniscience."[23] With these words the Bodhisatva elephant dies. The story ends in a double tragedy. Upon receiving the tusks and learning that Chhaddanta is dead, the queen of Benaras has a fit of remorse and also dies in grief.

5.5 The *Chhaddanta Jataka* is illustrated in this masterful painting behind the front wall of Cave 17 at Ajanta, 5th century CE. In this story the Bodhisatva appearing as a six-tusked white elephant commits the ultimate sacrifice by assisting the hunter sent by his former queen to cut off his tusks.

The *Chhaddanta Jataka* is illustrated in every major Buddhist monument. A railing medallion at Bharhut shows the hunter with his saw getting ready to remove the tusks of Chhaddanta as Mahasubhadda stands behind. The Amaravati carving shows a kneeling Chhaddanta helping the hunter cut his tusks, while the southern gateway of the Great Stupa at Sanchi has a more elaborate depiction, along the central panel, of Chhaddanta and his herd of elephants as they roam the Himalayan forests. At the extreme right of the panel the six-tusked elephant is shown standing alone under a tree, presumably the moment seized upon by the hunter to let loose his poisoned arrow. The piece de resistance is, however, in the artistry of Ajanta that is believed to have been executed in the 5th century CE under the Vakatakas, during the period of the Gupta rule at Pataliputra. Behind the front wall of Cave 17 the entire story unfolds in fading, multicoloured splendour inside the dimly-lit hall (figure 5.5). At the top we see Chhaddanta roaming with other elephants of his herd. Below this to the right the Bodhisatva offers his tusks to the hunter, while to the left the hunter presents these to the queen and other members of the royal household. Finally, as the queen gazes at the tusks she faints upon recalling her previous birth in which she was the consort of the six-tusked Chhaddanta, whom she has had slain. This 1,500-year old painting, surely a masterpiece of all time, captures a range of emotions – from the cruel and wanton killing of a self-sacrificing, noble animal to the drama of human envy and greed, and final grief.

***

Two hundred years after the death of the Buddha his doctrine had become established as a separate religion. The ruler most well known for his adoption and propagation of

5.6 Elephant carved out of rock at Dhauli near Bhubaneswar, to commemorate King Ashoka's victory over Kalinga in about 260 BCE.

Buddhism is the Mauryan emperor Ashoka who ruled circa 272–232 BCE. The ambitious conquests of Ashoka's grandfather Chandragupta Maurya and father Bindusara had extended Mauryan rule over a large region, possibly even into the Deccan as far south as Karnataka. Yet, Kalinga on the east coast was still independent.

Ashoka set his sights on Kalinga to usurp its resources and gain unrestrained access to trade routes along its coast. The bloody climactic battle was fought in about 260 BCE, an event that eventually changed the course of Indian and, more particularly, Buddhist history. Ashoka himself had the following account inscribed in one of his famous Rock

5.7 Elephant etched on Ashoka's Rock Edict at Kalsi near Dehra Dun, 3rd century BCE, with the word *gajatame* meaning "supreme elephant". Note the two lines between the eye and the ear clearly depicting the musth condition.

Edicts: "When he had been consecrated eight years the beloved of the Gods, the King Piyadassi [i.e. Ashoka] conquered Kalinga. A hundred and fifty thousand people were deported, a hundred thousand were killed and many times that number perished...."[24]

History books commonly portray a repentant Ashoka experiencing a change of heart virtually on the battlefield of Kalinga, and turning to Buddhism and non-violence, but a more accurate story, recorded in one of the edicts, is that this transformation took over two years. Ashoka actively spread the Buddhist doctrine far and wide across the subcontinent and even into the island of Sri Lanka. His rock edicts and pillar edicts, written mainly in the Brahmi script, reflect an ethic that has parallels in Buddhism, but also go beyond to accommodate the beliefs of a culturally and socially complex society. In fact, the edicts do not directly speak of the doctrine of Buddhism, not to mention the finer points of its metaphysics.

The doctrine of *ahimsa* or non-violence to humans and animals alike emerges strongly from Ashoka's edicts. The edicts speak of a ban on animal sacrifices in his capital as well as the killing of certain species, the regulation of animal consumption, planting of trees, cultivation of medicinal plants, and reserves for the protection of elephants and fish. We begin to see the emergence of vegetarianism in a major rock edict that states, "Formerly in the kitchen of Beloved-of-the-Gods, King Piyadasi, hundreds of thousands of animals were killed every day to make curry. But now with the writing of this *dhamma* edict only three creatures, two peacocks and a deer are killed, and the deer not always. And in time, not even these three creatures will be killed."[25] Another edict mentions that the former hunting expeditions of the king had been replaced by tours to spread *dhamma* to the people. A pillar edict lists a variety of creatures from queen ants, boneless fish, and tortoises to birds such as parrots and wild ducks, and mammals including deer, porcupines, squirrels, and wild asses – in short "four footed creatures that are *neither useful nor edible*" [emphasis mine] – that were protected.[26] This is a veritable potpourri of biodiversity that was conserved, not because it was directly useful to humans, but for its intrinsic value. The same edict goes on to state that during these [auspicious] days animals are not to be killed in the elephant reserves or the fish reserves either. Another edict mentions that sightings of "auspicious elephants" had increased under the emperor's rule, no doubt a reference to the sacred white elephant of Buddhist legend.

The sacredness of the elephant, implicit in the conception story, was reinforced by Ashoka. After his victory over Kalinga, Ashoka had a life-size elephant (said to represent the Buddha) carved out of the rock above his inscription at Dhauli near Bhubaneswar (figure 5.6). The rock inscription at Kalsi, near Dehra Dun in Uttarakhand, has something more explicit in this regard – a line drawing of a tusked elephant in musth with the word *gajatame* or "supreme elephant" below the etching (figure 5.7). The Ashokan pillars are all surmounted by animal capitals. The famous pillar at Sarnath with its four-lion capital, adopted as India's national emblem, also has four other creatures, including the elephant, between the four wheels of dharma fashioned below each lion. The pillar at Sankissa is surmounted by an elephant figure (figure 5.8).[27] Some scholars believe that the elephant atop the Sankissa pillar represents the Buddha himself.[28] It is likely that under Ashoka the elephant became a symbol of state as well as of religion. The erection of elephant pillars continued in Buddhist art after Mauryan times, as seen in the gateways of the Great Stupa at Sanchi.

The sacredness of the elephant is thus firmly established in early Buddhist times. The elephant festivals (*hastimangala*) and the worship of an elephant figure (*hatthimaha*) referred to in the *Jataka*s, the mention of auspicious elephants (*hastidasana*) and the supreme elephant (*gajatame*) in Ashoka's rock and pillar inscriptions, plus the reference in early Pali Buddhist literature to a group of people named *hatthivatika*s who worshipped the elephant, all clearly point to the elevation of the animal to sacred status. Indeed, the elephant had become a symbol of Buddhism itself. Rulers who adopted Buddhism strove to live up to the ideal of the *chakravartin* (universal monarch) for whom the seven jewels of royal power included the elephant, a symbol of the strength of the mind.

Around the time of the decline of the Mauryas and the rise of the Shungas, new invaders had begun to penetrate the Hindu Kush in the northwest. The Indo-Greeks (or Indo-Bactrians) came first in about 200 BCE and occupied the northwest, followed by the Shakas (Scythians) who controlled large portions of the north, the west, and upper Deccan for 400 years, the Parthians (Pahlavas) during the 1st century CE, the Kushans who established a large empire across the north in the early centuries CE, and the Indo-Sassanians who settled in the lower Indus. These foreign entrants soon absorbed the local culture, lost their identity and became completely Indianized. Their rulers embraced both Hinduism and Buddhism, and it is sometimes difficult to separate the two influences in their cultural life. The famous Kushan emperor Kanishka clearly patronized Buddhism, but other Kushan rulers worshipped Shiva or Vishnu. Increased contact with Central Asia stimulated trade and cultural exchange, eventually bringing changes to the practice of Buddhism; a new form of the religion known as Mahayana Buddhism or the Great Vehicle now differentiated from the older and more puritanical form known as Hinayana Buddhism or the Lesser Vehicle. Under the Kushans new centres of art arose at Gandhara and Mathura, the former incorporating elements of the Central Asian style.

Buddhism spread across the entire country with the exception of the extreme south before beginning to fade from about the 6th–7th centuries CE. Although it coexisted for long periods with the Brahmanical religion it also faced hostility from the Shaivites as well as from invaders such as the Hunas during the 6th century.[29] Confined to the east from this period, it virtually disappeared after the Muslim invasions of the late 12th century. On the other hand, Buddhism had spread outside India, to the south into Sri Lanka, the north into Tibet and onward into China and Japan, and eastwards into Burma (Myanmar), Siam (Thailand), and other regions of Southeast Asia where it has continued to flourish until present times.

***

5.8 Sankissa pillar capital, 3rd century BCE, showing the elephant.
Courtesy: Archaeological Survey of India, New Delhi.

5.9 Stone elephant at a Jain temple at Ellora, circa 9th–10th century CE.

Jainism does not boast of as rich a textual or visual representation of the elephant during the early centuries of its development in India as compared to its contemporary competitor. Buddhism had a headstart in this respect as its founder was directly identified with a sacred elephant. However, the elephant does figure significantly in the Jain tradition (figure 5.9). The symbol of Ajitanatha, the second of the 24 Jain *tirthankaras* or *jinas*, is an elephant and thus the elephant is depicted in several Jain temple carvings along with the symbols of other *jinas*. The 24th *jina*, Vardhamana Mahavira who lived circa 599–527 BCE, was conceived by a brahman woman, Devananda, after which she had 14 auspicious dreams. The first of these was of a great four-tusked elephant marked with auspicious signs (though very rare, four-tusked elephants are known in modern times). The god Indra, realizing that Devananda had conceived the last of the *jinas*, sent his commander Harinegamesi to take the embryo from the womb of Devananda and place it in the womb of Trishala, as she was a kshatriya and the *jina* should be born to a kshatriya. That night Trishala had the same 14 dreams, the first one being of the elephant (figure 5.10).[30] After the birth of Vardhamana, Indra and Indrani came on their white elephant Airavata and took the baby up to Mount Meru where he was ritually bathed/lustrated before being restored to Trishala. A similar episode occurs in the life of the first *jina* Rishabhanatha.[31]

There are a few other allusions to the elephant in the Jain tradition. Asurakumara, one of the great world rulers who are considered subordinate deities in the service of the *jinas*, is associated with Indra, and is depicted with Six Jewels, one of which is the elephant.[32] The *yakshi* Sulochana has an elephant *vahana*.[33] The *yaksha*s Purnabhadra and Parshva are sometimes depicted in elephant-headed form.[34]

The oldest Jain monuments that feature elephant carvings seem to be the rock-cut caves at Udayagiri and Khandagiri near Bhubaneswar (in fact, the twin hills are now virtually surrounded by the expanding city). In the 1st century BCE Kalinga was still smarting from the removal of a Jain cult object (Kalinga-Jina) by the Nandas about 300 years earlier, and from the humiliating defeat at the hands of the Mauryan emperor Ashoka a century after that. A powerful dynasty, the Chetis (or Chedis), whose rulers called themselves Mahameghavahanas, came to power at this time. The third king of the dynasty, Kharavela, converted to Jainism and excavated, in the 13th year of his rule, several caves at Udayagiri and Khandagiri for use as dwelling places by Jain monks. Cave excavations continued during later periods with some of these converted into shrines. Two scenes among the several elephant images in the Udayagiri-Khandagiri complex are noteworthy for their uniqueness and possible insight into the social status of women.

The largest of the caves, named Rani-gumpha, at Udayagiri also features some of the most elaborate sculptures of the elephant, in both lower and upper storeys. A remarkable scene involving elephants is carved between the cave arches in the better preserved upper storey (figure 5.11). To quote art historian Debala Mitra's description:

> [This] is a forest...at the foot of the hill is a lotus lake in which is a herd of three wild elephants, one of them confronting a party of one man and ten women. The story seems to be as follows. A party having come to a lotus lake for sporting, meets a herd of elephants, whose favourite resort it was. The consternation and panic created by this unexpected encounter are delineated forcefully. Three of the party - the man along with two women – are bravely trying to repulse the attack and also to drive the elephants away with whatever objects they could procure, the man holding a staff-like object with both hands, the first woman with disheveled hair, throwing a ring-like object, which may even be her anklet (two such objects are already sticking to the body of the front elephant) and the second holding a twig....[35]

I offer alternative interpretations of the scene. It is unlikely that one man and ten women would have gone to a lake for a picnic. The lotus lake is more likely a village tank situated at the foot of a forested hill frequented by elephants. A herd of elephants has come to the fringe of the village to raid the crops near the village tank. The man and the women guarding their fields are desperately trying to chase the elephants away with various weapons or implements; it is entirely likely that the women – who enjoyed a higher social status in Jain Kalinga – could have also been responsible for protecting their crops from animal depredation. However, since the man and the women seem to be wearing ornaments it is also likely that a party from a village proceeding on foot through the jungle has encountered a group of aggressive elephants. Whatever be the tale depicted in this frieze, this is possibly the earliest visual depiction of "elephant-human conflict", as it is termed today.

That the social status of women was exalted in Jain Kalinga can be seen in a noteworthy frieze on the upper back wall of Ganesha-gumpha, another cave at Udayagiri (figure 5.12). Mitra feels that this scene depicts the popular story of the elopement of the Ujjayini princess Vasavadatta with king Udayana of Kausambi.[36] Three persons riding on an elephant are being pursued by a party of armed soldiers. One of the elephant riders is clearly a woman holding an *ankush* (goad) in her right hand. This could only mean that she is the elephant's mahout; the frieze is again unique for its depiction of a woman mahout in ancient India. The panel continues with the tale of the elopement that is mentioned in Buddhist, Brahmanical, and Jain literature. Incidentally, the figure of Ganesha in the right cell of the cave belongs to a much later period in Kalinga history, a theme that I return to in the next chapter. The two large, tusked elephants holding branches of a mango tree over a lotus were also added at a later time (figure 5.13).

5.11 Frieze of wild elephants being confronted by a group of people at the upper level of the Rani-gumpha at Udayagiri, Bhubaneswar, 1st century BCE. This image may be the earliest known visual representation of conflict between elephants and people.

5.12 Frieze of elephant with riders on the back wall of the Ganesha-gumpha at Udayagiri, 1st century BCE. The mahout is clearly a woman, indicating perhaps their exalted status in Jain society two millennia ago.

5.13 Two stone elephants holding branches of a mango tree over a lotus outside the Ganesha-gumpha at Udayagiri, 1st century BCE. These sculptures were probably added at the time the figure of Ganesha was carved inside, several centuries after the cave was originally excavated.

The caves at Udayagiri and Khandagiri also depict royal elephants, recognized by their holding an umbrella or a lotus, elephant processions, and other associations of elephants and people. Interestingly, the king is shown leading an army of foot-soldiers, horse-based cavalry, and elephants. As Mitra points out, a horse-drawn chariot is depicted only once, and that too not in actual battle.[37] The use of chariots in war had clearly declined by about 2,000 years ago. The Ananta-gumpha at Khandagiri also features a frieze of Sri or

Lakshmi standing in a lake entwined by lotus stalks, being bathed/lustrated by two tusked elephants holding pitchers in their trunks and standing on lotus flowers (figure 5.14), a common motif in Brahmanical and even Buddhist art.

The caves merely testify in their architecture to the rigours of the life of Jain ascetics; they do not illustrate the religious mythology of the faith as do the Buddhist monuments.[38] The early cave reliefs do offer some insights into the social, cultural, and political life of the people of those times. The Jainism of that period did not involve the worship of any images; the carvings of the *tirthankaras* all pertain to a later period. In the course of time it is natural that some of the *tirthankaras* became associated with the elephant; as we have seen, the elephant became a symbol of Ajitanatha. A 7th-century relief on a stone slab from Mathura shows Rishabhanatha flanked by elephants (figure 5.15). A story of the 22nd *tirthankara*, Neminatha, relates how this handsome prince riding a decorated elephant, on his way to his wedding ceremony, ordered the release of caged animals and birds kept for slaughter before he decided to renounce the world and become an ascetic.[39]

Of all the major religions it is possibly Jainism with its considerable emphasis on *ahimsa* that is most sensitive to the concerns of protection of all animals from the tiniest insect to the largest mammal. The *Sutrakritanga Sutra*, a canonical text going back to about the 3rd century BCE, makes a brief mention of particular behaviour towards elephants practised by a socio-religious group opposed by the Jains. This group of people believed in deliberately killing an elephant and living off its products for the rest of the year. Silanka, a commentator of this text from the 9th century CE, termed these people as "elephant ascetics" or *hastitapasa*.[40] In the words of Paul Dundas, the *hastitapasa* "advocated a dietary modus vivendi, which whimsically could almost be styled proto-environmentalist, in that it seems to have involved an unwillingness to overexploit the natural world from which sustenance derives, of a type which can be found in similar form among many nomadic groups to this day".[41] The reasoning of the *hastitapasa* was that it is better to preserve a larger number of smaller creatures by killing just one individual life in the form of an elephant. The elephant ascetics and the Jains seemed

5.15 Stone slab from Mathura showing Rishabhanatha, the first *tirthankara*, flanked by elephants, 7th century CE.
Photographed at the Government Museum, Mathura.

to have engaged in a philosophical debate over the destruction of life form, the former arguing that the Jains, too, destroyed plant life or even some animal life in the mere act of wandering, and the latter countering the killing of even one elephant because a host of smaller life forms was also destroyed in the act of cooking its flesh. Whatever the veracity of this story, contemporary debates over which sections of society are greater champions of conservation spring to mind!

From the Gangetic region Jainism spread to western India and to the south in the region of Karnataka. Most of the later sculptural images associated with Jain monuments are of the *tirthankaras* or of Brahmanical deities absorbed into the Jain pantheon. The odd image of Ganesha occurs, as in Cave 7 at Khandagiri, in association with other Brahmanical deities. In the Jain group of rock-cut caves excavated during the 9th and 10th centuries CE at Ellora, the *yaksha* Matanga, an attendant/guardian of Mahavira, is shown riding an elephant in several scenes.[42] (In fact Matanga means elephant.) An impressive elephant, sculpted in the round, stands in the open courtyard of Cave 32 (the name Indra Sabha is a misnomer because the image of Matanga riding an elephant had been wrongly identified as that of Indra). Elephant sculptures were also incorporated in latter-day Jain temples as with the marble elephants in the Luna Vasahi dedicated to the 22nd *tirthankara* Neminatha in 1230 CE at Dilwara in Mount Abu, Rajasthan.

Neither the Buddhist nor the Jain texts provide much information on the distribution of elephants in the subcontinent. The mention in the Buddhist tales of large herds of wild elephants in the forests of the Himalaya obviously refers to the region of eastern Uttar Pradesh, Bihar, and Nepal from which today elephants have practically disappeared. Elephants were more useful for deployment in war or as transport in the moister forested tracts of the east as compared to horses that proved their mettle in the dry, dusty plains of the northwest. The moister eastern tracts of the Himalayan foothills extending into Bengal and Assam continued to be the main sources of supply of elephants for the rulers of northern India for several centuries from early Buddhist times. It is thus not surprising that the horse culture of northwestern India was displaced by an elephant culture as one proceeded eastward.[43] This is reflected in the profusion of elephant images, even in those Buddhist monuments such as Sanchi outside of the eastern region, as compared to the paucity of depictions of horses and chariots. We can, however, rely on the Kautilya *Arthashastra* for the most comprehensive description of elephant distribution in the subcontinent about two millennia ago (see Chapter 3).

***

As Buddhism spread beyond India, it first reached the shores of Sri Lanka, named variously as Lanka in the Buddhist literature, Simhala in classical Sanskrit, Taprobane by the ancient Greeks, and Ceylon in modern times. The credit for bringing Buddhism to the island goes to Mahinda who is believed to be either the son or the brother of Emperor Ashoka. According to the Buddhist tradition of Sri Lanka, Mahinda and his sister Sanghamitta, children of Ashoka, adopted the religious life of their father as they grew up at Pataliputra. Some years after Ashoka hosted the third great Buddhist council, Mahinda departed for Sri Lanka where he was graciously received by its ruler Devanampiya Tissa (r. 307–267 BCE).

An indigenous elephant culture already existed in Lanka by the time Mahinda reached the island during the second half of the 3rd century BCE. Wild elephants were found practically all over the island. Stone Age rock art at several places depicted the creature (see Chapter 1). The ancestors of the Sinhalese are believed to have migrated from northern India beginning around the 6th century BCE. They would undoubtedly have brought with them the subcontinental skills of capturing and taming elephants.[44] The

5.16 A large tuskless bull or *makhna*, common in Sri Lanka, walks purposefully across a dry tank bed at Minneriya in the northeast of the island (2006). Megasthenes states that the elephants of Taprobane (as the island was known in ancient times to the Greeks) were larger than Indian elephants and better suited for use in war.

Sinhalese, however, captured elephants by the pit method, unlike the stockade method that was in vogue in northern India, suggesting that they had absorbed the southern tradition in the course of their migration to the island or imbibed a local tradition.

Ancient Greek sources such as Megasthenes (3rd century BCE) refer to the elephants of Taprobane as being larger than those in India (figure 5.16);[45] Arrian adds that they are more powerful and intelligent, and that they were exported by boat to Kalinga presumably for use in war.[46] Further, the Pali chronicles of Lanka such as the *Mahavamsa* record that the Pandyan king of Madurai in southern India gave King Vijaya, the first ruler of the island (who along with his followers reached there in 483 BCE according to tradition), his daughter's hand in marriage along with many valuable gifts including a retinue of elephants.[47] The Sinhalese ruler may have already had local expertise in managing these animals, or else they may have been accompanied by mahouts from the mainland. Thus, a two-way movement of elephants between Lanka and peninsular India was in vogue well over two millennia ago.

Devanampiya Tissa gratefully accepted the gift of the *dhamma* from the *thera* Mahinda. Seeing the great number of people eager to hear the missionaries, the king arranged for the elephant stables at Anuradhapura to be cleaned as they were large enough to hold the crowd.[48] Obviously, Devanampiya Tissa maintained many elephants in captivity. Eventually, even this space was insufficient and the sermons had to be shifted to the Nandana park outside the city.[49]

As in Buddhist India, the state or royal elephant was not only an important requirement for the use of the king but also an auspicious animal (*mangalahatthi*) to be used in ceremonial occasions.[50] After a very successful season of preaching and conversion of the islanders, Mahinda expressed a desire to enshrine the Buddha's relics within a stupa to which Devanampiya Tissa readily agreed. When the right collarbone of the Buddha eventually arrived at Anuradhapura, the state elephant was deployed to carry the urn containing the sacred relic. According to tradition this wise animal trumpeted joyfully in recognition of the holy relic, carried it safely to the most suitable spot outside the walls of the city to be enshrined, and guarded it zealously until the stupa was constructed. Mahinda's next task was to bring the *theri*, his sister Sanghamitta, to Anuradhapura so that the women of the island could be admitted to the Buddhist order. Sanghamitta arrived with a branch of the sacred Bodhi tree, specially selected by Ashoka to be planted at Anuradhapura. King Tissa established nunneries for her residence including one at Hatthalhaka-vihara (the convent of the elephant post) used for tethering the state elephant.[51] Two elephants mentioned by name, Mahapaduma and Kujara, the first such instance in Sri Lankan history, were used by the king to mark the boundaries of the Mahamewna Uyana or park in Anuradhapura.[52]

These descriptions in the *Mahavamsa* of the early period of Buddhist history in Lanka certainly point to an elephant culture in the process of elaboration during the second half of the 3rd century BCE. There is no mention as yet of the use of elephants in war, but this was to change a century later.

If King Puru had the mighty elephant Ajax to face Alexander, and if Hannibal had the dependable one-tusked Surus to negotiate the Alps in his march towards the Romans, the Sinhalese king Kavantissa (205–161 BCE) had the supreme war elephant Kandula.[53] According to the Sinhalese legend the elephant Kandula appeared mysteriously on the island the same day that the queen Viharadevi gave birth to the prince Dutthagamani.[54] A noble elephant of the six-tusked race brought a newborn elephant to the shore where a fisherman named Kandula found him and reported it to Kavantissa. The king sent his trainers to bring the animal to be reared at his palace, and named it after the fisherman. The reference to the six-tusked elephant who delivered Kandula to the shores of Sri Lanka is undoubtedly related to the tale of the noble Chhaddanta of the *Jatakas*.

Dutthagamani and Kandula were inseparable from a young age. In spite of the king's desire for peace with his neighbours across the Mahaweli river, the prince Dutthagamani was trained in the skills of riding and handling elephants, horses, and the use of sword and bow. Kandula's training is not narrated but he was "foremost in strength, beauty, shape and the qualities of courage and swiftness and of mighty size of body...";[55] elsewhere, we are told that he was a tusker.[56] After the king's death, Dutthagamani and his younger brother Tissa had a quarrel, in spite of having taken an oath before their father that they would never do so. In their first battle, it was Tissa who rode Kandula, presumably because he had possession of the famous elephant, while Dutthagamani rode the mare Dighathunika.[57] At first, Dutthagamani fled on his mare pursued by Tissa on the elephant, but later his mare leapt over the elephant enabling him to shoot an arrow that grazed Kandula's skin. The humiliated elephant shook off Tissa and promptly went over to his rightful owner Dutthagamani.

Dutthagamani began a campaign against the Damilas (Tamils) who inhabited the land across the Mahaweli. Riding the redoubtable Kandula, he notched up victory after victory, though the elephant's actual role in these battles is hazy until the king reached the fort of Vijithanagara, identified by some scholars as present-day Polonnaruwa, a highly fortified city protected by three moats, a high wall, and gates made of wrought iron.[58] It took him four months to capture the city. At one stage in the long-drawn battle, Kandula was sent to break the southern gate. We are told that "placing himself upon his knees and battering stones, mortar and bricks with his tusks did the elephant attack the gate of iron. But the Damilas who stood upon the gate-tower hurled down weapons of every kind, balls of red hot iron and molten pitch. When the smoking pitch poured on his back Kandula, tormented with pain, betook him to a pool of water and dived there."[59]

Kandula was not offered any respite, notwithstanding his discomfort. The warrior Gothaimbara, presumably in charge of the animal, urged him, "Here is no sura-draught for thee, go forth to the iron gate, destroy the gate!"[60] Trumpeting loudly the proud elephant came out of the water to get his wounds washed and anointed by the veterinarian before the king himself cheered him with the words, "To thee I give, dear Kandula, the lordship over the whole island of Lanka."[61] Clad in a seven-folded buffalo skin and armour, Kandula now went for the final assault "roaring like thunder"[62] to bring down the city's gate. Merlin Peris, professor of classics at Peradeniya University, makes the point that the exploits of Kandula should be taken as representing the achievements of the entire elephant corps of Dutthagamani's fourfold army.[63]

Dutthagamani was not yet finished; after the fall of Vijithanagara he marched to the outskirts of Anuradhapura where he confronted his arch rival Elara riding his elephant Mahapabbata. Outside the south gate of the city, the two elephant-riding kings fought to the finish, with Kandula thrusting his tusks into Mahapabbata at the same time that Dutthagamani hurled his spear at Elara, to decisively fell the king and his beast.[64] This is the first description in the *Mahavamsa* of one elephant fighting another in war (figure 5.17). In the meantime Bhalluka, based in India, arrived on the scene to rescue the Damilas with a large force of 60,000 men and many elephants. Strangely, we are told that Kandula backed off slowly along with the army at the sight of the advancing force to stand within the precincts of the Mahavihara.[65] When a puzzled Dutthagamani asked his archer Phussadeva the cause of Kandula's retreat for the first time after 28 battles, he got the reply "Victory lies behind us, O king; looking at the field of victory the elephant draws back, and at the place of victory he will halt."[66] This was obviously a tactical retreat by a wise animal! In the end Dutthagamani prevailed over Bhalluka to become the supreme ruler of the island.

According to Sinhalese chronicles, Dutthagamani felt remorse at the death and destruction he had caused in his numerous wars, much as Ashoka had felt after his bloody Kalinga campaign.[67] He devoted his energies to promoting Buddhism and building many monasteries and shrines. The first Buddhist monument he began was the Mirisavathi *dagaba* (stupa) that greatly exceeded in size the stupa built by Devanampiya Tissa. Elephants were used in the construction of the Mahathupa, the present-day Ruwanweliseya *dagaba* at Anuradhapura, initiated during the reign of Dutthagamani in the 2nd century BCE. The *Mahavamsa* states that the stones broken by soldiers with hammers were "stamped down by great elephants whose feet were bound by leather".[68]

Dutthagamani also organized an elaborate ceremony for enshrining the holy relics of the Buddha in which dancing women, caparisoned elephants, horses, troops, and his state chariot participated. The splendid Kandula, holding the golden casket under a white parasol, was undoubtedly the cynosure of all eyes.[69] This ceremony seems to be a forerunner of the extremely popular Perahera (festival) held annually at Kandy since the late 18th century CE. Dutthagamani died in 137 BCE after a reign of 24 years when he was in his early 50s.

5.17 The war elephant Kandula (right), ridden by the Sinhalese king Dutthagamani confronting the elephant Mahapabbata carrying the Tamil king Elara, from an 18th-century fresco at Cave 2, Dambulla, Sri Lanka.

By the beginning of the Common Era in Lanka, therefore, the use of the elephant as a royal mount and in war, with all the trappings associated with ceremony and battle, was firmly established. It was desirable for the king himself to ride an elephant in battle. The concept of the *chaturanga sena* was well known, though the elephant force of the Sinhala rulers was much smaller than those of mainland India.[70] The establishment included veterinarians with knowledge of caring for and treating elephants. The sacredness of the elephant is also implicit in the story of the six-tusked elephant (never mind that it was a bull!) bringing the newborn Kandula to the island, as also in its role as the carrier of the sacred relics of the Buddha.

Although the king had monopoly over the capture and trade in elephants, other citizens such as nobles and merchants also owned elephants.[71] It is even possible that a special tax was levied on owners of elephants; a rock inscription of King Vasabha (64–110 CE) mentions a term *hati-pati* that has been interpreted by scholars to refer to such a tax or perhaps revenue from elephant hunters.[72]

Elephants were prominently depicted in the architecture of the colossal *dagaba*s that were built at Anuradhapura between the 2nd century BCE and 3rd century CE. These *dagaba*s rose on massive basal platforms with elephants sculpted along the outer face of the supporting walls. I can do no better than reproduce verbatim C.W. Nicholas' description of the depiction of elephants on the Ruwanweliseya whose construction was initiated by Dutthagamani:

5.18 The modern (2011) facade of the Ruwanweliseya *dagaba* at Anuradhapura, Sri Lanka, featuring a concrete replica of the original stone sculptures of an array of 344 life-size, tusked elephants in bas-relief. Elephants were used in the construction of the *dagaba* initiated during the rule of Dutthagamani in the 2nd century BCE.

This architectural feature was called the *hatthipakara* or "Elephant Wall". Projecting from the immense platform and all around it were figures of elephants (head, tusks, trunk, and forelegs) in relief, equidistant and close together, giving the illusion to the spectator that the array of elephants was supporting the whole gigantic structure on their backs. The uppermost of the three circular terraces built around the base of the domes of these dagabas also carried, on its edge, projecting heads of elephants placed at regular intervals. The ornamental *vahalkadas* (inadequately rendered in English as "frontis-pieces") built against the cardinal faces of all the large dagabas, exhibited, above their basements, a course of stone-carved elephants, all kneeling and with their heads and forelegs protruding in full relief; some having the trunks uplifted, others curled to one side. The lofty, decorative stelae flanking the *vahalkadas* were carved on their exposed faces with various motifs with which were combined figures of men, women, elephants, and other animals, both real and mythical. Surrounding the tallest stelae on the eastern side of the dagaba were stone figures, carved in full round, of kneeling elephants: thus the elephant symbolized the East, the direction of the rising sun.[73]

This impressive representation of the elephant cannot be seen today because the ancient crumbling structure of the Ruwanweliseya has been built over in the process of restoration in recent times.[74] The modern facade of the *dagaba* features the original sculptures in concrete with an array of 344 life-size, tusked elephants in bas-relief along the outer wall of the basal platform (figure 5.18).

The array of sculpted tusked elephants at the Ruwanweliseya in ancient times raises the question of whether tusked bulls were common on the island 2,000 years ago. There are two diametrically opposite views on this matter. Some researchers believe that depictions of tusked elephants in rock art (see Chapter 1), and sculptures such as these at Anuradhapura at the temple of Isurumuniya (figure 5.19) are evidence that the Lankan population of wild elephants would have comprised essentially tusked males two millennia ago as in southern India.[75] The preferential capture of tuskers by the rulers of the island for use in the army would have gradually reduced the frequency of tusked males with a corresponding increase in tuskless males in the wild population.

The Greek monk Cosmas Indicopleustes, who may have visited India, wrote during the 6th century CE that "the King of Sielediba [i.e. Ceylon] obtains for purchase both the elephants and horses.... The price he pays for the elephants depends upon the number of cubits they reach in height."[76] Presumably, the Sinhalese imported elephants from India, because Cosmas goes on to state that the kings of the mainland catch their elephant locally. In another passage Cosmas also hints at the small tusks of the elephants of Taprobane (Ceylon), and that India imported tusks from Ethiopia.[77] Nicholas thus contends that the Lankan population of elephants comprised mostly tuskless males by the 6th century CE.

The early Greek references to large and powerful elephants could also be an indirect reference to tuskless bulls. It is common belief among elephant observers even today that tuskless bulls are larger and more powerfully built than their tusked counterparts.[78] It is possible that such descriptions of the elephants of Lanka could be a pointer to its mainly tuskless bulls.

Nicholas explicitly believes that the "most rational surmise appears to be that since tuskers...were rare among the indigenous elephants, these were the animals that were sought for and purchased abroad. Presumably, efforts were made to increase the proportion of tuskers in the local race by using some of the imported tuskers for breeding purposes...with a view to establishing a tusked race in Ceylon."[79]

Even if the historical sources are ambiguous about whether tusked or tuskless bulls predominated the wild population in ancient Sri Lanka, there is little doubt that the tusker represented the ideal phenotype to the human mind. The state elephant or royal mount was invariably a tusker, and even in recent times the rulers of the island have always sought tuskers from India for use in ceremony. It is thus reasonable to assume that considerable numbers of tusked bull elephants have been imported by Sri Lanka from the mainland over the ages, especially since the 6th century CE. The complex and extensive trade in elephants between Sri Lanka and Burma, southern India, and Kalinga[80] certainly makes this quite plausible. Some of these tuskers could have escaped or been deliberately set free, as Nicholas surmises, and infused the tusk gene into the wild population. Computer-based models show that this scenario is not outside the realm of possibility, though the alternative scenario of selective attrition of tuskers through capture may also have occurred.[81]

The use of elephants in war continued in Sri Lanka during the medieval period with mixed results as was the case with battles in the subcontinent; after all, the Roman historian Livy aptly termed the war elephant as *genus anceps* or a double-edge sword that was as liable to turn upon friend as upon foe in the heat of battle.[82] If the king rode an elephant, as many Sinhalese rulers preferred to do, he also unduly exposed himself to the enemy's arrows. Several Sinhalese rulers took their own lives if they lost a battle from riding an elephant;[83] among these were King Kassapa I (r. 473–495 CE) who cut his neck after his elephant veered off course in the heat of battle against his brother Moggalla

5.19 Tusked elephant carved on the rock face at the 3rd century BCE temple of Isurumuniya at Anuradhapura. The sculpture itself seems to be from a much later renovation during the late 5th century CE. However, neither this nor figure 5.18 is conclusive evidence for the presence of substantial numbers of tusked wild elephants on the island, though some scholars may think so. Rather, tusked elephants imported from India since ancient times could have represented the ideal phenotype for sculptural depictions.

5.20 A large herd of elephants drinking at a water tank at Minneriya in north-central Sri Lanka (2006). The extensive system of irrigation in the Mahaweli basin created by the rulers of Sri Lanka beginning in the 4th century CE also proved to be a boon to the elephants of the region.

causing his troops to flee,[84] and Mahinda, brother of Sena I (r. 833–853), who cut his own throat sitting on his elephant after being cornered by the Pandyan king.[85]

From the 4th century onward the Lankan rulers embarked upon constructing a series of irrigation projects – tanks, canals, weirs, spillways – that transformed the northern and eastern parts of the island.[86] These engineering works continued until the 10th century though their scale and frequency seems to have declined from the 8th century onwards. Large tracts of jungle lands were brought under agriculture as a result of the water that was harnessed. For the elephant this was a bonanza in more than one way; the tanks were a welcome source of water, the cultivated crops an additional source of food and, eventually, the secondary growth in the abandoned lands an attractive place for foraging. The present-day distribution of wild elephants on the island corresponds almost precisely to these areas (figure 5.20).

The Cholas of southern India invaded Lanka during the 10th century and set up their capital at Polonnaruwa, but were eventually repelled by Vijaybahu I. His grandson Parakramabahu I (1123–86) executed a grand irrigation scheme, the Parakrama Sumudraya, at Polonnaruwa, and several other architectural marvels including Buddhist temples. The Polonnaruwa Vatadage is one such structure that is believed to have enshrined the sacred tooth relic of the Buddha. The moonstones at the four entrances to the Vatadage feature friezes of elephants (figure 5.21). Parakramabahu's son Nissanka Malla (1187–96) probably renovated the structure. A stone inscription of Nissanka Malla close to the Vatadage records that elephant fights were organized for the entertainment of the king and the nobles (figure 5.22).[87]

5.21 Moonstone featuring a frieze of elephants at the entrance to the Vatadage at Polonnaruwa, Sri Lanka, 12th century.

5.22 This stone inscription of Nissanka Malla (1187–96) close to the Polonnaruwa Vatadage records that elephant fights were organized for the entertainment of the king and the nobles.

5.23 Samantabhadra, a Bodhisatva in Mahayana Buddhism and a member of the Shakyamuni trinity, is usually shown riding an elephant:
a He was well known in Tibet as Puxian Pusa, depicted in this rare painting from the second half of the 10th century.
b In Japan he was known as Fugen Bosatsu, depicted in this image probably from Heian, circa the first half of the 12th century.
Both images photographed at the Musée Guimet, Paris.

There was unexpected friction between Lanka and Burma during the 12th century when the king of Ramanna (Pegu in lower Burma) began to heap insults on the Sinhalese by first imprisoning their envoys, then usurping their gifts including elephants and money but giving nothing in return, and finally seizing a princess on her way to Kamboja (Cambodia).[88] This disrupted the age-old practice of harmonious trade between the two countries. In fact, each time a Sinhalese vessel visited Burma it carried expensive gifts and received an elephant in return; the Sinhalese also had the option of purchasing as many elephants as they wished at a fixed price.[89] An enraged king Parakramabahu sent a naval force to invade Pegu and bring its ruler Alaungsithu to his right senses. The Burmese agreed to the demand of the Sinhalese for a treaty to maintain the customary exchange between the two lands. The export of elephants from Burma to Lanka resumed; the possibility even exists that some of the present-day wild elephant populations on the island may have derived from such imports from Burma.[90]

Polonnaruwa was abandoned as the capital by the Sinhalese kings during the 14th century, presumably because it was susceptible to invasions from southern India. The elephant culture continued to flourish under the later kings who ruled from other centres. Some of them may have maintained a royal monopoly on the use of elephants as seen from a stone inscription of the early 16th century which states that the people would desist from "trading in elephants, [and] riding on elephants" in deference to the king.[91] With the arrival of the Portuguese on the island around this time, the Sinhalese rulers had to mobilize their elephant force to counter the colonizers from Europe (Chapter 8).

***

During the 1st century CE or even earlier Buddhism had reached China,[92] possibly through monks travelling with traders on the famous Silk Route. A six-tusked elephant on a bas-relief from T'eng-hsien dating to the middle of the 1st century is evidence that the depiction of the Bodhisatva in the form of a sacred elephant was known here from an early period.[93] Samantabhadra, a Bodhisatva in Mahayana Buddhism and a member of the Shakyamuni trinity shown riding an elephant, was well known in Tibet and China as Puxian Pusa, and in Japan as Fugen Bosatsu (figures 5.23a and b). At the Wannian monastery in Mount Emei, western China, a late 10th-century image of Puxian riding a white elephant is worshipped by the people of this mountain region. A late 12th-century gold and silver painting of a Buddhist sutra from the Heian period in Japan shows Fugen on a lotus-shaped pedestal borne by a six-tusked elephant descending to earth.[94] Puxian is also a favourite subject in Chinese porcelain and bronze images from the Ming period (14th–17th century). Porcelain vases of the Ming and the Qing dynasties also commonly feature stylized elephant handles (figure 5.24). Paintings on silk from the later Ming period, one showing a caparisoned elephant with an attendant and another the Shakyamuni on an elephant (figure 5.25), point to the decline of the elephant in China as the artists obviously had no first-hand knowledge of the elephant.[95]

We do not know much of the status of the elephant in China during the first millennium CE except that it continued its rapid retreat south of the Yangtze Kiang, though some still survived in the central part of the river valley.[96] Elephant flesh was consumed in the far south of the country; writings from the 5th century CE confirm that the trunk was a delicacy that tasted like piglet meat, and was "fatty and crisp".[97] The obsession with eliminating crop-raiding elephants continued throughout Chinese history. A 12th-century report from Zhangzhou in the southeast mentions that the peasants inhabiting the narrow river valleys amidst the mountains suffered greatly from the ravages of elephants. Some of

them killed elephants to rid themselves of the damage but when local officials demanded the feet and tusks in return for permitting them to eliminate the elephants, the peasants apparently stopped killing them in indignation.[98]

The elephant was deployed to a limited extent in warfare as seen from sporadic references in the historical records of southern China. Chengdu used elephants in its defence against the founder of the Ming dynasty in the 1370s but was defeated by the opponents' use of firearms.[99] The rebellion against the Ming from the southwest in 1388 likewise used more than 100 armoured elephants but was overcome by an overwhelmingly superior force of Ming cavalry. The Ming captured 37 elephants and used these for ceremonial purposes, as did the succeeding Qing dynasty. The year 1622 has the last reference to the use of war elephants in imperial China. By this time the wild elephant was confined to the extreme south, in the regions of Yunnan, and possibly a remnant population further east along the coast.

***

Buddhism had also spread along with Hinduism to Southeast Asia during the early centuries of the Common Era. The golden age of Burma began with the rise of Pagan (Bagan) during the mid-9th century CE. The story goes that the Hindu king Anawrahta defeated the southern city of Thaton in the mid-10th century and led the Buddhist Mon king and 32,000 Mon prisoners, along with sacred books and relics, on 32 white elephants back to Pagan.[100] The skilled Mon builders and carvers began to raise the great Buddhist and Hindu monuments of Pagan that eventually became a worthy rival to Angkor in its grandeur. The kingdom of Pagan was consolidated by Kyanzittha (1084–1113) and Alaugsithu (1113–67) who brought in Mon culture and Theravada Buddhism. The great Ananda temple built by Kyanzittha features 80 bas-reliefs relating the life story of the Buddha,[101] while 500 glazed tiles each with a Mon or Pali inscription explain the *Jatakas*.[102] Frescoes on another nearby 11th-century temple, Nagayon, illustrate "kings and courtiers, elephants and horses".[103]

During the late 13th century Pagan faced a challenge from Kublai Khan, the Mongol ruler of China. Marco Polo (circa 1254–1324), the Venetian merchant who travelled through Asia provides a detailed account of the great Khan's court and his campaigns.[104] Kublai was already familiar with elephants from his campaigns in neighbouring lands to the south and even possessed considerable numbers of them. Marco Polo records that in one of his local battles the Khan was "there on a hill, mounted on a great wooden bartizan, which was borne by four well-trained elephants".[105] During this period the ruler of Pagan was reputed to have 2,000 elephants in his army, possibly exaggerated because Marco also states that on each of these "was set a tower of timber, well framed and strong, and carrying from twelve to sixteen well-armed fighting men", an impossibility for even the strongest elephant.[106] In an act of bravado in 1277, King Narathihapate of Pagan sent a force that included many elephants through hilly terrain into Kaungai, a Siamese protectorate of Kublai. The advancing Mongol horses were initially alarmed upon seeing the elephants, but the archers dismounted and let loose a hail of arrows at the giant beasts which panicked and bolted, some of them falling down the hill slopes. Marco states that the Mongols captured 200 of the Burmese elephants, possibly an inflated figure again.[107] The Mongols retreated in this instance but finally sacked Pagan in 1287.

Further south, the Siamese had asserted their independence from the Khmers during the 13th century and had even invaded Angkor a century later. Discovered in the ruins of Sukhothai in the upper central plains of Thailand, the Ramkhamhaeng Stele, a stone obelisk controversially dated to 1292, provides the first historical account of this country in the Thai script.[108] It speaks of a thriving Sukhothai in which elephants were freely

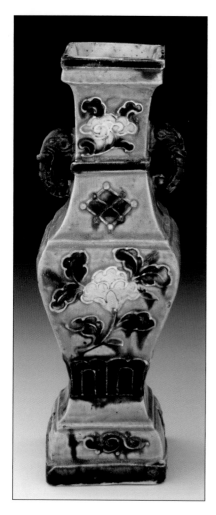

5.24 Porcelain altar vase featuring stylized elephant handles and "fahua-type" decoration made in Jingdezhen, Ming dynasty (circa 1436–64), China.
© *Trustees of the British Museum, London.*

5.25 Painting on silk from the later Ming period (16th–17th century), China, showing the Buddha Shakyamuni on an elephant. © *Freer Gallery of Art, Smithsonian Institution, Washington DC: Gift of Charles Lang Freer.*

5.26 Indra riding Erawan, as Airavati is known in Thailand, is ubiquitous in the art and architecture of the country as in this 20th-century Buddhist shrine at Bangkok.

5.27 Drum slab from Amaravati, Andhra Pradesh, mid to late 1st century CE, carved in limestone with images of the *chakravartin* or universal, righteous monarch flanked by four attendants, his horse, and his elephant. The possession of white elephants was important for a *chakravartin* to gain this recognition from the people.

© *Trustees of the British Museum, London.*

traded by the common people. Status was clearly defined by the possession of elephants; upon a man's death his son inherited, in order of importance, his "elephants, wives, children, granaries, groves, and so on".[109] Victorious rulers routinely dispossessed the vanquished of their elephants. The name Ramkhamhaeng, meaning Rama the bold, was earned by the king when, as a young man defending his father's kingdom, he rode a mighty elephant to victory against a superior enemy. Homage to the Buddha in the numerous temples was conducted by the people with the ruler riding a caparisoned white elephant.

The white elephant as a sacred symbol and a royal monopoly caught on quite early in Buddhist Burma and Thailand. The *chang pheuak* (literally, strange-coloured elephant) reached its pinnacle in Thai art, architecture, religion, and politics.[110] If Indra had changed his mount from a horse to the celestial Airavata in post-Vedic India, in Thailand he mounted the white elephant Erawan who possessed three or sometimes 33 heads. The depiction of Indra riding Erawan is ubiquitous in the art and architecture of Thailand (figure 5.26). The *Traibhumikatha*, a seminal Buddhist text originally compiled in the 14th century, idealized the concept of *chakravartin* or a universal, righteous monarch to whom the possession of white elephants was important for gaining this recognition from the people (figure 5.27). As only one ruler could be the *chakravartin* at a given time, the urge to be the "Lord of the White Elephant" resulted in a series of wars, popularly called the White Elephant Wars, across Burma, Thailand, southern Laos, and Cambodia, during 1549–1769 to gain control of these sacred animals.[111] These power struggles, accompanied

5.28 Depiction of elephants at Borobudur, 8th–9th century:
a Episode from the Manohara story in which Prince Sudhana and the Kinnari Manohara reunited, sit in a pavilion; an attendant holding a flywhisk, seated courtiers, and an elephant and horses appear in the background.
b Prince Sudhana, an umbrella held up over him, walks up to mount a royal elephant, escorted by guards, with celestial beings above.

by palace intrigues of shifting allegiances and betrayed love that rival the plots in Bollywood films, would fill an entire volume. A tragic incident for the Siamese was the unintentional death of queen Suriyothai who was killed by a spear aimed at her husband, King Mahachakrapat, when she rode her elephant towards the general of an invading Burmese force in 1594. Even though the Siamese managed to hold on to their capital Ayutthya they had to part with two white elephants to sue for peace. The establishment of the Chakri dynasty in 1782 brought stability to Siamese rule. Interestingly, the present monarch of this dynasty, Bhumibol Adulyadej (b. 1946), has possessed 17 white elephants (of which 11 have been alive at a given time) – as many as any former ruler has owned in Thai history.

We finally move closer to the equator, to the islands of Southeast Asia, to briefly look at a stupendous Buddhist monument that features elephants by the dozen. Buddhism reached this region, known in ancient times as Suvarnadipa (lit. golden isle), through the maritime trade.[112] The ancient history of this region is still quite hazy but we know that the thalassocracy of Srivijaya, centred on Sumatra, gained control of much of the region beginning the late 7th century CE. Two influential families, the Hindu Sanjaya and the Buddhist Shailendra, seem to have vied for control of the kingdom though they also intermarried in the process. Borobudur was built under the Shailendra dynasty during circa 760–830 CE. Standing on a small hill in the Kedu plains of central Java, this unique monument rises from a broad, square base as "a series of concentric terraces of decreasing size that rise like steps to a central peak".[113] About 1,460 carved stone panels in the galleries illustrate the life of the Buddha and various Buddhist stories including the *Jataka*s and the *Avadana*s (figures 5.28a and b). The elephant is depicted in a number of panels; it appears in the conception story of Queen Maya, as a royal mount, and as a wild creature along with other denizens of the forest such as peacocks and monkeys. Whether Java had an indigenous population of elephants or not in historical times has intrigued zoologists (see Chapter 8). Decorated elephants with parasols indicating royal status, or animals ridden by mahouts holding *ankush*, realistically carved, are evidence that the Javanese artists had first-hand knowledge of captive elephants. Some bas-reliefs clearly depict wild elephants, but whether this indicates the presence of free-ranging animals, or should be taken as artistic licence in placing the creature within its natural habitat in the original land of the Buddha, is a moot point.

The kingdom of Srivijaya weakened following the invasion of Rajendra Chola from southern India in 1025, and was finally conquered by east Java's Majapahit kingdom during the late 13th century. The conversion to Islam in a significant way beginning the 13th century was the last phase in the Indianization of the Southeast Asian islands and the Malay Peninsula before the European colonial influences and Chinese settlements took over from the mid-16th century.[114] The elephant would now be viewed through a different cultural lens.

CHAPTER 6

The Elephant
in Hindu Culture

THE TWO GREAT EPICS, *Mahabharata* and *Ramayana* are replete with references to the elephant, as we saw in Chapter 2. This animal also appears significantly in the Sangam literature of the Tamil land of southern India. Fairly independently of the north, the Tamils had developed a distinct language and a sophisticated culture that undoubtedly included a close relationship with the elephant (figure 6.1). They were, however, not immune to the winds of the Vedic culture that had begun blowing from the north during the first millennium BCE.

Peninsular India may well have established trade through the sea route with Africa and West Asia in ancient times.[1] The Old Testament states that the navy of King Solomon (9th or 10th century BCE) brought gold from Ophir, and further that "Once in three years came the navy of Tharshish, bringing gold, and silver, ivory, and apes, and peacocks."[2] Solomon also made a great throne of ivory, and overlaid it with the best gold. Some scholars believe that Ophir and Tharshish refer to ports in India, but it is not known whether the ivory came from Africa or India.[3]

An Ashokan rock inscription (No. 13) of the 3rd–2nd century BCE specifically refers to the people of the south as the Cholas, Pandyas, Keralaputra (Cheras), Satiyaputras, as well as Tambapanni (Lanka).[4] The Kalinga king Kharavela's famous (though somewhat defaced and thus obscure) inscription at Hathi-gumpha in the Udayagiri complex, dated to the mid-2nd century BCE, speaks of the ruler sending a force towards the river Krishna against a century-old confederacy of Tamil kingdoms (*Tramiradesasanghatam*) that become a threat to his kingdom. Kharavela obtained pearls from the Pandyas and, given the considerable stocks of elephants in his kingdom mentioned in the inscription, quite possibly elephants as well.[5] Ancient Greek sources such as Megasthenes also make reference to the Pandyan country. Clearly, the reach of the Tamils was considerable, as George Hart has suggested.[6]

For our purposes the earliest literary sources of the Tamil land are the poems of the so-called Sangam period.[7] The extant Sangam literature comprises eight anthologies and ten songs, and a total of 2,381 poems by 473 poets, including 102 anonymous poems, written between the 1st and 3rd centuries CE. The poems can broadly be categorized into those that cover *agam* (interior) or the relationship between man and woman within the family, and *puram* (exterior) or man's interaction with the outside world, especially martial heroism. The *Tolkappiyam*, a work on grammar and poetic technique, from a later period has also survived.

The Sangam anthologies have numerous references to the elephant that provide glimpses into its distribution, ecology, and behaviour.[8] The Tamils had already developed an indigenous elephant culture – remember the elephants that the Pandyan ruler sent along with his daughter to King Vijaya of Lanka in the 5th century BCE, or the Chola king Elara who invaded the island during the 2nd century BCE and ruled from Anuradhapura for half a century before he was defeated by Dutthagamani in an elephant-to-elephant combat (see Chapter 5). Obviously, the Tamils had the means to transport elephants across the seas much before the Sangam period. An important environmental concept that emerges from the *Tolkappiyam* is the *tinai* (place or region) that is used not merely to describe a distinctive landscape but also represents a "highly formalized ecology"[9] (figure 6.2). Five *tinai*s are described – *kurinji* (mountain), *mullai* (pastoral land), *palai* (arid land), *marutam* (riverine tract), and *netyal* (coast). The elephant is mainly associated with the *kurinji*, where hunting-gathering was a way of life and millets were cultivated (as is the case presently) and, to a lesser extent, the *palai* as well as possibly the *mullai*, a land of shifting cultivation. The *vengai* (*Pterocarpus marsupium*) tree was common in the *kurinji* land; the bright yellow flowers of the *vengai* falling on an

6.1 This 16th-century sculpture from Thogur, Tamil Nadu, of the deity Aiyanar riding an elephant illustrates the elephant culture of the Tamils that goes back to the first millennium BCE.
Courtesy: Government Museum, Chennai.

6.2 An elephant family moves through the forested hill landscape of the Sigur plateau in the Nilgiris, Tamil Nadu (2006). The *Tolkappiyam*, an ancient Tamil work, introduced the concept of the *tinai* (place or region) to describe a distinctive landscape. The *kurinji* (mountain) is one such landscape with which the elephant is associated.

elephant's back made it resemble a tiger's skin.[10] When elephants in the arid *palai* tract did not find any water in the pools they resorted to feeding on the mosses that grew along the moist edges.[11] The elephant's association with the densely forested hills and some arid lands also suggests that the cultivable plains of the south had already been settled by the Sangam period.

Elephants are described as inhabiting the Vengadam hills and beyond in the Eastern Ghats of Andhra Pradesh from where they have since disappeared. Similarly, the Chera country, the present-day southern Western Ghats of Kerala and Tamil Nadu, possessed elephants in abundance. A poem praising a local chieftain of the Chera country has been translated as follows: "Did this beautiful hill praise Andiran who wields the sharp sword and wears the wreath of *curapunnai*? How is it this hilly forest is full of male elephants?"[12] The pointed reference to male elephants can only mean that tuskers which could be captured and trained were common (figure 6.3). It would not be out of place to mention here that ivory poaching in recent times has greatly depleted the Chera land of tusked male elephants (see Chapter 9). It would also be pertinent to add that the hill tribes of the south not only hunted elephants for their tusks but also consumed elephant meat in the Sangam period.[13] In fact, tuskers were so plentiful that the hill people used the harvested tusks as fence posts for their small abodes in the forest! The women also used the tusks as pestles to pound millets and other grain.[14]

The ancient Tamil literature does not boast of a text equivalent to the *Gajashastra* of northern India (see Chapter 2 and the account later in this chapter). However, an intimate knowledge of the elephant is indicated by some very astute observations about the animal as well as the large number of names used for the elephant and its body parts.[15] The *Nigandu*, an old Tamil poetical lexicon, has no less than 45 names for the elephant, apart from several terms for female elephants, young elephants, and body parts such as forehead, extremity of the eye, trunk and its tip, tusk and its mid-point, back, foreleg and hindleg, and tail and its parts. In all, more than 75 terms in the Tamil texts refer to the elephant or a specific part of the animal.

Poetic similes relate various parts of the elephant to human attributes and other objects in nature.[16] Thus, an elephant's trunk is compared to the braided hair of a maiden or to a woman's thigh,[17] as well as to the ears of ripening millet or a palmyra stem. The sprouting tusks of a young elephant, tinged red at the edges, are like the slightly reddened eyes of a lady in love. An elephant's foot has the appearance of the *mattalam*, a musical instrument. The dignified walk of a Pandyan king on the battlefield is compared to the majestic gait of the elephant. The compelling metaphor of monsoon clouds and elephants is common to both Sangam and Sanskrit poetry. Thus, in Tamil poems an elephant drenched black by the rains is a monsoon cloud, while a dark cloud that drifts slowly across the sky is a black elephant anointed with oil[18] (figure 6.4).

More than once the Sangam poems refer to pearls produced from an elephant's tusks.[19] E.S. Varadarajaiyer, who examined the Sangam literature in detail for references to the elephant, and George Hart who has translated many of the Tamil poems have both concluded that these descriptions are merely the result of poetic imagination.[20] However, there may be a biological basis for this mention of pearls within elephant tusks. Hart correctly surmises that these could be excrescences that grow within tusks. While these could be very rare occurrences not formalized in scientific writings, such hard, round structures about the size of a thumbnail seem to be excrescences produced at the base of elephant tusks, according to experienced veterinarians. Having the appearance of precious stones, these objects known as *gajamukta* in the trade are much sought after for their magical properties (figure 6.5).[21]

6.3 A tusked male elephant along the Mudumalai-Bandipur border in the southern Western Ghats (1980). The Sangam texts make a pointed reference to the abundance of male elephants, undoubtedly tusked ones, in the land of the Cheras.

6.4 Dark monsoon clouds gather over the river Kabini as an elephant herd moves across the open landscape to the nearby woodland. In the Sangam poems the dark monsoon cloud and the elephant are effectively used as metaphors for each other.

6.5 A true *gajamukta*, much prized among traders for its supposedly medicinal or magical properties, may be formed out of excrescences produced at the base of elephant tusks. This object at the Forensics Laboratory of the Wildlife Institute of India, Dehra Dun, is however bone.
Courtesy: S.P. Goyal.

6.6 An adult female elephant feeding on bamboo at Mudumalai in Tamil Nadu (2009). The Sangam texts observe that a pregnant cow elephant that fed on young bamboo shoots would abort its foetus.

The sounds that elephants make are described as resembling particular musical instruments.[22] A sleeping elephant produces a sound like the *tumbru*, a wind instrument;[23] it is obvious that the poet had heard a sleeping elephant snoring.[24] The roaring of an elephant is like crashing thunder.[25]

The feeding preferences of the elephant are mentioned in several poems.[26] The animal fed on grasses, the pith of the palmyra stem, the branches and leaves of the *murungai* (Horseradish tree, *Moringa oleifera*), *vetpalai* (Ivorywood tree, *Wrightia tinctoria*), and *omai* (Charcoal tree, *Trema orientalis*). When green fodder was not available, elephants would even feed on the dry branches of trees such as *maramaram*, a very apt observation. That elephants feed on bamboo is a sufficiently common occurrence that a layperson knows well (figure 6.6). A Tamil poem however states that when a cow elephant in advanced stage of pregnancy feeds on the tender, leafless shoots of bamboo, it aborts its foetus.[27] This is a remarkable observation; we know today that young shoots of plants including bamboos produce cyanogenic compounds that are toxic to animals.[28]

The elephant's fondness for the bark of many trees is mentioned, especially in the context of *agam* or the man-woman relationship (figure 6.7). Thus, a bull elephant uproots the *omai* tree in order to appease the hunger pangs of its mate.[29] We know that bull elephants have a distinct inclination to push over trees but only feed sparsely on their bark or leaves before moving away; this behaviour is likely to be a social display.[30] It is entirely possible that other elephants in the vicinity, including cow elephants, would then come over to feed on the felled tree.

In another poem a lady confides in her maid that she expects her lover to bestow affection upon her as a male elephant would on his mate by breaking the branches of the *ya* tree to satisfy her hunger.[31] In an instance of unfulfilled love we learn that the heroine strokes her hair, devoid of flowers, with these words:

6.7 A bull elephant debarking a tree, as in this picture, is used as a metaphor in the *agam* category of Sangam poems to describe man-woman relationships.

Has he forgotten me?
He left me to weep
and goes on long, barren paths
where an elephant,
not bearing to see the suffering of his mate
staggering as she walks,
gores a high *yā* tree so it is ruined,
takes its white fibrous bark with his trunk,
tastes it,
and trumpets, his heart filled with pain.[32]

In this verse the gored *ya* tree is a metaphor for the heroine who has been abandoned after the hero has enjoyed her pleasures.[33]

The behaviour of mating elephants also finds interesting descriptions in Sangam literature even if the poet stretches his imagination to some extent. The bull elephant is often depicted as being affectionate to its mate.[34] Apart from bringing food for its mate to eat, some interesting passages refer to bull elephants in arid lands carrying water in their trunks to their mates, for pouring on their heads or to drink.[35] We know that on a hot day elephants have the habit of storing small quantities of water in pouches inside the throat that they can withdraw with the trunk and spray on themselves.[36]

Musth in the bull elephant is well recognized though its significance is not as well described in the Tamil texts as in their Sanskrit counterparts. Bulls with musth fluid oozing from their temples find mention in several poems. The relationship between musth and mating in elephants is seen from a passage that speaks of a mighty bull elephant, with musth fluid flowing down its temples, resting its trunk on its shining tusks, as it pairs off with its mate within a forest grove.[37] On the other hand, a musth bull that has

6.8 The bull Mudumalai lies in the waters of the Moyar river in total abandon as it is being bathed by its mahout and a young assistant (2010). The Tamil woman poet Avvaiyar who lived during the Sangam period praises the great bull elephant gently settling in the water where children bathe, to have its tusks cleaned.

killed its adversary, the tiger, also roams the jungle in wrath without joining its mates.[38] That bull elephants could be temperamental, gentle by nature but ferocious in musth, also comes out in a verse by the great Tamil poet Avvaiyar singing praises to her patron Adhigaman Neduman Anji:

> As is a great elephant settling into the water [figure 6.8] to clean
> his white tusks at a bathing site for the little children
> of a town, so sweet you are for us, O greatness! But like
> that elephant when he has entered into rut,
> dangerous to touch, O greatness, you are other than sweet to your enemies![39]

Elephants and tigers were rivals and, on occasion, an elephant fell prey to this predator that ranged over the hill forests where the *vengai* tree was common. More often, a bull elephant overcame the tiger as this poem evocatively describes:

> Oh! Lord of the hilly tract where the elephant which ate the branches of the bamboo
> with its kith and kin, vanquished the tiger with true fighting spirit which lay in wait
> to attack the elephant near the water-pool, and after wiping out the blood in its
> tusk, walked slowly and magnanimously and full of pride in having overcome its
> adversary, got united with its mate and lay asleep with the humming bees hovering
> round it in the hill full of plantain trees.[40]

The bees were hovering around the elephant because it was in musth; this observation is also common in Sanskrit works and may refer to the attraction of insects to particular chemicals secreted from the temples.[41]

The crocodile was considered the only adversary capable of catching and killing a mighty elephant.[42] This observation has parallels to the well known *gajendra-moksha* story of the *Bhagavata Purana*, discussed later in this chapter.

Solitary elephants, obviously bulls, could be vicious towards humans. Several passages speak of such animals waiting to ambush people walking along a forest path.[43] As often happens on forest roads even today, a Tamil poem mentions "the place where the leader

6.9 A young elephant being lifted from a disused pit it has accidentally fallen into in Kerala. The pit method was used since ancient times almost exclusively in southern India; fewer elephants were captured by this method than through the *kheddah*s used in the north of the country.

Photograph by Jacob Cheeran.

of the gang [group] gets separated from its kith and kin and lies in ambush in the roadside in order to get at passers by".[44] The poet mistakenly assumes that a bull elephant is the leader of an elephant group, though the greater tendency of a solitary bull to attack people is correctly recognized.

The tendency of wild elephants to raid cultivated crops such as millets and sugarcane finds frequent mention in the Sangam poems.[45] Apart from the legend of Palakapya, these passages are the oldest references I could find on elephant depredation of crops. One passage makes a pointed reference to a solitary bull elephant "with fiery eyes, alone and separated from its mate" approaching the fields in the *kurinji* land.[46] It is now well established that adult bulls are chronic raiders and enter cultivation much more frequently than do female-led groups.[47] The farmers kept vigil from raised platforms, much as they do today, and used drums, slings, and bows to chase away the marauders. In one instance the loft was made of "the hide of the tiger which never quails before the elephant's might".[48] As with recent experiments in the use of tiger urine and playback calls to deter crop-raiding elephants, the cultivators of the Sangam age believed that if an intruding elephant spotted or smelt the tigerskin it would keep away from their fields. Finally, one poem mentions how elephants managed to sneak into the millet fields after the guardians became drunk and fell into a stupor.[49] Nothing much seems to have changed in the Tamil land for over a millennium and a half!

The Tamil people captured elephants, including young ones, and trained them for use in battle.[50] Capture in pits, filled with soil and brush to soften an elephant's fall, was the preferred method of securing elephants (figure 6.9). There is no mention in the Sangam classics of elephants being driven into stockades as in the kingdoms of the north. The celebrated poet Tiruvalluvar's *Kural* (or *Tirukkural* as this classic text on ethics is better known) has an interesting reference to a tame elephant being used to capture a wild elephant.[51] This could imply some northern influence in the method of capture.

6.10a Coin (obverse) issued by Bactrian king Demetrius (2nd century BCE), depicting him wearing an elephant scalp crown or helmet.

© Trustees of the British Museum, London.

b Coin (reverse) issued by Indo-Greek king Apollodotus I (2nd–1st century BCE), with an elephant and a Greek legend.

Courtesy: The Trustees of Chhatrapati Shivaji Maharaj Vastu Sangrahalaya (CSMVS), Mumbai.

c Coin (obverse) issued by Indo-Greek king Lysias (2nd–1st century BCE), showing the ruler wearing an elephant's scalp.

Courtesy: The Trustees of Chhatrapati Shivaji Maharaj Vastu Sangrahalaya (CSMVS), Mumbai.

d Gold coin (obverse) of the Kushan king Vima Kadphises (circa 100–128 CE) showing the king riding an elephant.

© Trustees of the British Museum, London.

e Copper coin (obverse) minted by the Kushan ruler Huvishka (154–192 CE), showing the king on an elephant.

© Trustees of the British Museum, London.

f Gold coin (reverse) of the Kushan king Kanishka I (circa 128–151 CE), depicting him as a four-armed deity (Shiva) holding a trident, thunderbolt, water-pot, and elephant goad, and with an antelope skin draped over his shoulder.

© Trustees of the British Museum, London.

Gifting of elephants among chieftains was common during the Sangam period.[52] The state elephant was gorgeously caparisoned and could be identified by the parasol and the royal flag it carried,[53] a fairly standard practice in the subcontinent. Its tusks fitted with sharp metal caps, the mighty bull elephant was used to break down the gates and walls of enemy forts.[54] Although some of the Tamil chieftains may have possessed considerable numbers of elephants, the Sangam texts do not indicate any large-scale deployment of this animal in war as compared to the kingdoms of the Gangetic basin. This is not to deny the existence in the Tamil land of the organized fourfold division of the army as in the north; several passages in the Sangam texts allude to this concept.[55]

During the early centuries of the Common Era there are thus similarities and differences between the elephant cultures of the north and the south. A more formalized body of knowledge relating to the science of elephants had emerged in the north; the south too had considerable knowledge of the animal as seen from the Sangam classics, though in contrast no compendium seems to have existed. In the north elephants were captured through a variety of methods including the *kheddah*; this also allowed the build up of large stocks of elephants for mass deployment in war. In the south elephants were captured in smaller numbers, mostly through the pit method, though they also seem to have used *mela shikar* (tame elephants to capture wild ones) to a limited extent. Thus, the chieftains of the south used mainly tuskers in their battles. Gifting of elephants was common in both regions, as was the pride of place given to the royal mount.

***

From the deep south we now move to the northern theatre of the subcontinent where the elephant culture during the 2nd century BCE–3rd century CE seems to have largely maintained its continuity with the late Vedic and early Buddhist periods. Hinduism and Buddhism vied with each other for followers among commoners and kings. The Mauryas and the dynasties following it adopted one or the other religion, but often patronized both, their rulers even alternating between them. As Benoy Behl states, "the first 600 years of surviving art with Buddhist themes was all made under the rule of Hindu Kings".[56] In course of time the process of syncretization made it difficult to sometimes distinguish one culture from the other.

There are few literary leads to the elephant culture of the north around the turn of the Common Era when Central Asians began entering the subcontinent from the northwest. However, coins issued by the rulers between the 1st century BCE and the 2nd century CE often feature the elephant, implying that they had eventually absorbed the local elephant culture. Coins issued by the Bactrian king Demetrius during the 2nd century BCE depict an elephant crown (figure 6.10a). This followed the standard Greek design of representing the king's bust on the obverse and various divinities or other objects on the reverse. The Indo-Greeks of the northwest continued this tradition; King Apollodotus I issued a coin with an elephant and a Greek legend on the reverse (figure 6.10b), while King Lysias minted a coin showing the ruler wearing an elephant's scalp on the obverse (figure 6.10c). It was not difficult for the Parthians (Pahlavas) to imitate this coin design, though no such coin has been found in the north and this elephant motif is otherwise confined to a single sculpture from the Pallavas of the south. The first Indo-Scythian (Shaka) ruler in India, Maues (circa 90–60 BCE), minted coins showing an elephant wearing a bell, while a later Shaka king Rudrasimha I (2nd century CE) also issued a copper coin with an elephant, crescent, and the sun on the obverse.

An early Kushan king Vima Kadphises (circa 100–128 CE) was the first to introduce gold coins in India. His coins mostly portray Shiva and the bull, though one coin shows the king riding an elephant (figure 6.10d).[57] A later Kushan ruler Huvishka (154–192 CE)

minted a similar coin, while the great Kanishka (circa 128–151 CE) portrayed himself as Shiva with an elephant goad as one of his attributes (figures 6.10e and f).[58] Like the Vedic people of two millennia earlier, the new Central Asian tribes came with horse-based cavalry but then assimilated the elephant culture of the subcontinent. The Satavahanas of the Deccan also issued coins that feature the elephant.

Among literary works, the controversial *Manu Smriti*, a foundational work on ancient Hindu law or *Dharma Shastra* ("the laws of righteous conduct"), exhorts the king that "on even ground let him fight with chariots and horses; in water-bound places with boats and elephants".[59] This advice is similar to that given by Bhishma to Yudhishthira in the *Mahabharata* (see Chapter 2). It is difficult to assign a precise date to *Manu Smriti* but it is believed to have been composed sometime between the 2nd century BCE and the 3rd century CE[60] as "a commentary arising from the insecurity of the orthodox in an age of flux".[61] At the same time, it is also clear that during the Kushan period not only chariotry but also elephantry declined, with cavalry playing the major role in the army.[62]

The Guptas wrested control of Pataliputra from the Kushans in about 275 CE. Often described as the "golden age" of Indian history and culture,[63] three prominent kings, Chandragupta I (319–334 CE), Samudragupta (335–380), and Chandragupta II (380–412) successively took Gupta rule to greater heights of achievement. Art and literature flourished under their patronage. Although the Guptas were probably vaishyas, they came to be regarded as kshatriyas, and actively patronized Brahmanical Hinduism, several important Buddhist monuments such as a temple at Gaya were developed with their concurrence.[64] The paintings at Ajanta, too, pertain to the Gupta period, though the royal patrons were the Vakatakas of the northern Deccan region (in today's Maharashtra and

6.11 A wild bull elephant with its left tusk broken has a dust bath in the Mudumalai forests (2006). The 5th-century poet Kalidasa observed that such elephants were particularly prone to trouble the inmates of ashrams inside the jungle.

Madhya Pradesh). Overall, Buddhism clearly declined during the reign of the Guptas. These rulers made generous land grants to brahmans who became wealthy; this opening of uncultivated land,[65] obviously forest, undoubtedly resulted in further decline of the natural vegetation of the Gangetic basin.

Unlike the Mauryans, the Guptas had a smaller standing army. Faxian, the Chinese traveller who wrote an account of the Buddhist lands during that period, does not mention the size of the Gupta army but it is probable that a major portion of the troops came from feudatory states.[66] In the course of their interaction with the Kushans, they too seem to have taken to superior cavalry to the further detriment of chariots and elephants. I would add here that the process of deforestation of the Gangetic basin would have been practically completed by this time. Centuries of past exploitation of elephants could also have reduced their numbers in the fringe areas along the Himalayan foothills as well as the Vindhyas. Wild elephants were certainly a feature of the Gupta empire but possibly much less so than during Mauryan times.

The Gupta age is notable for the efflorescence of secular literature in Sanskrit and Prakrit. Kalidasa, who probably lived in the 5th century CE, is undoubtedly the most celebrated poet and dramatist of this period. The elephant finds mention in many of his poems and plays. In his lyrical poem *Meghaduta* (Cloud Messenger), that describes the journey of a cloud carrying a message from a lovelorn *yaksha* in the Vindhyas to his wife on Mount Kailasa in the Himalaya, the dark monsoon cloud is compared to an elephant (as in the Sangam poems):

Some months were gone; the lonely lover's pain
Had loosed his golden bracelet day by day
Ere he beheld the harbinger of rain,
A cloud that charged the peak in mimic fray,
As an elephant attacks a bank of earth in play.[67]

Again in Kalidasa's *Ritusamhara* (Ode to Seasons) that describes the six seasons, we find a connection between the rains and the elephant:

The rain advances like a King
In awful majesty.
Hear, dearest, how his thunders ring
Like royal drums, and see
His lighting-banners wave; a cloud
For elephant he rides,
And finds his welcome from the crowd
Of lovers and of brides.[68]

Kalidasa's most famous play is *Abhijnanashakuntalam* (Of Shakuntala Recognized by a Token). Dushyanta, king of Hastinapura, is hunting in the forest when he chances upon the beautiful Shakuntala at the hermitage of the sage Vishvamitra. An elephant, undoubtedly a solitary bull, is terrifying the inmates of the hermitage:

One tusk is splintered by a cruel blow
Against a blocking tree; his gait is slow,
For countless fettering vines impede and cling;
He puts the deer to flight; some evil thing
He seems, that comes our peaceful life to mar,
Fleeing in terror from the royal car.[69] [figure 6.11]

Later, the king himself is compared to a majestic bull elephant wandering in the open under a blazing sun, not an uncommon sight, while a family group is taking rest from the heat amidst a dense patch of jungle close by.[70]

Vatsyayana, who is also believed to have lived during the Gupta age, compares a woman's body, gait, and behaviour to that of an elephant, in his well-known *Kama Sutra* (aphorisms on love).[71] He describes four kinds of women, one of whom is *hastini*, the elephant woman. This does not necessarily mean that Vatsyayana had any detailed knowledge of elephant behaviour; in one passage he states that elephants mate only in water,[72] a mistaken belief that is common among people even today.

The encyclopaedic *Brihat Samhita* of Varahamihira (early 6th century) provides only a cursory treatment of the elephant in a single, short chapter that classifies the elephant into the traditional body types of *bhadra*, *manda*, and *mriga*, with the addition of the *sankirna* that represented the intermingling of the other three classes.[73] The most auspicious elephant was one that had between 18 and 20 nails,[74] a belief that is persistent even today among those who purchase elephants. Its prescription that a captive bull's tusks should be trimmed at a length that is twice the circumference of the base[75] is a sound rule of thumb to avoid exposing the root to infection. The *Brihat Samhita* also recognizes the *gajamukta* or "elephant pearl" that originates in the tusk of the animal,[76] though it is not this but the "pearls" that originate in the hood of the cobra (*nagamani*) that are said to bring fortune and victory to the ruler.[77]

***

One of the most important elements of Indic civilization is the use of elephants in mythology. The Vedic god Indra had switched from the horse to the elephant as his favoured mount by the middle of the first millennium BCE, as seen from passages in the *Ramayana*. Interestingly, Indra was worshipped as the Rain God, and the elephant was a symbol of rain and rain clouds since early times. Also, as we have seen, Indra appears in Jain scriptures as well. The earliest visual representation of Indra riding the fabled Airavata interestingly seems to be a relief flanking the doorway to a rock-cut cell at Bhaja, the site of a Buddhist *chaitya-griha* (prayer hall) and *vihara*s (monasteries), that dates to the mid-2nd century BCE during Shunga rule.[78] While Indra sports an elaborate headdress, garland, and jewellery, Airavata holds an uprooted tree aloft in his trunk (figure 6.12). The sculptural style is apparently similar to that of the terracottas and stone carvings of the Shunga period, several of which show the king, sometimes with an attendant, riding a bedecked elephant (figure 6.13).

Sri or Lakshmi, the goddess of fertility and wealth, is the consort of Vishnu, the supreme preserver, in Hindu tradition. Although the concept of a Mother Goddess goes back to the pre-Vedic Harappan civilization, the association of elephants with Lakshmi seems to have developed during late Vedic or post-Vedic times. The image of Gajalakshmi seated or standing on a lotus, flanked by two (or four) elephants pouring libations on her head, is a familiar icon in most Hindu households. Hindu, Buddhist, and Jain cultures of ancient times seem to have adopted this elephant-related imagery in religious iconography. The representation of Gajalakshmi in Hindu monuments is common (figure 6.14). In Chapter 5 we saw depictions of a similarly lustrated female divinity, identified as Mayadevi, in early Buddhist structures such as the Pithalkora caves and at Bharhut and Sanchi (see figure 5.2). We also saw an early depiction of Gajalakshmi in Cave 3 (Ananta-gumpha) of the Jain monuments at Khandagiri (see figure 5.14).

V.S. Naravane interprets the association of Lakshmi, elephants, and lotus as follows:[79] Lakshmi personifies the cosmic lotus containing the seeds of creation, and in Hindu tradition elephants are the *diggaja*s or "supports of the directions", holding the very cosmos on their heads. That elephants commonly frequent lotus-filled ponds in the forest is evocatively described in the *Ramayana* (see Chapter 2). Water is also considered as a necessary element of fertility; in one story when Lakshmi sat next to Indra he poured

6.12 Indra riding Airavata at Bhaja caves, near Pune, the earliest visual representation of Indra on an elephant, from the Shunga period, mid-2nd century BCE.

6.13 Railing crossbar from Mathura, Uttar Pradesh, showing a king and an attendant riding a decorated elephant, Shunga period, 2nd century BCE. *Photographed at the National Museum, New Delhi.*

6.14 Seated on a lotus, Gajalakshmi is flanked by four elephants, two of them lustrating her, at the entrance to the Kailasanatha temple at Ellora, Rashtrakuta period, second half of the 8th century. Above her is an umbrella and *vidyadharas* are seen flying in the sky.
Photograph by Hamsini Sukumar.

down rain so that the crops in the field flourished. In the famous churning of the ocean story of Hindu mythology, when the gods used the snake Vasuki as a rope around Mount Mandara to churn the ocean, it not only yielded the elixir of immortality but also other precious things including Lakshmi who arose seated on a lotus, whereupon the elephants bathed her with holy water (figure 6.15). Incidentally, the four-tusked white elephant, Airavata, was also among the many sacred objects that were thrown up by the churning of the ocean; each of his tusks signifies a divine quality – *prabhu* (sovereignty), *mantra* (counsel), *utsaha* (joy), and *daiva* (prosperity) – thus causing Indra to change his mount from a horse to the elephant.[80]

We may mention here the epithet *gajendra gamini* (she whose walk is graceful as an elephant's) used for Radha, the consort of Vishnu in his Krishna avatara.

A unique elephant-related symbolism arose in northern India during the Kushan period and became a popular deity during the Gupta period. This icon that rose to godhead and captured the imagination of the people as few other deities have done in the history of religion is, of course, the elephant-headed god Ganesha.[81]

Animal-headed deities have an important place in Hindu mythology – from Vishnu's vehicle Garuda who has an eagle's beak and wings, to Varaha with boar's head and Narasimha with lion's head (Vishnu's third and fourth avatars). However, Ganesha is very different – standing, sitting, or even dancing, a pot-bellied, comical elephant-headed *gana* (the *gana*s were impish dwarf attendants of Shiva), legs stunted, his left tusk broken, trunk twisted with its tip dipping into a bowl of sweets, holding his broken tusk, an elephant-goad, a rosary, sugarcane, and riding the lowly rat – seemingly a most unlikely god. Wendy O'Flaherty summarizes the essence of Ganesha in these terms: "Ganesa has everything that is fascinating to anyone who is interested in religion or India or both: charm, mystery, popularity, sexual problems, moral ambivalence, political importance, the works. One can start from Ganesa and work from there in an unbroken line to almost any aspect of Indian culture."[82]

The origins of Ganesha are shrouded in veiled literary references and obscure architectural depictions of elephant-like figures in the subcontinent.[83] It is not even clear if the true antecedents of Ganesha are Vedic, Buddhist, or neither. The *Ramayana* and the *Mahabharata* do not mention Ganesha (though we should recall that the latter, the world's longest poem, is said to have been written non-stop by Ganesha, using his broken tusk as a pen, at the dictation of the legendary sage Vyasa). Some of the later Vedic texts mention deities such as Dantin (one with tusks), Ekadanta (he of one tusk), Vakratunda (he of the twisted trunk), and Hastimukha (one with an elephant's face) that are obviously elephant-related, but these seem to have independent traditions without direct relationship to Ganesha,[84] though scholars like M.K. Dhavalikar think there is a connection.[85]

A coin issued by the Indo-Greek ruler Eukratides (170–150 BCE) shows the Greek god Zeus with an elephant head to his right and a mountain to his left.[86] Another Indo-Greek coin issued by Hermaeus around 50 BCE features an elephant's head.[87] Some scholars thus believe that a tradition of the sacred elephant existed in Gandhara before the 2nd century BCE. The Kushans would have encountered this tradition en route to India, but took it a step further by fashioning early forms of Ganesha. Three such images at the Mathura Museum show the elephant-headed deity carved in the round, a specialty of Kushan artists, standing in the nude with the trunk reaching into a bowl of sweets (figure 6.16).[88] Interesting elephant-headed figures dated to the early centuries of the Common Era are also seen on railings in Mathura and Amaravati.[89] I must mention one more sculptural depiction of an elephant-headed figure, a circa 2nd–3rd-century frieze of

Narayana

Mt Mandar

asuras

suras

vasuka

Kurm Raja

Lakshma Goddess of abundance

Churning of the World

Doonurm God of Water

6.15 The ocean churning story of puranic Hinduism is shown in great detail in this painting from Thanjavur (circa 1820). At the centre is Mount Mandara resting on the back of the Kurma (turtle) avatar of Vishnu. Coiled around the mountain is Vasuki the snake used as a rope by the *asuras* (holding its tail) and the *devas* (holding its head) to churn the ocean. Among the precious objects that emerge from the ocean depths are Lakshmi seated on a lotus (bottom left) and the four-tusked elephant Airavata, the mount of Indra (bottom left).
© Trustees of the British Museum, London.

ganas, one of them elephant-headed and receiving offerings in the Amaravati style, on a stupa at Mihintale in Sri Lanka.[90] What role these prototype elephant-headed images played in eventually defining Ganesha is not clear.

The classical image of Ganesha with the paraphernalia we are familiar with today emerged during the Gupta period. Two of the earliest images are the Ganeshas from Bhumara and Udaygiri near Vidisha in Madhya Pradesh dating to the end of the reign of Chandragupta II (401 CE).[91] The Ganesha outside Cave 6 at Udaygiri is a simple squatting figure, two-armed, with the trunk resting on a bowl of sweets (figure 6.17). Ganesha seems to be guarding the Shiva linga inside the cave. From this period onward we see a rapid elaboration and spread of the iconography of Ganesha to the familiar classical style. During the 6th century CE Ganesha appears at Elephanta, an island off the coast of Mumbai,[92] and at the Ravana Phadi Cave of the temple at Aihole in Karnataka.[93] Ganesha is well represented in the 7th-century rock-cut temples at Ellora. The most intriguing of the images is the *saptamatrika* (seven mothers) panel within Cave 14 with Ganesha seated in *lalitasana*, a tusk and axe in the upper hands and a sheaf of grain and a plate of sweets in the lower hands (figure 6.18); standing next to him is Kala (the god of death). By this time Ganesha had not only reached the south of the country where a shrine was dedicated to him at Tiruchirapalli during the reign of the Pallavas,[94] but also journeyed across the ocean to Thailand, Indonesia, Cambodia, and Vietnam.[95]

From the literary evidence scholars generally agree that a group of malevolent deities or Vinayakas, mentioned in several ancient texts,[96] played a role in eventually defining Ganesha. By the 3rd century CE the four Vinayakas, who were propitiated to avoid

6.16 One of the earliest known sculptural representations of the elephant-headed god Ganesha, sculpted in the round and standing nude, from the late Kushan period, circa 4th or 5th century CE.
Photographed at the Government Museum, Mathura. (Two other such Ganesha images are known from the same museum.)

6.17 Ganesha outside Cave 6, guarding a Shiva linga inside, at Udaygiri, Madhya Pradesh, dated as 401 CE from the Gupta period.

personal ills, were merged into a single Vinayaka appointed as the leader of Shiva's *gana*s.[97] Vinayaka and other epithets for Ganesha such as Vighnesha derive from *vighna*, meaning obstacle, and thus the potential of this deity to create trouble is implicit. The *vighna*-related epithets also have the dual connotation of malevolence (*vighna-karta* or creator of obstacles), and benevolence (*vighna-harta* or remover of obstacles) as Ganesha is popularly considered. Historian of religion G.S. Ghurye was puzzled at this flip-flop when he observed that "Only one step further, and that a very radical transformation, was needed to enthrone Ganesa being the 'Lord of Obstacles', as the 'Destroyer or Remover of Obstacles'. Such transformations inhere in the very nature of early religio-magical systems of beliefs. One who is the lord of anything can be trusted to control and subdue the thing he is lord of.... So Vinayaka, the trouble-maker, becomes the much-prayed-to trouble-averter Ganesa."[98] This metamorphosis seems to have been completed by the Gupta period when the classical images of Ganesha emerged. The classical Ganesha is well represented in the Hoysala temples in Karnataka (figure 6.19).

The rise of a benevolent Ganesha from malevolent antecedents demands an explanation, not merely in the evolution of religious iconography or literary imagination, but also in the sociopolitical context and ecological milieu of the subcontinent. I have attempted an explanation elsewhere,[99] and shall discuss this only briefly here. The elephant would have been a very negative force to small agricultural societies, including shifting cultivators, in the largely forested landscapes of ancient times. From Anga in the north to the Vengadam hills in the south, wild elephants ravaged the crop fields of the people or even killed them on occasion. It is thus not surprising that ancient societies worshipped a malevolent, elephant-headed spirit to avoid misfortune. The taming of the elephant and its use as a war-machine, however, meant that it was also a very positive force to the chieftains and the kings; as early as the Mauryan period Kautilya exhorted the ruler to set up sanctuaries for the protection of elephants that were needed for his army. By the early centuries of the Common Era the Vedic people had almost completely opened up the Gangetic basin for cultivation and settlement; the problem of crop raiding by elephants was naturally solved over this vast tract with the exception of the periphery.

6.18 Ganesha seated in *lalitasana* along with *saptamatrika* (seven mothers) in Cave 14 at Ellora, circa 8th century. Standing next to Ganesha is Kala, the god of death.

6.19 An elaborately sculpted classical image of Ganesha from the Hoysaleshvara temple at Halebid, Hoysala period, 12th century.

It is easy to imagine that for the elite of Vedic society the elephant was a positive force. For them Ganesha was a deity waiting to be invented, though not necessarily so for the common people who suffered elephants' depredation. Ghurye is very explicit as to who invented Ganesha: "He [i.e. Ganesha] represents the Brahmanizing process in excelsis... the raising of Ganapati to the position of being a component of the pentad [of the Hindu pantheon] is a romance enacted by Brahmins and Brahmins alone."[100] Whether through a brilliant flash of inspiration or a more gradual process of change and acceptance, a popular icon was raised to supreme godhead. I would even surmise that Ganesha was Brahmanism's response to the *gajatame* and *mangalahatthi* of Buddhism or, perhaps, a force in the former religion's resurgence and the latter's decline in the age of the Guptas. Many centuries later, Ganesha was to play a similar role in the subcontinent's resistance to its colonial rulers (see Chapter 8).

The ecological pressures from a large human population, and the spread of Buddhism and Jainism with their emphasis on *ahimsa* or non-violence towards all creatures, would have challenged the meat-eating elite of Vedic times. A taboo on the consumption of beef, established in Brahmanical society during the early centuries of the Common Era, was perhaps a response to this ecological and moral challenge.[101] The ban on killing elephants in Mauryan times also implies a taboo or restriction on the consumption of elephant flesh, though remember that hill tribes in the south did not have any such compunctions during the Sangam period. With the exception of the northeast, elephant meat possibly ceased to be consumed across the subcontinent along with the spread of Ganesha worship. The Arab scholar Al-Biruni who spent more than a decade in India during the early 11th century observed that consumption of elephant flesh, and that of a number of other "useful" animals, was forbidden.[102]

The mythology of Ganesha diversified greatly into the realm of fantasy in the *puranas*, a collection of Sanskrit poetical works dating from the Gupta period.[103] The puranic legends of Ganesha's origins are sufficiently well known and will only briefly be described here.[104] Ganesha had to be first installed in a respectable position in the Hindu pantheon, and what could confer better status than being considered the son of Shiva, the supreme destroyer? In the most popular legend of Ganesha he was fashioned out of clay by Parvati, the consort of Shiva, as her son. One day when Parvati was in her bath the great lord himself arrived at her doorstep but the little boy refused him entry. In the fight that ensued Shiva cut off the boy's head whereupon Parvati was filled with grief and anger. Realizing that he had to pacify his consort, Shiva instructed his *ganas* to go out and bring him the head of the first creature they encountered. Soon they returned with an elephant's head that Shiva used to restore the boy to life. Thus Parvati's son came to acquire an elephant's head; the bottom line of the episode was that peace reigned once again in the Parvati-Shiva household and Ganesha took his rightful place as their own son. There are innumerable variations and elaborations of this legend of the elephant-headed deity who came to command adulation among the masses probably unmatched by any other deity in the Hindu pantheon.

In one variation of the puranic legends Shiva as Gajasura-samhara cut off the head of the demon elephant Gajasura who happened to be standing nearby and placed it on the decapitated youth's body. In yet another version, popular in temple iconography, Gajasura (whose father Mahisha had been killed by the goddess Durga) performed extreme austerities for which Brahma, the supreme creator, granted him a boon of invincibility. The rampaging elephant demon soon alarmed the gods who approached Shiva for help. When Gajasura came to Kashi where Shiva lived, the supreme destroyer engaged the demon in a fierce battle and danced his terrible *tandava* on the elephant's head. A defeated Gajasura praised the destroyer and pleaded with him to wear his skin. Shiva agreed to this and transformed the demon into a linga. Dancing Shiva with the elephant skin stretched over his back is seen more than once in the Hindu cave temples (6th to 8th century CE) at Ellora (figure 6.20a). However, the most outstanding sculptural depictions of Shiva dancing on the demon elephant's head are surely those in the Hoysala temples (12th to 13th century) in Karnataka (figure 6.20b). In a variant southern Indian version it was Pillaiyar (Ganesha) who defeated Gajamukha (Gajasura),

6.20 Shiva defeats the elephant demon Gajasura and dances the *tandava* with the elephant's skin stretched over his back. This myth is represented in these two master sculptures from:
a Cave 16 (the 8th-century Kailasanatha temple) at Ellora.
Photograph by Hamsini Sukumar.
b The Hoysaleshvara temple at Halebid, Hoysala period, 12th century.

whereupon the demon transformed himself into a rat and became the elephant-headed deity's vehicle.

As if to make amends for ignoring the other supreme Hindu deity – Vishnu the preserver – in the origin of Ganesha, several *purana*s also attempt to make such a connection. In the well-known *gajendra-moksha* story of the *Bhagavata Purana* and *Vishnu Purana*, the elephant king is trapped by a crocodile when he enters the ocean of milk. Efforts by other elephants in the herd to rescue him go in vain. Finally, Gajendra

prays to Vishnu for assistance whereupon the preserver comes to his rescue (figure 6.21). In another tale it is Vishnu who transfers the head of Gajendra to Ganesha, and restores Gajendra with another elephant's head. The story of a crocodile clenching an elephant's leg in its powerful jaws is obviously quite plausible in the natural habitat of these creatures.

6.21 *Gajendra-moksha*, or Vishnu coming to the rescue of the king of elephants from the grip of the crocodile demon, in a Kota painting of *Vishnu Purana*, circa 1750.
Courtesy: National Museum, Delhi.

***

We now move on to 7th-century India where the break-up of empire had given rise to several smaller kingdoms jostling for space and power. The medieval history of the subcontinent over the next several centuries is too complex to be related in this account. I shall therefore pick up only a few threads of the elephant culture of the Hindu kingdoms as seen in the superb temples that were carved out of rock, or rose to towering heights block by block, across peninsular and central India. We again begin in the deep south where the Cholas, the Pandyas, and the Cheras were involved in internecine struggles and a new dynasty, the Pallavas, had gradually risen to prominence with their capital at Kanchipuram. Various theories have been proposed on the origin of the Pallavas as being from the north or from the Deccan, but for our purposes the most intriguing postulation is that they had Persian ancestry. The phonetic similarity of the term "Pallava" and the Iranian "Pahlava" is the most obvious starting point for this argument.[105] At the Vaikunthaperumal temple in Kanchipuram there is a sculpture depicting Nandivarman Pallavamalla's ascent to the throne in which the monarch's crown resembles an elephant's head.[106] This is similar to the elephant crown used by Bactrian kings of the 2nd century BCE and depicted on coins issued by Demetrius (see figure 6.10a).

Whatever the true origin of the Pallavas, they created stupendous rock-cut temples and sculptures that prominently feature the elephant. The monolithic monuments to Hindu gods and heroes of the epics at the coastal town of Mamallapuram (Mahabalipuram), not far south of Chennai (Madras), are also among the earliest examples of Hindu temple architecture.[107] The name Mamallapuram derives from the title "Mamalla" of the Pallava ruler Narasimhavarman I who sent a successful naval expedition to Lanka around the mid-7th century CE from this port town. Narasimha's father Mahendravarman I (circa 600) began excavating simple cave temples on rocky hillocks at places such as Vallam (between Mamallapuram and Kanchipuram), Pallavaram (near Chennai), and Tiruchirapalli. Interestingly, neither Mahendra nor Narasimha created any monuments at Mamallapuram itself, contrary to what most history books state. It was only from about 690, during the reign of Rajasimha, that Mamallapuram witnessed a burst of artistic activity that lasted nearly 40 years.[108] Then, with the death of Rajasimha the renaissance of Mamallapuram came to a rapid end, leaving behind unfinished works; the year 730 marks "the date of artistic collapse" in this coastal town.[109]

Among the most famous of the monoliths at Mamallapuram is a cluster of five shrines or *rathas* popularly known as the "Pancha Pandava Rathas". A larger-than-life stone elephant, sculpted in the round, stands imposingly near the Nakula-Sahadeva *ratha* (figure 6.22). The roof of this *ratha* is an example of the so-called *gajapristakara* or elephant-back style. The most sublime expression of the Pallava artists is, however, reserved for the great bas-relief known as the Descent of the Ganga or Arjuna's Penance. Sculpted on a rock surface over 30 metres long and 15 metres high, the relief is a virtual potpourri of over 90 figures including celestial beings, ascetics, *gandharvas*, *ganas*, hunters, lions, tigers, monkeys, and many other animals in a landscape of hills, forests, and the river Ganga. Art historians have offered various interpretations of this complex panel that captures the essence of Shaivite Hinduism. By far the most striking aspect of this ancient masterpiece on rock is the scene of an elephant family with two life-like

6.22 Stone elephant near the Nakula-Sahadeva *ratha* at Mamallapuram, Pallava period, late 7th or early 8th century.

6.23 Elephants on the bas-relief "Descent of the Ganga" at Mamallapuram, Pallava period, late 7th or early 8th century, described as the largest open-air relief of its kind. These life-size elephants are arguably the most realistic representation of the species in stone.

6.24 Caryatid tusked-elephants supporting the huge *jagati* of the 8th-century Kailasanatha temple at Ellora.

6.25 Gigantic stone elephant in the northern courtyard of the Kailasanatha temple at Ellora, 8th century. A similar sculpture in the southern courtyard has been considerably mutilated.

6.26 Sculpted elephant on an extended parapet above the entrance to the Kandariya Mahadeva temple at Khajuraho, Chandella period, first half of the 11th century.

elephants, the animal in front a magnificent tusked bull, the perfect *koomeriah* (to borrow a Sanskrit term), its swollen left temple indicating musth, followed by a mature cow elephant with upcurled trunk and raised left foot, and calves gambolling amidst the bull's legs in front, arguably the most realistic representation ever of the species in stone (figure 6.23).

The Chalukyas were the proximate northern neighbours and competitors to the Pallavas. The 7th-century Chinese pilgrim Xuanzang recorded that the Chalukyan king organized his army very meticulously and followed the rules of warfare scrupulously. In battle array the "several hundred savage elephants [are given] intoxicating spirits to drink, till they are overpowered with it...his foes are thus without fail put to flight".[110] During the 7th and 8th centuries the Chalukyas constructed several fine temples in Dravidian style at Aihole, Pattadakal, and Badami in northern Karnataka that are regarded as the cradle of Hindu temple architecture. Elephant-related motifs are seen in several of these early temples. The Durga temple at Aihole also features the so-called *gajapristakara* or elephant-back style in its longitudinal and barrel-vaulted roof. The Virupaksha temple at Pattadakal has a remarkable animal carving designed to look like an elephant from one angle and a buffalo from another perspective. Shiva as Gajasura-samhara is also illustrated at this temple that was built around 740–745 to commemorate the victory of the Chalukya king Vikramaditya II over the Pallavas. Figures of Ganesha are seen at the Ravana Phadi Cave Temple at Aihole and Cave Temple 1 at Badami. Small sculpted elephants mark the entrance to the now fallen *mandapam* of the Azar Shivalaya temple at Badami.

Further north, the Rashtrakutas fashioned a rock-cut temple of mammoth size at Ellora that gloriously captures the concept of the *diggaja*s or elephants supporting the dwelling of the gods themselves upon their shoulders.[111] Built during the reign of king Krishna I (757–772) and dedicated to Lord Shiva, the Kailasanatha temple stands on a high plinth along which are carved an impressive array of caryatid tusked-elephants supporting the huge *jagati* that towers 30 metres high (figure 6.24). The large courtyard features two gigantic stone elephants, one to the north and the other to the south (now mutilated), along with *dhvajastambha*s or victory pillars (figure 6.25).

The idea of an array of elephants as the bearers of temples now spread across central and peninsular India, and became commonplace in the architecture of the great Hindu temple complexes that arose over the next 800 years. Vikramajit Ram makes a very relevant distinction between *gaja-pitha* and *gaja-thara*, the former referring to an elephant-platform at the base or plinth of a temple featuring elephants facing frontally towards the viewer as in the case of Ellora's monolith, and the latter describing a horizontal frieze of elephants in procession as in many temples that were built during the second millennium.[112]

The Chandellas who ruled the north-central region of Bundelkhand raised the Khajuraho complex of temples, described as a consummate architectural achievement of medieval Hindu India, mainly during the 10th and 11th centuries.[113] Both the *gaja-pitha* and the *gaja-thara* forms of the elephant are featured in the Khajuraho temples.[114] The Lakshmana temple founded by King Dhanga in 954 was raised on a high rectangular platform decorated on all sides with *gaja-thara* friezes of a procession of elephants, horses, soldiers, battle scenes, and the life of the common people. Above this along the base of the temple the *gaja-pitha* elephants alternate with men wielding staffs. Sculpted elephants (figure 6.26) stand on extended parapets above the entrance to the Kandariya Mahadeva temple built during the reign of Vidyadhara (1017– 29).[115] We know that the Chandellas maintained considerable numbers of elephants in their army; when Mahmud

6.27 The pyramidal *shikhara* of the great Brihadishvara temple at Thanjavur, built in the early 11th century, soars 70 metres high in the evening sky. The monolithic dome at the top, weighing about 80 tonnes, is believed to have been dragged on wooden rollers up a 2-kilometre-long ramp using elephant power.

of Ghazni threatened the region, Vidyadhara was able to successfully counter him without direct military engagement by mobilizing a force of 145,000 foot-soldiers, 36,000 horses, and at least 640 elephants.[116]

Following the decline of the Pallavas in the south, the Cholas once again rose to prominence and held sway over the entire region during 837–1267. This maritime power used elephants extensively, including transporting them overseas by boat, to achieve their imperial ambitions. Temple construction in the south reached a grandeur and sophistication during their reign unmatched in any other period. The great Brihadishvara temple at Thanjavur, whose foundations were laid in 1002–03 during the rule of Rajaraja I, boasts of a pyramidal *shikhara* that towers 70 metres high and is capped by a monolithic *stupi* (finial) weighing about 80 tonnes.[117] It is believed that an earthen ramp several kilometres long was made to drag the weighty monolith on wooden rollers using elephant power (figure 6.27). Lions and elephants sculpted on the granitic wall form a line of guards around the temple. The magnificent Chola bronzes from this period, famous for the masterful rendering of Shiva's cosmic dance, include images of Ganesha, either alone or in the company of his parents, Parvati and Shiva. The Cholas declined during the 13th century following raids from their traditional rival, the Pandyas of the south, as well as the Hoysalas from the north.

An obscure people from the hill-forests, the Hoysalas became powerful in Karnataka by the early 11th century and held sway over a large area of the peninsula until the mid-14th century. The temples they built are unmatched in their refined sculptures and reliefs carved in dark steatite.[118] The temples at Belur and Halebid are the best known, but several other fine ones were built by the Hoysalas including a jewel of a monument at Somnathpur and another at Hoshaholalu that is not so well preserved.

Gaja-thara elephants along the base of the temple are a recurring feature of Hoysala architecture. The succession of friezes along the outer wall of the temple begins with a procession of elephants at the bottom and typically illustrates the three divisions of the army, the other two being cavalry and foot-soldiers, with ornamental mouldings and other carvings such as lions at higher levels. The Hoysala elephants have decorative

6.28 The basement of the outer walls of the 12th- and 13th-century Hoysala temples of Karnataka typically feature horizontal rows of animal and floral design, with the elephant occupying the lowest tier. These pictures show:
a The Chennakeshava temple at Belur featuring bedecked elephants as in ceremonial procession but without riders.
b The Hoysaleshvara temple at Halebid featuring elephants with mahouts and warriors as deployed in battle.

features distinct from those of elephants in other styles of temple architecture.[119] Although all these four temples feature elephant friezes along the base of the outer wall, not all are of war elephants. The Chennakeshava temple at Belur depicts only a procession of decorated elephants, the Lakshminarayan temple at Hoshaholalu shows a procession with the odd mahout in between the marching animals, the Keshava temple at Somnathpur has reliefs of elephants with riders, while the Hoysaleshvara temple at Halebid features elephants ridden by mahouts and warriors in actual battle scenes (figure 6.28). Chariots had disappeared by this period but the depiction of the odd vehicle on wheels in some of the Hoysala friezes indicates that it may still have been used to a limited extent in war or for ceremony. The Hoysala temples also have outstanding sculptures of Indra and his consort on Airavata, Bhima fighting Bhagadatta's elephant Supratika, Shiva dancing his terrible *tandava* on the elephant-demon Gajasura, Ganesha in all his pot-bellied glory, and finely sculpted caparisoned elephants standing guard at the entrance or the corners of shrines and pavilions (figure 6.29). The importance of war elephants in the Hoysala army can be evidenced not only from their profuse depiction in these temples but also from a record that the Hoysalas had to surrender 36 mighty elephants to Malik Kafur, the general of the Khalji sultans, during the early 14th century (see Chapter 7). Hoysala power eventually declined from the Islamic onslaught.

In the ancient land of Kalinga on the east coast, a distinct variation of the Nagara style of temple architecture had begun to take shape from the late 7th century in a burst of creativity.[120] The scale of temple building prompted the observation that "there are more temples now in Orissa than in all the rest of Hindustan put together".[121] The elephant is represented in the early temples of Orissa, though not as frequently as one would have expected. A unique stone relief from an unknown 11th-century temple at Bhubaneswar illustrates elephants being transported by boats across the ocean, evidence of the active maritime trade in this animal by the rulers of this region (figure 6.30).[122]

We however need to skip over the rich medieval history of Orissa to examine the majestic Surya temple at Konarak, known to ancient seafarers as the Black Pagoda, to examine its elephant-related iconography. The ruined temple, restored during the

6.29 Sculpted caparisoned elephants standing guard at the entrance of a shrine within the Chennakeshava temple complex, Belur, Hoysala period, 12th century.

6.30 Stone relief from an unknown 11th-century temple at Bhubaneswar illustrating elephants being transported by boats across the ocean. Ancient Kalinga was an important source of elephants for the complex maritime trade in this species.
Photographed at the Orissa State Museum, Bhubaneswar.

6.31 A pair of huge lions rampant on recumbent elephants that hold human figures, at the eastern entrance to the pillared *nata-mandira* at the Surya temple, Konarak, Eastern Ganga period, mid-13th century.

20th century, was designed as a giant chariot with 12 pairs of wheels, drawn by seven spirited horses. Built during the mid-13th century by Narasimha I, a prominent ruler of the Eastern Ganga dynasty that held power between the 11th and 14th centuries, this medieval colossus makes up for any earlier deficiency in the temples of Orissa in depicting the elephant. A pair of huge lions, mouths open, eyes protruding, tongues lolling, rampant on recumbent elephants that hold human figures between their forelegs and trunks, greets visitors at the eastern entrance to the pillared *nata-mandira* or dance pavilion (figure 6.31).[123] The symbolism of this sculpture is open to a number of interpretations; the tourist guidebooks claim this to represent the triumph of a resurgent Hinduism over Buddhism, a philosophical view is that it depicts a pious human striving for liberation from the bonds of nature,[124] while a more sober historian would construe this perhaps as a sign of a triumphant king. We know that ancient kings took on titles of strong and powerful animals such as the elephant (*gaja pati*) and the lion (*simha raja*) to flaunt their superiority. An entire dynasty of Orissan kings that ruled during 1434–1541 was known as Gajapati. I must mention here that a similar theme of a lion prevailing over an elephant is sculpted as a pillar capital in the Hoysala temple at Hosaholalu. Konarak also features two near life-size stone elephants, each clasping a warrior in its trunk, that originally may have stood guard at the northern entrance of the porch and are now relocated on a raised platform further away (figure 6.32).

The imposing *jagamohana* or assembly hall of the main temple is replete with elephant friezes at various levels. The entire base of the profusely embellished outer wall of the high platform features an unbroken procession of about 1,700 *gaja-thara* elephants, each individual uniquely depicted in its stance and behaviour, some in battle-gear, others being driven into a stockade, yet others roaming the jungle, socializing or mating (figure 6.33). The elephant friezes continue at successive levels of the much-admired pyramidal roof of the *jagamohana*. A unique illustration at Konarak is that of a king, possibly Narasimha I himself, mounted on an elephant and receiving a delegation

6.32 Stone elephant clasping a warrior in its trunk at the Surya temple, Konarak, Eastern Ganga period, mid-13th century.

6.33a and b Row of elephants along the base of the Surya temple, Konarak, Eastern Ganga period, mid-13th century. A detail from another panel shows elephant capture in a stockade.

6.34 A king, possibly Narasimha I, mounted on an elephant and receiving a delegation from east Africa with a giraffe as a present, at the Surya temple, Konarak, Eastern Ganga period, mid-13th century.

6.35 *Gaja-simha* represented on an ivory throne, Eastern Ganga period, 13th century.
© *Freer Gallery of Art, Smithsonian Institution, Washington DC: Gift of Charles Lang Freer.*

from east Africa with a giraffe as a present (figure 6.34). Konarak also features in profusion the *gaja-vyala* or *gaja-simha*, a creature that has the head and trunk of an elephant but the body and hind parts of a lion, perhaps signifying the combined strength of the two animals.

Ivory *gaja-vyala*s supporting the royal throne are also known from the Eastern Ganga dynasty (figure 6.35). The *patta* paintings from Orissa going back to the 14th century include the *gaja-rasa* or *nari-kunjara* in which a flute-playing Krishna is seated on an illusory elephant that has been cleverly depicted by painting the mutually interlocked bodies of nine *gopis*.[125]

Our final stop in this tour of the elephant in the Hindu world of the subcontinent is the fabulous Deccan city of Hampi, the capital of the Vijayanagara kings, who resisted the Islamic rulers of the north for over two centuries from 1336 CE when Harihara I ascended the throne.[126] Both Muslim and European travellers to the kingdom described the grandeur of Hampi in glowing terms. Elephant sculptures abound in the ruins of Hampi.[127] Mutilated elephant balustrades flank the steps leading up to the front hall of the unfinished Vitthala temple, "the most splendid building in the city",[128] which was consecrated in 1513 during the reign of Krishnadeva Raya (1509–30), the greatest of the Vijayanagara kings. Decorated elephants in front of the famous stone car in the courtyard of the temple seem to be drawing the gigantic structure (figure 6.36). The walls of the Throne Platform are profusely carved with processions of elephants, horses, other animals, dancers, and other themes; this arena was the venue of the grand, nine-day festival of Dussehra conducted annually at Hampi (figure 6.37).

The Elephant Stables, a picturesque, elongated building with eleven stalls and domed roofs with a distinct Islamic character, is reputed to have provided the housing for the royal elephants (figure 6.38). Doubts have been expressed about this purpose, because of the absence of iron rings or bars in the floors or walls to tie up the elephants.[129] However, we have the first-hand account of Abdur Razzak who states that the choicest elephants were maintained in this *pilkhana* close to the king's palace, and that the elephants were secured "with chains, the end of which is strongly fastened to the top of the roof",[130] apparently because otherwise they could undo their bonds! This is quite possibly the most elaborate housing ever provided for elephants in ancient times. The elephants were looked after very well and fed twice a day with balls of cooked rice, pulses, salt, and sugar, much like we see in some modern-day elephant camps. Each year about 1,000 elephants, that "presented the appearance of the waves of the sea", were paraded at a grand festival. Some of the elephants performed circus feats such as balancing themselves with all four feet upon three blocks of wood, their trunks raised and swinging to the tunes of musicians and dancers, or even being hoisted into the air with a stone counterweight for the show.[131] Razzak also records the presence of a "white elephant" in the royal court at Hampi; this animal with "grey spots like freckles" was paraded before the king every morning as a good omen.[132]

Vijayanagara has been described as "perhaps the nearest approach to a war-state ever made by a Hindu kingdom" because of the large standing army consisting of an elephant corps, cavalry, and infantry, in addition to the smaller but similar forces maintained by the *nayak*s or military chiefs for deployment by the king in war.[133] When Krishnadeva Raya was on a campaign against the Gajapati kings of Orissa, the Bijapur ruler Ismail Adil Khan recovered the Raichur doab from Vijayanagara. Krishnadeva marched against him in 1520 with a huge force of soldiers, cavalry, and 551 elephants whose tusks were fitted with sharpened knives, according to the chronicle of Fernão Nuniz.[134] The raja's elephants not only "worked amongst them mischief without end, for they seized men with their trunks and tore them into pieces" but also waded into the Krishna river and caught the escaping enemy. In the final stages of the battle Krishnadeva rode a horse against the sultan who fled for his life on an elephant.

The mighty Hindu bastion in the Deccan crumbled about half a century later when Husain Nazim Shah, the sultan of Ahmednagar, formed an alliance with the sultans of Bijapur and Golconda to challenge

6.36 Decorated elephants in front of the stone car in the courtyard of the Vitthala temple at Hampi, consecrated in 1513.

6.37 Wall of the Throne Platform at Hampi (early 15th century) carved with elephant, lion, dancers, and other themes. This platform is believed to have been used by the Vijayanagara king and the nobles to watch ceremonial processions during the nine-day annual festival of Dussehra.

6.38a Elephant Stables, consisting of 11 chambers with lofty domed roofs in Islamic architectural style, at Hampi, early 15th century.
b The iron ring on the ceiling to which elephants were tied, according to the description of the Persian ambassador to the Vijayanagara empire, Abdur Razzak.

6.39 Hathi Pol, the gateway to the Chhatar Mahal at Bundi, built in 1607–31. *Photograph by Soonoo Taraporewala.*

the might of the octogenarian Vijayanagara king Rama Raya. The battle was joined on January 23, 1565, by a Muslim force superior in skilled horsemen equipped with long spears and metal bows capable of dispatching arrows to a greater distance, and a Hindu force that fielded a large number of soldiers and elephants. In an ironic twist of fate, the battle ended when the old Rama Raya, who could neither mount a horse or an elephant, was captured by an elephant-mounted general of the sultan and decapitated by Nazim Shah himself. The only redeeming feature for the Hindu kingdom seems to have been the escape of Rama Raya's brother Tirumala with all the treasures carried on the backs of 1,550 elephants.[135]

The war elephant of ancient and medieval times now began to fade from military history. The increasing use of more sophisticated firearms during the Mughal period had gradually rendered the elephant a liability rather than an asset in direct battle.[136] A commander seated on a tall elephant was a conspicuous target of guns that could even be fired by swift-moving horsemen. The elephant was now reduced to being a baggage carrier, a hauler of heavy cannon, and a ceremonial object.

The Marathas of the northwestern Deccan, who effectively challenged the Mughals and other Muslim powers under the dynamic leadership of Shivaji (1627–80) and his successors, employed a military strategy of maximizing mobility using horses and minimal baggage to harass the enemy rather than engage them in direct battle.[137] The elephant obviously had no role in such war tactics; in any case, the wild elephant had disappeared from the forests of the Maratha stronghold. However, the later Marathas acquired elephants from their conquests in neighbouring lands. There is an interesting anecdote of 1759 when the Peshwa ruler Shahji, doing an Archimedes, weighed an elephant by placing it on a boat and noting the displacement of water, then loading the boat with stones of known weight to obtain the figure.[138] Grant Duff, a soldier in the British East India Company, describes the Maratha army that was raised under the leadership of Sadashivrao Bhau to counter the Afghan forces in the north at this time: "The equipment of this army was more splendid in appearance than any Mahratta force that ever took the field…. The lofty and spacious tents lined with silks and broad cloths, were surmounted by large gilded ornaments…vast numbers of elephants, flags of all descriptions, the finest horses, magnificently caparisoned…seemed to be collected from every quarter…[it was] an imitation of the more becoming and tasteful array of the magnificent Moghuls in the zenith of their glory."[139] The Marathas had obviously succumbed to the temptations of replacing their light and mobile force with a ponderous one that reeked of pomp and splendour. On January 14, 1761, this vastly encumbered Maratha army was routed by the Afghans at the third battle of Panipat. Towards the final stages of the battle Sadashivrao dismounted from his elephant and mounted his Arab charger but was eventually killed.[140] Hindu resistance to Muslim forces faded with this shock defeat accompanied by great slaughter. It is another matter that by now it was not the Muslim rulers but the British who were gradually but decisively taking control of the subcontinent.

The elephant had by now disappeared almost completely from western Maharashtra while only a few stray herds remained in the east. The real animal was symbolically replaced by the Ganapati festival that began under the Peshwas during the 18th century (see Chapter 8). If the Marathas celebrated the extinction of the wild elephant with a new religious fervour, the Rajputs celebrated the absence of the wild creature in their land by immortalizing it in their art and architecture. Nowhere, perhaps, is this depicted more dramatically than in the Hathi Pol, the enormous stone gateway built in 1607–31 to the Chhatar Mahal at Bundi, spanned by a pair of elephants with their tusks locked

6.40 Elephants are an important element in the royal procession of Raja Man Singh (1803–43) of Jodhpur, depicted in a painting, Jodhpur, circa 1810 CE.
Courtesy: National Museum, New Delhi.

in duel (figure 6.39). The elephant is depicted in murals of the palace's Chitrashala that features a fascinating gallery of court scenes, hunting, festivals, processions, animals, and the life of lord Krishna. As with the Mughal miniatures from which the Rajput artists drew inspiration, the Rajasthani miniature paintings also have fine portrayals of captive elephants in various contexts – royal elephants in the court, the king riding an elephant, and elephant fights (figure 6.40). The *chhatri*s (cenotaphs or domed pavilions built over funerary sites) at Bundi and elsewhere have numerous and life-like carvings of elephants in action along the platforms. The elephant is dead; long live the elephant!

***

The *Gajashastra* or science of elephants that is believed to have originated with the mythical sage Palakapya continued to be elaborated in various texts in medieval Hindu India. Of particular significance is the *Manasollasa* ("delight of the mind") believed to have been composed by the Western Chalukyan king Somadeva III in the 12th century. This encyclopaedic work in Sanskrit has elaborate descriptions of the characteristics of elephants, their geographical distribution, their capture and training, their diseases and treatment, and their use in sport by the king.[141] While borrowing heavily from the earlier texts, the *Manasollasa* also adds to the knowledge of the elephant in ancient times. In the first reference to the elephant, the *Manasollasa* repeats the assertion of the *Arthashastra* that an elephant forest is the best type of forest, but with the rider that the king should protect it with the help of forest dwellers (and not a *Nagavanadhyaksha* or "Superintendent of the Elephant Forests" as stated in the latter).[142] This paradigm shift was perhaps recognition by the Chalukyan rulers of the knowledge and skills of tribes inhabiting the hill forests, a process that would be termed today as a participatory approach to management of wildlife. Five methods of capturing elephants are described: *vari bandha* (*kheddah* or drive into stockade), *anugata bandha* (*mela shikar* or noosing after chasing with trained elephants), *vasha bandha* (luring with the help of female elephants), *apata bandha* (noosing suddenly with specially made stout ropes), and *avapata bandha* (trapping in pits), with the observation that the last two should be discarded because of the increased risk of injury and death of the elephant.[143] These

6.41 The *Hastividyarnava* describes the various types of physical characteristics in elephants and their uses in great detail. In these palm-leaf illustrations a *makhna* and a tusked bull are shown. Almost every description of male elephants in this early 18th-century manuscript is of tusked elephants, implying that these were preferred for capture and use by the king as a royal mount or in war.

Courtesy: Publication Board, Guwahati, Assam.

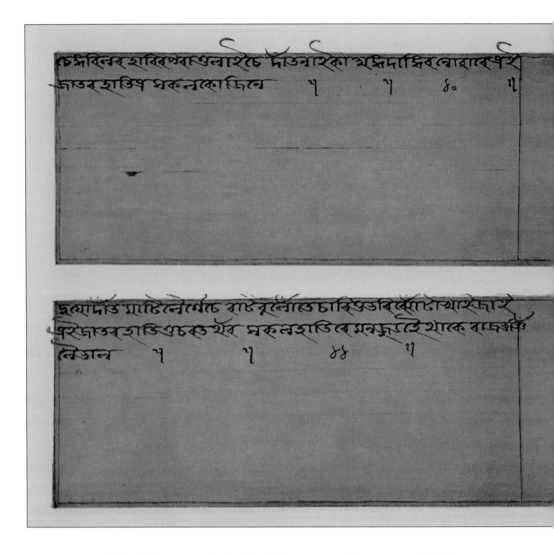

statements and the elaborate methods of training, care, and treatment of elephants indicate that the rulers of the period valued these animals. The *Manasollasa* again repeats the *Arthashastra*'s assertion that a king desiring victory in war should develop a strong elephant corps.[144] For the first time an ancient Sanskrit text also provides elaborate detail of *gaja-vahyali* or elephant sport for the exclusive pleasure of the king. Not only would elephants compete against other elephants, horses, or men in races, they would also be pitted against each other in a no-holds-barred fight unto death.

The *Manasollasa* lists the eight *gajavana*s or elephant forests of the country as in the *Arthashastra* and the *Gajashastra*, but interestingly rectifies the lack of information in the latter texts about elephant distribution in the extreme south.[145] Thus, the *Manasollasa* extends the description of the Kalinga Vana to include the Dravidadesha or land of the Tamils. This perhaps reflects better knowledge among the Chalukyans, a peninsular kingdom, about the geography and fauna of the south during the 12th century. Interestingly, the *Manasollasa* adds the Aparanta Vana to the Saurashtra Vana and Panchanada Vana as being inferior forests for elephants. The Aparanta Vana or region of the northern Sahyadris in Maharashtra would have already been substantially degraded by this period and lost most of its elephants.

Two other undated Sanskrit texts, the *Gajagrahananaprakara* and the *Gajashiksha* are available at the Oriental Research Institute of the Sri Venkateswara University at Tirupati.[146] The former text provides descriptions of ten methods of capturing elephants

including the *salila bandha*, a variation of the *vari bandha* in which wild elephants were driven into an area surrounded by a moat filled with water, the *panchalika bandha* or luring juvenile elephants with the help of dummies of young elephants, and the *udyana bandha* or luring young male elephants with the help of adult females. It also makes recommendations for the construction of stalls for elephants; an east-facing stall was the most auspicious, while a west-facing stall would reduce the strength of the enemy (recall the west-facing Elephant Stables at Hampi).

Finally, I must mention the *Hastividyarnava*, a comparatively late treatise composed in 1734 by Sukumar Barkath under the patronage of the Ahom king Siva Sinha and his queen Ambika Devi.[147] Beautifully illustrated with miniature colour paintings, this treatise elaborately describes elephant morphology with fine distinctions made between body types and other features (figure 6.41). It also provides an account of elephant training and treatment of diseases and other health conditions. By the 18th century Assam, along with the surrounding hill forests of the northeast, was the last great bastion of the elephant in the subcontinent. A distinct culture of training and managing elephants had begun to develop here, a culture that is still prevalent today, perhaps the only region in India that still retains the skills of capturing, training, and keeping elephants in captivity.

***

Vedic Brahmanism had given way to what has been called "Puranic Hinduism" during the Gupta period,[148] with the evolution and adoption of a new genre of religious literature as well as active royal patronage. Along with Buddhism, Hinduism spread to Southeast Asia where large areas of present-day Burma, Thailand, Cambodia, Vietnam, Malaysia, and Indonesia were influenced by the Indian religion, and its art and architecture.[149] The elephant culture of India, too, reached these distant lands, and had an impact on the native practices of capture and use of the animal and its representation in temple art. As during a certain period in Indian history, the influences of Hinduism and Buddhism are difficult to distinguish in several of the Southeast Asian monuments. Thus, the temples at Angkor in Cambodia feature sublime images of the Buddha along with a galaxy of Hindu gods.

Some Indian merchants who travelled to the east established trading settlements which influenced the indigenous cultures. Ancient Chinese sources refer to an Indianized settlement of Funan[150] during the 3rd century CE in the lower Mekong delta of Indochina. Funan apparently had a practice of sending tributes to the Chinese courts. In 357 CE a mission from Funan arrived at the Eastern Chin dynasty in southern China with a retinue that included trained elephants.[151] The Chinese emperor was alarmed at seeing the elephants, and "considering these animals from distant lands as a source of danger to the people, ordered them returned".[152] These sources and later Sanskrit and Khmer inscriptions trace the founding of Funan to an Indian by the name Kaundinya, possibly a brahman or a Chola noble, who married the daughter of a local *naga* king, who then built a capital for the couple and named it Kamboja.[153] By the 5th century CE Funan had a Hindu ruler and Sanskrit was adopted as the court language. Funan and a neighbouring state Zhenla (that wrested control over Funan by the late 6th century CE) were the predecessors to the great Khmer civilization whose glorious Angkor period lasted well over 600 years from the early 9th century to almost the mid-15th century.[154]

Beginning with Jayavarman II (circa 770–850), a succession of over two dozen kings ruled over a large area of Thailand, Cambodia, Laos, and Vietnam until the collapse of Khmer supremacy around 1430–32 CE. During this period the Khmers built dozens of temples, mostly Hindu but also some Buddhist, over an area of 200 square kilometres, temples that "startle with their splendour and perfection, but beyond the emotions they evoke lie complex microcosms of a universe steeped in cosmology", to quote art historian Dawn Rooney.[155] As could be expected of an Indianized civilization that grew and flourished amidst a tropical jungle teeming with elephants and other creatures, the elephant is a prominent part of the art of Angkor. Indeed, many of the gigantic temples such as the Angkor Wat and Bayon could not have been built without the use of elephant labour.

Temple construction at Angkor began as early as the 6th century CE but these pre-Angkor structures as well as the early Angkor temples (of the early 9th century) are mostly in ruins. Jayavarman III (circa 834–870), successor to the first Khmer ruler, had a passion for hunting elephants that were undoubtedly plentiful in the forests of the lower Mekong basin. The Rolous group of temples dating to the late 9th century depict elephants; at the Bakong temple, constructed in 881 CE during the rule of Indravarman I, sculpted elephants of diminishing size stood at the basal corners of the central sanctuary. This style of elephants supporting the four directions (*diggajas*) of a temple-mountain symbolizing Mount Meru is also seen in the better preserved East Mebon temple built in the mid-10th century when Rajendravarman II ruled Angkor (figure 6.42). The Hindu god Indra riding his mount, Airavata, shown as three-headed in Angkor art, springs out of lintels at East Mebon and many other temples, including Banteay Srei (second half of the 10th century), widely regarded as the loveliest surviving Angkor temple for its intricate sculptures (figure 6.43).

6.42 One of the elephants that support the four directions (*diggaja*s) at the East Mebon temple, Angkor complex, Cambodia, mid-10th century.

6.43 Indra riding his mount, Airavata, shown as three-headed in Angkor art, at Banteay Srei, Angkor complex, Cambodia, second half of the 10th century.

6.44 Sculpted elephants of 10th-century Champa, at Tra Kieu, Quang Nam province, Vietnam. The kingdom of Champa was at war with the Khmers during the 12th century.
Photographed at Musée Guimet, Paris.

The colossal Angkor Wat, the centrepiece of the Angkor complex, was built in the first half of the 12th century during the rule of Suryavarman II, though it was probably completed after his death. The artistic wonders of this masterpiece of Khmer architecture are too complex to be related here beyond making a brief mention of the gallery of bas-reliefs that features, in addition to other themes from Hindu mythology, the battle of Kurukshetra (*Mahabharata*), the battle of Lanka (*Ramayana*), and the churning of the ocean of milk (*puranas*).[156] Commanders riding elephants direct the battle operations at Kurukshetra, a monkey-warrior seizes the tusks of an elephant at the battle of Lanka, and Airavata rises from the ocean of milk at the climax of the churning. The war elephant par excellence is depicted in the panel illustrating the army of King Suryavarman II. In this relief the king, wearing a conical headdress and holding a sword across his shoulder, is standing on the royal elephant, as commanders on elephants march with their troops against the enemy. In fact, Angkor has some of the greatest reliefs in the world of elephants on the march.

By the 12th century it is clear that the Khmer army was organized in the familiar Indian style of foot-soldiers, horses, and elephants, though the Khmers did not seem to have a permanent standing force but raised it specifically for their military campaigns.[157] Although the Khmer rulers could easily mobilize large numbers of elephants in view of their abundance in their kingdom, the figure of 200,000 elephants in the Khmer army claimed by the Chinese traveller Zhao Rugua in the 13th century is clearly hyperbole. Another Chinese source, the mandarin Ma Tuan-lin, was shipwrecked off the coast of Champa (southern Vietnam) when the Chams were at war with the Khmers. Ma Tuan-lin apparently advised his hosts that they should rely more on cavalry and less on elephants in their war (figure 6.44). He even claims to have trained Cham soldiers in using the bow-and-arrow more effectively from horseback.[158] We know that a Cham naval fleet that sneaked up the Tonle Sap scored a surprise victory against the Khmer ruler Tribhuvanaditya in 1177 CE. This Cham victory was short-lived as another strong Khmer ruler Jayavarman VII (1181–1218) soon expelled the enemy forces.

Jayavarman VII built a new capital city, Angkor Thom, within whose walls burst forth a new wave of Khmer architectural genius. At the centre of the "Mighty City" rose Bayon,

6.45 Khmer commanders mounted on tusked elephants amidst a procession of foot-soldiers marching against the invaders, depicted at Bayon, in Angkor Thom, the new capital of Jayavarman VII (1181–1218), Cambodia.

not quite as large as Angkor Wat but certainly equally awe-inspiring, with a different purpose, design, and decoration. Scholars have debated as to whether this enigmatic temple was Hindu or Buddhist, and as to the significance and identity of its giant, sculpted faces with an enigmatic smile, now believed to be of Jayavarman VII himself as the Bodhisatva Avalokiteshvara. The southern face of the south gallery of bas-reliefs at Bayon depicts successive stages of the battle between the Chams and the Khmers along the Tonle Sap. Several beautifully carved scenes show the Khmer commanders mounted on tusked elephants amidst a procession of foot-soldiers marching against the invaders (figure 6.45).

The Terrace of the Elephants at Angkor Thom, possibly built during the time of Jayavarman VII, with later additions and renovations, is a grand showpiece in the elephant story of the ancient Khmer civilization (figure 6.46). Extending over 300 metres (nearly 1,000 feet) in length, and located directly in front of the east *gopuram* (entrance tower) of the royal palace's enclosure wall, the stairways and facade are decorated with sculpted elephants, nearly life-sized, with riders on their backs, using their trunks to fight or hunt while tigers confront them. It is not difficult to imagine Jayavarman VII and his court sitting in a pavilion on the terrace, viewing his war elephants, cavalry, and troops marching in ceremonial procession, much like the parades one witnesses today at Rajpath in New Delhi or Tiananmen Square in Beijing. The Chinese visitor Zhou Daguan who came here during the reign of Indravarman III (1295–1308) describes the king going out in ceremony: "When the prince goes out, troops head the escort.... Then there are the girls of the palace carrying lances and shields, who comprise the private guard of the prince.... The ministers and princes are mounted on elephants; in front of them one can see from afar their red parasols, which are innumerable. After them come the wives and concubines of the king, in palanquins, in carts, on horses and elephants. They have, certainly, more than a hundred parasols flecked with gold. After them is the sovereign, standing on an elephant and holding the precious sword in his hand. The tusks of the elephant are also sheathed in gold. There are more than twenty white parasols flecked with gold, with handles of gold. Numerous elephants crowd around him, and there are more troops to protect him."[159]

6.46a and b Sculpted elephants at Terrace of the Elephants, Angkor Thom, built at the end of the 12th century. The Khmer rulers used the terrace as a viewing platform for ceremonial processions in which elephants participated.

6.47 Standing Ganesha wearing a *sampot*, Cambodia, 7th century. *Photographed at the Metropolitan Museum of Art, New York.*

The specific circumstances of the collapse of the Khmer empire are not clear; it is believed that Angkor was temporarily abandoned in 1369 CE following an onslaught of invading Siamese forces, with the final retreat possibly occurring in 1430–31 CE. At the same time, the Khmer civilization may have been already weakened by environmental degradation of the forest resources they depended upon, and depleting soils in cultivated areas.

Ganesha accompanied the spread of Hinduism to Southeast Asia and soon appeared in the iconography of the region as early as the 6th century CE.[160] Burma was the first

6.48 Seated Ganesha at a shrine inside the 9th-century Shiva temple at Prambanan, Java, Indonesia.

6.49 Tantric Ganesha, Java, 12th–13th century.
Photographed at the National Museum, Jakarta, Indonesia.

6.50 Six-armed Mahakala trampling Ganesha as the demon of obstacles, a 15th-century Tibetan bronze.
Courtesy: Norton Simon Art Foundation.

stopover for Indian traders and priests and, thus, several images of Ganesha, known locally as Mahapeinne, are known from this region. The Shwesandaw temple built by King Anawrahta in Pagan during the late 10th century had images of Mahapeinne at the corners of each of the five terraces. It is in Cambodia, however, that the best representations of the early Ganesha can be seen, possibly from the late 6th century. These are seated forms of the elephant-headed deity, fashioned like a squatting elephant, curved trunk reaching into an (empty?) bowl held in the left hand, resembling the Indian Ganeshas of the early 5th century.[161] Standing images of Ganesha from Cambodia date to the 7th century (figure 6.47), a major difference with the Indian Ganesha being that the former is not naked but wears the Cambodian *sampot* (cloth wrapped around the lower body).[162] That Ganesha was considered an independent god in Cambodia by this period is also seen from mention of the exclusive temples dedicated to him at Angkor.[163] By the 8th century Ganesha was well established over a large area including Thailand and Vietnam, with not just Hindu but also Buddhist influences on his iconography. Ganesha also appears at several of the grand temples at Angkor, including East Mebon, Angkor Wat, and Bayon (10th to 13th century). In Indochina Ganesha was generally regarded in his positive role as a remover of obstacles.

Java has yielded the richest haul of the elephant-headed deity's images in the Sunda islands. The earliest Ganesha images of Indonesia, dating to the 8th century, come from the Dieng plateau in central Java,[164] which is also the site of a group of the oldest Hindu temples, constructed during the 7th and 8th centuries. The Ganesha idols of Java broadly pertain to two regions, periods, and styles. The early style (8th to 10th century) is seen in central Java, of which the best known is the massive Ganesha inside an independent shrine within the Shiva temple at the Prambanan complex constructed by the Hindu Sanjaya dynasty beginning about 850 (figure 6.48), resembling in most respects the contemporary Indian images.[165] In east Java Ganesha took on a demonic character as tantric practices spread during the 12th–13th century; in one large sculpture of this style at the National Museum in Jakarta, Ganesha is seated on a base of human skulls, the right knee partly raised, the upper right hand holding an axe, the upper left hand a rosary, curved trunk reaching into a bowl (or is it a split skull?) with many skulls decorating his headgear and body (figure 6.49). An interesting variation of the 13th-century Indonesian Ganesha is the *kalamukha* iconography, in which the *kala* face is sculpted at the back of the elephant's face; this representation signifies the dual role of Ganesha as a creator and a remover of obstacles and is placed at temple doorways to allow the worthy to enter and keep away the unworthy.[166]

Ganesha also spread from India mainly through the vehicle of Buddhism into Nepal, ancient Tibet, China, and even Japan.[167] In Buddhist iconography Ganesha, interestingly, maintained a dual role as the creator and the remover of obstacles.[168] Images of several Vajrayana Buddhist deities trampling an elephant-headed figure, typically a two-armed *vighna*, are known; of these Vighnantaka and Mahakala are frequently encountered in Nepal and Tibet (figure 6.50). I would interpret such iconography as reflecting not only an underlying tension between Buddhism and Hinduism, but also the occasional nuisance value of the elephant in mountainous lands such as Buddhist Nepal where the animal had no great utility unlike in the Gangetic region. The Tantric Ganesha of Java and the helpless *vighna* of Nepal eventually point to the potentially destructive character of the elephant, one that prevailed over people in the former and had to be overcome in the latter context.

The surprisingly early entry of Ganesha into China, where an image dated to 531 CE is known from the Buddhist temple of Kung-hsien, could perhaps be attributed to the Chinese traveller Faxian, who returned home from India in the 5th century, or one of the other Buddhist priests of this period.[169] Ganesha also took on a tantric form in Tibet and China, quite unknown in India, and was placed as the protector of the four entrances of Buddhist monasteries. During the 9th century the monk, Kobo Daishi, brought the cult of Ganesha from China to Japan where the god similarly became a protector of Buddhism. One of the forms of Ganesha in Japan (again originally from China) is the dual image known as Kangiten ("deva of bliss") which shows two elephant-headed figures in embrace. The most astonishing aspect of this evolution of Ganesha in East Asia was the identification of the female elephant with the Bodhisatva Avalokiteshvara.[170] Just as the Buddha was eventually adopted by Hinduism as the ninth incarnation of Vishnu, a popular Brahmanical icon had been usurped by Buddhism in a foreign land.

CHAPTER 7

Elephants in
the Islamic Period

THE PROPHET MUHAMMAD was born in Mecca in 570 CE – interestingly a year regarded by the Arabs as the "Year of the Elephant". The story goes that, before the birth of the prophet, Abraha al Ashram, the Christian ruler of Saba (Yemen), was jealous of the shrine at Mecca known as Ka'aba that had been built, according to legend, by Abraham and his son Isaac of the Old Testament. Abraha thus sent an army with elephants (or an elephant) to destroy the Ka'aba. There are different versions of what happened thereafter. According to one version the elephant refused to enter Mecca in spite of much persuasion and enticement. Indeed, when the animal was turned around to face Mecca, it knelt down as if in worship of the shrine. A short account of this elephant legend is found in the *Quran*.[1]

In the year 622 CE, Muhammad and his followers emigrated from their native town of Mecca to the northern city of Medina, both located in present-day Saudi Arabia. Muslims generally consider this year to be the birth of a new social, political, and religious order we now call Islam. The ensuing conflict between Mecca and Medina is well known and need not be elaborated upon here; interestingly a painting from the 14th-century Turkish manuscript *Siyer-i-Nebi* (Life of the Prophet) shows the Mecca army attacking Medina with some elephants – which is quite unlikely (figure 7.1).

Soon after the birth of Islam in 622 CE, Muslim Arabs arrived in western India and by 711 an Arab general, Muhammad bin Qasim, had captured Sindh to found the first Muslim kingdom in the subcontinent. However, Arab traders had close contacts with settlements along the west coast of India much before the time of Muhammad. It is thus entirely possible that Muslims reached peninsular India not long after the birth of Islam; there is certainly evidence of such settlements during the 8th century CE. The Mappilas (or Moplahs) of Kerala are believed to be descendants of Muslim settlers or converts much before the Muslim invasions of India through the northwest. Curiously, during this early period of trade, ivory was undoubtedly one of the commodities that the Arabs sourced from Africa for the Indian market.

The next major foray by a Muslim ruler into the subcontinent came from Ghazni, now in Afghanistan. Mahmud of Ghazni, whose father Sabuktigin had already wrested the trans-Indus region from the Shahiyas, turned his attention at the beginning of the 11th century CE to the Indus plains and beyond.[2] The standard school textbook begins its account of the Islamic history of India with Mahmud of Ghazni and his plundering raids over a period of nearly three decades. The elephant is an integral part of this political history culminating with the eventual disintegration of the Mughal empire during the 18th to 19th century. As with the Hindu rulers, earlier and subsequently, the Muslim conquerors and rulers of India shared a passion for the elephant. Although their military successes are usually attributed to their superior organization of horse-based cavalry, several of the Muslim rulers, notably the Mughals, raised the art of the war elephant to new levels.

The Ghaznavids made their first thrust into India in November 1001 when Mahmud marched his forces towards Peshawar against the Shahiya ruler Jayapala. The Shahiya army had a considerable number of elephants; after defeat and capture by the Ghaznavids, Jayapala had to secure his release by handing over 50 elephants to Mahmud. Jayapala immolated himself after this humiliation. His successor Anandapala faced a second invasion by Mahmud in 1008. On this occasion the Shahiyas had the assistance of forces from the Hindu kingdoms of Ujjain, Gwalior, Kalinjar, Kanauj, Delhi, and Ajmer. The battle was apparently going against the Ghaznavids when Mahmud sent his elite soldiers to attack Anandapala's elephant that fled the hail of burning naptha balls and arrows.[3] The valiant soldiers of the confederacy lost their morale upon seeing the flight of

7.1 The attack on Medina, painting from a Turkish manuscript *Siyer-i-Nebi* (Life of the Prophet) by Mustafa bin Yusuf of Erzurum, 1388.
Courtesy: Topkapi Palace Museum, Istanbul.

7.2 Rustam slays the maddened white elephant, illustration from a *Shahnama* manuscript of the early 14th century. Firdausi, the Persian poet who composed the *Shahnama* between 977 and 1010, visited the kingdom of Ghazni.
© Freer Gallery of Art, Smithsonian Institution, Washington DC: Gift of Charles Lang Freer.

a hapless Anandapala and, needless to say, the battle of Waihind was lost along with 30 elephants.

This emboldened Mahmud to launch a series of notorious raids on Hindu religious towns – Kangra, Mathura, Thanesar, Kanauj, Kalinjar, and the most famous of all Somnath in 1026, after the loot of which he returned to Ghazni where he died in 1030.

Ghazni attracted a large number of scholars and poets owing to Mahmud's munificence, and soon emerged as a rival to Baghdad itself in this regard. Besides the Persian poet Firdausi (figure 7.2) who is said to have visited the kingdom of Ghazni, a remarkable Arabic scholar, Abu Raihan al-Biruni (or Alberuni), was ordered in 1017 to spend ten years in what is now Pakistan. Al-Biruni actually spent 13 years in India

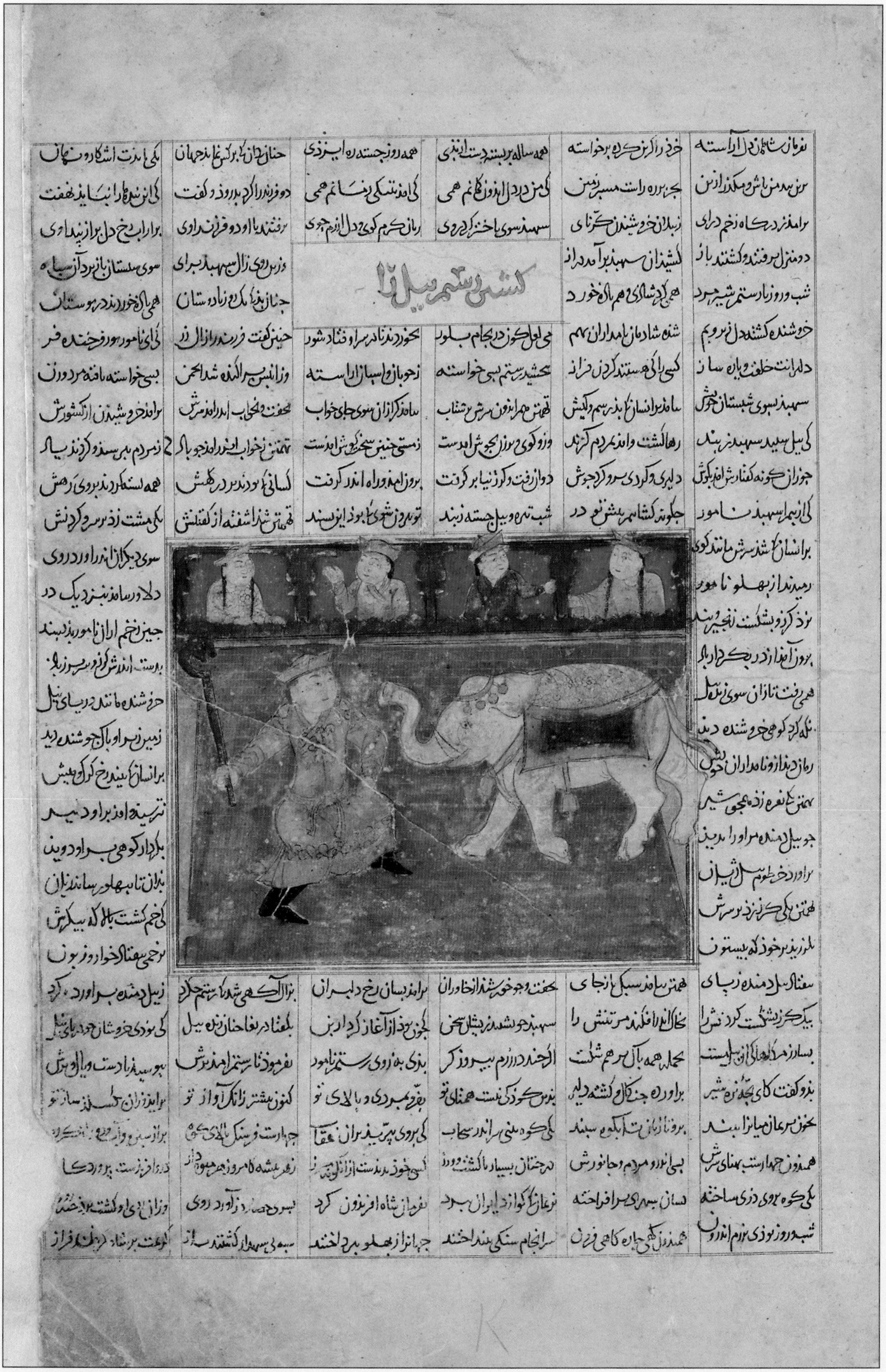
کشتن رستم پیل را

before returning to Ghazni where, during the reign of Mahmud's son Masud, he wrote the *Tahqiq-i-Hind*, an insightful, erudite, and objective account of Indian social customs, religion, and the sciences, especially mathematics and astronomy.[4]

Al-Biruni does not mention elephants as frequently or in as much depth as one would have liked; nevertheless, he does make some pertinent observations for our purposes. Al-Biruni was familiar with Hindu myths relating to the elephant, including Indra's fabled Airavata and the elephant-headed Ganesha who wrote the *Mahabharata* non-stop as dictated by the sage Vyasa.[5] He makes a pointed reference to the story of Ashwatthama, the elephant that died in the Mahabharata war, and of Yudhishthira's deception in conveying this news to Drona. He also goes on to describe verbatim the *akshauhini*, the standard unit of field deployment of the army by the Pandavas and the Kauravas – the former reputedly fielded seven and the latter 11 units, each comprising 21,870 chariots, 21,870 elephants, 65,610 cavalry, and 109,350 foot soldiers,[6] clearly hyperbole repeated through the ages by other sources including the *Arthashastra* and *Manu Smriti*. Al-Biruni was also aware of a treatise on elephant medicine; based on this he observes that some male elephants excel man in cunning.[7] Also, he writes that it is considered a bad omen if a person stands at the head of a herd of elephants – not an unreasonable belief when you consider the risks, even to experienced mahouts, from ill-tempered bulls.

It is not clear how much personal knowledge Al-Biruni had of elephants. He gives an accurate description of the Indian one-horned rhinoceros (*ganda*) which he seems to have observed on more than one occasion, and goes on to relate an incident of a young rhinoceros attacking an elephant, possibly a wild one, by thrusting its horn on to the latter's forefoot with such force that it fell to the ground.[8] Such encounters between rhinoceros and elephant are not uncommon even today in northeast India (figure 7.3).

As mentioned in the previous chapter, Al-Biruni also comments on the food taboos in the country, clearly pointing to a cessation of consumption of elephant meat along with that of cows, horses, mules, asses, and camels, all of them animals useful to humans.[9]

The Ghaznavids possessed a large number of war elephants. Mahmud is reputed to have inspected 1,300 elephants during the muster of 1023–24, while his son and successor Masud inspected 1,670 elephants in 1031. While these numbers seem excessive, historian Simon Digby feels they are reliable.[10] The Ghaznavids captured considerable numbers of tamed elephants during their Indian campaigns – 350 from Kanauj and 150 from Mahaban in 1018–19, and 580 from the Chandella raja Ganda the following year. At the same time, the wild elephants of northern India could have been overexploited and, for all practical purposes, wiped out during this period by the local rulers.

The early 12th century witnessed a struggle between the Ghaznavids and the Ghurids, and in 1173, Muiz-ud-din or Muhammad Ghuri as he is better known in Indian history was given charge of Ghazni by his brother Ghiyas-ud-din, the sultan of Ghur. Muhammad Ghuri now set his sights on India, not primarily with the intention of loot as in the case of Mahmud of Ghazni, but rather with the aim of political suzerainty over northern India. After wresting control of Multan and Lahore, he faced opposition from Prithviraja III, the Chauhan ruler of Ajmer, famed for his Lochinvar-style elopement with the daughter of the king of Kanauj. At the First Battle of Tarain in 1191 Prithviraja's forces that included 3,000 elephants defeated Muhammad Ghuri decisively.[11]

Muhammad Ghuri regrouped his forces comprising Turks, Persians, and Afghans, and returned the following year to serve Prithviraja an ultimatum through a messenger. The Persian historian Ferishta (1560–1620) reproduces Prithviraja's retort from the battlefield at Tarain as follows: "To the bravery of our soldiers we believe you are no stranger, and to our great superiority in numbers which daily increases, your eyes bear witness!

7.3 An elephant family warily watches a rhinoceros moving purposefully in front of them at Kaziranga, Assam (2011). Al-Biruni rightly observed that a rhino could attack and seriously injure a wild elephant.

You will repent in time of the rash resolution you have taken, and we shall permit you to retreat in safety; but if you are determined to brave your destiny, we have sworn by our gods to advance upon you with our *rank-breaking elephants* [emphasis mine], our plain-trampling horses, and blood-thirsty soldiers, early in the morning to crush the army which your ambition has led to ruin."[12] As many as 150 Rajput princes with their combined forces amounting, by the lowest and most moderate account, to 300,000 horses, 3,000 elephants, and a great body of infantry assembled at the same battlefield at Tarain.

Prithviraja's proclaimed might, however, did not work on this occasion. Muhammad Ghuri, after making a humble and false plea for time, caught the Rajput army by surprise in the early hours of the decisive Second Battle of Tarain (1192). By sunset Ghuri's elite force of 12,000 horsemen made a desperate charge through the Hindu camp killing many Rajput princes.[13] Prithviraja was disheartened and got down from his elephant to try and escape (perhaps on horseback) but was captured. This battle is held up as another example of the superiority of horse-based cavalry over an elephant-based force, though the more charitable viewer of the elephant would quip that Prithviraja lost the battle after he had abandoned his elephant. Muhammad Ghuri too undoubtedly possessed considerable numbers of elephants but whether and how these were used at Tarain is not clear.

The Second Battle of Tarain is generally regarded as a watershed in Indian history with the Muslim Turkish forces wresting complete control over the upper Gangetic basin from the Hindu rulers. With this was established the Delhi Sultanate that lasted for over two centuries under the Slave dynasty, Sultan Balban, the Khaljis, and the Tughlaqs, before its crushing defeat at the hands of the Central Asian warlord Amir Timur in 1398. Several smaller sultanates also sprang up in other regions of the subcontinent as in the Deccan, Gujarat, and Bengal, independent of the Delhi Sultanate.

Historians have long debated not only the seeming superiority of the early Muslim invaders but also the continued military success and endurance of the Delhi Sultanate over the 13th–14th centuries. A theory popular among some historians was that the invading forces were welcomed by the lower sections of Indian society in order to liberate themselves from the oppression of the higher Hindu castes. Others have sought to explain this in terms of the technological superiority of the invading forces, in particular the use of mechanical devices such as the stirrup and the horseshoe, or weapons such as long-range bows. Simon Digby, on the other hand, has sought an explanation in the supply of the principal war animals, the elephant and the horse. He argues that, while the utility of the horse is indisputable, the elephant was perhaps equally important as evidenced from the strenuous efforts of the Delhi sultans to ensure sufficient supplies of this animal for their armies. Digby brought the evidence together in his classic work *War Horse and Elephant in the Delhi Sultanate* and it is worth summarizing this account.[14]

The Delhi sultans considered the elephant primarily as a war machine and prepared the animal for battle in elaborate manner.[15] The customary howdah was covered with gilt or inlaid with steel armour in times of war or with various types of silk in peacetime. The mahout sat in front while the tower behind him carried six to ten men, rather excessive for even a full-grown elephant. The tower had openings through which the men fired arrows and flung flasks of Greek fire (a combustible mixture of naphtha, nitre, and sulphur) at the enemy. Foot-soldiers helped clear the path for the advancing elephants and protect them from enemy cavalry. The war elephants generally occupied the front rank, presumably for their intimidating effect on the opponents, and were placed in the centre.

The Sufi mystic and poet, Amir Khusro Dehlawi (1253–1325), wrote in awe of elephants closing in for battle:

The rank of elephants was like a line of baneful clouds,
Each cloud with lightning to attack, swift like the wind,
In its swift motion each elephant like a splendid mountain,
The armour upon it like the cloud upon the mountain;
On the back of the elephant Turks with arrows by their thumb-rings...

and poignantly of the elephant in defeat:

From arrows the elephant was grafted with arrow-notches
Like a porcupine with its back full of quills:
From the elephant its driver was hanging,
His body hanging and his life fled.[16]

The Delhi sultans seemed to have acquired most of their war elephants through capture from their enemies or as tribute. There are few indications of organized captures from the wild; one such account refers to the capture of eight wild elephants in the jungles of Jajnagar (Orissa) by Firoz Shah Tughlaq (1351–88).[17] On the other hand, there is ample evidence that the sultans got most of their elephants from captive stocks already available in the subcontinent.[18] Fourteen elephants were captured in 1192 during the conquest of Delhi, Kuhram, and Ajmer at the time of the establishment of the Sultanate. Soon after, in 1194, an expedition to Kanauj acquired between 80 and 100 elephants from its ruler Jitachandra. Considerable numbers of elephants came from Bengal as tribute – 30 elephants in 1225, two from Lakhnavati in 1259, and about 60 elephants in 1264 to appease Balban (1264–87) soon after he became the sultan of Delhi. Orissa also seemed an important source of supply; Balban's expedition of 1281–82 to Jajnagar captured 20 elephants while the ruler agreed to surrender a further 50 elephants.

The Khalji sultans continued this tradition of obtaining elephants from their opponents. In 1295 a raid upon Devagiri yielded 31 elephants for the future sultan Ala-ud-din whose general, Malik Kafur (a Hindu convert from Gujarat), was especially successful in augmenting the Sultanate's *pilkhana* (elephant stables). Kafur obtained 17 elephants after sacking Devagiri in 1308–09 and, the following year, at least 100 elephants from the *rai* or ruler of Warangal, in addition to three exceptionally large elephants which had been hidden outside the fortress. The slave general's third Deccan expedition (1301–12) yielded a rich haul of elephants – 23 animals from the *rai* of Tilang, 36 "huge elephants" from the Hoysala ruler at Dhorasamudra, 108 or 120 elephants from the Pandyas at Kandur (unidentified, but possibly present-day Kannur in Kerala), and another 250 elephants at Brahmapuri (Chidambaram or Kanchipuram in Tamil Nadu), but only two or three animals at Madurai, the seat of the ruling family.[19] Malik Kafur thus added 512 elephants to the sultan's *pilkhana* on his return to Delhi apart from 20,000 horses and considerable quantities of gold and jewels. Ziaud din Barni indicates that Alauddin Khalji's *pilkhana* already had 1,500 elephants in 1299 much before the Deccan expeditions.[20] Referring to Alauddin's possessions, a wise man once remarked that "Elephants and wealth when held in great abundance are the cause of much strife. Whoever acquires them becomes so intoxicated that he does not know his hands from his feet."[21]

The elephant stables of the Delhi sultans were perhaps best stocked under the Tughlaqs. Al-Umari's accounts of the reign of Muhammad-bin-Tughlaq (1325–51) indicate that around 1340 the sultan had 3,000 elephants of different kinds and sizes and for the expenditure on their food the revenue of a large kingdom would hardly suffice, an apt observation indeed. Such high figures of elephants in the sultan's *pilkhana* may be questioned but, as Simon Digby points out, only about a fourth of this number (750 in this case) would be elephants fit for use in war, the rest being younger elephants used merely as pack animals or juveniles under training. The historical accounts too support such a build up. Muhammad-bin-Tughlaq's predecessor, Ghiyas-ud-din, had acquired great spoils from his Bengal campaigns including "all the elephants of the country" (in Barni's words), an area known to be a rich capturing ground for elephants.[22] Muhammad's successor Firoz Shah extracted more elephants from the sultan of Bengal, capturing 47 animals during his first campaign in 1354, and later imposing an annual tribute of 40 elephants (but at the same time presenting him 500 fine horses in a deal obviously perceived as favouring Firoz Shah – remember that an elephant was considered the equal of 500 horses in Hindustan). As mentioned above, he also mounted an expedition to Jajnagar primarily to acquire elephants; it was during this campaign that he captured eight wild elephants, the only recorded instance of a Delhi sultan resorting to capture from the wild. These elephants were captured by the *kheddah* or stockade method well known in the north. It is thus clear that the Delhi sultans did not make any serious effort to develop the art of capturing wild elephants but relied on the other Indian rulers' skills in obtaining them from the wild. This is contrary to the pursuits of the latter-day Mughal kings such as Akbar.

7.4 The defeat by Timur of the Sultan of Delhi, Nasir Al-Din Muhammad Tughlaq, in the winter of 1397–98, illustrated folio from the *Zafarnama* of Sharaf Al-Din 'Ali Yazdi, circa 1595–1600, from the Imperial Library of Emperor Akbar. Now in a private collection that has been in England since the 1940s.

From a peak of 3,000 elephants in the *pilkhana* (or about 750 war elephants) around 1340, the number of war elephants came down sharply to only 120 animals in 1398 when the dreaded warlord Amir Timur of Samarkand invaded Delhi. The power of the Delhi sultans had weakened considerably as a result of internal struggles after the exit of Firoz Shah Tughlaq. Control of the *pilkhana* was still uppermost in the minds of the warring factions. During the decade preceding Timur's invasion, Sultan Muhammad, the second son of Firoz Shah, tried desperately to gain control of Delhi but failed; one reason for this according to Digby was that his opponents still controlled the *pilkhana* and used its elephants to repel him. The *pilkhana* itself was probably located within a large, walled enclosure (at Firoz Shah Kotla) in close proximity to the Yamuna river. Sultan Muhammad was eventually invited to resume the throne at Delhi but had to use deceit to gain complete control over the *pilkhana*. In any case the *pilkhana* was now a pale version of its former glory. The intrigues at Delhi became even more complex and murky after Sultan Muhammad's death three years later in 1393. Eventually, the *pilkhana* came under the control of one Mallu Khan who was aligned with Muhammad's son Mahmud when Amir Timur's forces approached the gates of Delhi in 1398 with a battle-hardened force of 90,000 men.

Timur was well aware of the war elephants of India; indeed, his men had heard dark stories of these strange beasts clad in steel and ridden by flame-throwers, archers, and crossbowmen in protective turrets. Like that other terrible conqueror, Alexander of Macedon, who had faced an elephant army at the Jhelum nearly 1,700 years before, Timur had to come up with strategies to counter the dreaded elephants. He first ordered his men to erect palisades and to dig deep trenches to protect them from the elephants – the latter is the standard (though mostly ineffective) means today to keep wild elephants away from agricultural fields. He then took measures that would have surely horrified animal lovers – he asked his smiths to make caltrops, three-pronged iron stakes, to be thrown in the elephants' path, had buffaloes tied together with leather thongs as a protective barrier, and ordered camels to be roped together with bundles of dried grass and wood on their backs.[23]

On December 17, 1398, Timur's chronicler Nizam al-din Shami records that "Malikzada Sultan Muhammud with Mallu Khan and other leaders and commanders of the land of Hind, with 10,000 horse and 20,000 fully armed foot [soldiers] and 120 war-elephants, surging like the ocean and trumpeting like thunder clouds, armoured and with structures placed upon their backs" marched out of the walled city of Delhi to do battle with the Mongols.[24] The elephants were placed in the centre as was typical with the Muslim armies of the day. In spite of their elaborate preparations, the Mongols were sufficiently alarmed at the sight of the elephants for Timur to hastily summon a maulana and offer prayers to reassure them. In fact, Timur's physicians were so terrified of the elephants that they requested to be placed "in the same place as the ladies and women".[25] As the elephants lumbered forward in tight formation, Timur's archers aimed their arrows at the mahouts riding in front. Seeing that this did not stop the elephants, Timur ordered the camels with their dry fuel load to be set on fire. The elephants panicked upon seeing the burning camels rushing towards them, only to injure themselves on the vicious caltrops as they retreated. One of Timur's grandsons, Prince Khalil, even managed to overcome an elephant along with its riders and march it to Timur as a present. Sultan Muhammad and Mallu Khan fled the scene and Delhi was taken by Timur's forces (figure 7.4).

After two weeks of loot and slaughter, Timur and his entourage began the return journey laden with unimaginable treasures, accompanied by the enslaved master-craftsmen of Delhi and, significantly, several of the 120 captured war elephants that even carried carved stone to adorn the great mosque at Samarkand. The sculptures do not seem to have actually reached Samarkand as none has been discovered there. The elephants that made it to Samarkand were paraded before a delirious crowd.

Meanwhile a shattered Delhi revived under the sultans of the Sayyid (1414–51) and Lodi (1451–1526) dynasties. The last of the Lodis, Ibrahim, was defeated in 1526 at the First Battle of Panipat, another watershed in Indian history. The victor was Babar, a descendant of Timur as well as of Genghis Khan, who founded the Mughal (Persian for Mongol) dynasty.

***

Babar was already familiar with the elephant; in the northwest he had ordered his men to put a rhinoceros and an elephant together in the hope of watching a fight between these two large beasts but the rhino refused to confront the elephant. His son Humayun had captured eight elephants from Ibrahim Lodi's advance force, prior to the battle at Panipat. Babar records in his memoirs that Lodi and his amirs fielded a much larger army than his, including "nearly a thousand elephants" (obviously a gross exaggeration; the historian Percival Spear places the number at only a tenth of this figure).[26] In any case, Babar's superior military tactics, his highly manoeuvrable cavalry and new artillery from Turkey that included firearms – the first time these were used in India – gave him a decisive victory. A large number of elephants with their mahouts also fell into Babar's hands. Thus began the Mughal rule in India that was to last for over two centuries in all its glory before gradual decline and extinction.

The chronicles and memoirs, often painstakingly illustrated, of the Mughal rulers are a rich source for understanding their relationship with the elephant. As with the Delhi sultans, the Mughals continued the tradition of maintaining large numbers of elephants in their armies – indeed this may have reached an all-time high in Indian history during their rule though, ironically, the relevance of the elephant in the battlefield was also completely lost at this time. The engagement of the Mughals with the elephant also changed qualitatively compared to earlier Muslim rulers; the Mughals learnt and used the Indian art of capturing elephants. Some of them developed personal bonds with their animals. As in some modern studies of elephants, individual animals had names and distinct characters in the Mughal accounts.

In his memoirs (*Tuzuk-i-Babari/Babarnama*) Babar gave descriptions of the fauna and flora of Hindustan. He first wrote about the elephant, being impressed by the large size, power, and great sagacity of a creature that understood humans and carried out their bidding. Some 30 to 40 villages in the region of Karrah and Manikpur (west of Allahabad along the Ganga) were engaged solely in the occupation of capturing and training elephants.[27] Indian rulers invariably kept elephants in their armies. Two or three elephants could drag a gun carriage that would otherwise need the exertion of 400–500 men.[28] This creature was unequalled as a pack animal, especially when transporting heavy loads across deep or rapid streams and rivers.

Babar died in 1530 just four years after his conquest of northern India. His son and successor Humayun, described as "elegant, clever, and fascinating",[29] does not seem to have had any special engagement with elephants. He suffered repeated defeats during 1539–40 at the hands of the Afghan chief Sher Shah whose army reputedly had 5,000 elephants (another gross exaggeration, obviously). A fugitive Humayun finally wrested control of Delhi in 1555 from Sher Shah's son. The elephant Dilsankar that Humayun presented to his son Akbar made a lasting impression on the young boy who commenced a virtual love story with the species that was to last several decades. Akbar inherited the

7.5 Emperor Akbar riding an elephant, 18th century painting. His biographer Abu'l Fazl records that the emperor revelled in taming and riding bull elephants in musth.
© *Trustees of the British Museum, London.*

Mughal throne in early 1556, at the tender age of 13, following his father's sudden death due to an accidental fall. He however had to wait for more than three years to take over the reins from the de facto ruler, his regent Bairam Khan.

Jalal ud-din Mohammad Akbar has been described as someone infatuated with elephants, as a connoisseur of elephants (figure 7.5). Given the richer textual and pictorial material for this period in Indian history we are obviously on firmer ground with respect to describing the relationship between a ruler and the elephant than for earlier periods.[30] Puru's faithful elephant Ajax had saved him from death on the battlefield, Ashoka had elevated the elephant to supreme status, Hannibal's elephant Surus had carried him safely across the Alps, Dutthagamani's Kandula had never tasted defeat in battle, but Akbar's engagement with this creature bordered on mania. Not only did Akbar maintain 101 elephants at any given time for his personal use, he revelled in taming the fiercest elephants. His chronicler Abu'l Fazl writes that "he rode more than a hundred times in *mast* [i.e. musth], elephants which had killed their drivers and were men-slayers, and were capable of smiting a city or perturbing an army and engaged them in fighting".[31] Even today, captive elephants in musth are apt to kill their mahouts if handled carelessly.

Akbar's early initiation in the world of elephants stood him in good stead during his lifelong engagement with the animal. He fought many battles with his prized elephants and had a keen eye for the best animals, whether he spotted them during his "elephant hunting" expeditions, received them as tribute, or captured them from his enemies. One of Akbar's favourite elephants, Hawa'i ("the rocket") was captured from Himu, the brilliant Hindu general of the Afghan ruler, Muhammad Adil Shah, a nephew of Sher Shah. Himu had won all the 22 battles he had fought for his ruler in the course of the Afghan internecine struggles. When Humayun died suddenly in 1556, Himu saw his opportunity to wrest control of the Mughal seat of power. Accordingly, he marched towards Delhi with a large force reportedly comprising 1,000 elephants in addition to 50,000 horses, 51 cannon, and 500 falconets. At Tughlaqabad, a short distance to the south of Delhi, Mughal forces under Tardi Beg, the governor of the city, gave battle to a vastly stronger Afghan force and beat them back, even capturing 400 elephants. Sensing victory, the Mughal officers began to disperse in order to plunder the enemy camp. Himu had kept aside 300 of his choicest elephants for the second assault.[32] He now suddenly charged Tardi Beg with this reserve force. The Afghan elephants were some of the most fearsome beasts of the land as conceded even by Mughal historians of the day. The Mughal officers and their men fled upon seeing "the impetuous advance of the huge beasts" and Tardi Beg lost the battle.[33]

The young Akbar was at Jalandhar in Punjab when news of the defeat at Tughlaqabad reached him. With his guardian Bairam Khan, his commanders, and their forces, he set out at once to confront Himu at the second battle of Panipat fought on November 5, 1556.[34] The advance Mughal cavalry led by Ali Quli Khan initially surprised an advance Afghan artillery force but Himu was undeterred. He marched at the head of 30,000 Afghan and Rajput horsemen, and 500 choice war elephants protected by metal armour, their trunks armed with spears and knives, to evoke shock and fear among the Mughals. In the words of Abu'l Fazl, each of these 500 *sira* elephants was "a paragon for swiftness and dexterity. In might and courage they were exemplars, and the running of those active athletes could not be called running, for though the race-horses of Iraq (i.e. Arabia) be swift they could not outstrip those elephants. In truth each one of those famous elephants was capable of disordering a large force."[35] There was the first-rate Ghalib Jang, the one-in-a-thousand Gaj Bhanwar, the powerful Jor Banyan, Fauj Madar, and Kali Beg that Himu had ridden during many battles. On this day, however, Himu rode the lofty

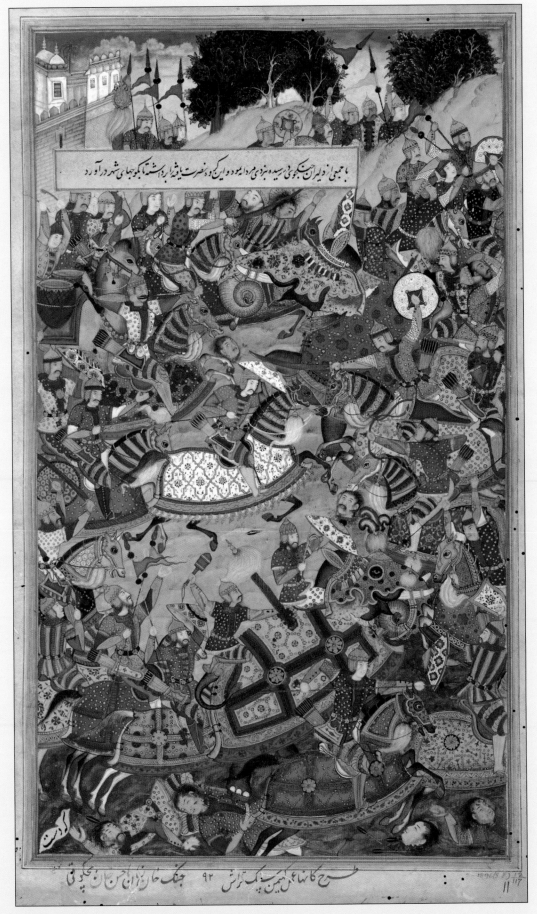

7.6 The victory of Ali Quli Khan on the river Gomti, illustrated folio from the *Akbarnama*, painted by Kanha and Khiman Sangtarash, circa 1590–95.

Courtesy: Victoria and Albert Museum, London.

Hawa'i as he launched the first attack on the main Mughal forces. The "mountain-like and dragon-mouthed elephants" swept aside even battle-hardened Mughals but, rather than directly confront the huge beasts, the survivors made a strategic detour to take on the Afghan horsemen.

By this time the advancing Mughal centre reached a secure piece of ground protected by a deep ravine that could not be negotiated by the enemy's elephants and horses. Flanking parties of Mughal horsemen now began harassing the Afghans from the rear, slashing at the elephants' legs with their swords and picking off their mahouts with their arrows. An unfazed Himu gathered "a band of fierce elephants [and] showed every stratagem which his powerful capacity could conceive...and dislodged many strenuous soldiers of the sublime [i.e. Mughal] army". The battle was evenly poised when an arrow ("from the bended bow of divine wrath", in the words of Abu'l Fazl) pierced Himu's eye. Pulling the arrow out, Himu bravely urged his men to continue fighting even as he fainted inside the howdah. The Mughal commander Shah Quli Mahram had by now reached the scene but seemed unaware that Himu had fallen; his goal was to kill the impressive Hawa'i's mahout and capture the beast when "the helpless driver, who had neither the helmet of loyalty nor the cuirass of courage, from fear of his life, pointed out his master". Along with the prized Hawa'i, the betrayed Himu was marched off to Akbar's camp where Bairam Khan promptly beheaded him.

By all accounts, the battle could have gone either way – a chance arrow and a disloyal mahout perhaps changed the course of history. Abu'l Fazl makes an interesting observation of Himu's reliance on his choice elephants: "In the drunkenness of infatuation, he could not understand that he who is supported by the driver of the elephant will assuredly prevail over him whose trust is in the elephant." Five years later, the Mughals would defeat the Afghans again, this time at Jaunpur, and capture several more war elephants (figure 7.6).

At Panipat, about 1,500 elephants including the mighty Hawa'i fell into Mughal hands. Hawa'i has been immortalized in a colourful miniature composed by Basawan, a leading master at Akbar's atelier, and painted by Chetar.[36] This double-page scene shows Akbar riding a ferocious Hawa'i in pursuit of the nearly equally impressive elephant Ran Bagha across the river Yamuna (figure 7.7). Abu'l Fazl describes this incident in the *Akbarnama*: "The elephant Hawa'i was a mighty animal and reckoned among the special elephants. In choler, passionateness, fierceness and wickedness he was a match for the world. Strong and experienced drivers who had spent a long life in riding similar elephants mounted him with difficulty...that royal cavalier and tiger-hunter [i.e. Akbar] one day without hesitation mounted this elephant, in the very height of its ferocity...and executed wonderful manoeuvres. After that he pitted him against the elephant Ran Bagha which nearly approached him in his qualities."[37] Akbar's subjects had never witnessed anything like this before and his dumbfounded courtiers were wondering how they could dissuade the emperor from this deadly pursuit. Ran Bagha was in musth as seen from Basawan's composition, while Hawa'i too would have been in peak musth as inferred from Abu'l Fazl's account (Hawa'i is shown flapping his ears in the painting and thus his musth gland is not visible). Akbar was only 19 years old when he indulged in this particular mad pursuit, a hobby that had commenced in his youth and continued throughout his life. When a musth elephant in his *pilkhana* had killed its mahouts or other people, Akbar would mount the animal from the front by placing his feet upon its tusks – a direct challenge to the raging animal.[38] He would then smilingly take his seat upon the elephant and goad the animal to fight with another musth elephant, sometimes even leaping from his own elephant to the other if the latter's mahout lost control. When Akbar was only

7.7 Emperor Akbar riding the elephant Hawa'i in pursuit of Ran Bagha across a bridge of boats on the river Yamuna in 1561, by Basawan and Chetar, 1590–95. *Courtesy: Victoria and Albert Museum, London.*

7.8a The Mudumalai elephant camp (1985) showing prescribed rations of cooked grain for feeding the captives, a system that had begun during Mughal times.
b Animals such as this large bull capable of coming into musth are provided the highest quantities of cooked rations.

14 he had mounted the bull Jhalpa in musth and engaged in battle with another musth elephant. That contest had ended in a draw.

To continue the story of the incident on the Yamuna,

...the lion-hearted Shahinshah calmly went on with his terrifying pursuit until the elephant Hawa'i by the strength of a hidden arm, and the divine fortune, got the victory over his opponent. Ran Bagha let fall the strong cable of steadfastness and turned to flee. Hawa'i looked neither behind nor before and disregarded heights and hollows and went like the wind in pursuit of the fugitive. His Majesty, a rock of firmness, continued to sit steadily and to watch the ways of destiny. After running a long way the elephant [Ran Bagha] came to the edge of the river Jamna...[and] in his confusion went on to the bridge, and Hawa'i with [Akbar] on his back came upon the bridge behind him. Owing to the great weight of those two mountain forms the pontoons were sometimes submerged and sometimes lifted up...the elephants...traversed the whole of the bridge and got to the other side...Ran Bagha ran off, carrying his life.[39]

This racy account of a contest between two titans surging with testosterone, one of them goaded by a man who is obviously experiencing an adrenaline rush, is reminiscent of accounts by field biologists observing a contest between two dominant bull elephants in musth. A direct confrontation in the wild could easily result in the death of one of the combatants but more often, as in the case of Hawa'i and Ran Bagha, the subordinate animal flees for its life.

The emperor took very good care of his elephants. He paid personal attention to the conduct and management of his large elephant establishment,[40] and himself classified the imperial elephants into seven types on the basis of his personal knowledge of the age and utility of those animals[41] (this was different from the one based on morphology that I shall mention later). *Mast* elephants were young and strong animals possessed of the "peculiar heat". *Shegir* or tiger-seizing elephants were likewise youthful and alert, while *sadah* elephants came close to the former in usefulness. *Manjholah, karha, p'handurkiya,* and *mokal* elephants were progressively inferior or younger animals, the last-mentioned ones not yet fit for use. Daily rations were prescribed for each of these elephant classes.[42]

7.9 A young adult bull exhibiting symptoms of musth during the dry season. The *Ain-i-Akbari* makes the interesting observation that bulls of different body types come into musth at different seasons.

Needless to state, those capable of coming into musth received the highest quantities. The *khasa* elephants (i.e. the 101 animals "appointed for the exclusive use of His Majesty") received a diet that was similar in quantity but superior in quality. In addition to the standard rations of grass, hay, and leaves, these chosen giants were fed cooked rice mixed with spices, ghee, and jaggery (figure 7.8). When sugarcane was available they got 300 canes each, while some privileged few were even given milk. For each *halqah* or group of 10, 20, or 30 elephants, Akbar appointed a *faujdar* (superintendent) to look after their health and training.[43] The *faujdar* also had to teach the elephants to be bold and not panic at the sight of fire or the sound of artillery during battle. Further, each elephant in the imperial stables had the customary *mahawat* (mahout) to direct the animal, a *bhoi* who sat upon the rump and assisted the driver in battle and, depending on its quality and size, one or more *met'h*s or servants to fetch fodder and assist in dressing up the elephant. A large musth bull had "three and a half" *met'h*s – presumably four, one of whom would be attached to more than one elephant.

An elaborate system of fines ensured that the attendants did not become careless or lazy.[44] Upon the death of a *khasa* elephant the *mahawat* and the *bhoi* were fined three months' wages; this fine was increased to the cost of the animal if the death was due to gross neglect. The attendants had to pay special attention to the health of tuskers and the condition of the tusks – if a tusk broke and its root was infected, the entire team led by the *faujdar* had to shell out a fine equal to one-eighth the price of the animal. Daily reports on the condition and behaviour of the animals had to be maintained, and each week the emperor sent his emissaries to inspect these reports. Further, a trustworthy clerk in charge of the finances of the *pilkhana* ensured that His Majesty's orders were carried out and that the elephants were paraded in a particular order. Akbar personally inspected the elephants during the muster and fixed their ranks.

The Mughals adapted many older accoutrements but also designed several new ones for controlling or adorning their captive elephants.[45] As many as 31 devices are described in the *Ain-i-Akbari* but several more existed as it was "impossible to describe all the ornamental trappings of elephants". Akbar seemed to be conscious of his animals' welfare; at least two types of harnesses were discontinued because they were found to cause injuries to the elephants.

The *Ain-i-Akbari* makes some interesting observations on the biology and behaviour of elephants. On the basis of morphology four kinds of elephants were recognized.[46] This classification was obviously adapted from the ancient Hindu system of categorizing elephants based on body structure. The Mughals recognized the *bhaddar* (*koomeriah* in the traditional Hindu system), a well-proportioned elephant with an erect head, a broad chest, large ears, and a long tail. This thoroughbred elephant was bold, indefatigable, and much sought after for use in battle. There were also the *mirg* (the *mriga* of the Hindus), the *mand* (possibly the *dwasala*), and a new category *mir* to describe a small, easily frightened elephant. The Mughals also recognized intermediate types that arose from the mixture of these four basic kinds of elephants. Further, they recognized three behavioural types among their bull elephants by adopting the Hindu differentiation of dispositions of the human mind. An elephant in which *sat* predominated was handsome, submissive, moderate in eating, practically celibate, and enjoyed a long life. An animal with a *raj* disposition was savage in looks and behaviour, a voracious eater, and sought sensual pleasures. An elephant full of *tam* was self-willed, destructive, sleepy, and also voracious in appetite.

The *Ain-i-Akbari* also observes that in a female elephant the breasts and the womb resemble those of a human female. The testicles in the male are placed inside the body.

Cows in oestrus rub themselves against the bull, smell its urine and dung, and are jealous of other females who may approach the male. The gestation period is calculated as 18 lunar months, not too far from the observed figure of 18–23 calendar months. A premature delivery was possible during the 17th lunar month.

As mentioned earlier, Akbar had a craze for controlling elephants in musth and, unsurprisingly, Abu'l Fazl often refers to this dangerous predilection, though he does not seem to have much direct knowledge of musth – his account of elephant biology merely makes frequent reference to the Hindu texts. It may be mentioned here that the observations of musth in the much older *Gajashastra* are more detailed and factual. The *Ain-i-Akbari*, however, makes a very interesting observation about when elephants come into musth. Elephants of different body types came into musth at different times of the year.[47] Thus, "the *bhaddar* ruts in Libra and Scorpio, the *mand* in spring, the *mirg* in Capricorn and Sagittarius, the *mir* in any season." We know today that such spacing over time in the expression of musth among bull elephants in a population is a means of minimizing serious conflicts – indeed, game theory has been applied to explain such phenomena in the animal world (figure 7.9).[48]

The Mughal rulers were fond of hunting and Akbar was no exception. Abul Fazl mentions that the emperor preferred to mount elephants to hunt lions and wild pigs (figure 7.10), trapped cheetahs and trained them to hunt antelope and ibex, and used hawks to hunt other birds. Their "elephant hunts", interestingly, refer exclusively to expeditions for capturing elephants and not for killing them. Perhaps the Mughal rulers respected the prevailing Hindu sentiments of the sacredness of the elephant, though the utility of the animal as a war machine would undoubtedly have been the reason for capturing them. Abu'l Fazl describes the four basic methods of catching elephants – the *kheddah* or drive (though Abu'l Fazl does not mention a stockade), the *chor kheddah* in which a tame female elephant is used to enter a herd and noose a wild elephant, the *gad* or camouflaged pit, and the *bar* or digging a ditch around the resting place of elephants leaving only a single opening with a gate (an obvious modification of the stockade). Abu'l Fazl goes on to state that Akbar invented a new method of "remarkable finesse". In this method several tame female elephants were used to lure male elephants from a wild herd into an enclosure where they were captured.

During one such "hunting" expedition in the province of Malwa, Akbar and his men first captured a herd of nine elephants that included two or three males, and later a large herd of 70 elephants in the forests of Narwar (figures 7.11 and 7.12).[49] This must have been a difficult expedition because the monsoon was at its peak; during the crossing of the swollen Chambal river the waters swept away the special elephant Lakna. The Mughals seemed mindful of the welfare of the elephants they captured. As Abu'l Fazl explains, "The real method of taming every animal is gentleness, and the exhibition of what is agreeable to him such as grass, grain and water." For Akbar a hunting expedition, whether to kill certain animals or capture elephants, was not merely a pleasure trip; it was also a means of increasing his knowledge of the natural world besides inquiring into the condition of his citizens and his armed forces.

The elephant forces of the Mughals were effectively deployed in several battles including those in which their opponents had good numbers of war elephants too. After Akbar had established himself firmly at Delhi and the north, he turned his attention to the region of Bihar and Bengal that had come under the control of the Afghan house of Karrani. Akbar himself led his forces during the siege of Patna in August 1574. Daud Karrani who had foolishly proclaimed his independence from the Mughals fled the region leaving behind some of his elephants in Akbar's hands. Before returning to his capital

7.10 Prince Salim, out hunting on a richly caparisoned elephant, surprised by a lion, circa 1595–1600, attributed to Miskin.

Formerly in the Eckstein collection, present whereabouts unknown. Reproduced from Christie's catalogue, 1981.

Akbar used Daud's elephants to amuse himself by engaging them in fights. The following year, Mughal forces led by an ageing Munim Khan faced Daud Karrani at the battle of Tukaroi.[50] The Mughals did not wish to fight on a particular inauspicious day but Daud precipitated the battle by ordering his elephant force under the command Gujar Khan to make a surprise charge upon the Mughal vanguard. "As the tusks and necks of the elephants were covered with black yak-tails and the skins of the animals" they evoked fear

7.11 Emperor Akbar inspecting the newly captured elephant Gajpati outside Sipri fort, *Akbarnama* painting by La'l and Sanwala, 1590–95.
Courtesy: Victoria and Albert Museum, London.

7.12 Elephants captured at Narwar being driven into the Banayan fort, by La'l and Khem, 1590–95.
Courtesy: Victoria and Albert Museum, London.

among the Mughal cavalry. In spite of this initial setback, the Mughal forces eventually prevailed over Daud.

A year later Akbar turned his attention toward Rajasthan where Rana Pratap Singh posed a challenge to Mughal supremacy. The final showdown took place on June 18, 1576 at the famous battle of Haldighat.[51] The Rajputs had the Afghans on their side, the Mughals had firearms, and both sides had their elephants. The contest was deadlocked and could be resolved only by the use of their choice war elephants. Pratap Singh deployed his "rank-breaking Lona" to clear a path, and the Mughals countered this move by sending Gajmukta, their "pearl among elephants". Abu'l Fazl describes the clash of these giants: "The shock of these two mountain-like forms threw the soldiers into trepidation and the imperial elephant [i.e. Gajmukta] was wounded and about to fly when...a bullet struck the driver of the enemy's elephant, and he turned back."[52] At this critical stage of the battle the Rajputs brought in Ram Prasad, their foremost elephant, but the Mughals faced him with Ran Madar and Gajraj. As luck would have it, Ram Prasad's mahout was thrown to the ground by an arrow. Seizing this opportunity the Mughal commander Hussain Khan leapt onto its back from his own elephant and secured the prized animal for Akbar's court. At the end of the day the Rana's forces lost a hard-fought battle.

Akbar's military exploits with his elephants are too numerous to recount here. Figures compiled by historian Shireen Moosvi suggest there were about 5,000 captive elephants in the Mughal *pilkhana* around 1595.[53] By this time Akbar had also secured Gujarat (1573), the great Rajput forts of Chittor and Ranthambhore (1568–69), Kashmir (1586), Orissa (1592), and Sindh (1595). The following ten years he was engaged in capturing territories of the Deccan kingdoms. His elephants no doubt played important roles in these conquests. Akbar had gone to such great lengths to acquire, train, and maintain elephants that it is unthinkable not to assign a major role to these animals in his establishment of empire.

Following Akbar's death in 1605 of a sudden illness, his sole surviving son Salim or Jahangir, as he is better known, ascended the throne. Jahangir was not as passionate about elephants or indeed about military conquest as his illustrious father, but he was a keen naturalist.[54] It has been remarked: "had he been the head of a natural history museum he would have been a better and happier man".[55] His memoirs contain descriptions of a variety of plants and animals. He once observed a female elephant in the *pilkhana* giving birth and ordered investigations into the gestation period of the species. The answer he obtained (18 months for a female calf and 19 months for a male calf) reflects the figures given in the *Ain-i-Akbari*. Based on first-hand observation he wrote, "In contrast to human babies, which usually come from the mother's womb head first, an elephant calf usually comes out feet first. When the calf was separated from the mother, the mother kicked dust on it with her feet and began to show love and reassure it. The calf remained down for an instant, and then it got up and went for the mother's udders."[56] Incidentally, elephant calves normally come out head first and not feet first as in this case. Jahangir was also familiar with the African elephant and its differences from the Indian species. He had received a young elephant from Ethiopia and remarks that the "Ethiopian's ears are larger than the ones here, and its trunk and tail are longer".[57]

Jahangir participated in an elephant capture operation near Dohad in Gujarat. Two hundred female elephants with their expert mahouts from the Jariya tribe were used to form a circle around the wild elephants, but the latter broke through this cordon and 12 of them ran in Jahangir's direction as he watched from a tree-top platform. Some of them, including two splendid elephants were lassoed and taken to the Mughal *pilkhana*. Eventually his party led by Gajpat Khan, the superintendent of the *pilkhana*, and Baludi Khan, the chief scout, captured 185 elephants (73 males and 112 females) from this region.[58] The pick of the Dohad catch was Pawan Gaj, a young tusker of good proportions with a pair of light-coloured ears.[59]

As had his father, Jahangir maintained many choice elephants that were illustrated by his master-painters. While many of these portraits cannot be identified,[60] two of them have been – Gaj Ratan, in the Indian Museum, Kolkata and Alam Guman, in the National Museum, New Delhi (figures 7.13a and b). Once the chief elephant of Rana Amar Singh of Mewar, Alam Guman ("Arrogant of the Earth") was presented to Jahangir by his son, Prince Khurram, in 1614. According to D.K. Lahiri-Choudhury, Gaj Ratan, shown standing under a canopy with attendants cooking his food, is the same Gajraj of Haldighat fame now in "mellow retirement".[61] Jahangir presented this elephant to Khan Jahan in 1621.[62]

Prince Khurram became known as Shahjahan on succeeding his father in 1627. While Shahjahan continued the family tradition of maintaining elephants he does not seem to have had any special affinity to them. Nevertheless, the painters of his atelier continued to produce outstanding images of his choice elephants.[63] One of these elephants, Mahavir Dev (previously named Khus Khan) that was presented to Shahjahan by Adil Khan, was valued at 300,000 rupees, perhaps the highest value ever recorded for an elephant. Another painting shows Prince Aurangzeb taming the giant elephant Sidhkar, much like Akbar did when he was young (figure 7.14). A third painting shows Shahjahan watching an elephant fight, along with two of his sons, at the Red Fort in Agra (figure 7.15). Shahjahan used his elephants to give vent to his vindictiveness – a story by the European traveller Francois Bernier speaks of how the emperor let loose a vicious elephant upon a Persian visitor who had not paid due obeisance to him; the visitor and his followers escaped by shooting a volley of arrows at the elephant.[64]

Among the royal Mughals, Aurangzeb seems to have come closest to the illustrious Akbar in his engagement with elephants. As a 14-year-old, the prince was charged by a violent elephant Sudhakar when he along with his three brothers and their father were watching an elephant combat on the banks of the Yamuna outside Agra Fort on May 28, 1633.[65] This tusked elephant Sudhakar had been victorious in combat over its tuskless rival Suratsundar when it turned upon the young princes who were watching from horseback. While his three brothers fled, Aurangzeb managed to steady his horse and struck the elephant on its forehead with his spear (see figure 7.14). The elephant gored the horse with its tusks but Aurangzeb leapt down from the saddle to face the elephant. At this crucial moment Suratsundar returned to the fray; Sudhakar fled the scene and the emperor presented Aurangzeb with 5,000 gold coins and the elephant Sudhakar for this brave act.

Following Shahjahan's debilitating illness in September 1657, an internecine struggle for the control of the Mughal throne ensued among his four sons, from which his third son Aurangzeb emerged victorious. The elephant was again to play a prominent role in these battles.[66] At the last stage of the battle of Samugarh, Aurangzeb's vanguard fell upon his brother Dara Shikoh who was seated on an elephant. An alarmed Dara changed to a horse and his troops fled upon seeing an empty howdah, thinking that their leader had fallen – a familiar conclusion in subcontinental battles involving elephants.

Aurangzeb imprisoned his father and crowned himself emperor at Delhi on July 21, 1658. Soon he faced a challenge from his brother Shuja, governor of Bihar and Bengal. The opponents met on January 5, 1659 at Khajwa in Fatehpur district. Sayyid Alam at the head of Shuja's right wing drove three musth elephants towards the imperial left wing, each elephant brandishing a heavy iron chain in its trunk and scattering the opponents

7.13a Gaj Ratan standing under a canopy, painter unknown, circa 1621. *Courtesy: Indian Museum, Kolkata.*
b Alam Guman, the chief elephant of Rana Amar Singh, with other elephants, painter's name illegible, circa 1614. *Courtesy: National Museum, New Delhi.*

7.14 Prince Aurangzeb controlling the musth elephant Sidhkar (possibly the renamed Sudhakar), detail of an illustration from the *Padshahnama*, 1630–40.
The Royal Collection © 2011, Her Majesty Queen Elizabeth II.

7.15 Emperor Shahjahan, accompanied by two of his sons, watching an elephant fight at the Red Fort in Agra, possibly on the occasion of his lunar birthday on October 23, 1632. An illustration from the *Padshahnama*, 1630–40. The tradition of staging elephant fights goes back to at least the time of the 12th-century Chalukyan king Somadeva III who staged the *gaja-vahyali* or elephant sport for the exclusive pleasure of the king (see Chapter 6).

The Nasser D. Khalili Collection of Islamic Art MSS 900. © The Nour Foundation. Courtesy: The Khalili Family Trust.

in its path. One of them came right up to Aurangzeb but the emperor chained his own elephant to prevent it (and his troops) from fleeing as he faced the threatening bull calmly. One of his soldiers in the meantime shot down the musth bull's driver and a mahout jumped on the elephant's back to bring it under control. At the final stage of the battle Shuja, sensing defeat, got down from his elephant and mounted a horse. Needless to say, his army fled thinking that their master was dead.

Several of Aurangzeb's decrees did not go down too well with the people. In 1679 he revived the *jazia* or poll-tax on non-Muslims; when a crowd of poor people blocked a road in protest Aurangzeb used elephants to trample and scatter them.[67] Through another ordinance (in March 1695) he forbade all Hindus with the exception of Rajputs to "carry arms or ride elephants, *palkis*, or Arab and Persian horses".[68] After hearing of an elephant-fight organized by his eldest son, Aurangzeb issued a decree that "ordering an elephant-fight is the exclusive prerogative of kings".[69]

The internecine struggle for the Mughal throne continued after Aurangzeb's death in 1707. His eldest surviving son Muazzam Shah Alam (crowned as Bahadur Shah I) fought his younger brother Muhammad Azam Shah (both quite old men actually) at Jajau, south of Agra. There was heavy loss on both sides, including scores of elephants that died from wounds and from the June summer heat. Unlike earlier battles in the subcontinent in which few elephants seemed to have perished, the high death toll in this Mughal battle could be attributed to the increasing role of gun power.

The Muslim armies of the 18th century continued to use the elephant, albeit unsuccessfully, against superior firearms whose design was influenced by imports from Europe. These armies used bullocks to draw their artillery guns with an elephant giving a push when needed with such heavy equipment. The Mughal empire disintegrated rapidly during the 18th century, splitting into several independent or semi-independent states. Independent Muslim states were established in the Deccan, Awadh, and Bengal. The Rajputs, the Sikhs, the Jats, and the Marathas reasserted themselves against the much-weakened Mughals. To add insult to injury, Nadir Shah the Persian sacked Delhi in February 1739 and carried away astounding riches, including the famous Kohinoor diamond, Shahjahan's peacock throne, 10,000 horses, and 300 elephants. His successor Ahmad Shah Abdali invaded India no less than six times, the last in 1764, each raid further crippling the much-reduced Mughal empire. The Mughals tottered along for another century until the last ruler, Bahadur Shah Zafar, was deported to Burma by the British on suspicion of assisting the so-called Sepoy Mutiny or the Indian revolt in 1857.

***

We can now take stock of the status of the elephant and its decline during the centuries of Muslim dominance of the subcontinent. We have little direct evidence for the distribution of wild elephants during the 11th century when Muslim presence began to be felt in India. Al-Biruni's observations of a rhinoceros attacking an elephant indicates that the latter was present in the former's specialized habitat, the floodplains of the Indo-Gangetic basin. Much, if not the rest, of this region was under the plough or settled and, thus, the elephant would have been restricted to the forests and floodplains of rivers along the Himalayan foothills in the Siwalik range, perhaps extending west into Punjab as far as present-day Pakistan.

Elephants would have been plentiful in Bengal, an important source of captive stock for later Muslim rulers, as well as in the Brahmaputra valley and the surrounding hill ranges. They would also have been widespread in central and peninsular India, with the possible exception of major river valleys that had been under settlement and cultivation in Andhra and Tamil Nadu, as well as perhaps the driest tracts of the interior Deccan.

7.16 An elephant herd near Kalpi, a stray folio from an Akbari-period *Babarnama*. Composition by Kanha and painting by Ikhlas.
Collection of Aga Khan, Geneva.

The Western Ghats were undoubtedly a stronghold of the elephant, while the species may already have become more isolated in the scattered hills of the Eastern Ghats of the peninsula.

The large numbers of elephants held by rulers of the north certainly indicates plentiful supply from a variety of sources in the wild. The 1,670 elephants possessed in 1023–24 by the Ghaznavids, whose kingdom lay entirely outside the range of the elephant's distribution in the subcontinent, would only have been possible if the local rulers too held large stocks that could be replenished from nearby sources. The early Muslim rulers, including the Ghaznavids and the Ghurids, or even the Delhi sultans, seemed to have made no attempt to organize the capture of elephants for their armies. Their stocks came entirely from capture during war or as tribute from subordinate rulers. Thus, the systematic capture of wild elephants and their training seems to have been the exclusive domain of the Hindu rulers of the subcontinent during the 11th to 14th centuries. The only exceptions were the sultans of Bengal who seemed to have assimilated and used the local expertise in capturing elephants.

The coming of the Mughals changed this situation, though not immediately. The first campaign of a Mughal ruler to capture elephants seems to be that of Akbar in the province of Malwa during the monsoon of 1564. A distinct Mughal elephant culture evolved under the patronage of Akbar and continued under his successor Jahangir.

The memoirs of the Mughal rulers help us reconstruct the distribution of wild elephants in central India. Most of their observations pertain to a region where elephants are largely absent today. Babar noted that the elephant "inhabits the [western?] borders of the Kalpi country [i.e. district], and becomes more numerous in its wild state the further east one goes" (figure 7.16).[70] Kalpi in southern Uttar Pradesh is devoid of elephants but the west-east gradient that Babar referred to was a very accurate observation. The *Ain-i-Akbari* gives the distribution of elephants as follows:[71] the district of Agra (the forests of Bayawan and Narwar where Akbar captured them) as far as Barar, the district of Allahabad, the region of Pattah (Bhatta or Rewa in Baghelkhand), Ghoraghat, Ratanpur, Nandanpur, Sargachh (Sarguja), and Bastar, the region of Malwa near Handia, Uchhod, Chanderi, Satwas, Bijagarh, Raisen, Hoshangabad, Garh, and Haryagarh, places in Madhya Pradesh/Chhattisgarh from where the wild elephant soon disappeared. The presence of elephants further east, in Bihar/Jharkhand, Orissa, and southern Bengal up to Hugli is also mentioned.

This covers a wide region in central India where elephants have been wiped out (though elephants have recently immigrated into Chhattisgarh). In addition, the Mughals were familiar with the presence of wild elephants in Jharkhand, Orissa, and Bengal. The elephants of Pattah were believed to be the best. Jahangir adds to this information; his elephant capture operations at Dohad in eastern Gujarat possibly indicate the western extremity of elephant distribution in this part of the subcontinent.

We should also take stock of the numbers of captive elephants held by the Mughals and other rulers in the subcontinent. Shireen Moosvi estimates that Akbar's *pilkhana* held about 5,000 elephants in the year 1595.[72] Various zamindars subordinate to the Mughals held at least 1,772 elephants, according to an incomplete census, of which the major holdings were in Bengal (1,170) followed by Allahabad (323), Agra (221), Malwa (90), and Awadh (59). Perhaps about 1,000 elephants were held by the jagirdars. Further, the Portuguese traveller Fernão Nuniz writing circa 1535–37 mentions that the Vijayanagara emperor hired 3,000 men to take care of his elephants[73] that Moosvi interprets as not more than an equal number of elephants. To this can be added an estimated 1,000 elephants in the Deccan kingdoms and 2,000 elephants held by the rulers (*nayaka*s) and temples in the

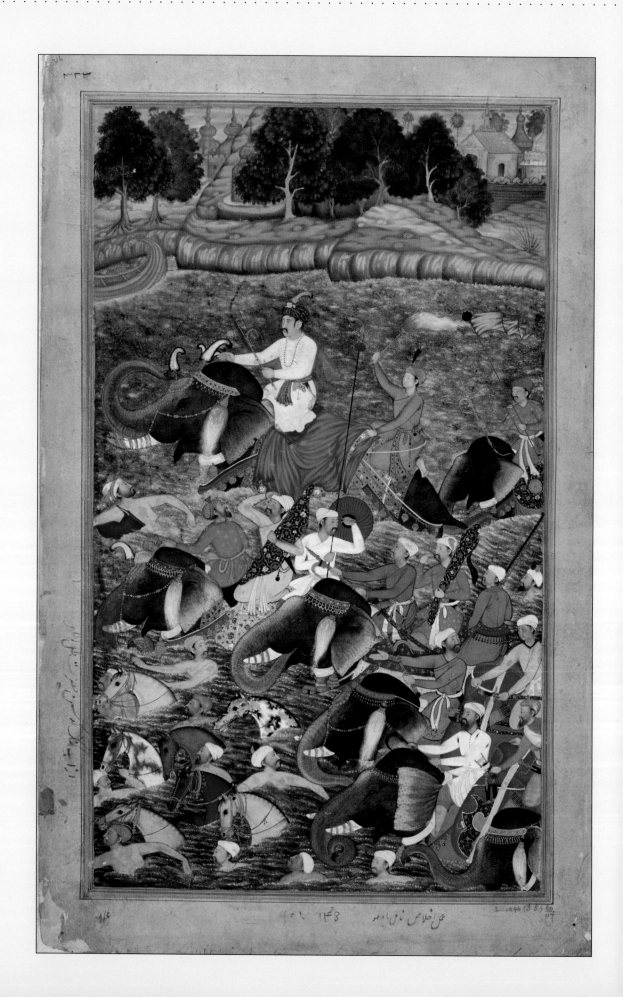

south, for a total of perhaps 17,000 captive elephants for the subcontinent during the late 16th century. While this seems reasonable on the whole, I would add that Vijayanagara had fewer elephants, possibly about 1,550 animals at the most (see Chapter 6).

The number of captive elephants in the subcontinent possibly reached its peak during the time of Jahangir. The French navigator Francois Pyrard de Laval who visited Bengal and the Malabar during the first decade of the 17th century recorded that the king of Bengal possessed 10,000 elephants, while he had heard from "many Indians and others" that the great Mughal king maintained as many as 30,000 elephants.[74] These figures are suspect if applied to only captive animals but is not an unreasonable estimate of captive and wild elephants in the subcontinent within the region of Bengal and the Mughal empire; remember there would still have been large numbers of elephants in the northeast and in the extreme south that were not a part of the territories of Bengal and of the Mughals.

An important development for elephants at the height of Mughal power was that, for all practical purposes, the wild elephant populations of central India, with the exception of the region of Orissa and Bihar-Jharkhand, were wiped out. A part of this population in the present-day states of Gujarat, Maharashtra, southern Uttar Pradesh, Madhya Pradesh, and Chhattisgarh, in any case, would have been rather isolated by Mughal times, and all that the Mughals probably did was to deliver the final blow.

Before we close this chapter we must reconsider the true efficacy of the elephant as a war machine. Most historians have argued that the Indian rulers' faith in the elephant in this regard was rather misplaced, and that horse-based cavalry was consistently superior on the battlefield. A.L. Basham summed up this view in the following words:

> The great reliance placed on elephants was, from the practical point of view, unfortunate.... The pathetic Indian faith in the elephants' fighting qualities was inherited by the Muslim conquerors, who, after a few generations in India, became almost as reliant on elephants as the Hindus, and suffered at the hands of armies without elephants in just the same way.[75]

To the contrary, Digby argues that the tactical importance of the elephant was much greater than has been conceded by military historians. For instance, the size of the elephant force was an indicator of the strength of the sultans of Delhi – they were thus able to control vast areas of northern and eastern India, as evident in their collection of war booty and tribute, when their *pilkhana* was well stocked with several thousand elephants. To reinforce this viewpoint, Digby further points out that the decline and defeat of the Delhi Sultanate at the hands of Timur occurred after its *pilkhana* had been reduced to a pale version of its former glory.[76] This horse-versus-elephant argument may never be completely settled, but we have to acknowledge that the elephant was indispensable in hilly terrain and moist tracts where the horse had its limitations (figure 7.17). Indeed, much after the direct use of the elephant in the battlefield had died out, the animal continued to play an indirect role in warfare in Asia until the late 20th century, as we shall see in the following two chapters.

7.17 Emperor Akbar crossing the Ganga on the back of an elephant in 1567, by Ikhlas and Madhav, 1590–95.
Courtesy: Victoria and Albert Museum, London.

CHAPTER 8

The Elephant in Colonial Asia

WITH THE ARRIVAL OF THE PORTUGUESE EXPLORER Vasco da Gama in India in 1498, a new chapter began in the story of the Asian elephant that would have unfortunate results for the animal. As in the past, the primary use of the elephant for warfare continued unabated into modern times. The Portuguese were followed by the Dutch, the British, and the French in quick succession and the capture and deployment of elephants in war by both the native rulers and the new arrivals with their imperial ambitions increased the misery of the animals. The continuing demand for the pachyderm as a war machine or a beast of burden, as well as for its new role in logging the rich Asian forests, increased the capture and trade in the animal on a large scale; the elephant now became an important trade commodity not only in the subcontinent including Ceylon (Sri Lanka) but also in Burma (Myanmar) and Southeast Asia. Moreover, the colonial powers introduced a vicious regime of big-game hunting or shikar which further led to the unrestrained slaughter of the animal and trade in ivory. Finally, a new dimension was introduced in the capture of the animal on a much greater scale than in the past, to supply elephants for European and American (a new player from the 18th century) entertainment in circuses and spectacle in private menageries and zoos, and many other forms of public and private uses, that also spread on the subcontinent itself and other parts of Asia. This phase of the Asian story opened up the inevitable confrontation between man and beast for resources and habitats that continues to the present.

We saw in Chapter 4 that expeditions by Afonso de Albuquerque to Cochin during 1510–14 took back at least four elephants to Portugal, one of which was gifted to Pope Leo X. The Portuguese trade in Asian elephants from India, however, seems to have been rather limited, perhaps as they did not get a strong foothold in the region of Kerala where elephants could be easily sourced. On the other hand, they established themselves firmly in the island of Ceylon which was at that time divided among several warring groups, with the Moors controlling the sea trade. The Portuguese also had a foothold at Goa in southwestern India when, in 1505, their "Viceroy" in the country, Don Francisco de Almeida, sent his son Don Lorenzo to intercept the Moors.[1] Lorenzo landed at Galle, to the south of Colombo, where he found the Moors loading their ships with cinnamon and elephants. The following year King Manuel of Portugal instructed Francisco de Almeida to establish a fort in Ceylon because here were "all the elephants in India, in addition to fine cinnamon, pearls and many other wares of great value and profit".[2]

The island to the south of India had acquired fame several centuries ago as the breeding ground for robust war elephants; this was now reinforced with the arrival of the Portuguese in South Asia. In fact, Vasco da Gama himself had recorded in the journal of his first voyage, on the basis of secondary sources, that "the King of Ceylon has many elephants for war and for sale".[3] The Ceylon elephant figured positively in the accounts of several Portuguese voyagers to the East. The Portuguese historian João de Barros summarized this reputation as follows: "The Ceylon elephants, of which a good number are bred, are those with the best instinct in the whole of India, and because they are notably the most tameable and handsomest they are worth much."[4] Duarte Barbosa adds that elephants from Ceylon reached the king of Cambaya (Cambay) through Malabar (figure 8.1).[5]

After Don Lorenzo's maiden landing in Ceylon in 1505, it was another 12 years before the Portuguese visited the island again to establish a fort at Colombo after concluding a treaty of peace and commerce with the Sinhalese king of Kotte that included the promise of annual tribute of elephants. In the words of Nicholas, "Next to cinnamon, elephants were the major attraction which impelled the Portuguese to establish themselves in Ceylon."[6] Two years later, following a breakdown in the peace, the Portuguese had their first encounter with Sinhalese elephants in battle. Twenty-five elephants, including four tuskers

8.1 The King of Cambaya besieging the fortress of Diu on elephantback. Painting from the *Códice Casanatense*, a Portuguese manuscript produced in India in the 16th century, Folio 43/44.
Courtesy: Biblioteca Casanatense, Rome.

with swords fitted to their tusks, charged the Portuguese who were initially discouraged at the prospect of facing these lethal giants. The Portuguese guns and gunpowder, however, caused the Sinhalese elephants to panic and trample their own infantry. This encounter may have been the first time that war elephants were repulsed with gunpowder[7] whose increasing use in subsequent wars in South Asia proved to be their nemesis.

In spite of this setback, the Sinhalese rulers persisted with their large elephant forces. Rajasinha I of Sitawaka built up a force of 200 war elephants that the Portuguese found difficult to fight on plain ground such as at Mulleriyawa in 1562.[8] The Sinhalese ruler also used his large elephant force during the siege of Colombo in 1579–81, and again in 1587–88.[9] The latter was an especially hard-fought war of attrition, the elephants being used as battering rams to break down the gates, walls, and fortifications of Colombo. The Portuguese countered the elephants with muskets, fire balls, gunpowder, and long fire-lances to blind the animals.[10] Apparently the elephants had got accustomed to the din and smoke of battle but remained vulnerable to the horrific injuries they suffered. The siege of Colombo fort eventually failed.

The Portuguese were clearly not interested in training their elephants for use in war but rather acquiring them for trade. They soon established a flourishing trade in elephants for export to India. At this time the kingdoms of Kotte, Sitawaka, and Kandy already had a thriving trade in the export of elephants[11] perhaps to the extent of about 100 animals each year.[12] By controlling the main ports on the island, the Portuguese ensured themselves a near-monopoly over sea-borne trade. The tribute of two elephants annually agreed upon in 1540 by the ruler of Jaffna increased to 12 elephants in 1591. The Portuguese also began to capture and tame elephants for purposes of export.

At this time the Sinhalese already had an elaborate state establishment for capturing elephants. The various tasks of capturing, taming, and maintaining the elephants were entrusted to different groups of people.[13] The Panikkayas were responsible for capturing elephants, the Pannayas for feeding them, and the Kuruwe people for caring for the animals after capture. Elephants were captured by the pit method but with an interesting variation – a cow elephant acting as a decoy was tied to a tree close to where the pit was dug and camouflaged. This may have been a method to selectively capture bull elephants that were attracted to the vicinity.

The Portuguese seem to have introduced the corral or *kheddah* method of capturing elephants, possibly having learnt it from their experience in India.[14] While early Portuguese writers describe the pit capture as the method of securing elephants, a century later the historian Paulo de Trinidade graphically describes how 1,000 people, many armed with muskets and arrows, were mustered to construct a stockade of stout logs and drive an entire herd of elephants through its narrow entrance. The Sinhalese in the meantime persisted with the traditional pit method as they perceived the drive method to be too dangerous to life and limb. C.R. de Silva adds a new dimension to the Portuguese preference for the corral method of capturing elephants.[15] The elephant was merely a trading commodity for which a "new production technique", to use the language of economics, that maximized the number of animals acquired was highly desirable. The corral method enabled them to acquire entire herds at lower risk of injury to or death of the elephants, as opposed to the solitary animal or at most two or three individuals, often injured by the fall, obtained by the pit method.

The Walawe Ganga, a part of the Portuguese Disawany of Matara in the south and an important elephant habitat, was the main region of captures.[16] The elephants were exported almost entirely to India by marching them to the northern ports of Mannar and Jaffna from where special boats called *champana*s carried them across the shortest sea route. The animals were either auctioned at Kotte, Mannar, and Jaffna, or were sold in India to agents of the rulers of Vijayanagara, Bijapur, Golconda, Thanjavur, Madurai, and Bengal. The Mughal empire with its capital in the north was another major destination for the elephants during the 17th century.[17] The elephants were valued principally according to their height, carriage, and other points such as presence of tusks. The best animals fetched 500–1,000 xerafims in Ceylon, with the amounts doubling or quadrupling in India.[18] Based on an incorrect figure of an elephant's weight, de Silva estimates that the weight of the elephants exported exceeded that of the other major traded commodity, cinnamon.[19]

In the meantime, the Dutch had firmly established themselves on the Indonesian island of Java. Rajasinha II, the Kandyan king of Ceylon, invited the Dutch in 1636 to help him oust the Portuguese. In return he promised them a fort at Kottiyar or Batticaloa plus expenses of their fleet.[20] Seeing this as an opportunity to also wrest the cinnamon trade, the Dutch East India Company sent envoys to the Sinhalese court in 1637 for negotiations, and finally laid siege to Colombo in 1655–56. The siege inflicted terrible suffering on the Portuguese within the fort; of the 15 elephants they had with them they were forced to kill all but one animal to ward off starvation (incidentally, even human flesh was secretly consumed).[21] The sole survivor, Horatala, was a handsome animal that had been used to capture wild elephants. The "affection that all [Portuguese] had for him" apparently saved his life. Horatala lived to a ripe old age after being passed on to the Dutch who captured the fort; the story that the same animal witnessed the Dutch capitulation to the British nearly a century and a half later[22] is obviously a tall one.

Once the Dutch wrested control of the maritime provinces from the Portuguese by 1658 they, too, began to covet the lucrative trade in elephants, second only to cinnamon as with the Portuguese.[23] Three documents from the Dutch historical records provide valuable insights into their thinking on this matter. The first is a 1667 directive from Holland to their governor and council in Ceylon which states: "We consider the promotion of agriculture to be a good object and calculated to bring about great tranquility, but on the other hand, as Ceylon would then require little rice from outside, this would act prejudicially against our elephant trade...."[24] The directive goes on to explain that traders from Bengal and the Coromandel who brought rice to Ceylon and took back the elephants would be discouraged to do so. This would force the Dutch East India Company to organize the hazardous transportation of elephants to the west coast of India, an undertaking clearly not desirable when the company was "so much in need of funds and the elephant trade is such a fruitful source of income". This was also the reason why the Portuguese had paid so little attention to cultivation.

The second reference to elephant trade is taken from the memoirs of Ryclof van Goens, Governor of Ceylon (1675–79).[25] It begins by stating that "The sale of elephants is a clear source of profit, as they can be captured in any place in Ceylon, and the lack is not of elephants but of purchasers." It goes on to say that wars along the Indian coast, presumably among the jostling European powers, and robberies by the French had injured this trade. The price of elephants had to be reduced to attract buyers who were principally the "Oramis, Loury, Pirmal, and Tinmersja Neyks". Interestingly, van Goens candidly admits that "the amount paid was almost all of it pure profit for the company, as *forced labour* [emphasis mine] played a large part in the elephant hunts, and even the feeding in the stables had to be done free by the inhabitants." Elsewhere, it is also stated that a profit of 150,000 to 200,000 guilders (a considerable sum) was made each year through the sale of elephants in Jaffna and Galle alone.

The Dutch took over the elephant trade almost with a vengeance. Not only did they demand annual tribute from the chiefs of the Wanni in the north, they also successfully organized the capture of large numbers of elephants in the south of the island (figure 8.2). The Dutch *kraal*s, though similar in design to the Portuguese corrals, were more rounded than triangular with a broader funnel to drive the elephants. In 1666 they captured 96 elephants in a single *kraal*,[26] while close to Colombo 160 elephants were secured in another operation.[27] When capturing elephants in the Kandyan kingdom they greatly exceeded their permitted annual quota of 20–30 animals by rounding up 150–200 animals each time.[28] While they continued to use the elephant stables at Matara, the Dutch also held annual sales of elephants at Jaffna in the north. The scale of the trade can be gauged from the fact that, at its peak, Jaffna had 1,500 stalls to house elephants.[29]

The third document dated 1697 is the memoirs of Thomas van Rhee, the Dutch governor of that period.[30] By this time the Dutch had set up elaborate machinery for the capture, training, and sale of elephants. Four permanent *kraal*s had been set up in the district of Matara for the trade. Local inhabitants were compelled to assist in the capture and maintenance of the elephants. Four classes of people to assist in the capture of elephants, and eight classes of people entrusted with tasks relating to training and maintenance of the elephants are described;[31] this is reminiscent of the elephant establishment during Mauryan times described in the *Arthashastra* (see Chapter 3). In 1697 the stalls at Matara had 97 elephants.[32]

During the early decades of the 18th century, the Dutch made an average profit of 100,000 florins a year, a figure that rose to 250,000 florins during 1711 and 1715. The number of elephants sold each year was 75–90 animals, dropping to only 25 or rising to 120 animals; for the year 1740 the Dutch set a target of 100 elephants to be acquired from various regions of the island on the assumption that about 90 of these would survive by the time they were sold.[33] The Dutch also designed special flat-bottomed boats to transport the animals to waiting ships at sea.[34] Merchants from Golconda and the Coromandel coast of India were the main purchasers of elephants during the later Dutch period.[35]

The Kandyan rulers of the island slowly adopted the Portuguese-Dutch method of

Hunc feruant morem Naturæ inftinctu Elephantes:
In foueam incautus cecidit fi forte gregalis,

Auxilium accelerant alij conferre, et in antrum
Moles, ac ramos, terrǽq; immittere glebas.

the *kraal* to capture elephants. The Dutch in the meantime had imposed a ban on other forms of capture; in 1716 the governor Hendrick Becker issued the following order: "The use of pits and nooses has now been forbidden because they injure the animals."[36] The Kandyans, however, ceased to use the elephant in war, recognizing its limitations against muskets and cannon. Rather they began to use their elephants for ceremonial purposes; even today the elephant is the star attraction of the Perahera (festival) at Kandy that had its beginnings during the late 18th century. In 1707 the Kandyan king is reputed to have possessed 300 tuskers,[37] a very high number considering the paucity of tusked male elephants on the island. Either this figure is exaggerated or else the ruler imported many tuskers from India and Burma.[38]

Once the Dutch had established control over the entire Ceylon coastline, following a treaty with the island's rulers in 1766, the encircled Kandyans found their normal trade with the outside world disrupted. They began secret communications with other European nations such as the French for help to evict the Dutch from the island. Eventually it was the British, already established in India, who occupied Ceylon.

***

8.2 Engraving on paper of elephants helping each other to escape from a trap; while one elephant emerges from a pit, six other elephants lift rocks and branches with their trunks. This print made in Antwerp by Jan Collaert II sometime after 1596 was possibly based on accounts in western Europe of elephant capture in an Asian location littered with palm trees. The artist obviously did not have first-hand knowledge of the animal. The Portuguese and later the Dutch actively traded in elephants from Ceylon.
© *Trustees of the British Museum, London.*

8.3 A group of elephants from a timber camp in the Pegu Yomas in Burma, being bathed by their mahouts at a jungle stream (1995). Pegu has a long history in capturing and exporting elephants to places in India and Ceylon.

Before we move on to the British engagement in Asia that lasted for about two centuries, we need to journey to the Sunda region in the east to consider some interesting developments there for the elephant. The trade in elephants was not confined to India and Ceylon. Burma was an important player in the trade as well for several centuries, while other regions such as the Malay Peninsula, Sumatra, and even Java in the Sunda shelf participated to some extent. The kingdom of Pegu in south-central Burma was the most active in capturing and exporting elephants to India and Ceylon (figure 8.3). The ban imposed in the 12th century by king Ramanna of Pegu on the export of elephants, primarily to Ceylon,[39] may have been relaxed or ignored sooner rather than later. Elephants were being captured regularly in the kingdom of Pegu, famous as the land of the White Elephant, during the 16th century as well as being exported to the kingdoms of Narsyngna (Vijayanagara), Malabar, and Cambaya (Gujarat) at this time.[40] There is no reason to believe that elephants were not being sent to Ceylon as well. Ralph Fitch, a pioneer English voyager to India, Ceylon, and Burma during the late 16th century, records that the king of Pegu had "aboue [about] fiue [five] thousand elephants of warre [war], beside many other which be not taught to fight".[41] Interestingly, the Burmese elephants are described as "monstrous huge" as compared to the Ceylonese elephants, though the latter were superior in fighting in spite of their small size.[42]

Sunda states such as the Malay Peninsula, Sumatra, and Java had a thriving elephant culture that died out during precolonial or colonial times. The Aceh region in northern Sumatra had an indigenous elephant culture that later disappeared. The sultan of Malacca

8.4 A young bull elephant captured from the wild at the Lok Kawi Wildlife Park in Sabah, Borneo (2008). Note the characteristic long tail with bushy hair that touches the ground. The origin of the wild Bornean elephant is a mystery with the possibility either that these originated in Java or that they have been isolated on the island of Borneo for about 300,000 years.

(Melaka) in the Malay Peninsula rode an elephant in ceremony during the 15th century.[43] As in South Asia, the elephant was a state animal in the Malay Peninsula and islands of the East Indies. When the Portuguese invaded Malacca in 1511, the Malays opposed them with 20 war elephants,[44] though the elephants may have come from elsewhere. Java imported elephants from Kedah in 1651 and from Johore in 1682,[45] while the Dutch governor of Batavia sent elephants from Perak in 1752.[46] Further, elephants from Aceh and Perak were exported to India during the 17th–18th centuries.[47] Thus, a complex maritime trade in live elephants existed both regionally and between South and Southeast Asia during the 15th–18th centuries. The trade originally set up by local rulers and merchants was later appropriated by the colonial powers.

The most interesting aspect of this trade in elephants relates to the origin of elephants on the island of Borneo. The wild elephants here are confined to the northeastern part of the island, in the Malaysian state of Sabah (figure 8.4), with small numbers extending their range south into the Indonesian province of Kalimantan.[48] This mystery has engaged the attention of zoologists and writers since the 19th century.[49] The maritime trade in elephants in this region has a major bearing on resolving this mystery.

The presence of elephants on the island of Sulu, in the southern Philippine chain, was known since the later half of the 16th century.[50] This was obviously a feral population of elephants descended from captive animals imported onto the island. It is recorded that two elephants from the Hindu raja of Java were presented to Raja Baginda of Sulu in 1395, and may have eventually established a feral population at the western end of the island. The Spanish governor of Manila sent an expedition in 1579 with the intention of procuring two or three tame elephants from the sultan at Jolo, the port city of Sulu. European travellers of the late 18th and early 19th centuries noted the presence of considerable numbers of wild-living elephants that ravaged the agricultural crops; in fact, John Hunt recorded that in 1814 the Sulu people "no longer venerated [the elephant] under their new religion [i.e. Islam]", and destroyed them whenever they encountered the elephants and even "instituted a grand hunting match every year" for this purpose.[51] By 1848 the elephant had disappeared from Sulu.

The historical trade in elephants had not bypassed the island of Borneo. As early as 1521 delegates from the ship *Victoria*, a part of the Spanish navigator Magellan's fleet that reached Brunei, were taken to the ruler's palace on caparisoned elephants. No elephant seems to have been present at the royal court of Brunei during the late 18th and early 19th centuries. At the southern end of the island the sultan of Banjarmasin was reputed to ride a royal elephant during the late 19th century.

We now return to the question of where the sizeable population of elephants in Sabah came from. It is impossible for captive elephants from Brunei or Banjarmasin to have colonized Sabah. Two other possibilities have been debated. First, the elephants of Sabah could be a remnant of an indigenous population that was isolated during the glacial cycles accompanied by drastic changes in sea levels during the Pleistocene (see Chapter 1). Second, the elephants may have originated from captive animals that a mid-18th-century sultan of Sulu, who also controlled a large area of northeastern Borneo, released from stocks on his island or from a gift received from the East India Company.[52] His motive may have been to assert his suzerainty over a part of Borneo or divert an unwelcome gift in order to avoid the nuisance value of elephants already present in Sulu.

The fossil evidence for the presence of elephants in Borneo during the Pleistocene is rather equivocal. The single molar tooth of an elephant supposedly from a cave in Brunei, and taken by D.A. Hooijer as support for past distribution, has since been questioned.[53] In 2003 a widely publicized study by Prithviraj Fernando and associates came to the conclusion that the Bornean elephant was native to the island, genetically distinct from other Asian elephant populations, and had evolved independently after it split from a common ancestor in the Sunda region at least 300,000 years ago.[54]

The story does not stop here. P.S. Shim has marshalled the historical evidence to suggest that the elephants of Sulu, and of those in northeastern Borneo if derived from the former, would have most probably originated in Java.[55] Fossil teeth of elephant, dated to only a few thousand years ago, found in cave deposits at Sampoeng in Java suggest the occurrence of a now-extinct race named *Elephas maximus sondaicus* by palaeontologist P.E.P. Deraniyagala.[56] That the elephant persisted on the island into historical times can perhaps be inferred from its representation in superb carvings at the 8th–9th century Buddhist monument of Borobudur (see Chapter 5). Based on these considerations as well as new historical material on the genealogy of the sultans of Sulu, Shim concludes that Java is the most likely source for the Borneo elephant.[57]

I have examined the bas-reliefs at Borobudur in some detail. Most of the carvings depict captive elephants associated with a story of the Buddha. However, a few scenes show what seem to be free-ranging elephants along with other creatures such as monkeys in the forest (figure 8.5). The elephant depictions, captive and free-ranging, are very realistic, suggesting that the artists of Borobudur had intimate knowledge of these animals. They could not have created such superb carvings otherwise. Could these depictions be taken as evidence that wild elephants were present in Java at that time? I am not sure; it is possible that the master carvers of Borobudur were merely translating

8.5 Depiction of wild elephants in a forest scene on a bas-relief at Borobudur in central Java, 9th century CE. As compared to many other reliefs featuring royal elephants or animals with riders, the elephants in this scene are clearly not captive animals.

their first-hand knowledge of captive elephants in Java to illustrate Buddhist stories, and perhaps imagining a natural forest scene with creatures they used in their depictions. It is also possible that some of the carvers came from lands outside of Java where they were familiar with elephants. The jury is still out on this issue.

***

We now return to India, Burma, and Ceylon which had the largest populations of wild elephants in Asia. The British engagement with the animal took on a different colour from that of the earlier European powers or of the local rulers. Rather than trading in elephants, the British began to capture them in order to use them in the military and in exploiting the rich timber resources of the region, or to indulge in their favourite sport of big-game hunting.

As the East India Company infiltrated the subcontinent, the British realized the value and importance of elephants to achieving their goal of exploiting the natural resources of the land (figure 8.6). Sujit Sivasundaram's insightful analysis of the Company's relationship with the elephant is an importance source for examining this period in the elephant's history.[58] As the British began to observe the pervading influence of the elephant in the social, economic, political, and cultural life of the land they had occupied, they appropriated this knowledge and transformed it to fulfil their needs. By the time the colonial era came to an end in Asia about two centuries later, the British had reinvented an elephant culture in which a strange anthropomorphism first clashed with but then yielded to the emerging revolution in the natural sciences.

The British began their engagement with the elephant by using it for military transport during the late 18th century.[59] In the preceding decades, the Mughals had received their elephants from the zamindars of Sylhet and Dhaka in eastern Bengal (presently Bangladesh). The British focused on controlling the supply of elephants from this region. The Company initially organized the capture of elephants; however the capture operations soon became too expensive and so the Company turned to the local market for its supply. Many British officers apparently took advantage of this new arrangement to organize the captures themselves and sell the animals to the Company,

BREED against BULK or the Bucks attack on the Leadenhall Street Elephants

8.6 Satire on the East India Company, represented by men seated on two elephants. This print made by Charles Williams and published by S. Knight in 1813 is titled "Breed against bulk or the Bucks attack on the Leadenhall Street Elephants". The Ministry attacks the Company by sending a stag, representing Lord Buckinghamshire, laden with documents inscribed "India Bill". One of the elephants has seized the India Bill in its trunk as one of the ministers exclaims "Zounds how that Animal tosses the Bills about by the God of Physick they'll all be lost."

© Trustees of the British Museum, London.

making considerable personal profit in the process.[60] Two officers, William M. Thackeray, the first collector of Sylhet in 1772, and his successor Robert Lindsay seem to have particularly benefited from the capture and sale of elephants in addition to the shooting of tigers. Thackeray, in fact, even won a legal battle against the Company for its refusal to pay him for 66 elephants, including 50 that died, that were transported from Patna in the north to Belgaum in the south.

Elephants were sent to the south presumably to strengthen the Company's military presence there. The British had successfully kept their old rivals, the French, in check but still had to deal with two important Indian powers, the Marathas and the Muslim rulers of Mysore. Haidar Ali, a highly successful military commander of the Wodeyar rulers of Mysore, usurped the kingdom in about 1761. Haidar possessed many elephants including a "white elephant" that he rode on ceremonial occasions.[61] His son Tipu Sultan who succeeded the Mysore throne in 1782 built up a formidable army to challenge several powers in the peninsula including the Marathas and the Nizam of Hyderabad. In 1790 Tipu's army was reported to possess 700 elephants; in fact a British officer wrote in 1798 that Tipu has "as many elephants, camels and draught and carriage cattle as he ever can require" (figures 8.7 and 8.8).[62] Many of these elephants undoubtedly came from captures in the rich forests of the Western Ghats. Tipu had a formidable presence in the forests of Mysore, the Nilgiris, and the Wyanad that are still home to an abundant population of elephants. He used his elephants not only for carrying baggage but also to terrify or

8.7 Mural at the Daria Daulat or Tipu's summer palace (1784–91), Srirangapatana, depicting the use of the elephant as a royal mount in battle. A young Tipu inside a howdah on elephantback accompanies his father Sultan Haidar Ali, also on an elephant (outside the frame), in the battle of Polilur or the Second Mysore War against the British forces led by Colonel Baillie. *Photographed with the kind permission of the Archaeological Survey of India.*

execute his enemies by tying them to the foot of an elephant and dragging them over the ground, a gruesome practice that is undoubtedly much older (figure 8.9).[63] Tipu defied the British in many ways such as changing the calendar, introducing new weights and measures, and even issuing new coins some of which featured the elephant.

In 1790, the British governor-general Cornwallis concluded treaties with the Maratha Peshwa and the Nizam to launch an offensive against Tipu. His preparations included collecting 28,000 bullocks from the Carnatic and 100 elephants from Oudh (Awadh in central Uttar Pradesh).[64] The army had at least another 50 elephants to fight Tipu.[65] The British seemed anxious to ensure that their elephants were well fed and fit for work. For this purpose they first gathered information of how Tipu maintained his large elephant stocks. Captain Barclay who was in charge of elephants observed that it was essential to offer them ghee (clarified butter) and gur (jaggery) for their well-being.[66] With this powerful force Cornwallis managed to dent Tipu's defences at Seringapatam (Srirangapatana, an island on the Kaveri river) sufficiently to force the latter into agreeing to a humiliating peace that included handing over two of his young sons as hostages. Tipu was finally killed at Srirangapatana in 1799 by the British under the leadership of Wellesley in a landmark victory that brought the large kingdom of Mysore firmly under their control. The Mysore kingdom was restored to a child prince of the former Wodeyar dynasty. And the defeat of the Marathas in 1817–18 now brought virtually the entire subcontinent under British rule.

8.8 This satirical print titled "Good News from Madras" was published by William Holland at London in 1791. The imaginary scene shows a victorious Tipu, seated on an elephant which tramples and rends British soldiers, receiving the sword of Lord Cornwallis who has surrendered. A well-dressed man watches the scene while the inscription beside him reads "The Patriot's eye in a fine phrensy rolling...".
© *Trustees of the British Museum, London.*

8.9 Trained elephants executing the followers of Khan Zaman, an enemy of the Mughal emperor Akbar, in a painting conceived by Miskina and completed by Banwali the Elder, from the *Akbarnama*, late 16th century.
Courtesy: Victoria and Albert Museum, London.

GOOD NEWS FROM MADRAS.

During the 19th century the British built up stocks of elephant mainly in the south and the east of the subcontinent, the two most important regions for wild elephant populations. Once Mysore was under their control, the British too were swayed by the long-standing belief that Ceylonese elephants were superior to local ones. In 1800 the Company set up an agreement with the British government of Ceylon for the supply of elephants to augment their stocks at Mysore. This experiment was however short-lived. Many of the imported elephants died in passage or after reaching Mysore. British financial prudence soon overcame all other considerations; the auditor-general of the military noted that Ceylonese elephants costing 2,000 rupees each need not be purchased when Bengali elephants could be procured for only 250 rupees each.[67]

The increasing use of sophisticated firearms had made the elephant superfluous in direct battle. Elephants were however needed to haul heavy guns, and as baggage carriers in swampy and mountainous terrain (figure 8.10). The mapping of India (the Great Indian Arc of the Meridian), that began in 1800 at the southern tip of Kanyakumari and was completed nearly 50 years later in the snowclad peaks of the Himalaya, was achieved

8.10 British army elephants drawing heavy artillery along the Khyber Pass at Campbellpur, photographed by William Jackson Henry, 1895.

Courtesy: Library of Congress, Washington DC.

only through the use of elephants not to carry the surveyors but also the heavy survey equipment weighing half a ton. At the swollen river Krishna, George Everest noted the fortunate presence of "these powerful animals" that "were more at home in the water than any other quadruped", which enabled the surveyors to achieve the crossing safely with men and theodolite.[68]

The British established a military commissariat by 1810 in Bengal; one of its responsibilities was to maintain a stock of elephants. Elements of a standardized management of elephants now began to emerge. The British borrowed heavily from Indian traditions, especially Mughal, of elephant management, but over the decades also incorporated new principles based on the emerging European science of veterinary medicine.[69] One of the recommendations made to the commissariat was to capture elephants from Awadh as an alternative to Bengal.[70] Record-keeping and reporting were important requirements of the new regulations. These were vital to the aim of increasing the efficiency of managing the Company's elephants many of which were dying of ill-health.[71]

The Company soon found that they also had to deal with the problems of people affected directly by wild elephants. In 1822 the collector of Coimbatore in the Madras Presidency admitted that nearly half the area of the district was "subject to the ravages of the elephants".[72] The scenario was similar in the district of Madurai whose collector sent a note to his counterpart at Coimbatore with advice on how to trap elephants.[73] The Company had in the meantime done away with the services of 7,000–8,000 guards employed specifically to keep wild elephants away from cultivation. Efforts to reintroduce this system at Coimbatore seem to have failed. Instead, elephant trappers from Chittagong were brought in to train a select group at Coimbatore in the northeastern method of capturing the animal.[74]

British control of a tropical land rich in natural resources also opened up possibilities of exploiting these to feed the expanding imperial power.[75] As a seafaring nation the British shipyards back home and at Bombay needed timber for the construction of vessels, and the forests of India and Burma provided high quality timber in plenty. The opening of the Indian railways in 1853 likewise created an enormous demand for teak, sal, and deodar wood to be used as sleepers.[76] Timber was also needed for the construction of buildings at hill-stations at various locations that provided cooler climes for respite from the torrid summer heat of the plains.

In 1807 the company appointed a conservator of forests "to preserve and improve the protection of teak and other timber suitable for shipbuilding".[77] A monopoly over timber resources in the Malabar and Travancore region was soon established; in addition, the company began experiments with raising teak plantations at Nilambur. During the first half of the 19th century the British procured timber largely from merchants. For instance, during the 1830s an important region of supply was the Dangs in the west. A British agent at Surat would be entrusted with the purchase of teak for use in the naval dockyards at Bombay.[78] The unregulated exploitation of forests caused concern and ultimately resulted in the introduction of scientific forestry, based on German and French schools of this discipline. In 1856, Dietrich Brandis, a German botanist, was appointed superintendent of forests in Burma. This was soon followed by the creation of the Indian Forest Service in 1864, half a century before anything similar was set up in Britain itself.

The elephant was vital to British forestry operations in India and Burma. Thus the "timber elephant" was born, an epithet that continues to persist in the literature today even after the animal's role in dragging timber has diminished or disappeared altogether in most parts of Asia.

The Indian revolt of 1857 brought sweeping changes to the political administration of the subcontinent. The following year the rule of the East India Company was transferred to the British crown, ushering in the Raj. In the meantime the British were also gradually gaining control over Burma after a series of wars beginning in 1823–24 that culminated in Burma being attached to the British Empire on January 1, 1886.

While the army continued to maintain elephants for military purposes, the capture and management of elephants seems to have become the responsibility of the newly emerged forestry service during the mid-19th century. The British possibly initially made use of the elephant stocks maintained by the rulers of Nilambur to extract timber from the moist forests in the Malabar region before setting up their own elephant establishment.[79] The wasteful exploitation of timber and depletion of the Malabar forests during the first half of the 19th century spurred the British to explore more efficient means of extraction; elephant power was possibly one such means to achieve sustainable forestry. The elephant command language, incorporating Urdu and Assamese words, still prevalent today in the elephant camp in the Anamalai forests of the south suggests that aspects of a northeastern system of elephant management were introduced here by the British quite early.[80]

The major elephant-catching establishments were naturally in the northeast and in the south of the country, the two regions with the largest wild elephant populations. Of these the northeast was by far the more important, with capturing operations in the forests of Chittagong, in Assam and, later, Jalpaiguri.[81] Dacca (Dhaka) was the headquarters of the Bengal *kheddah*, under the charge of a permanent superintendent, responsible for holding the animals captured in the region. G.P. Sanderson, a British officer based at Mysore, who held temporary charge as the superintendent of the Dacca elephant-catching establishment during 1875–76 describes the *kheddah* as follows:

8.11 *Kheddah* painting by Rama Varma (b. 1879) at the Jaganmohan palace, Mysore. Elephants are shown inside the stockade being roped by mahouts on trained elephants as spectators outside the stockade watch the operations. *Photographed with kind permission.*

The Peelkhána, or elephant depot, is situated just outside the town, and covers an area approaching one quarter-mile square. It consists of an intrenched quadrangular piece of ground in which the elephants' pickets are arranged in long rows. At each picket is a masonry flooring, with a post at the head and foot, to which the animals are secured. The flooring is necessary to prevent them kicking up the earth. Along one side of the quadrangle is a shed several hundred feet long, in which the elephants can be kept during the heat of the day. There is also a hospital for sick elephants; houses for gear and stores; a native doctor's room for treating the attendants; a shelter for howdahs and ropes, &c. The depot is situated close to the river for convenience of bathing and watering the elephants, and also that fodder may be brought by boats.[82]

The Dacca establishment maintained 50 *koonkie* elephants, curiously all of them female, for use in capturing wild elephants generally during the winter months of December–March. Sanderson records that during 1936–39 an annual average of 69 elephants were captured, while during the seven years prior to his tenure (1875–76) this averaged 59 elephants.[83]

From these levels of capture during the mid-19th century, the rates of capture increased dramatically by the last quarter of the century.[84] The annual captures averaged 168 elephants during 1876–80 in the Dacca hills alone[85] in addition to 400 elephants each year in the Garo hills during the late 19th century.[86] This pattern of large-scale capture in the northeast continued into the first half of the 20th century. During 1911–14 the captures in the Garo hills averaged 85 elephants annually while a whopping 621 elephants were captured during two years (1916–17) in the forests of Goalpara in Bengal.[87]

8.12 The last *kheddah* operations at Kabini in Mysore during 1970–71. Mahouts on elephants are seen driving a wild herd of elephants along the river, and eventually into a stockade where they would be restrained and roped.
Courtesy: R. Anandakrishna.

The story was the same in the Sibsagar-Naga hills where 900 elephants, or an annual average of 300 animals, were captured during 1934–36.[88] In the dozen years (1937–50) before India became a republic, a total of 3,026 elephants were taken from the forests of Assam.[89]

In contrast to the northeast the scale of capture in the south was modest. Part of the reason was that elephants were captured in small numbers, usually totalling under 10 animals a year in the Madras Presidency and 20 animals a year in Mysore, by the pit method.[90] Sanderson introduced the *kheddah* method of capture to the princely state of Mysore in 1874, but even here the captures averaged less than 30 animals a year (figures 8.11 and 8.12).[91]

Haidar Ali, the first Muslim ruler of Mysore, had attempted to capture elephants within a stockade in the jungles at Kakanakote but failed. He had apparently pronounced a curse on anyone trying to do so. Sanderson's first attempt in November 1873 in the Biligirirangans failed, as prophesied by Haidar, but the following year he succeeded in securing 53 elephants in a *kheddah* operation at the foothills of this range.[92] *Kheddah* captures continued in the Biligirirangans until 1947; in the meantime similar operations had already begun in the jungles of Kakanakote.[93] Over a period of nearly a century since the first *kheddah* in 1874 in the south, a total of nearly 2,000 elephants were captured at these two Mysore sites.[94]

In the meantime, the British took over the *kraal*s of the Dutch in Ceylon. After organizing two captures during 1800–01 near Tangalla and Negombo, the British seem to have realized their own limitations and accepted the skills of the Kandyan chiefs in this venture;[95] we do know however that these chiefs organized *kraal*s exclusively in their own provinces. In 1828 the British passed a law prohibiting the capture of elephants, except on behalf of the government, only to repeal it three years later.[96] The British also brought in elephant-catchers from Bengal sometime during the early 1840s for employment in the Ceylon Elephant Establishment.[97] The captured elephants were used by the Company for clearing the jungle and hauling loads. The death rate among the

8.13 Elephants dragging timber along a river in Burma, depicted in a 20th-century mural from a building at Yangon. *Artist unknown.*

elephants seems to have been very high at this time. Historian James Tennent records that, of the 240 elephants in the service of the government, a large number died within two years.[98] The elephant department began to be neglected over time and was finally abolished in 1882, though the Kandyan chief continued to capture elephants.[99] The scale of captures can be gauged from the figures of elephant exports gathered by Jayantha Jayewardene from the British administration reports; these total 3,243 elephants between 1853 and 1894.[100]

The task of procuring elephants to exploit the great teak forests of Burma seems to have been vested with the Bombay Burmah Trading Corporation (BBTC). Set up in India in 1863, BBTC soon became the leading producer of teak in Burma and one of the leading companies in Siam (Thailand). Burma itself came entirely under British control in 1886. On the other hand, Siam remained free from colonial rule; the Siamese king Mongkut, however, signed a treaty of friendship and commerce with Britain in 1855, and later with several European powers. Siam also granted teak concessions to many European firms including the BBTC.[101] At the turn of the 20th century the BBTC had 2,000–3,000 elephants.[102] Nearly half a century later, between 6,000 and 7,000 adult elephants were at work in the Burmese timber industry; to this has to be added another 4,000 sub-adult elephants they would have held (figure 8.13).[103] No estimates are available on the numbers of elephants completely outside of the timber industry but this could have been another 5,000–10,000 animals just prior to World War II.[104] Such large captive stocks are corroborated by available figures of elephants captured in Burma during the first half of the 20th century; between 1910 and 1950 at least 12,080 elephants were captured, with another 3,370 or more elephants destroyed.[105] Elephants for timber operations in Burma also came from Siam and Assam.

Records of death or serious injury to elephants caught in pits are not available. The pit method was confined to southern India, mainly the Madras Presidency. It should be possible to reconstruct some of these data from archival records but we have a clearer idea for the *kheddah* captures in Mysore. The 285 deaths recorded among the 1,977 animals captured during 1873–1971 amounts to a casualty rate of nearly one in seven captures.[106] The death rate was especially high during the earlier period. Among the approximately 1,000 Commissariat elephants in Bengal in 1874–75, Sanderson records that 114 elephants died in one year, a rate that can be taken as "a fair annual average".[107] The Burmese *kheddahs*, too, presumably took a heavy toll, though reliable figures are not available.

The British were concerned at the high rate of mortality and morbidity among the elephants during capture and post-capture. Although the British officers in charge of the elephants did not necessarily dismiss the traditional knowledge of elephant care, they began to question the efficacy of several traditional practices.[108] Drawing upon the emerging European science of veterinary medicine, especially the experience in rearing of horses, the British began to reinvent elephant husbandry in India and Burma. As early as 1841 William Gilchrist, assistant surgeon of the company's army at Hunsur in Mysore, published an encyclopaedic survey of elephant diseases with the aim of increasing the usefulness of elephants to the army.[109] Adoption of the emerging veterinary science in the treatment of elephants was obviously slow. Wilberforce Clarke of the Royal Engineers observed in 1879 that in "the treatment of elephants, the subject seems to be chaotic and empirical…no scientific attention seems to have been paid to the subject. There seems to be room for great improvement…. From an economic point of view, ignorance regarding such a costly animal is very costly, as from it arise (a) invaliding of the animals for long periods of time and (b) high mortality."[110] At the turn of the 20th century it became standard practice for a veterinarian from Britain to be attached to each timber elephant establishment; later Indian and Burmese veterinarians began to take over this role. A landmark publication from Burma, *Elephants and their Diseases*, by G.H. Evans in 1901 became the bible of the new science of elephant health care in the colonial establishment.[111]

Elephant husbandry in the 20th century now incorporated elements of the traditional and the modern. An enlightened British officer, A.J.W. Milroy, made perhaps some of the most radical changes in the post-capture treatment and training of elephants.[112] Working in Assam, Milroy ended the practice of starving newly caught elephants, replaced the vicious metal objects used to control them with sharp sticks, and brought in many positive changes in the management of animals in the stockade.[113] The British continued with several ayurvedic medicinal preparations but also tried to discontinue the use of others such as *ganja* (*Cannabis sativa*) for sedation and control of recalcitrant bulls in musth.[114] Vaccination for anthrax, a major cause of death among forest-based elephants was introduced in 1926 in the Madras Presidency, and in 1935 in Burma. A more scientific diet of cooked food to supplement the fodder obtained from the forest was introduced. Strangely, the Malabar practice of feeding cooked goat's meat to elephants in poor condition seems to have continued in the Madras Presidency through the British period. Necropsy procedures were introduced; these presumably helped in the scientific diagnosis of ailments for further improvements in management. Most important, the British introduced systematic record-keeping in the establishments under their direct control. The result was certainly much improved elephant husbandry in the forest-camps during the 20th century even after the British had departed. For instance, an analysis of reproduction, health, and longevity among the elephants in forest camps of the Madras Presidency showed that these were among the best maintained captive groups globally.[115]

Continuing in the tradition of scientific husbandry of elephants introduced by the British, two Indian veterinarians, S. Gopalan (in the early–mid-20th century) and V. Krishnamurthy (1927–2002), played critical roles in the success of captive elephants in the Madras Presidency. Indeed, the experienced Assam elephant-catcher P.D. Stracey, writing in 1963, states that "nowhere have I seen elephants so well maintained and so well cared for as in the south".[116] The Burmese management of elephants, too, excelled as seen from potentially self-sustaining populations; for instance, when the BBTC's stocks reached about 2,000 animals it was seen that births balanced the deaths, and it was no more necessary to obtain animals from the wild.[117] Before the onset of World War II about 70% of Burma's 6,000 working elephants had been born in captivity.[118]

***

We now examine a rather dishonourable facet of the colonial relationship with the elephant in Asia, namely, the slaughter of the elephant for sport. Two thousand years ago the hill tribes in southern India had killed elephants for meat and ivory; several centuries later the sultans of Delhi and the imperial Mughals had hunted lions, tigers, and wild pig from elephantback and the Mughal "elephant hunts" were restricted to capture of the animals. Even today the elephant is killed across Asia for ivory, and in many regions elephant meat is consumed. The British period in Asia, however, introduced a new ethos in the elephant-human relationship in the form of killing for sport or fun.

British historian John MacKenzie has identified three qualitatively distinct phases in the pursuit of hunting by Europeans in southern and central Africa.[119] The first was commercial hunting for ivory and products such as skins. The second was what he describes as "subsidy for the second level of European advance, the period of acquisition, conquest, and settlement".[120] The third and most interesting aspect was hunting as a socio-cultural phenomenon or a "contemporary rediscovery of medieval chivalry" linked to ritualized warfare.[121] This is a useful framework for examining the hunting of elephants in Asia during the British period.

The shikar genre of English literature is vast; indeed much of the natural history accounts of colonial lands were in the context of hunting. Lahiri-Choudhury has brought together a sample of these elephant shikar writings with an insightful introductory essay on hunting as a way of colonial life.[122] Commerce was obviously on the minds of early British officials such as William Thackeray and Robert Lindsay, collectors of Sylhet during the late 18th century, who made elephant capturing a private enterprise for personal profit. On the other hand, commerce from ivory was probably not that important – remember that female Asian elephants do not carry tusks (but only small tushes) and many males too do not have tusks; in contrast both females and males of the African elephant possess tusks and yield far greater volumes of ivory. The slaughter of large numbers of elephants, in the hundreds or even in the thousands, would obviously have yielded quantities of ivory of some value. For instance, Thomas Rogers who shot elephants in Ceylon during the mid-19th century is credited with having "bought his successive steps in the army, from a subaltern to a major" using the value of the ivory he obtained.[123] Some value was also extracted by the locals from tail hair (used in bracelets fashioned by goldsmiths; commonly believed to be a lucky charm even now) or teeth (fashioned into objects such as knife-handles and presse-papiers). However, Tennent states that the "incessant slaughter of elephants by sportsmen in Ceylon, appears to be merely in subordination to the influence of the organ of destructiveness...."[124]

The wanton slaughter of elephants by colonial hunters had elements of what MacKenzie refers to as European conquest and subjugation of a strange land. Environmental historian Mahesh Rangarajan reinforces this view. According to him the elephant, like the tiger, was to the British just another large denizen of the jungle whose killing symbolized the conquest of a vast subcontinent by a small group of men.[125] This was not necessarily the case during the early period of British occupation of South Asia. Lahiri-Choudhury points out that Thomas Williamson had written in his *Oriental Field Sports* (1807) that "no native of Bengal nor any European resident there, would undertake such a piece of rashness as to go out shooting elephants".[126] Thus the idea of sport hunting of elephants in Asia became ingrained in the British upper classes after 1807.

Lahiri-Choudhury suggests that elephant hunting as sport had become accepted in Ceylon before 1826 in contrast to the strict protection accorded to the animal by the Kandyan rulers.[127] For Samuel White Baker, whose *Rifle and Hound in Ceylon* (1854) became "a manifesto of English big-game hunters", elephant hunting was "the most dangerous of all sports". Baker and his friends shot dozens of elephants during their sporting trips into the Ceylonese jungles but these figures pale in comparison to what some of their contemporaries achieved. The name of Major Thomas Rogers figures prominently in any discussion of sport hunting of Asian elephants. This "sportsman" killed upwards of 1,200 elephants in Ceylon during the mid-19th century.[128] Two other army men, Captain Gallwey and Major Skinner between them killed at least an equal number of elephants on the island. The colonial government also offered bounty of a few shillings per head and this was claimed for 3,500 elephants over a 3-year period (1845–48) in the northern province and 2,000 elephants during 1851–56 in the southern province of the island (figure 8.14).[129] We thus have a total of over 8,000 elephants slaughtered in Ceylon within a short period during the mid-19th century – a mind-boggling figure considering that this possibly exceeds the number found on the island today.

Such indiscriminate slaughter of elephants was perhaps relatively less in India and Burma, but this is a topic that is yet to be systematically researched. Gun licences seem to have been issued rather freely by the British authorities for control of crop-raiding elephants. As early as 1919, a British resident of Tellicherry (Thalassery) in the Malabar region wrote of "a grand elephant hunt next month, in the hills between here and Coimbatore; ordered by Government to check the elephants' crop damage; last such hunt was in Tippo's time; Tippo's vast dyked area of several miles at Coimbatore now being made ready again...."[130] We know that during the 1820s the administration at Coimbatore was grappling with the issue of protecting crops from raiding elephants.[131] In Burma the thousands of guns distributed among villagers for keeping away elephants from their fields were also used rather indiscriminately for poaching other animals.[132] Incomplete figures suggest that between 1928 and 1941 at least 3,770 elephants were destroyed in the country under crop-protection measures.[133] Presumably both peasants and sportsmen had a part in the destruction of elephants.

AN ELEPHANT HUNT IN CEYLON

8.14 An elephant hunt in Ceylon:
1. Kottiar canoes passing "Round Island",
2. The village of Kottiar, 3. Native bridge
over a river, 4. The first shot, 5. The
second shot, 6. The death, 7. The return
– crossing the river by raft, 8. A Veddah
who offers his services, 9. Kanda Kandu,
the ferryman, 10. The hunter (identified
simply as Mr J.M.) posing between two
natives, Sinnacooty and Allah Pitchei.
From The Graphic, *London, December 3, 1887.*

At the peak of colonial expansion, hunting was elevated to "the Hunt", with a capital H, a distinct cultural movement in "pursuit of manliness and moral edification through sportsmanship" as MacKenzie puts it.[134] The analogy that MacKenzie draws between the Hunt and medieval practices of ritualistic warfare and chivalry is perhaps not too farfetched, nor is the element of sexual selection lost on a society "increasingly obsessed with social Darwinism and notions of eugenics".[135] Indeed, the Hunt gave rise to a distinct moral code for late 19th- and early 20th-century European society in fields as diverse as literature, education, iconography, and military training.

There were some differences in the practice of the Hunt in Africa and in Asia. The former was still largely a wilderness teeming with wildlife in the savannas that could be easily disposed off by the hundreds with the gun; thus administrators, missionaries, traders, explorers, soldiers, famous personalities such as Randolph Churchill – in short, almost every European visitor or settler – indulged in hunting big game. The meat itself was often used to compensate native labourers, usually starved of protein, who built the railways and raised the colonial settlements. In Asia sport hunting seemed to be the prerogative of a more exclusive club of senior administrators, military men, and visiting royalty. For one, game was more restricted across the Asian continent in comparison to Africa. Second, the strong cultural abhorrence of meat as food over a large part of the Indian subcontinent, at least among the upper classes, would have rendered meat less attractive as a currency. In fact, one question that begs an answer is how the British managed to get away with sport hunting of the elephant, a creature widely revered in mainstream Hindu and Buddhist cultures, a sentiment respected by even the Islamic

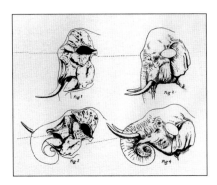

8.15 "Diagrams shewing the position of the Elephants Brain", obviously referring to the point where a hunter should take aim to shoot it.
Line drawings from Sanderson (1878).

rulers. It was one thing to hunt deer or wild pig, it was entirely another matter to hunt the sacred elephant. A possible answer is that rural people could have seen the destruction of the elephant as bringing them relief from a creature that ravaged their crop fields. The famous novelist George Orwell confesses that, as a young police official in Burma, he was "hated by large numbers" of people; it was only after reluctantly shooting a rather truculent elephant that had killed a labourer that he became a hero in local eyes.[136]

The colonial sportsmen evolved their own rules of conduct in hunting, ostensibly to assert a moral superiority in the manner that animals were killed. Thus, Samuel Baker wrote that "there is a great difference between elephant-killing and elephant-hunting; the latter is sport, the former is slaughter".[137] Sport hunting was for the gentleman, killing was the handiwork of the savage. The shikar literature is also obsessed with conveying to the reader the perfect way to stalk and shoot an elephant with a single shot that penetrated the skull through to the brain; thus a knowledge of the anatomy of the animal, especially its skull was important, so that the various angles from which it could be shot cleanly was understood and mastered (figure 8.15). Sportsmen after all should not draw too much blood and make a mess of this blood-sport. The obsession with bagging an animal with the most impressive trophy, the tusks in the case of the elephant, was justified as merely culling an individual past its reproductive stage. Modern scientific studies certainly do not support this assumption as regards the elephant; we know that reproductive success increases with age in bull elephants,[138] that bulls with longer tusks may be more resistant to parasites and diseases,[139] and that trophy hunting would reduce the genetic quality of many large mammalian populations.[140] Nevertheless, the myth that sport hunters are merely eliminating useless individuals persists to this day.

Not all prominent Britons were hunters. Historian James E. Tennent, whose piece on the elephant is a prominent part of his tome on Ceylon, confesses that persons like himself "are not addicted to what is called 'sport'...a pursuit which presents nothing but the monotonous recurrence of scenes of blood and suffering". He goes on to rubbish several of the claims of sportsmen who would have others believe that they are "tender-hearted men, who shun cruelty to an animal".[141] At the same time, Indian royalty too indulged itself on occasion in hunting elephants during the 20th century, though most of the animals shot seem to have been "rogue" bulls.[142]

Faced with the prospects of rapidly declining elephant stocks in the wild, the Madras government had issued a ukase in 1871 against the killing of elephants, the earliest official attempt to protect a mammal in British India.[143] The Madras Presidency followed this up the following year by passing a law, which came into effect in October 1873, to halt the indiscriminate killing of elephants. Troublesome elephants could, of course, be killed under licence. The Elephant Preservation Act of 1879, first covering India and later extended to Burma, gave protection to elephants, but more important also established the British government's monopoly over an important economic resource, as Lahiri-Choudhury points out.[144] Legal attempts at conservation of elephants in Ceylon seem to have begun with an ordinance in 1891 to prevent the wanton destruction of various game including the elephant.[145] More effective legislation came only in 1938 with the Flora and Fauna Protection Ordinance (1937) that also helped create two national parks, Wilpattu in the north and Yala in the south of the island. These legal measures possibly provided some respite in the large-scale hunting of elephants in British India, Burma, and Ceylon, but hunting under licence and as sport, as well as the capture of elephants, continued as evidenced from available records.

The colonial period also witnessed major transformation of the elephant's habitat across South Asia. Selective logging of moist forests for teak, sal, and other trees would

8.16 An elephant herd moving through a tea plantation in the Valparai plateau in the Anamalais, southern India (2005).
Courtesy: Anand Kumar.

have opened up the canopy, increased the frequency of ground fires, and allowed bamboo, perennial grasses, and other weedy plants to invade the forest floor, thus creating secondary vegetation more attractive to elephants.[146] At the same time the raising of monoculture plantations of teak or other timber trees would have rendered the habitat less attractive to elephants.[147] The more serious change was the large-scale loss of habitat as a result of converting forests into commercial plantations of coffee and tea beginning the early to mid-19th century. The history of colonial cultivation of coffee in South Asia goes further back in time than does the cultivation of tea. The Dutch cultivated coffee in Ceylon as well as the Malabar region of India during the 17th century. In 1860 Ceylon was the largest coffee-growing country in the world. It was however during the British period that large-scale cultivation of coffee, and later tea, commenced in Ceylon and southern India. The systematic replacement of natural forest with tea bushes in India began in Assam with experimental planting during the 1930s.

A report of 1862 states that thousands of acres were being cleared of forest every year for this purpose.[148] From Assam tea cultivation spread to northern Bengal and by the 1850s to the Nilgiris, and later the Anamalais, in southern India. Planting of tea on a large scale in Ceylon seems to have begun after a series of coffee blights during the late 1860s through to the 1880s resulted in tea replacing coffee almost entirely.[149] By 1900 there were about 4,000 tea estates in India and 2,000 estates in Ceylon. The movement of elephants through these plantations further intensified their conflict with people, in this instance the planter community that was culturally less tolerant of elephant depredation (figure 8.16). This was further excuse for the elimination of elephants.

✻✻✻

The increasing engagement of Europeans with the elephant in Asia also naturally resulted in the export of this and other exotic beasts to menageries back home as objects of public display and performance. As we have seen, the early Portuguese explorers had taken elephants from Malabar to Europe. The Czar's court of 17th-century Russia maintained a menagerie with elephants obtained from Samarkand[150] that had probably imported

8.17 Poster showing performing elephants at the Ringling Brothers and Barnum & Bailey circus in the USA, second half of the 20th century.
Courtesy and copyright: Feld Entertainment, Inc. All rights reserved.

these animals from elsewhere in Asia. There was a steady trickle of elephants into Europe during the 17th and 18th centuries but the total never exceeded a few dozen animals. The circus featuring acrobats and animal trainers was revived at the beginning of the 19th century in Britain and spread to continental Europe; in these shows the novelty of the elephant was simply in the animal being exhibited or ridden. Baba the elephant became a star at Paris' "Cirque Olympique". German circuses sprung up by the mid-19th century. Eventually, it was in America that grand displays of large numbers of elephants became an established feature of circuses (figure 8.17).

The first elephant to reach American shores was apparently a two-year old female Indian elephant procured from Calcutta in 1796. Sold to the showmen Pepin and Brechard, this elephant brought enormous profits from its display abroad. "The elephant was now ruled by the dollar" in a land of successful pioneering settlers starved of adequate entertainment.[151] The number of circuses grew rapidly in the New World and in Europe. Phineas T. Barnum, who set up a giant circus company in the USA, once quipped that "elephants and clowns were the linchpins on which circuses depended".[152] Barnum merged with its rival Bailey to create an even larger circus spectacle; during an 1887 show at New York's Madison Garden, Barnum, Bailey, and Forepaugh put on a display that brought 160 elephants into the ring at the same time. Circuses expanded into South America, with Brazil boasting of 40 large companies. In Europe the circus pioneer was undoubtedly Carl Hagenbeck of Germany who creditably tried to incorporate concerns about the animals' psyche into the training of elephants for the modern circus.[153]

Circuses had by now become elaborate shows that travelled from one country to another. Elephants drew the greatest applause from admiring audiences as they performed stunning feats for so large a beast – walking upright on hindlegs, walking a tightrope, doing a headstand, balancing on a ball, a drum, and even on a pair of bottles with hindlegs suspended – clearly a suite of ill-conceived, unnatural, and cruel tricks under fear of punishment. Large numbers of elephants often performed in a coordinated fashion in these grand displays. The emphasis clearly was on human control over an intelligent giant beast from a strange land, much like the ancient Roman displays of these animals. As each company tried to outcompete its rivals in the circus game, the imports of elephants into Europe and America increased sharply during the late 19th century. Both African and Asian elephants were imported but the preference was clearly for the latter, given the established systems of its capture and trade as well as its reputation, real or imaginary, of being the more trainable of the two species. The British authorities liberally issued licences for the export of elephants from India and Ceylon; between 1866 and 1886 Hagenbeck imported 300 Asian elephants, including 65 animals from Ceylon during 1883 alone.[154] Many of these elephants were sold to American circus companies. Hagenbeck used the profits from his business to build the first zoological garden with spacious, open-air enclosures for elephants, so far confined to cramped cages in the menageries. The gentler methods of training elephants he incorporated, using his observations of animal behaviour and ideas from Indian mahouts, brought much-needed respite from cruelty to zoo and circus elephants under his care. After Hagenbeck's death in 1913 his family has continued to maintain high standards in the upkeep of elephants (figure 8.18).

Many other elephants in Western facilities were not so fortunate. When bulls in musth became intractable and injured or killed people they were dealt with mercilessly, being cast in chains or put down immediately. There were many such incidents across Europe and America.[155] At the turn of the 19th century a travelling elephant was put down in Venice but its mistress went on to acquire another for her show. This elephant too became difficult to handle in Geneva and had its head blown off with a cannon after the use of the poisonous prussic acid and arsenic oxide failed to have the desired effect.[156] Another animal that attracted wide publicity was the Indian bull elephant Chuny who was taken from Bengal to Britain by ship in 1809–10 by the East India Company.[157] Chuny first performed in the Covent Garden Theatre and later at the Exeter 'Change Menagerie.[158] He earned a reputation from the public and prominent people alike of being a very affable creature. At the age of 22 Chuny began to exhibit signs of musth ("strong symptoms of madness") and killed his keeper, seemingly accidentally when ordered to turn around.[159] When the "madness" erupted again in the spring of 1826 Chuny was executed by firing 152 bullets under the supervision of two surgeons familiar with elephant anatomy. Charles Knight who published an entire volume on the elephant in *The Menageries* describes Chuny's last moments: "In the greatest access of his fury, when bullets were striking him from every side, he obeyed the voice of his keepers who ordered him to kneel, in the belief that he might be more easily shot in that position."[160] Students of anatomy in London clamoured to be present at the dissection, while people made offers to be provided chunks of Chuny's meat.[161]

Captive elephants in America did not fare any better. An Asian bull named Tusko in the Barnes Circus during the late 1920s earned the reputation of being "the most chained

8.18 Elephant being led by a trainer at Hagenbeck Zoo, Hamburg, Germany, 21st century. This zoo has maintained high standards in its management of captive elephants as have some others such as the Rotterdam Zoo in the Netherlands.
Photograph by Uwe Wilkens, courtesy Hagenback Zoo.

elephant in the world".[162] It was eventually acquired by a famous handler George 'Slim' Lewis who fortunately restored sanity to the animal. In 1902 a bull named Mandarin and, some years later his apparent daughter Columbia, were strangulated with neck nooses because they had killed people. Some of the offending elephants were virtually executed in military style; as an example, the bull Black Diamond was killed in 1929 by Texan shooters who fired 170 bullets at him as if in target practice. The execution in 1941 of the bull Teddy of Linderman Circus was no less dramatic as policemen fired 107 shots over a 45-minute period; either they were unaware of the finesse achieved many decades ago by British sportsmen in putting down an elephant with a single bullet penetrating through to the brain, or else were acting in a bloodthirsty frenzy reminiscent of the Roman arena two millennia ago. Either way the bull elephant just did not belong to the modern American circus and practically disappeared by the mid-20th century.

The elephant had earned high reputation among the public in Europe and America quite early. Few creatures were better suited for humanizing than the elephant; thus anthropomorphism became the order of the day in countries such as Britain when referring to the elephant.[163] The execution of an elephant thus did not go down too well with the public.[164] Describing Chuny's death, one British newspaper referred to it as the "noble animal of India" while another observer called it "the only peaceful one among us cruel wretches".[165] Charles Knight observed of Chuny, "Thine was a sagacious and noble nature...."[166] Indeed, the terms "sagacious" and "noble" seem to be the most common descriptors of the elephant in the early 19th century. Elephanticide in the New World, too, was followed by outrage among the media and the public.[167] The murder of Old Bet, without any provocation whatsoever, by an ill-tempered gunman named Daniel Daniel in 1816, was reported with a deep sense of shame in a virtual panegyric to the animal: "...as the Elephant was passing through this town [i.e. Alfred], he was waylaid by some diabolical miscreant, and shot dead with a brace of musket balls.... Ah! noble, generous, high minded, intelligent animal justly classed among the wonderful works of God! Thou hadst past from the banks of the Ganges.... And here thou hast come to fall by the hand of a miserable unknown caitiff, who only lives to disgrace his species – to dishonour God, and to be a scoundrel to his country."[168] There has been much soul-searching in recent times about the treatment and role of elephants in Western zoos and circuses.

Sujit Sivasundaram uses the Asian elephant as an example of how a colonizing power, in this case Britain, "appropriated" local knowledge and tradition even as it sought to invent a new objective science of the natural world. Increasingly aware of the pervasive influence of the elephant in local systems of warfare, hunting, trade, and religion, the British incorporated elements of ancient Sanskrit knowledge and Mughal tradition into their own systems of elephant husbandry after establishing control over this important resource. Back home in Britain, the elephant was held in high esteem by the public and more serious observers, but the creeping anthropomorphism of the animal, with substantial elements of Indian tradition, was seen as being too "heathen" in a land whose worldview was supposed to be based on rational Christian theology.[169] New objective science sought to replace this anthropomorphism and tradition but, in truth, the two knowledge systems operated concurrently. Indeed, when it comes to the elephant, Sivasundaram concludes that "the newly objective science was built in part on what Britons learnt in India".[170]

***

The Second World War broke out in Europe in September 1939 and soon spread to other parts of the globe including Asia. On the side of the Axis powers, Japan made rapid advances in Southeast Asia before making a decisive thrust into Burma during the winter of 1941–42. Outside the Chindwin river valley and the plains of the great Irrawady, Burma is a rugged land of mountains and dense tropical forest. Much of the war had to be fought in these hilly jungles, a far cry from the European plains or the North African desert. Here in Burma the elephant was still king when it came to war. While armoured tanks were engaged in fierce battles across Europe and North Africa, the elephant was patiently dragging timber for the British war effort; carrying soldiers, refugees, and food; and building bridges across the numerous rivers of Burma's treacherous terrain. With the outbreak of war the upsurge in demand for timber by Britain had to be met from all possible sources including Burma. The entry of the Japanese further spurred this demand for timber and elephants. As the Japanese advanced rapidly through Burma, the British hurriedly organized an evacuation of their forces along with their families through the difficult hill route in the Upper Chindwin region into India. A great number of refugees, mostly Indians, also joined the long and arduous journey north across the virtually impenetrable mountain barrier between India and Burma. Hundreds of Burmese elephants became the saviours of this retreating mass of people (figure 8.19), a story made popular in the poignant account *Elephant Bill* by a British army officer J.H. Williams.[171]

The Japanese too realized the value of the elephant and managed to take control of considerable stocks as they moved up to the Indian border and made a thrust towards Imphal. In March 1944 they crossed the Chindwin with a column of 350 elephants that eventually suffered from overwork and indifferent management.[172] Williams makes a pointed reference to the Japanese interest in elephants – their passion for ivory resulted in almost every tusked elephant having its tusks sawn off as close to the nerve as possible. This made it very difficult for them to be used in dragging timber but the Japanese interest was in using them as transport across the rugged northern terrain. It is unclear how many captive elephants actually died in the course of the war but it is certain that this numbered several thousands.[173] Many of the elephants died as a result of being directly bombed by the Royal Air Force to prevent them from being used by the Japanese; in one such raid alone 40 elephants were killed.[174]

8.19 Burmese elephants with people and baggage moving through a hilly, forest trail at Alaungdaw Kathapa National Park, 1994. During World War II the elephant was much sought after by both the British and the Japanese for its utility as a beast of burden in Burma's inhospitable jungles.

A NEW MAP OF INDIA FROM THE LATEST AUTHORITY.

From an estimated 6,500 full-grown timber elephants available during the pre-war years in Burma, only 2,500 animals seem to have survived by the end of the war in 1945.[175] It is of course possible that many of the elephants were dispersed across the country, or even stayed back in India and, thus, were not registered at the end of the war. Either way, the Asian elephant had clearly been a direct victim of the global conflagration that originated in Europe.

Winds of freedom were to soon blow strongly across colonial Asia. The destiny of the elephant would now be decided by independent nation states even as they struggled to shed the colonial legacy and raise living standards for people in one of the most densely populated regions of Asia.

The elephant, often used by British satirical artists to represent India (figure 8.20), had its moment of triumph in the struggle for Indian independence. The nationalist leader Bal Gangadhar Tilak (1856–1920) deployed the elephant-headed god Ganesha as a powerful symbol in the early independence movement.[176] The Ganapati festival that had begun during the 18th century under the patronage of the Peshwa rulers was now revitalized as a focal point to rally the masses (mainly of Bombay and Poona) against the British. The British were considerably alarmed at this development. Thus, M.M. Underhill wrote in 1921, "The growing interest among students in politics, and the adoption of Ganesa as their patron god, have united to connect him closely with the nationalist movement."[177] Mountstuart Elphinstone, the governor of Bombay, was even more forthright when he wrote "One talisman [i.e. Ganesha] that while it animated and united them all, could leave us without a single adherent. This barbarism is the name of religion, a power so obvious that is astonishing that our enemies have not more frequently and systematically employed it against us."[178] India's independence, that triggered movements for independence in other Asian countries, could thus be considered as the triumph of the nationalist elephant over the imperial lion.

CHAPTER 9

The Elephant
in Independent Asia

TWO DAYS AFTER THE SURRENDER of Japan in August 1945, the charismatic Indonesian nationalist leader Sukarno declared independence from Holland. However, it took over four years of struggle before the Dutch recognized an independent Indonesia. In the meantime the British granted independence to India but not before partitioning the land into two countries, India and Pakistan. A short while before Indian independence was heralded in on August 15, 1947, another charismatic Asian leader Jawaharlal Nehru proudly proclaimed "Long years ago we made a tryst with destiny.... At the stroke of the midnight hour, when the world sleeps, India will awake to life and freedom.... It is a fateful moment for us in India, for all Asia and for the world...."[1]

These two newly independent countries, India and Indonesia, were home to perhaps the two most significant populations of the Asian elephant, significant not just because of their sizes but also because of their association with a rich biological diversity. India and Indonesia were thus vested with a special responsibility of ensuring the continued survival of this charismatic creature. The post-colonial economic and social history of these countries would determine the eventual fate of the elephant. Many other Asian neighbours, too, were soon freed of the colonial yoke – Ceylon and Burma from Britain in 1948, Laos and Cambodia from France in 1949 and 1953, respectively, a partitioned Vietnam from France in 1954, and the Federation of Malaya from Britain in 1957. Within a decade the onerous responsibility of safeguarding the elephant along with the rich biodiversity of the region had truly been turned over into Asian hands.

We can trace the fate of the elephant in post-colonial Asia across three distinct regions that have shared roughly similar histories in their political, social, and economic spheres. These regions are South Asia comprising India, Sri Lanka, Nepal, Bhutan, and Bangladesh (that emerged out of Pakistan in 1971); continental Southeast Asia including Burma, Thailand, Laos, Cambodia, Vietnam, and a small part of China where the elephant clings on; and the equatorial Southeast Asian countries of Malaysia and Indonesia. At the end of the colonial period none of the Asian range countries could match up to even a decent fraction of the prosperity of their erstwhile European masters. Economic growth to lift the masses of one of the most populous regions of the world was thus an imperative for the Asian rulers. The course of economic awakening in each of these regions post-independence has, however, been rather different and, along with it, the fate of the elephant.

***

The equatorial range countries, Indonesia and Malaysia, were among the first in the region to witness a spurt in economic development. Indonesia's rulers decided that people from overcrowded islands such as Java would be moved to Sumatra in a government-sponsored "transmigration" programme. Between 1949 and 2000 the government resettled an estimated 5–7 million people while many others moved without sponsorship.[2] Since 2000 the government-sponsored transmigration has largely collapsed. Most of the resettlement occurred initially in southern Sumatra but then spread to the central region of the island. The major environmental consequence of the transmigration programme has been the rapid and massive deforestation of Sumatra. From the estimated forest cover of over 80% of the land area in 1900, the figures came down to under 50% by 1985, and further to 35% by 1997.[3]

The clearing of Sumatra's forests has been accompanied by not only the expansion of human settlements and agriculture but, most notably, the planting of oil palm (*Elaeis guineensis*) on an extensive scale (figure 9.1). In 2006 the area under oil palm in Indonesia was estimated to be 6.1 million hectares of which 70–80% was in Sumatra.[4] That year Indonesia also overtook Malaysia as the world's largest producer of palm oil.

9.1 A newly transformed landscape in the wake of the transmigration programme, with rainforest being replaced by oil palm plantations in the Aceh province of Sumatra, Indonesia (1999).

During the early 1980s the area under rubber plantation even marginally exceeded the area under oil palm.[5] Shifting cultivation has been another major cause of deforestation.

The once contiguous forest cover of Sumatra began to fragment rapidly. Charles Santiapillai and Widodo Ramono described the distribution of elephants in Sumatra as comprising 44 "discrete populations" during the early 1980s.[6] The largest of these were believed to be in the northern province of Aceh, the central province of Riau, and the southern province of Lampung. The range of 17 of the 44 populations lay within 28 Protected Areas that covered over 48,000 sq. km while the remaining populations were mainly found in production forests. Given the difficulties in estimating elephant numbers in dense tropical forests the best estimate available at that time was a minimum of 2,800 and a maximum of 4,800 elephants across the island.

Some of the smaller populations had already begun disappearing; as an example, a UNDP/FAO survey had reported elephants to be present in the Kerumutan Baru Nature Reserve, Riau province in 1982, but only a few years later there was no trace of them here.[7] Indeed, the province of Riau in central Sumatra was to suffer one of the highest rates of deforestation and attrition of elephant numbers on the island.[8] In the southern province of Lampung, in which 12 populations of elephants were believed to exist during the mid-1980s, surveys by Simon Hedges and colleagues indicated that only three populations were extant by 2002.[9]

The increased fragmentation of habitat also resulted in a sharp increase in elephant-human conflicts across the island.[10] The Indonesian government decided on a policy during the early 1980s to capture elephants systematically in an attempt to reduce conflict.[11] By 1993 at least 310 elephants had been captured in various provinces, nearly half of them in Lampung. Further, the authorities proposed to capture another 715 elephants between 1994 and 1998. Elephant training camps (ETCs) were set up in various regions.

The capture and training of elephants was a new experiment for Indonesia in recent times. The historical elephant culture in northern Sumatra had declined by the late 19th century and eventually disappeared during Dutch colonial times.[12] The Indonesian

9.2 A young elephant captured from Sumatra's southeastern province of Lampung under training at Way Kambas (1990). Such methods of training using sharp metal objects inflict unnecessary injuries and trauma upon the animals.

9.3 Captive elephants at the Elephant Training Centre, Way Kambas, Sumatra, performing for tourists (1990).

authorities thus brought in mahouts and trainers from Thailand to handle the captured elephants. The policy of capturing an endangered animal in such large numbers soon became mired in controversy.[13] A significant proportion of the elephants died during the process of capture itself. A disproportionate number of the elephants captured were juveniles and sub-adults, as these were the easiest to catch, even though the trouble-makers were usually adult bulls or matriarch-led herds. Once in the camp the elephants faced a host of health problems, many of which were related to injuries suffered during their capture, confinement, and training. Improper charge in dart guns and high doses of drugs used to immobilize the elephants were part of the problem. Wounds inflicted during capture became infected. The training methods used by the Thai mahouts were unnecessarily cruel and caused further injuries (figure 9.2). Many of the young elephants suffered from undernutrition; a recommendation to supplement the diet made by an experienced Indian veterinarian[14] who visited the ETC at Way Kambas was never implemented; lack of hygiene in the camps resulted in spread of parasites and diseases.[15] Several international NGOs and volunteers rushed in to assist with veterinary care but the battle seemed to be lost in the overcrowded ETCs.

In 1999 the Indonesian government apparently decided to stop capturing elephants for sending to the ETCs but kept the options open of capture for translocation or export. By the end of 2000 the six functioning ETCs held an estimated 391 elephants.[16] An equal or larger number had perhaps been captured, with most of them having died and a few exported to other facilities at Bogor and Bali (figure 9.3). The tourist revenues these elephants generated possibly resulted in better care and management. The offer by some

Australian zoos to take a few Sumatran elephants on loan became controversial with animal welfare groups vehemently opposing this move, and conservationists arguing that such arrangements would not help the overall cause of the Sumatran elephant.[17]

Between 2000 and 2005 at least 96 elephants in the ETCs died, according to official figures.[18] Elephants also continue to be captured in Sumatra, especially in Riau, and more than half of those captured have died, an extremely high rate of mortality.[19] The official figures also indicate that 42 people were killed by elephants, while about 100 elephants were eliminated in retaliation by farmers between 2002 and 2007. The province of Riau, where development has been most rapid, is the "hot spot" of elephant-human conflict, resulting in attrition of elephant numbers. Ivory poaching that was virtually unknown or rare in Sumatra in earlier decades also surfaced during this period, perhaps as an opportunistic spin-off from the elephant-human conflict.

Although wild population estimates are uncertain, it is clear that the Sumatran elephant has been among the worst sufferers of Asian elephant populations in recent decades. On the positive side the large network of Protected Areas covering nearly 10% of the island offers hope that several elephant populations will continue to persist in the coming decades and centuries. Only a few elephants are believed to be present in Kalimantan, adjoining Sabah in Borneo.[20]

In Malaysia the wild elephant populations are roughly equally divided between Peninsular Malaysia and Sabah on the island of Borneo. The story of the elephant in independent Malaysia is rather similar in some respects, but different in other features, to that of Indonesia. The economic awakening of Malaysia began soon after its independence in 1957. The clearing of pristine rainforest that had begun during the colonial period now hastened considerably. From an estimated forest cover of 84% of the land area of Peninsular Malaysia in 1958, the cover dropped quickly to 49% in 1971 and 44% in 1990.[21] By this time oil palm had been planted in over 2 million hectares while the other important commercial crop, rubber, covered an additional 1.8 million hectares. These two crops alone covered nearly 30% of the land area of Peninsular Malaysia. The creation of large reservoirs also meant loss of high quality river valley habitat for elephants; two such dams in the upper Perak state, the Kenering dam and the Temenggor dam, appear to have adversely affected the wildlife of the region.[22]

The familiar conflict between elephants and agriculture ensued in the wake of the rapid clearing of Peninsular Malaysia's forests as elephants became isolated in fragmented patches. Much of the conflict was with the oil palm plantations; after all elephants are known to favour a number of wild palms in Asia's rainforests and would not have disapproved entirely of this variety of palm that humans brought in plenty to their former natural habitat. The outcome of the conflict was the inevitable elimination of the elephant by poisoning, shooting, or capture. During 1959–69, for instance, the officials shot a total of 120 elephants in the central state of Pahang, a number considered too high to maintain the viability of the remaining population.[23] In Perak the population had been reduced to a very small number, while the elephant had disappeared from the west coast. By the early 1970s the elephant population in Peninsular Malaysia was an estimated 500–600 animals.[24]

The persisting or escalating conflict that accompanied the extensive land development led the Malaysian government to experiment with other forms of control and mitigation. In 1972 the government had enacted the Protection of Wildlife Act whereby it federalized, over the next four years, the administration of all the state game departments for more effective management. The Department of Wildlife and National Parks set up an Elephant Management Unit in 1974 to specifically address the problem of elephant-human conflict.[25] Among the tasks it took up was to establish a herd of captive, trained elephants to assist in dealing with problem animals. As with Sumatra, an older tradition of maintaining elephants in captivity had died out during colonial times in Peninsular Malaysia; hence, the government brought in mahouts and elephants from Assam in India to help train its park rangers to catch, train, and manage elephants. Attempts to capture wild elephants in the dense tropical jungle by using the Assamese method of lassoing them generally proved futile. Only one young female elephant that had entered a rubber plantation was caught at the end of a two-month operation.[26]

Plantation companies in the meantime had suffered huge financial losses from elephant depredation. The annual loss during the mid-1970s averaged 14 million Malaysian ringgit while this figure rose to 30 million ringgit the following decade.[27] The largest of the plantation agencies, the Federal Land Development Agency (FELDA), suffered particularly high levels of damage as it was "constantly on the pioneering frontier, and so constitutes the front line of attack on the elephant's habitat".[28] Indeed, a herd of nine elephants had cumulatively damaged plantation crops worth 37 million ringgit over five or six years or, to put it simply, Malaysia had created the "four million dollar elephant"![29]

The beleaguered plantation agencies began to experiment with a variety of measures from the bizarre to the high-tech to deal with the elephant problem. They hired the *bomoh* or practitioner of traditional medicine to "negotiate" with the elephants their peaceful withdrawal, they used "carbide cannon" to scare the elephants with loud noises, and they organized night patrols to chase elephants. When these gambits failed to pay dividends, the companies turned to other measures such as barriers. The trenches they dug around the plantations collapsed or got silted up in hilly terrain with heavy rainfall. Finally in 1978 they began erecting electric fences to jolt the elephants into compliance.[30] As elephants learned to negotiate an electric fence the design of the fence became more sophisticated. By the early 1990s about 1,000 km of fencing had been put up across Peninsular Malaysia.[31]

In the meantime the Department of Wildlife and National Parks adopted drug immobilization as the preferred means of capture of elephants for translocation.[32] The plan now was to round up as many elephants as possible from fragmented habitats and relocate them in the larger and more intact ranges, in particular, in the Taman Negara (National Park) and its surrounding forests (an extensive range of about 35,000 sq. km of forest spread over several states in central Peninsular Malaysia). The idea was to reduce conflict to the extent possible while, at the same time, integrating the isolated elephants with the more viable populations. The government went ahead with this singular goal in a professional manner by training and equipping the Elephant Management Unit to carry out this task. Capturing and transporting elephants in the dense rainforests of Peninsular Malaysia was no easy task. In some cases elephants were isolated on islands created within reservoirs by construction of dams; the rising waters of the Kenyir lake for instance had isolated a group of 40 elephants;[33] for the relocation of these animals the department used special rafts that could accommodate the captives as well as trained elephants (figure 9.4). According to official figures, 482 elephants were captured for translocation between 1974 and 2001 in Peninsular Malaysia.[34] Of these, 142 elephants were released in the Taman Negara. Sixty-one elephants were released in Belum State Parks in Perak to the northwest and 37 elephants in the Endau-Rompin State Park in the south. The rest presumably died or were retained in captivity.

Unlike the Sumatran situation, the Malaysian elephant capture and translocation programme has not attracted criticism for several reasons. Most of the elephant deaths

9.4 An elephant being transported by boat across Kenyir lake to the Taman Negara in Peninsular Malaysia (2007). This animal was captured in Jerantut district, Pahang state, as it was in serious conflict with oil palm plantations and villages.
Photograph by Shariff Daim.

took place during the early years of the operation. Learning from the experience, the Malaysian wildlife authorities markedly improved their record in later years. They did not maintain large numbers of undernourished, injured, or diseased elephants in captivity where public visibility would have been high. There was also appreciation in conservation circles of their plan to integrate the small, non-viable groups into larger viable populations.

Peninsular Malaysia's forest cover seems to have stabilized at about 45% of the land area,[35] with 6.6% under Protected Areas.[36] The latest estimates of the elephant population place the number at nearly 1,300 individuals or over twice the estimates during the 1970s.[37] A recent report indicates that Taman Negara alone holds nearly half the present population of the elephant.[38]

Whether the elephant was native to Sabah, one of the states of the Federation of Malaysia, or had been introduced from Java during the 18th century (see Chapter 8), the story of land development and deforestation of its habitat is similar to that of the Peninsula. In 1953 about 85% of Sabah in northern Borneo was under natural forest cover; by 2001 this had dropped to 58% cover including degraded or secondary growth.[39] Again, oil palm was the main commercial crop replacing Sabah's rich tropical rainforest at a frenetic pace as in other parts of Southeast Asia. By 2004 oil palm had been planted

9.5 A wild elephant herd from the Lower Kinabatangan region, Sabah, Malaysia (2007). This is the best place to sight Bornean elephants as they are confined to a narrow strip of forest along the river.

Photograph by Raymond Alfred.

on 1.17 million hectares or nearly 16% of the land area of Sabah, an increase of 322% from 1990.[40]

The problem with oil palm for the elephant in Sabah was not so much the area planted but where and how it was planted. Land development cut large swathes through the natural forest, severely fragmenting the range of the elephant. To control the ensuing elephant-agriculturist conflict the Sabah Wildlife Department shot about 300 elephants between 1960 and 1994; since then capture and translocation has been the preferred option with 25 elephants moved to Tabin Wildlife Reserve and another 15 elephants elsewhere (up to 2001).[41] A small number have also been exported to zoos abroad while a few have been retained in local facilities. Legislation to protect Sabah's wildlife came much later than in Peninsular Malaysia. The Wildlife Conservation Enactment of 1997 also placed the elephant in Schedule II[42] unlike in the Peninsula where it was accorded a higher Appendix I status.[43]

Sabah's elephants are now distributed in four distinct areas or "Managed Elephant Reserves" (MERs).[44] The largest of these extending over an area of 10,800 sq. km in southern Sabah bordering Kalimantan is loosely termed as the Deramakot-Ulu Segama-Kalabakan MER. Some of Sabah's best preserved rainforests such as in the Danum Valley Protection Forest Reserve are found in this MER but considerable areas are also managed for timber production. The Tabin Elephant Range in the east comprising logged dipterocarp forest is completely surrounded by oil palm plantations but retains a few hundred elephants. The Lower Kinabatangan MER along Sabah's largest river has a highly visible but modest population of about 100 elephants (figure 9.5). This range is also the most tenuous, given that it is a narrow strip of secondary forest along the Kinabatangan, with oil palm plantations on either side. The Ulu Kalumpang–Tawau hills MER is a hilly region that has also been cut off from other elephant ranges; the long-term viability of this population of about 80 elephants is in doubt. Overall, it is estimated that 1,127–1,623 elephants may be found in Sabah, not an inconsiderable number given the possible history of introduction of the animal less than three centuries ago.

***

The Asian elephant has perhaps been most impacted in recent decades in the Indochina region of Vietnam, Cambodia, and Laos.[45] Hardly had these countries won independence from French colonial rule after the first Indochina War (1946–54), than they were plunged into another war, involving mainly Vietnam. The US operation "Rolling Thunder" carpeted North Vietnam with a million tonnes of missiles, rockets, and bombs. The bombing extended to the famous Ho Chi Minh trail that ran through the jungles of Cambodia and Laos. American forces also sprayed the notorious herbicide, Agent Orange, believed to cause cancer and banned in the USA, on an extensive scale to defoliate the forests, expose enemy convoys, and decrease their food supplies.[46] Two million hectares or 20% of forests in South Vietnam suffered the spraying.[47]

The character of Indochina's forests along the war zone changed due to their defoliation, allowing deciduous and weedy plants to invade the evergreen forests. During my field studies in Cat Tien National Park in southern Vietnam, I found that large areas of the jungle were virtually impenetrable due to the invasion of thorny rattans and bamboos.[48] This transformation itself perhaps did not impact the elephants negatively because they are known to be partial to disturbed or secondary growth forest. But the war itself created terrible hunger in the region forcing the people to hunt wildlife for food, and to clear the forest for growing more food. If rising economic prosperity had spurred the destruction of forests in Malaysia and Indonesia, war, poverty, and hunger had done the job in Indochina.

Vietnam lost nearly 50% of its forests as a result of these forces unleashed by the war.[49] A forest cover of 43% of the land area of the country in 1943 declined to a low of 27% by 1990. It has since then increased to 37% by 2005, but as a result of raising industrial plantations not useful for wildlife.[50]

The elephants of Indochina also suffered directly from war. American planes bombed elephants along the Ho Chi Minh trail to prevent the Viet Cong using them as transport.[51] The earlier anecdotal accounts of elephants being targeted from the air have since been confirmed in several later stories coming out of Indochina. In 1966 US Marine pilots, for instance, strafed a column of 11 baggage elephants in the mountains near Danang, killing five animals while another five fell from injuries.[52] Elephants would undoubtedly have also died from landmine explosions.

Elephants were also hunted heavily possibly both during and after the war, and Vietnam is typical of the sad story of a once thriving wild elephant population being devastated by human violence. William Bazé described how one could see "vast herds of elephants lording it over the plain beyond the range of our rifles" in the La Nga floodplain region; on one occasion he counted from elephantback "175 adult males in two hours" a task that is impossible today in any part of the species' range in Asia, and perhaps even in Africa![53] This region held several thousand elephants during the wet season in the late 1940s. Vietnam's elephant population would certainly have been much larger at this time,

9.6 Thatched dwelling in a cashew plantation along the southern boundary of Cat Tien National Park, Vietnam, that has been flattened by the small group of wild elephants inhabiting the park (2001).

9.7 Elephants captured from the Tan Phu forest kept at the zoo in Ho Chi Minh City, Vietnam (1998). These elephants were captured as they were in severe conflict with the adjoining villages.

though one cannot hazard a guess as to the numbers. Estimates of 1,500–2,000 elephants during the immediate post-war period of 1975–80,[54] and of 400–600 elephants for 1990–92[55] are considered to be gross overestimates.[56] The magnitude of the real decline of the elephant in Vietnam stunned the conservation world when it was announced in 1998 that perhaps less than 100 wild elephants survived in the country.[57]

Even with such small numbers elephant-human conflicts were reported from nine of the 11 populations! The most dramatic of these conflicts occurred in the Tan Phu State Forestry Enterprise, a heavily-logged patch of forest separated from the larger Cat Tien National Park by a major highway (figure 9.6). Here, authorities initiated in 1993 the capture of a trapped herd of about 25 elephants using the services of a Singapore-based firm (figure 9.7). The operations were suspended after the head of the capture team was killed by an elephant. The remaining group of 12 elephants continued to be in serious conflict with agriculture and killed several people in the process. In 2001 these were captured and a few released at Yok Don National Park near the Cambodian border, but this experiment too failed as the elephants did not give up their earlier partiality for feeding in cultivated land.[58]

While local hunters undoubtedly contributed to much of the decline of wild elephants in Vietnam, hunters from Laos have wiped out the species in the northern areas – especially the Lai Chau province.[59] Ethnic minorities such as the M'Nong, Gia Rai, and E De in the highlands of Dak Lak province are also skilled in the capture and training of elephants which has been a tradition for centuries, with the men carrying out the operations being accorded high respect and esteem. The Dak Lak province has thus witnessed a steep decline in wild elephant numbers. Even its captive elephant population reduced from 502 animals in 1979–80 to just 138 in 2000, possibly due to neglect of the captives as the tradition has lost ground in modern times, or because of the sale of animals across the border to Laos and Cambodia. Many captive elephants have also been shot for their tusks when they are let out in the forest for feeding.

The Vietnamese government has passed several decrees and laws that prohibit the hunting of elephants.[60] With the exception of perhaps a few protected areas such as Cat Tien National Park, enforcement of the law has been weak because of lack of capacity. Vietnam became a signatory to CITES[61] in 1994; the illegal trade in ivory and ivory products, with most of the raw material coming into the country from Laos and Cambodia, however, continues to thrive at several cities across the country.[62]

Joe Heffernan and Trinh Viet Cuong summarized the overall elephant situation in Vietnam in 2004 by listing 11 small isolated groups or solitary elephants totalling just 59–81 individuals.[63] Only two of these populations offer even a glimmer of hope for short- to medium-term survival. These are the Nam Cat Tien population of 11–17 individuals in Dong Nai province in the south,[64] and the Dak Lak province in the southwest where a population of 17–32 elephants was reported to range in Yok Don National Park and adjoining areas.[65] There are still possibly over 100 captive elephants (165 in the early 2000s) in Vietnam, mostly in Yok Don province, making these a valuable resource for conservation.

Neighbouring Cambodia has fared somewhat better as regards the numbers of elephants. Although only the eastern region of Cambodia suffered directly from the ravages of the second Indochina war, the country was later torn apart by civil war during the notorious reign of Pol Pot and the Khmer Rouge (1975–79). During the period 1965–70 nearly three-fourths of the land area was under forest, much of it primary tropical dry forest as in the east, and moist forest as in the southwest.[66] It is not clear how the wars impacted the forests other than those along the Vietnamese border that suffered defoliation. Apart from some minor losses due to shifting cultivation, there may have been no major change in the quality or area of forests.[67] However, illegal logging became rampant with both the ousted Khmer Rouge forces, now in hiding in western Cambodia, and the rulers at Phnom Penh controlling the trade.[68] Logs or sawn timber were exported to Thailand, Vietnam, and Laos, much of the wood eventually reaching China. An official assessment of Cambodia's land cover indicated that the area under forest had come down to 60% by 1992,[69] and about 56% by 1995.[70]

The Cambodian government attempted to rationalize the timber industry by designating 7 million hectares of forest, or 38% of the country's area, for allotment to 30 logging concessionaires during 1994–97.[71] The consequences seem to have been disastrous with illegal logging continuing to be rampant. Three million hectares of concessions to 22 companies were cancelled in 2000 to try and curb the virtually uncontrolled exploitation. At the same time a move to promote community-based forestry was initiated. In 2002 Cambodia adopted a National Forestry Policy statement and a Forestry Law that designated the remaining forests as Permanent Forest Estate. A role for community-managed forestry and collective property rights was also defined especially in the context of shifting cultivators.

The indirect impact of logging through increased human activity and hunting has been far more devastating for the wildlife. Field surveys of Cambodia's wildlife regions since the mid-1990s began to reveal the true magnitude of the problem. Whether it was the tropical mixed forests of the biologically-rich Cardamom mountains bordering Thailand in the southwest[72] or the tropical dry forests of the Virachey-Lomphet-Phnom Prich complex of protected areas close to Laos and Vietnam in the east,[73] the story was similar. Evidence of poachers was visible everywhere. In fact, elephant surveys in the east found very low densities of the species, indicating that poaching was the biggest threat to the wildlife of the region.

Past estimates of wild elephant numbers in Cambodia have been pure guesswork, and the situation is not much better even now. In 1974 Pan Leang Cheav gave a figure of 10,000 elephants in the country in 1969;[74] the only message we can draw from this number is that the elephant population was perhaps in the thousands and not in the hundreds. For several years no new figures were forthcoming until the results of a questionnaire survey among hunters were presented at a conference in 1998.[75] The stronghold of the elephant was reported to be the Kravanh (Cardamom) mountains in the west covered with evergreen forests at higher elevation; 300 elephants still survived in this region. No estimates were given for the nearby Chuor Phnum Damrei (Elephant) mountains in the southwest. The second important region was the Mondulkiri province in the east bordering Vietnam, where 150 elephants were believed to survive. A few scattered herds totalling 50 individuals roamed the northern plains in the region around Siem Reap. The presentation concluded that the "elephant population of Cambodia is unlikely to be higher than 500".[76] This was later confirmed by a figure of 400–600 elephants in the country in 2004.[77]

Captive elephants too have not fared well in Cambodia. Jeff McNeely gave a precise figure of 582 captive elephants in 1975,[78] a number that was broadened to 300–600 in 1997.[79] A few years later a survey yielded only 164 captive elephants in the country,[80] mostly in the Mondulkiri and Ratanakiri provinces where the Phnong minority tribe has a long tradition of capturing and maintaining elephants. Because of fear of poachers killing their captive bulls for tusks, the Phnong apparently now preferred to keep only female elephants. This implies that many captive elephants have been killed or traded with neighbouring countries.

Having hopefully emerged from a long era of political conflict, the Cambodian government has been struggling to retrieve a seemingly hopeless situation for the country's wildlife. In 1993 the government established 23 Protected Areas through royal decree.[81] A chapter on wildlife protection was incorporated into the Forestry Law of 2002. Several *praka*s (regulations) under the existing laws give the highest level of protection to elephants. If Cambodia is serious about the protection of elephants the most favourable factor for their recovery is the availability of two relatively extensive tracts of forest, in the west and in the east. These afford scope for a substantial increase to viable and safe population levels.

Lao People's Democratic Republic (or Lao PDR) was once referred to as *meuang lan xang* or the "land of a million elephants", an exaggeration no doubt but a pointer to the teeming population of the species in the region. This has been perhaps the most difficult among the Asian range states for obtaining objective data on the status of the elephant. Forests covered about three-fourths of this mountainous nation in the 1950s. The extent of forest in this sparsely settled country when it emerged out of war is not clear. Statistics of forest cover reported in various sources are confusing, perhaps due to the difficulty in distinguishing in satellite pictures between natural vegetation and regrowth in areas of shifting cultivation. Indeed, the distinction may not be meaningful in a land where this form of agriculture has been extensively practised for centuries and so-called primary forest is only a small fraction of the total forest cover. FAO gives a figure of 53% of the land area as covered by forests in 2000,[82] while the government itself put out a lower figure of 42% forest in late 2002.[83]

No separate estimate for wild elephant numbers in Lao PDR was available until Venevongphet announced in 1988 that 2,100–3,300 individuals might be present across the country.[84] A decade later a clearer picture emerged at a regional conference where Khamkhoune Khounbouline presented the results of his questionnaire survey indicating at least 839 wild elephants in the country;[85] he revised this figure in 2004 to a minimum of 781 and a maximum of 1,202 individuals.[86] As expected these elephants were spread throughout the country with the maximum numbers in the north, especially the Sayabouri province (300 elephants), and declining as one proceeded southward to the border with Cambodia. The Nakai Nam Theun plateau in central Laos with 150 elephants and the Xe Piane region in the south with 100 elephants were among the larger populations. By the late 1990s the process of habitat fragmentation and isolation of wildlife populations, so common with the elephants across Asia, had already begun in Lao PDR that possibly held the most significant populations in the Indochina region.

Several ethnic tribes such as the Khamu in this country also have a tradition of maintaining elephants.[87] Lao PDR thus has the largest stocks of captive elephants in the region; an estimate of 1,020 captives in 1993[88] remains unchanged since then. An active cross-border trade in elephants has existed with animals from Lao PDR being taken into Thailand.[89] This was part of a more extensive illegal trade in ivory; during 1991–92 at least 42 elephants were reported killed in the Nakai Nam Theun region.[90] The ban on logging in Thailand had also driven timber merchants to seek supplies from Lao PDR and Myanmar.[91]

Lao PDR initiated legal measures to conserve wildlife quite late as compared to other countries in Asia.[92] The Prime Minister's Decree No. 164 established 18 National Biodiversity Conservation Areas (NBCAs) in 1993, while two more were added in 1995–96. Covering nearly 14% of the country's land area, these NBCAs offer the best hope for conservation of elephants that are found in 18 of the 20 areas.

This landlocked country has also been slow to wake up to the technological developments taking place in other parts of Asia but there are signs that this is changing.

9.8 White elephants along the brick-red basal wall of the late 14th-century Wat Chang Lom pagoda at Si Satchanalai Historical Park, Sukhothai, Thailand. The white elephant was considered sacred and worshipped in Thailand since ancient times.

Courtesy: Bigstock.com.

A bitter controversy erupted over the building of the Nam Theun II dam, funded by the World Bank, in the Nakai Nam Theun plateau some years ago.[93] With a water spread of 447 sq. km, the Nam Theun II reservoir is one of the largest such water bodies to be created in Asia, submerging biodiversity-rich river valleys in central Laos. This project may be the harbinger of a succession of hydroelectric dams as this mountainous country strives to unleash its economic potential. We can only speculate on the future of the elephant in such a scenario.

Thailand, a country that had not come under the colonial yoke and was the most prosperous among the nations in continental Southeast Asia, was perhaps the best placed in the region to consolidate its forests and wildlife by the mid-20th century. Outside of India and Sri Lanka, the elephant culture was most elaborated in Thailand. This was the "land of the white elephant", a divine creature upon which was lavished care and protection worthy of a monarch (figure 9.8).[94] Yet this excessive veneration of the elephant eventually proved to be its downfall, the obsession with the elephant as a cultural icon resulting in its transfer from the wild into captivity in alarmingly large numbers.

At the turn of the 20th century nearly 90% of Thailand is believed to have been under forest; by 1961, when Thailand came out with its first National Economic and Social Development Plan, the figure was about 55%,[95] and by 1990 the forest cover had come down to 30% of the land area.[96] During these three decades Thailand underwent massive deforestation as it took the path to rapid economic growth (figure 9.9).[97] Nature struck with a vengeance in November 1988 in the form of an exceptional storm that caused massive landslides, killed several hundred people, and destroyed thousands of homes in the Nakhon Si Thammarat province in the south. Public outcry over the perception that uncontrolled logging was responsible for this misery forced the government to impose a complete ban on logging in January 1989 effective a year later. To beat this deadline the "forest almost exploded with the roaring sound of chainsaws".[98] Logging was controlled eventually, but not before much of Thailand's forests had been terribly damaged. The FAO estimated that only 23% of the country was under forest cover five years after the logging ban.

Capture and training of elephants for work continued to be a thriving business with the Karens in the north, these traditionally-skilled elephant catchers and trainers controlling the flourishing trade in elephants. In addition to absorbing considerable numbers of the captured elephants in local enterprise, Thailand also sold more elephants abroad than did any other Asian country. Between 1950 and 1969 Thailand exported 1,138 elephants and during 1970–76 another 376 animals were sent abroad,[99] extremely high numbers for recent times considering the dire status of the wild population. An illegal cross-border trade in elephants, especially with Myanmar, also flourished. It is clear that wild elephant populations in continental Southeast Asia took a severe beating as a result of widespread captures. Correspondingly, the ratio of captive elephants to wild elephants turned decisively in favour of the former category, a pattern that Thailand unfortunately exemplified more than any other country.

Prior to World War II the population of wild elephants could easily have been a few tens of thousands considering the known size of the captive population. The rapid post-war deforestation of the country combined with the high rate of capture of elephants changed this situation. Boonsong Lekagul and Jeff McNeely gave an estimate in 1977 of between 2,600 and 4,450 wild elephants distributed in six areas across the country.[100] Mattana Srikrachang and her colleagues announced in 2004 that 3,000–3,500 elephants were present within an area of 55,000 sq. km or one-third of the forest cover of Thailand

9.9 An elephant at work pushing a log down a steep hill slope near Chiangmai in northern Thailand (1988). Extensive floods in the country forced the authorities to ban logging effective January 1989.

comprising a number of Protected Areas (PAs).[101] Practically no elephants were left in forests outside the PA network. Eleven PA complexes with elephants were identified; of these, the Western Forest Complex (incorporating the Huai Kha Khaeng Wildlife Sanctuary) with 1,000–1,200 elephants emerged as the most significant. Sizeable numbers were also found in the Lower Western Forest Complex (500–600 elephants),

9.10 This young elephant on the streets of modern Bangkok is the cynosure of passersby. The "street-begging elephant" became an international icon during the 1990s for the plight of Thailand's captive elephants that were out of work following the ban on logging during the late 1980s.

Photograph by Dheeraporn Saenthewee.

the Northeastern Plateau A (450–550 elephants) centred around the Khao Yai National Park, the Northeastern Plateau B (350–450 elephants) focused on the Phu Khieo Wildlife Sanctuary, and the Southeast Region (250–300 elephants). There were encouraging signs that some populations were recovering.

Nor has the high rate of captures sustained the population of captive elephants in Thailand. From 13,397 captive elephants in 1950 the number came down to 11,022 in 1972,[102] and thereafter steeply to 3,565 in 1994.[103] With the logging ban, many of these elephants lost their jobs. Unable to feed and take care of the elephants, some owners or mahouts found a new source of income in Thailand's thriving tourism industry; they took their elephants for tourist entertainment in cities such as Bangkok, Pattaya, and Chiangmai. Bangkok also earned the dubious reputation of being home to "street-begging elephants" (figure 9.10). In 1977 Bangkok's municipality moved to enforce a ban on the entry of elephants into the city but this was an exercise in futility.

Thailand's elephants in the meantime continue to be cash cows for the tourist industry with the ownership of many elephants having passed on to businessmen. The Surin elephant fair held annually in November in this northeastern province is the most famous of Thailand's elephant shows.[104] A big tourist attraction, the round-up brings in elephants from all over the country to demonstrate "in microcosm the former methods of elephant capture, the traditions of pageantry in which elephants participated, as well as the many skillful capacities and endearing attributes of this most intelligent of animals".[105]

As Thailand struggles to preserve its wild elephants and hold on to its rich elephant culture in a changing world, it has brought in new legislation to protect the animal's habitat. The Wild Animal Preservation and Protection Act 1960 and the National Park Act 1961 have helped develop the Protected Area system of Thailand. The existing and proposed PAs would cover one-fifth of the country's land area.[106]

Although a party to CITES since 1983, Thailand has not regulated the thriving illegal trade in ivory. Poaching for tusks has been a problem in this country, because of the easy availability of guns.[107] A survey in 2001 estimated that over 88,000 worked ivory items, from cheap curios to intricately-carved figurines, were available for sale in Thailand, more than in any other country in Asia or even Africa.[108] Indeed, Thailand is the hub of a major illegal trade in wildlife involving cross-border commerce with several countries. Some of the ivory items on sale may come from trimmed tusks of Thailand's large captive elephant population or from dead ones, allowed under local law, but certainly much of the ivory is illegal, involving also imports from Africa and from neighbouring countries.

After Burma's independence it enjoyed parliamentary democracy for about a decade and a half (1948–62) before coming under military rule. This largely forested and mountainous country with diverse ethnic groups has also remained very poor, practically frozen in time for over a century. The country was renamed Myanmar in 1989. Its extensive forests have continued to be an important source of state revenue with the "timber elephant" resisting the change that has overtaken its counterparts in neighbouring Thailand and India. At the time of independence it can be safely assumed that well over 50% of the country was under forest cover, a figure that seems to have come down to 36% by 1988.[109]

Myanmar is the only country that still retains the romantic aura of the "timber elephant", a legacy of the colonial period. The country maintains the largest numbers of captive elephants globally. This has also meant a substantial decline in the population of wild elephants. During the decades following independence population guesstimates of 3,000–10,000 elephants had been made.[110] Ye Htut of Myanmar's wildlife department carried out an extensive survey in the mid-1990s of elephant distribution and possible numbers by questioning villagers and officials. He came up with a tally of 4,155 wild elephants at a minimum across several disjointed populations.[111] A decade later U. Uga summarized the distribution of elephants in five distinct regions – the Northern hill ranges including Tamanthi Wildlife Sanctuary, the Western hill ranges or Rakhine Yomas with its northern extension comprising the Alaungdaw Kathapa National Park, the Bago Yomas in central Myanmar, the Tenasserim range in the south bordering Thailand, and the Shan state or eastern Yomas that probably held only a small population.[112]

From independence until the early 1990s Myanmar continued to capture wild elephants in sizeable numbers in order to maintain its stocks of timber elephants. Between 1950 and 1970 a total of 2,940 or an annual average of 147 elephants were captured; over the period 1970–82 the average captures per year came down only slightly to 130 elephants.[113] Over the next decade the captures dropped sharply from 44 animals during the year 1982–83 to only 13 individuals by 1993–94 according to official statistics.[114] The following year only two elephants were captured. This clearly points to a rapidly depleting wild population making it extremely difficult to detect and successfully capture elephants from the wild in Myanmar's hilly, tropical jungles.

The government enacted the "Protection of Wildlife and Wild Plants and Conservation of Areas Law of 1994" that gave elephants the status of a "completely protected" species.[115] In 1995 the government also imposed a moratorium on capture of wild elephants for the logging enterprise. This was the outcome of the visit of a delegation, of which this author had the privilege of being a part, from the IUCN/SSC Asian Elephant Specialist Group to initiate conservation measures for the species.[116] This change from the earlier policy of exploitation provided welcome relief for the wild elephant population, though licenses have been issued for capture and translocation of elephants that are in conflict with agriculture.[117]

For long Myanmar's elephants have suffered from hunting for ivory, meat, and other products, as well as illegal capture to meet local need and export to neighbouring countries such as Thailand. A recent survey by TRAFFIC shows that the trade in ivory or its products as well as the illegal capture of wild elephants are widespread in the country.[118] More serious, the study documented the illegal export of about 250 live

9.11 Elephants at a timber camp in the southern Bago Yomas, Myanmar (1995). These so-called "timber-camp elephants" are widely acknowledged to be among the best managed captive elephants globally.

elephants to Thailand for the latter's tourist trade in the decade following the moratorium on captures. It is clear that Myanmar's capacity for enforcing national and international laws pertaining to wildlife protection are weak. Large areas of the country such as the northern state of Kachin, parts of Shan state in the east, and Kayin, Mon, and Tenasserim in the south, are not under effective control of the government because of insurgency. Further, landmines are also widespread in regions facing insurgency, thereby escalating risks to people and wildlife.

It is widely acknowledged that the captive elephants in Myanmar are among the best managed in the world (figure 9.11). Graeme Caughley wrote in 1980 that "Veterinary treatment and training in Burma is modern, highly sophisticated.... Burma could teach other countries a lot about veterinary care of elephants but there is little or nothing on this subject that other countries could teach Burma."[119] During several visits to Myanmar during the 1990s I was extremely impressed with the system of management of its captive elephants. The blend of traditional and European systems of health care and training during colonial times had produced highly skilled elephants and mahouts. After the catastrophic declines during World War II the captive stocks seemed to have gradually recovered not just through captures but also through better management. Records compiled by Khyne U. Mar show that, independent of captures, births among the Myanma Timber Enterprise's elephants consistently exceeded deaths during 1980–87.[120] The year 1987 however seems to have been a turning point; from here on deaths among MTE's elephants exceeded births, resulting in declining stocks in spite of captures up to

9.12 Sculpted elephants with riders stand in front of an apartment block at Jinghong in the Yunnan province of China where a small population of wild elephants and an active elephant culture still survive (2009).

1995 when the moratorium was imposed. Khyne U. Mar pinpointed the cause as being a high death rate of calves at heel (those under five years old) possibly due to the taming process.[121]

Myanmar has also been slowly developing a network of Protected Areas that presently covers just over 2% of the country.[122] Significant among these has been the establishment of the Rakhine Yoma Elephant Sanctuary based on surveys carried out during the 1990s.[123] The potential for long-term conservation of the elephant is high in Myanmar if we consider the extensive habitat still available. To realize its potential, Myanmar has to ensure that its wild elephants are protected from poaching and illegal capture, that their habitats do not suffer fragmentation as in other range states, and that its captive elephants are healthier and put to more careful use in forestry operations.

We now turn briefly to China where the elephant had already disappeared over most of the country, barring a small region in the southern Yunnan province, by the mid-20th century. The rapid economic expansion of China has imposed pressure on its natural forests. The tropical forests of Xishuangbanna in southern Yunnan, the main habitat for elephants, reduced from 69% of the geographical area in 1976 to under 50% by 2003 with increase in forest fragmentation.[124] Road building has contributed greatly to this development, with resulting fragmentation of habitat and restriction of the movement of elephants.[125] A relatively stable population of 200–250 elephants survives in Yunnan province, mostly in the fragmented Xishuangbanna National Nature Reserve.[126] Smaller groups are isolated in the Lincang and Simao provinces further north. There are less than

50 captive elephants in China, most of them imported from neighbouring countries, but also a few caught locally as in Xishuangbanna.

China became a party to CITES in 1981 to regulate the illegal wildlife trade that is rampant in the country.[127] The Chinese Wildlife Protection Law places the elephant at the highest level of protection, while other regulations prohibit the conversion of elephant habitat within the nature reserves. The growing economic prosperity of China has, however, fuelled demand for ivory in recent years. As a consequence the market for illegal ivory has shifted decisively from Japan to China, as seen prior to the Beijing Olympics in 2008.[128] In spite of tremendous opposition from conservation groups, a standing committee of CITES approved, in July 2008, the sale of 108 tonnes of African elephant ivory to China.

The elephant culture still thrives in Yunnan province that has considerable numbers of ethnic minorities who have traditionally valued the animal. In the city of Jinghong elephant symbolism is ubiquitous in the form of decorations on buildings or as sculpture in public spaces and even the frontage of multi-storey apartments (figure 9.12). One can only hope that strong political will combined with local pride in the elephant will eventually save the creature from extinction in this large and tremendously diverse Asian country.

***

Sri Lanka and India, two countries in South Asia, have counterbalanced the substantial decline in wild elephants in Southeast Asia by maintaining stable populations, or even registering increases locally over the past half century. Yet, the conditions for the survival of the elephant have not necessarily improved here during this period but, in fact, have significantly deteriorated at many places. It would be interesting to see how the apparent stability of the elephant population has been achieved under such difficult circumstances.

I begin with the island of Sri Lanka (name changed from Ceylon in 1972), the "Pearl of the East" that maintained forest cover over nearly half its territory at the time of its independence, in spite of the antiquity of human occupation. The recorded forest cover of 44% of the land area in 1956 soon declined to 25% in 1981, and 22% by 1988, as agriculture and settlement expanded.[129] We must bear in mind that – with the exception of a few small areas – the vegetation of the island, especially in the eastern dry zone, is essentially manmade as a consequence of historical cultivation and slash-and-burn agriculture. The mosaic of artificial water bodies, secondary jungle, and agriculture supports the high density of elephants seen on the island.[130] Human transformation of the landscape has thus not been a complete disaster for the elephant population.

On the other hand, the nature of land development in Sri Lanka resulted in the "pocketed herd phenomenon" at several places.[131] Sri Lanka, in fact, pioneered the concept of wildlife corridors as early as the 1950s in order to link the major tracts of elephant habitat by narrow strips of jungle through agricultural areas.[132] The idea was abandoned by the government because of the practical difficulties in establishing such corridors. Later research on movement of elephants by fitting them with radio-transmitters indicated that such corridors were not essential for protecting their range; in contrast to elephants elsewhere in Asia, the elephants of the island typically had small home ranges of only 50–150 sq. km.[133]

Agricultural development of the Mahaweli river basin in the east has been a key aspect of the country's economic development since independence. In 1977 the government decided to hasten this process through the Accelerated Mahaweli Development Project. A series of large and small dams created water bodies that submerged over 120 sq. km, with the potential to directly irrigate up to 3,640 sq. km and generate 470 MW of

9.13 A large elephant herd being driven from an isolated jungle patch to a national park in northwestern Sri Lanka (2006). This country has used relocation of elephants quite extensively as a means to reduce elephant-agricultural conflicts, with mixed results.
Photograph by H.R. Janaka.

hydropower.[134] Given the spectre of isolated elephant groups the authorities planned two courses of action to mitigate problems such as conflict with agriculture. They drove the pocketed herds to larger habitats and also set up a system of protected areas in the Mahaweli basin including Somawathiya, Wasgamuwa, Flood Plains, and Maduru Oya National Parks totalling 1,237 sq. km to be connected by several nature reserves and corridors (figure 9.13). The idea of corridors for elephants did not really take off in Sri Lanka but, as explained earlier, this was perhaps not of immediate concern.

Given its high elephant density and the juxtaposition of cultivated land and settlement across the species' range, the conflict between elephants and people is considered the most serious conservation problem on the island. Apart from substantial damage to crops, about 50 people are killed each year by elephants. In retaliation, farmers shoot, electrocute, and poison crop-raiding elephants; between 1950 and 2003 at least 4,200 elephants or an average of about 80 animals each year perished in this manner (figure 9.14).[135] Agricultural development as a result of the Mahaweli project further complicated the already widespread conflict. To give a prominent example, the planting of sugarcane over an area of nearly 10,000 hectares in the environs of Handapanagala to the southeast led to sharp escalation in conflict.[136]

If Peninsular Malaysia has perfected the art of capture and relocation of elephants, Sri Lanka has been the champion in driving elephant herds over long distances.[137] Between 1978 and 1989, several drives involving about 500 elephants in total were organized, especially between the Mahaweli region and Wilpattu National Park and adjoining areas in the northwest and Uda Walawe National Park in the south. The drives however became "progressively more difficult and impracticable" because of the rapid land development in elephant habitats.[138]

A quarter century of armed conflict within Sri Lanka, that ended in 2009, also created several problems for elephant conservation in the north and the east of the country.[139] Elephants were probably not directly targeted in the conflict but an unknown number

9.14 Elephant killed after it damaged this flimsy dwelling and was obviously a threat to its inhabitants, in southeastern Sri Lanka (2003).
Photograph by H.R. Janaka.

of animals were injured or killed by landmines. This risk still remains in parts of the elephant's range.

In spite of the complex challenges facing the elephant in Sri Lanka, a heartening feature has been the relative stability of the wild elephant population. It is estimated that between 3,160 and 4,400 wild elephants are found on the island (as of 2000) with 2,100–3,000 of these ranging within Protected Areas.[140] The PA network covers 13% of the land area of the country. Given the very low frequency (about 7% of males) of tusked male elephants in the population, ivory poaching is not a serious issue, though some illegal sale of ivory from sawn tusks of captive animals still prevails.[141] Only about 300 captive elephants are now believed to survive in the country.[142]

The ancient elephant culture of the island associated with the Buddhist influence is still quite strong. A spectacular expression of this culture is the annual Kandy Perahera whose origins go back to 1775 during the reign of Kirti Sri Rajasinha.[143] Over 150 caparisoned elephants, including an impressive tusker carrying the sacred tooth relic of the Buddha, kept at the Dalada Maligawa (Temple of the Tooth), march through the streets of Kandy amidst performing dancers and drummers carrying fire torches at night (figure 9.15). The strong cultural affinity between the Sri Lankan people and the elephant has undoubtedly played a role in the survival of the species until the present.

We now move to mainland South Asia where the elephant is seen in Nepal, Bhutan, Bangladesh, and India. The elephant populations of the first three countries are quite small and shared with neighbours. Bangladesh, a low-lying, densely populated country drained by the vast delta of the Ganga-Brahmaputra rivers today has a natural forest cover of only 5% of its land area, most of it in the southeastern Chittagong region where hundreds of elephants were captured during the late 19th century.[144] Even after independence from colonial rule, the Chittagong region continued to be a source of elephants as seen from the records of 471 animals captured during 1947–62. Today, only about 200 elephants survive in Bangladesh, mostly in Chittagong and Cox's Bazar districts, and the Chittagong Hill Tracts along the border with Myanmar and India. Some

9.15 Tusked elephant at the Perahera at Kandy, Sri Lanka (2006). Traditionally, a magnificent tusker has always carried the sacred tooth relic of the Buddha at the Perahera whose origins go back to 1775.

elephants from the Indian state of Meghalaya also visit the Sylhet region of Bangladesh. The country had 94 captive elephants in 2004; most of these were being used to drag timber.

Bhutan is a mountainous country in the eastern Himalayan region. Famous for its high score in the index of Gross National Happiness,[145] nearly 60% of the land is under forest cover.[146] The country has an elaborate system of nature reserves termed as the Bhutan Biological Conservation Complex covering 35% of its land area.[147] The Royal Manas National Park bordering the Indian state of Assam is the main habitat for elephants along with adjoining forests to its west up to the Namgyal Wangchuk Wildlife Sanctuary. Land development for planting tea, cultivating sugarcane, settlement, and road construction on the Bhutanese side has fragmented the habitat.[148] Although no objective estimates are available of the population numbers, it is unlikely that the Bhutanese forests support more than 200–250 elephants, many of which are seasonal migrants from the Indian side. The new National Forest Policy of 1985 that aims to preserve a significant area of the country's biological wealth offers hope for the continued survival of the elephant and other wildlife in the country.

Another Himalayan country, Nepal too supported elephants historically only along its foothills. The moist region of tropical jungle and floodplains known as the terai was inhospitable to humans until malaria was eradicated during the 1950s.[149] This resulted in the inevitable influx of people from the hills and the clearing of jungle for settlement and agricultural development, with 80% loss of habitat for elephants. Nepal has taken a number of steps to strengthen its system of Protected Areas with external assistance; the considerable tourism potential of these parks was not lost on the government. Elephants are found in four of the 16 PAs in Nepal;[150] the Royal Bardia National Park with about 60 resident individuals holds about half the population, followed by Royal Suklaphanta Wildlife Reserve, Royal Chitwan National Park, and Parsa Wildlife Reserve. The upper figure in the estimate of 102–172 wild elephants in Nepal[151] is high considering that this includes the elephants moving in from India for only short periods. Nepal also holds a

9.16 Dams impounding water for irrigation and power generation, called "the temples of modern India" by Jawaharlal Nehru, have caused substantial loss of river habitats but at the same time provide a perennial source of water for wildlife. This picture shows the waters of the Parambikulam reservoir, the core of a Wildlife Sanctuary that harbours a large elephant population in Kerala (1986).

nearly equal number of captive elephants used mostly for tourist rides in parks.[152] Several illegally traded wildlife products including ivory move through Nepal, indicating poor law enforcement.[153]

We finally consider the fate of the Asian elephant in India that holds over 60% of the wild population and perhaps the key to the long-term survival of the species. Soon after independence in 1947, India embarked upon a system of centralized planning for economic development with the goal of ensuring equitable distribution of "the ownership and control of the material resources".[154] In the first of its five-year plans issued in 1951, the country's Planning Commission laid emphasis on agriculture to increase food production. At the same time, Prime Minister Nehru announced that "we have to industrialise India and as rapidly as possible"; in this context he also called for construction of dams which he termed "the temples of modern India" (figure 9.16).[155]

In a country with a large and mostly impoverished human population, food production could be increased only through clearing forest and constructing dams for irrigation as well as power generation. Needless to state, the forests of India, already exploited and fragmented over the centuries, shrank further. The system of record-keeping in British India notwithstanding, precise data on the forest cover of India at the time of independence are not available.[156] We do know that 4.13 million hectares of forest, or about 5% of the existing forest cover, was lost between 1951 and 1976 mostly for agriculture but also for river valley projects and other purposes.[157] All this had a disproportionately adverse impact on the habitats of the elephant as well as other wildlife in terms of the resulting fragmentation.

9.17 An elephant herd crossing the Ramganga at Corbett National Park (1994). The park lost habitat during the 1960s from the construction of a dam across this river.

The anti-malarial campaign during the 1950s[158] also opened up large tracts of forests for human settlement. This was most visible in the virtually uninhabited terai along the Himalayan foothills in the north where forests were rolled back and the moist land drained for cultivation. Uttar Pradesh and West Bengal were two states that benefited the most in terms of reduction in malarial deaths among humans. At the same time, the once contiguous (or nearly so) distribution of elephants along the terai from Uttar Pradesh through Nepal into northern West Bengal was now decisively broken.[159]

Elephants in the northern state of Uttar Pradesh[160] were soon confined to an area of about 1,000 sq. km in the forest divisions of Dehra Dun, Siwalik, Lansdowne, Kalagarh, Bijnor, Ramnagar, and Haldwani as a result of loss of forest to an equal extent following independence.[161] In 1966 V.B. Singh concluded on the basis of a systematic census that "the population of elephants in U.P. is not likely to be more than 400 in number".[162] By this time the conflict between elephants and people had intensified as a consequence of the "presence of men and machinery in every part of the forest" for construction of roads, hydel and irrigation projects, and the increase in cultivation.[163] A decade later, Singh listed four important factors that impacted the elephant population; these were a reduction in habitat area or its conversion to suboptimal plantations, clearance of forest in Nepal, construction of the Chilla-Rishikesh power channel, and filling up of the Ramganga reservoir within and near Corbett National Park (figure 9.17).[164] These developments caused changes in the movement patterns of elephants; thus, elephants from Nepal now began to move frequently into Dudhwa that had not been part of the species' range in recent decades.

9.18 An elephant herd at a salt lick at the Jaldapara Wildlife Sanctuary in northern West Bengal (2005). Some decades ago there were hardly any resident elephant groups at Jaldapara but presently some elephant families that have immigrated from outside range entirely within the sanctuary.

In 1992 the elephant population of this region was estimated at between 877 and 1,069 individuals,[165] suggesting a growing population. The most recent estimates vary from about 1,000 elephants to 1,600 elephants across the range, though fragmented into as many as six subpopulations in an area of about 10,000 sq. km comprising Rajaji National Park, Corbett National Park, Dudhwa Tiger Reserve, and other forest reserves.[166]

In the northeast of the country the range of the elephant extends from northern West Bengal eastward into Assam, Arunachal Pradesh, Meghalaya, Nagaland, Manipur, Mizoram, and Tripura, though elephants have virtually disappeared from the last three states.[167] Four years prior to independence, L.R. Fawcus who assessed the status of the elephant in Bengal, observed that "there were formerly large number of elephants in the Dooars, but due to the spread of tea and cultivation, the herds have become smaller and less numerous than before".[168] He further stated that "there is a regular elephants' high road along the foot of the hills in the Dooars...[running] for miles in a west–east direction" and estimated the elephant population to be between 100 and 200 animals. After independence elephants continued to be captured in the Bengal Duars; between 1947 and 1957 at least 29 elephants were rounded up in four *kheddah* operations.[169] The *mela shikar* technique of capturing wild elephants by chasing them with trained elephants was introduced here for the first time by the famous elephant-catcher P.C. Barua in 1957–58, and 93 elephants were captured over the next ten years.

The brief Sino-Indian war of 1962 had significant consequences for the forests of this strategic region. The Indian government gave a fillip to developing infrastructure and establishing military bases, which further fragmented the natural habitat. Not only did the elephants have to adjust their traditional west–east movement in the Duars, they also abandoned their occasional movement up the hills to altitudes of 1,000 metres; indeed, some bulls would ascend up to the snowline at over 3,000 metres.[170] In the words of Parbati Barua and S.S. Bist, "the response of elephants to these changes can be seen from the details of depredation in the annual reports of the Forest Department from 1965–66 to 1969–70".[171] Crop depredation increased, people were killed by elephants, and several elephants declared rogue and shot. P.C. Barua was invited to capture more elephants; a *kheddah* operation in 1971 failed but 117 elephants were captured (until 1981) through *mela shikar* that was selective in the removal of mostly sub-adult animals.[172]

During the 1980s northern West Bengal witnessed a surge in elephant-human conflict. There were several instances of large elephant herds rampaging through paddy fields and labour lines in tea gardens. With an average of about 50 people killed each year, the northern West Bengal region earned the notoriety of being a "hotspot" of elephant-human conflict.[173]

Since then the elephants have readjusted to the changed situation on the ground. Although levels of conflict are still high in terms of people killed, mostly by bull elephants, the instances of spectacular crop raids by herds seem to have subsided. A detailed study of the elephants of the northern West Bengal region during 2001–06 by my research team[174] found that the population was about 500 individuals, or higher than earlier estimates, over an area of about 2,000 sq. km. This could be explained by natural increase after elephant herds ceased to be captured since 1981[175] as well as influx from the forests of Assam. Elephant herds now began using habitats they had avoided in preceding decades; for example the radio-collars we put on two adult female elephants showed that these herds stayed entirely within the Jaldapara Wildlife Sanctuary,[176] an area that only a few bulls had frequented in earlier decades (figure 9.18).[177] Other elephants that were collared, some with satellite-linked transmitters, moved more extensively: one family group in the west described a home range of over 1,000 sq. km, including visits to Nepal during the two crop harvest seasons, while other families moved from Buxa Tiger Reserve in the east into Assam.[178] West Bengal state has declared a number of protected areas but the Buxa-Jaldapara complex is possibly the only viable habitat for the beleaguered elephants of this state.

A contiguous distribution of elephants still existed along the Himalayan foothills from Sankosh river eastward to the Brahmaputra river in Assam and the Northeast Frontier Agency (now Arunachal Pradesh) at the time of independence. Save for the Brahmaputra valley, forest cover was still quite high across the entire northeastern region and, hence, the elephant could still have enjoyed genetic contiguity south of the Brahmaputra into the other smaller states as well.[179] The entire region was fertile ground for elephants and possibly held the largest regional concentration of the species around 1950.

Post-independence, Assam continued to capture elephants in large numbers. The available figures indicate that about 1,200 elephants or an annual average of 200 animals were captured during 1955–60.[180] The same rate of capture continued in Assam over the following two decades; Lahiri-Choudhury records over 5,564 elephants captured for an annual offtake of 278 animals between 1961 and 1980, with a further 586 elephants declared "rogue" and shot in the northeastern states mostly from composite Assam.[181] This rate of capture and killing is likely to have depressed wild elephant numbers in the northeast.

The most significant influence on the elephant population of the northeast has been the attrition of its habitat from several causes. Slash-and-burn shifting cultivation or *jhum* has been a way of life for centuries among the inhabitants of the moist hilly tracts outside the Brahmaputra valley and sustainable at low human population densities.[182] Indeed the mosaic of vegetation in various stages of succession, maintained under rotation periods exceeding 20 years, was a boon for elephants that favoured bamboo, grasses, and other "weedy" plants in secondary growth.[183] The expanding human population post-independence resulted in a reduction in per capita availability of land and a shortening

9.19 *Jhum* or shifting cultivation being practised in the northeast Indian state of Meghalaya (2010).
Photograph by Asad Rahmani.

9.20 Tusked bull elephant and a *makhna* at Kaziranga in a test of strength (2008). There are about two *makhna*s for every tusked bull among adult elephants at Kaziranga today.

Photograph by Karpagam Chelliah.

of the *jhum* cycle in Meghalaya accompanied by land degradation.[184] At the level of landscapes intensive *jhum* areas are clearly suboptimal for elephants (figure 9.19).[185]

The northeast has been fertile ground for several insurgency groups. Assam has lost forest as a direct result of insurgency; the Bodo people agitating for an independent state, for instance, have cleared large tracts of forest since the 1990s, chiefly in the Kameng and Sonitpur Elephant Reserves.[186] Elephant-human conflict escalated in the wake of this rapid loss of habitat. Apart from enhanced crop depredation, elephants killed 34 people in this region while people poisoned 22 elephants during 2001–03.[187] North of the Brahmaputra several elephant herds virtually became nomads wandering widely through agricultural areas.[188]

Illegal capture and trade in elephants have been rife in the northeast, especially in Arunachal, though the extent of this problem has never been properly documented.[189] It is believed that some of the animals caught are taken into Myanmar while others end up for sale in the far south in Kerala. Given their low capacity for law enforcement, the northeastern states have also been happy hunting grounds for ivory poachers.[190] Because of the substantial numbers of tuskless bulls in the northeastern populations, the extent of ivory poaching has been lower than that in the south of the country; however, the changes seen in the relative proportions of tusked versus tuskless bulls point to a gradual attrition of tuskers.[191] Records of elephants captured in Assam during 1937–50 had indicated an equal number of tusked and tuskless bulls.[192] In the Kaziranga population this ratio has changed to two *makhna*s for every tusker among older bulls in recent years (figure 9.20).[193]

Consumption of elephant meat is still prevalent among certain tribes in the northeast. The Karbis and the Garos shun elephant flesh, but the Mizos, Kukis, and Nagas continue the tradition of consuming it. Vivek Menon recorded several instances of elephants, mostly females, being killed in Meghalaya during the 1990s by Mizos and Nagas, with the help of locals, for the specific purpose of extracting meat.[194] More disturbing were instances of elephant meat, whose long fibres reportedly preserve well in the humid tropics, being preserved and even canned for supply to militant groups in the region. It is pertinent to mention here that the wild elephant has, for all practical purposes, disappeared from Mizoram, while it is greatly reduced in numbers in Nagaland.[195]

Anwaruddin Choudhury's survey of the elephant's status in the northeast shows a very fragmented distribution.[196] Along the Himalayan foothills to the north of the Brahmaputra about 3,000–3,500 elephants are distributed from northern West Bengal into western Assam, Arunachal Pradesh, and Bhutan.[197] There are several threats to this genetic contiguity, chiefly in the region of Pakke Tiger Reserve in central Arunachal.[198] A decisive 20-kilometre break occurred beginning the 1970s in the east along the Dibang valley of Arunachal from cultivation and settlement.[199] To the south of the Brahmaputra a population of 1,100–1,200 elephants ranges over Arunachal, Assam, and Nagaland. The range of this population includes the Namdapha National Park, noted for its exceptional biodiversity. South of the Brahmaputra the Kaziranga National Park, located in the floodplains of the great river, is part of a large population of nearly 3,000 elephants. These elephants move south into the Karbi Anglong hills and beyond to the Jaintia hills during the monsoon period when Kaziranga is largely flooded, though the numbers and extent of movement are not known. The link between Kaziranga and Karbi Anglong is rather tenuous because of settlements, cultivation, and tea plantations along a major highway, leaving only a few narrow passages across the road at the western and eastern extremities. The fourth large elephant population in the northeast, estimated at 2,800–3,000 animals, ranges mainly in the Garo and Khasi hills of Meghalaya and adjacent areas in Assam. The northeast also has several smaller and scattered elephant populations, each numbering less than 50 individuals.

At the time of independence the east-central Indian states of Bihar and Orissa also had a sizeable population of elephants spread over the Chota Nagpur plateau and the Eastern Ghats. The Chota Nagpur Plateau featuring ancient Precambrian rocks and coal deposits (in the Damodar river valley) also has among the largest and most valuable concentrations of minerals, including iron ore, copper chromite, bauxite, mica, limestone, and apatite, in the subcontinent. Mining has thus been the bane of the once extensive Sal forests of this region,[200] fragmenting the elephant's habitat and polluting the rivers and streams on which they critically depend during the dry period (figure 9.21).[201] Nor has the mineral wealth of this region benefited the local people who remain impoverished in one of the least developed regions of India. In Bihar the state-owned Forest Development Corporation began replacing the Sal forest with plantations of teak, an activity that was resented by local people. An agitation for a separate state of Jharkhand intensified and culminated in such a state being carved out of the forested districts of southern Bihar in November 2000. In the course of this movement about 10,000 hectares of some of the best natural forests of the region were felled by the agitating people in the Saranda, Kolhan, and Porahat forest divisions of Singbhum during the late 1970s and early 1980s.[202] These forests also constituted some of the finest elephant habitats of east-central India. In the Eastern Ghats, particularly in southern Orissa, the intensification of shifting cultivation has likewise disturbed the elephant's habitat.

As the forests of the region degraded and fragmented, an interesting change in the elephants' behaviour occurred in the 1980s. A small population of about 50 elephants in the Dalma hills of southern Bihar had, until then, confined its range to these hills during the dry months, moving down to the plains during the monsoon, with some of them

9.21 Iron ore mining in the Keonjhar district of Orissa (2004). Significant areas of forest here and elsewhere in central India have been destroyed by open cast mining.
Photograph by Shanti and Ashish Chandola.

9.22 A solitary bull elephant emerges from a village pond at Kandi Nadia in Murshidabad district, West Bengal (2009). Both elephant groups and solitary bulls have been in serious conflict with agriculture in this region since the late 1980s.
Photograph by Subrata P. Chowdhury.

moving east to the West Medinipur district of West Bengal to feed on the paddy crop.[203] In November 1983 a herd of 40 elephants made a deeper foray into the state, reaching the Hugli district, within 50 kilometres of Calcutta city, before turning back.[204] During 1986–87 the problem became more serious when different herds from Dalma moved out in three directions, one herd going westward into Sarguja district of Madhya Pradesh while two others went northward and eastward into West Bengal (figure 9.22).[205] What triggered these long-distance movements or dispersal is not fully resolved. The elephants were obviously not living in ideal habitats in Bihar. However, I suspect that two major droughts that occurred in India during 1982 and 1986, coinciding with a global climatic phenomenon known as El Niño Southern Oscillation,[206] could have been the proverbial "last straw" that pushed the elephants out of southern Bihar to seek greener pastures.[207]

The herd of 18 elephants that dispersed into Madhya Pradesh caused terror among the villagers, killing 45 people and causing entire settlements to be abandoned before the authorities finally rounded up the elephants in a six-week long operation at Sarguja in 1993.[208] Immigration of elephants into this region – including Ambikapur, Jashpur, Korba, and Raigarh districts of the newly-formed state of Chhattisgarh – has continued since then.[209] These elephants, numbering over 125 individuals by 2009, have moved in from Jharkhand as previously, and possibly from Orissa as well. Damage to crops and houses, and loss of human life continues.

The elephants moving deeper into southern West Bengal have adopted a completely different lifestyle. They have discovered a landscape transformed by the successful regeneration of forests by local communities under the Joint Forest Management Programme. Such forest patches provide them convenient shelters during daytime for launching raids into nearby paddy and vegetable fields at night. My visit to this region in November 2009 showed that over 100 elephants now move here seasonally, and that the elephants are spending more time in this attractive landscape than earlier.

These recent changes in the movement patterns of elephants in east-central India have depleted the elephant population of Jharkhand, especially in the Dalbhum and Singbhum regions. One population that has not lost ground and possibly even consolidated is that of the Palamau Tiger Reserve. The elephants of this 1,000 sq. km tract of moist and dry deciduous forest, isolated from other populations, are descendants of captive animals released by the raja of Sarguja during the early 20th century.[210]

Orissa holds the largest regional populations of elephants but here again several changes have occurred in recent decades.[211] The state has about 1,000 sq. km of land under mining and about 4,000 sq. km of elephant habitat under shifting cultivation. Simlipal Biosphere Reserve in Mayurbhanj district to the northeast is the most intact habitat for elephants, and consequently suffers the least from elephant-human conflict. This population may number about 500 elephants. To the west of Mayurbhanj the forests between the Baitrani and Brahmani rivers, especially those of Keonjhar district, are under heavy pressure from mining and shifting cultivation. Nearly half of the state's mining area is located here, resulting in considerable disturbance and fragmentation. About 150 elephants are believed to inhabit this region. West of Keonjhar the forests of the Sambalpur region constitute another important habitat for elephants. Although in a better state than the forests of Keonjhar, the mosaic of reserve forests, cultivation, village forests, and fallow land has resulted in a fragmented landscape. There has been a virtual doubling of the elephant population to about 500 animals over the past two decades, largely due to immigration from adjoining forests. However, as we saw in southern West Bengal, in recent years elephants have been moving out of the Sambalpur forests – possibly due to disturbance from the presence of militant Maoists and illegal cultivation of *ganja* (cannabis) – into the heavily industrialized Jharsuguda district to raid the paddy crop at night, taking shelter in regenerating village forests during the day.[212]

The elephant range of Sambalpur maintains a tenuous link with another large tract of forest further south extending up to the mighty Mahanadi river. Although there are many settlements in this region, the forests are not disturbed by mining activity. The Satkosia Gorge Sanctuary forms the backbone of this elephant range that is believed to hold 450–500 elephants. South of the Mahanadi the extensive but highly disturbed and fragmented forests of southern Orissa seem to have lost their capacity to retain a viable population of elephants.

We finally turn to southern India that holds the largest regional population of elephants in Asia.[213] At the time of independence it is likely that the south had two populations of elephants separated by only the Palghat gap. Developments during the colonial period had already begun to fracture the habitats of both, but genetic continuity was still possible within each population. One population of elephants ranged to the north of the Palghat gap over the Western Ghats and Eastern Ghats in Kerala, Tamil Nadu, and Karnataka, with its northern limit in the North Kanara region of Karnataka bordering Goa and Maharashtra. The second population to the south of the gap ranged over the Anamalais, Nelliampathis, Periyar, and Agasthyamalai.

The Western Ghats were ideal terrain for generating hydroelectric power and the post-independence period witnessed a surge in dam construction in this stronghold of the elephant. The anti-malarial campaign of the 1950s also provided more conducive conditions for people from the plains to settle in the hill forests. The North Kanara district had more than 80% of its land under tropical evergreen and deciduous forest; the construction of the giant Kalinadi dam along with mining of iron and manganese ore changed this scenario rapidly.[214] The forests receded and degraded from the demands of people for fuelwood, manure for homestead gardens, and fodder for livestock. The escalating elephant-human conflict also resulted in elephants being eliminated; a bounty for killing crop-raiding elephants during earlier times had encouraged farmers to shoot them.[215] Submergence of river valleys and resettlement of people in adjoining forests soon isolated a population of about 50 elephants in northern Karnataka. More dams, iron ore mines, and coffee plantations further south along the ghats also meant that few elephants survived up to the Coorg (Kodagu) district. An exception was the Malnad Plateau, separated from the crestline of the ghats, where another isolated population of about 300 elephants survived. In Kodagu itself a vast swathe of coffee cultivation separated a sparse, western distribution of elephants in the rain-swept Pushpagiri and Brahmagiri range from an abundant, eastern distribution in the deciduous forests of Tithimathi, Nagarahole, and Kakanakote.

Elephant captures in the Kakanakote forests continued until 1971 when the rising waters of the Kabini dam submerged the *kheddah* site at Mastigudi. The resettlement of people necessitated by this reservoir in Karnataka, along with encroachment of 10,000 hectares of adjoining forests at Pulpally in Wyanad, Kerala, restricted the passage of elephants moving across the Kabini river (figure 9.23).[216] South of the Kabini the forests of Bandipur, the erstwhile hunting preserve of the maharaja of Mysore, constituted the core of what remained as a stronghold of the elephant, with Nagarahole to its north, Wyanad to the west, and Mudumalai in Tamil Nadu to the south. This 2,000 sq. km tract that held about 4,000 elephants was once proposed as the first interstate protected area, the Jawahar National Park,[217] an idea ahead of its time, but realized a decade later as the Nilgiri Biosphere Reserve in 1986 – an enlarged and more comprehensive concept of the biosphere reserve.[218]

9.23 Elephant herd at Mastigudi along the Kabini (2001) whose waters were impounded by a dam in the 1970s. Movement across the Kabini is now restricted to a 5-km stretch between the forests of Bandipur and Nagarahole.

During the 1950s developments to the east of Mudumalai to harness hydel power in the Sigur plateau threatened the link between the Western Ghats and the Eastern Ghats, but the main passages for the elephant fortunately survived.[219] The Sigur Plateau had historically been extensively settled, with its human population declining from disease and local wars. The developmental projects brought in a fresh wave of settlers.

Beyond, the rugged forested terrain of the Eastern Ghats had also been under much cultivation for centuries. The forests of the Biligirirangans, Madeshwaramalai, and the

Melagiris held another 2,000 or more elephants. A major expansion of settlement took place to the east of the Biligirirangans in Karnataka when Tibetan refugees were provided forested land at Bailur during the 1970s.

South of the Nilgiri massif, the forests of the Attapadi plateau in Kerala were rolled back for settlement and cultivation during the early 1970s, greatly reducing the mobility of the elephants of this region. A major conservation success was the stalling of the proposed dam across the Kunthipuzha in the rich evergreen forests of Silent Valley, to the

9.24 Evergreen forests along the Kunthipuzha river in Silent Valley, Kerala (1986), the proposed site of a major hydroelectric dam that was shelved during the 1980s following protests from conservationists.

9.25 Physical obstructions to elephant movement have contributed to fragmentation of habitat in India. This sequence of pictures shows examples of such obstructions including:
a Open-cut canal in the Anamalais, Tamil Nadu, that cannot be crossed by elephants. The person in the picture is veterinarian V. Krishnamurthy (see Chapter 8).
b Penstock pipes along the eastern slopes of the Dindugal Forest Division, Tamil Nadu, near Periyar in Kerala, that have completely obstructed the movement of elephants.
Photograph by N. Baskaran.
c The steep, concrete-lined sides of the Chila-Motichur canal in Uttarakhand that cannot be negotiated by elephants; the bridge in the background has been occasionally used by bull elephants and in recent years by family groups to cross the canal.

west of Attapadi in Kerala (figure 9.24). The campaign against the dam during the 1980s spearheaded by a people's science movement, the Kerala Sastra Sahitya Parishat, was instrumental in raising environmental consciousness among the Indian public.[220] A few hundred elephants range over Coimbatore division in Tamil Nadu, and Attapadi, Silent Valley, New Amarambalam, and Nilambur regions of Kerala.

That the Palghat gap had been a barrier to the movement of elephants for a considerable period of time was clear from genetic studies (figure 9.25).[221] South of the gap the Anamalai and Nelliampathi ranges constitute another stronghold of the elephant. The Parambikulam-Aliyar project, involving a series of dams along with associated canals and penstock pipes, has disrupted the traditional movement patterns of elephants in this region that now holds over 2,500 elephants.[222] Expansion of tea plantations in the Valparai plateau and the Munnar range has likewise fragmented the habitat.[223] The granting of leases by the Kerala government for planting cardamom in the forest undergrowth has also effectively separated the elephants of the Anamalai-Munnar region from the Periyar plateau to the south. A population of about 100 elephants is, however, isolated in the Idukki district around the forests of a massive dam commissioned here in 1976.

The Mullaperiyar dam constructed during the early 20th century impounds a reservoir that is the nucleus of the Periyar Tiger Reserve, famous for its population of over 1,000 elephants. Along with the forests of Srivilliputhur in the drier east, and the moister Ranni, Kanni, Achenkovil, and Punalur, this forest tract is the least fragmented in southern India and is estimated to hold about 2,000 elephants.[224]

Settlement and cultivation along the Ariankavu pass, through which run major road and railway lines, have now isolated a smaller population of 100–150 elephants[225] in the southern Ashambu-Agasthyamalai range centred around the Kalakad-Mundanthurai and Neyyar protected areas in Tamil Nadu and Kerala, respectively. Hydroelectric and irrigation dams, and tea and rubber plantations, have spread their tentacles across this

9.26 Ivory inlay on door, Madurai, Nayaka period, 17th century.
Photographed at Musée Guimet, Paris.

landscape considered to be the richest in biodiversity outside of the northeast of the country. Reports of sightings of "pygmy" elephants that appear in the media from time to time have not been supported as yet by scientific evidence.[226]

A brief mention must be made of the Andaman islands that have a feral population of elephants introduced post-independence.[227] In 1962 a timber company abandoned a small group of captive elephants in the Diglipur forests of northern Andamans, and another group of 40 elephants on Interview island (133 sq. km). On Interview island the elephant population has not increased but seems to have impacted many tree species.[228] Administrators face the dilemma of how to manage these feral elephants; the most pragmatic course at present seems to be capturing the elephants at Diglipur that are in conflict with agriculture, but retaining those at Interview island for the present.[229]

***

In February 1948, only a few months after independence at a time of great social turmoil in the country, Prime Minister Nehru actually found the time to send a letter to the administration at Junagadh on the need to preserve the remaining lions.[230] This strongly signalled his concern for the wild denizens of the country, quite apart from the imperatives of constructing dams to provide power for industry and irrigation for the peasants' fields. Ironically, the Ashokan lion crafted in Perso-Hellenistic style was selected as the national emblem,[231] and this animal symbolizing imperial rule became India's national symbol.[232] This was in spite of the eminent naturalist M. Krishnan arguing in 1952 that the elephant was the truly pan-Indian animal that deserved to be the national symbol.[233]

The Indian Board for Wildlife formed in 1952 set about addressing the challenges of conservation. The Wildlife Protection Act of 1972 was the first comprehensive legislation that categorized species on the basis of their charisma and the threats they faced; the elephant was placed in Schedule I or the highest category of protection. This effectively banned the systematic capture of elephants across the country. It was however the tiger – India's national animal – that attracted the greatest attention of conservationists and the government alike with the launch of Project Tiger in 1973.

In the meantime the elephant faced a new threat from ivory poaching, the consequence of a rather distorted import policy as well as a surge in global demand for "white gold".[234] Ivory carving was among India's many traditional crafts (figure 9.26). For nearly a century prior to independence, India had been the largest importer of ivory from Africa, much of this en route to markets such as Europe and China.[235] Substantial quantities of ivory were also used by the large pool of Indian carvers with the finished products finding a ready market abroad. After independence the import of African ivory began to decline steeply because of the government's fiscal policy that discouraged foreign imports of all consumer or luxury goods by imposing extremely high customs duties, ostensibly aimed at conserving foreign exchange in a poverty-stricken country.

The high landed cost of African ivory eventually put this out of the reach of Indian ivory importers. From the pre-independence figures of about 250 tonnes of ivory each year, the quantities imported came down to under 15 tonnes by the early 1980s.[236] During the 1970s there were at least 7,200 ivory craftsmen in the country, about half of them in the south turning out superior carvings by working with their hands as compared to their northern counterparts who worked mostly with electric lathes.[237] With the supply of cheap African ivory drying up, these craftsmen turned to tusks from Indian elephants supplied legally by state forest departments and illegally by poachers.[238]

A wave of ivory poaching hit the southern Indian elephant populations during the 1970s, beginning from the Periyar Tiger Reserve in Kerala and working its way northward

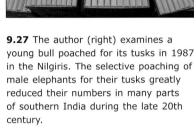

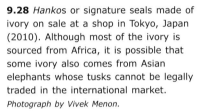

9.27 The author (right) examines a young bull poached for its tusks in 1987 in the Nilgiris. The selective poaching of male elephants for their tusks greatly reduced their numbers in many parts of southern India during the late 20th century.

9.28 *Hanko*s or signature seals made of ivory on sale at a shop in Tokyo, Japan (2010). Although most of the ivory is sourced from Africa, it is possible that some ivory also comes from Asian elephants whose tusks cannot be legally traded in the international market.
Photograph by Vivek Menon.

into Tamil Nadu and Karnataka, as tusked males soon became rare in the affected populations. The slaughter of far greater magnitude of African elephants during the 1980s only added to the misery of the Asian elephant (figure 9.27).[239] Japan was the final destination for the harvested tusks that were used not for expression of art but for manufacturing *hanko*s or signature seals (figure 9.28).[240] Further, Asian ivory fetched higher prices because of the market perception that this had superior qualities for working as compared to African material.[241] Vivek Menon's investigations of the Asian ivory trade showed that tusks were being smuggled from Kerala's coast to West Asia, in particular to Dubai, that served the East Asian markets through ports such as Singapore and Hong Kong. The international trade in Asian elephant ivory was banned by CITES as early as 1976 but this was being laundered along with legal African ivory. Only a few expert end-users could make out the difference between tusks from the two continents.

Based on my field work in southern India, I estimated that a minimum of 100 bulls, and perhaps up to 150, were killed each year during 1977–86 by poachers for an annual yield of 1.8 tonnes of ivory.[242] In November 1986 the government banned all domestic trade in Indian ivory but poaching still continued in the southern populations. Two years later the government abolished customs duties on imports of African ivory in an attempt to keep the local carvers supplied with legal tusks. By then most traders had already ceased to import tusks from Africa, and only 2,000 carvers still continued this profession.[243] The historic ban on international trade in African ivory imposed by CITES in 1989 resulted in a temporary crash in ivory prices and a collapse of the trade globally.

The Indian elephant had only a short respite. By the 1990s the populations in the south had been depleted of large tuskers and poachers were increasingly targeting sub-adult elephants, sometimes as young as four years. In Periyar there was less than one adult male elephant for every hundred female elephants,[244] a situation that has since improved to about 1:60 more recently.[245] Further north in the Nilgiris, the ratio of adult male to female skewed to about 1:25 by the end of the century.[246] Other major populations in the south such as Anamalai-Parambikulam and the Eastern Ghats, too, witnessed

9.29 One hundred and one caparisoned tusked elephants are paraded at the annual Thrissur Pooram festival in Kerala. The vast crowds thronging around the captive elephants ironically also symbolize the large human populations across Asia that now isolate the wild elephant populations into small forest patches.
Photograph by Balan Madhavan.

skewed sex ratios though clear figures are not available. It was only at Nagarahole and further north in Karnataka that the larger males were still spared, as seen from its 1:5 ratio,[247] but poachers had begun to discover this region as well.

During the 1990s ivory poaching also spread to other parts of the country.[248] Orissa was especially hard hit but the impacts here have not been studied as well as in the south. The large proportion of tuskless bulls or *makhna*s in the northeast conferred some immunity to the populations here from ivory hunters, but tuskers were still being picked off selectively. The male to female ratios here remained healthy, relative to the south, because of the sizeable numbers of *makhna*s. Vivek Menon has documented the modus operandi of the ivory poachers who used a variety of methods from high-velocity rifles to crude muzzle-loading guns, electrocution, and even arrows with poisoned tips to kill their prey.[249] A rash of elephant killings in 1994 in northern West Bengal was attributed to hunters using arrows smeared with poison from the crushed seed of *Aesculus punduana* and fired from bamboo pipe guns. These hunters had clearly come from the northeast. The poaching of six bulls in 2001 at Corbett National Park in the north was also by hunters from the northeast using poisoned arrows fired from a crossbow. During the past decade the levels of ivory poaching have come down, but at least 15–20 tuskers are still killed each year in the country, mostly in Orissa.

In 1990 the Indian government set up a task force to prepare an action plan for Project Elephant, a comprehensive framework for the conservation of this flagship species.[250] The task force made several recommendations for long-term and short-term measures to conserve elephants and their habitats.[251]

For this purpose it identified 11 elephant landscapes across the country, each of which was to be constituted as an Elephant Reserve (later changed to Elephant Range).[252] The key management action in each Elephant Reserve was to ensure the integrity of the overall landscape through protecting, strengthening, or creating corridors for the movement of elephants. The task force also addressed issues relating to mitigation of elephant-human conflicts, controlling poaching, building capacity within states for elephant management, promoting interstate coordination in conservation efforts, and improving the welfare of the considerable numbers of elephants in captivity. Project Elephant was formally launched in February 1992.[253]

The previous year India had begun to liberalize its policies to help unleash its potential for economic growth. The fear among conservationists now was that a new wave of development in the form of roads, railway lines, dams, canals, and mines would further fragment the range of the elephant. Growing conservation awareness however helped avert further damage on several occasions.[254] At the same time the welfare of captive elephants in the country, estimated at about 3,500 individuals,[255] has been under increasing public scrutiny.[256] With a ban on logging imposed by the Supreme Court of India in 1996, a Thailand-like situation has developed in parts of the country as regards the elephant. This gave the impetus for elephants from the northeast to be brought to places as far as Kerala in the south for sale. In Kerala itself the elephant has been increasingly commercialized for use in festivals, not only in temples but also in churches and mosques. The Pooram festival at Thrissur boasts of a grand display of 101 caparisoned tuskers (figure 9.29), while other temples put up more modest shows. The very use of the captive elephant is now being questioned, a paradigm shift from the taming of the beast about 4,500 years ago.

The continued pressures on the wild elephant population, and the emerging crisis with the captive elephant, prompted the Indian government to set up another task force in 2010 to take stock of the situation and make fresh recommendations in implementing elephant conservation.[257] The elephant also finally received at least the symbolic recognition it had long deserved – it was declared as the National Heritage Animal.

India has probably managed to hold on to the numbers of wild elephants it had at the time of independence, though with moderate loss of space, a more fractured landscape, and fewer tusked bulls. Indonesia has lost a much greater fraction of its forest cover and its elephant population post-independence, though it maintains (in Sumatra) a significantly larger proportion of its land under forest and protected areas than does India. Indonesia has struggled to reintroduce a culture of the captive elephant, while India has struggled to keep up its centuries-old relationship with the animal. It is not possible to spot a clear winner in the conservation-of-the-elephant contest post-independence. The important point is that both countries still hold reasonable numbers of the wild elephant to ensure its future survival.

CHAPTER 10

Ecology and Conservation
of Asia's Elephants

SINCE THE TIME OF PALAKAPYA, the ancient Indian sage who expounded his knowledge of the life of elephants to the ruler of Anga, we have made considerable progress in our scientific understanding of this subject. European science of the 19th century provided descriptions of elephant anatomy and disease, though the accounts of big-game hunters were more often misleading than enlightening when it came to the social life of the animal; an exception to this was G.P. Sanderson who was more an elephant catcher than a hunter.[1] F.G. Benedict's 1936 classic on the physiology of the Asian elephant, based on experimental work carried out on a single animal in America, is however still unmatched.[2] It was only after the mid-20th century that biologists began to use statistical tools and sophisticated laboratory techniques to study the ecology and behaviour of the elephant in the wild and in captivity.

In 1972 naturalist M. Krishnan provided an insightful account of the elephant's life based on years of field observation and photography in which he preceded the formal descriptions of infrasonic calls in elephants and female choice of mates.[3] Krishnan described sounds that were "throaty, audible" and "low pitched but clearly audible from a distance". Sanderson too had mentioned similar sounds made by elephants. Female choice in a large mammal was not a fashionable concept among biologists of the time but was later confirmed by studies of the African elephant. Although Krishnan was incorrect in applying the term "musth" to female elephants (this was also the case with some African elephant researchers), he was probably correct in attributing temporal gland secretion in cow elephants to pregnancy. Scientific studies of the ecology of the Asian elephant begun during the 1970s by biologists of the American-based Smithsonian Institution at places such as Wilpattu and Yala,[4] were later continued by Sri Lankan researchers at Ruhuna, Gal Oya, Somawathiya, and Wasgamuwa.[5] Simultaneously, surveys of elephant habitats began at various places in India.[6] These studies provided a basic picture of the status and structure of elephant populations, their ranging patterns, feeding habits, and various behaviours. This author's study during the early 1980s in the Biligirirangans of southern India provided the first account of elephant-human interactions in relation to the natural ecology of the species.[7]

Since then several studies in India and Sri Lanka have provided a more complete picture of the ecology of the elephant in tropical dry forests.[8] Less is known of the elephant in tropical moist forests simply because the dense vegetation makes it difficult to observe elephants that are also more thinly distributed as compared to their counterparts in dry habitats.[9]

Much has been written about the prodigious appetite of the elephant but this is rather misleading.[10] It is true that an adult elephant consumes several hundred kilograms of fresh plant every day but this is only about 8–10% of its body weight – a much smaller proportion than that consumed by smaller animals. Larger animals have lower metabolic rates than do smaller animals. Elephants have a bewildering array of plant species and parts to choose from in the biologically rich tropical forests and grasslands they inhabit, and they feast on these diverse offerings with great gusto. Leaf, stem, bark, pith, twig, root, tuber, fruit, flower, it would seem that nothing is spared to satisfy the appetite of this mega-herbivore. It is true that a tree pushed over by an elephant or a standing tree with its bark stripped is quite obvious to even a casual observer. But there are also signs of feeding by an elephant which are sometimes hardly visible to even an experienced observer, as when it dexterously plucks the tiny flowers, one at a time, of a touch-me-not herb (*Mimosa pudica*) with the tip of its trunk! As a creature that needs to consume a large quantity of food the elephant cannot afford to be too choosy, yet there is considerable choice in the type and the part of the plant it eats. It also changes its diet

10.1a-c Elephants feed on a wide variety of plant species and parts including grass, bamboo, leaves, and bark.

seasonally, eating tender, nutritious grass after the rains but switching to other plants when the land turns dry (figure 10.1).[11]

Some of the early studies in Sri Lanka concluded that elephants ate mainly grasses[12] but there was a problem with these results. The observers studied elephants mainly in grasslands where it was easy to view them, and the elephants obviously ate grasses in these habitats! What they ate when they moved into the woodlands, and how important this was to their nutrition, were open questions. I used a sophisticated chemical technique, known as the "stable carbon isotope" method, by which I traced the isotopic signature recorded in collagen present in elephant bone to see the relative importance of grasses versus browse (trees and shrubs) in its diet in the drier forests of southern India.[13] To my surprise I found that grasses contributed only about 30% of the carbon for synthesis of collagen protein in adult elephants, the remaining 70% coming from browse plants, on average. This not only meant that elephants were feeding a lot more on shrubs, trees, and bamboos than one realized but also that they were deriving more nutrition from these plants than from grasses.[14]

The elephant's penchant for feeding on agricultural crops has been noted since ancient times. Crop raiding by elephants can be broadly explained by habitat factors such as fragmentation that increases contact between elephants and cultivated fields, and by foraging theory which predicts that an animal should try to obtain the energy it requires in the least time possible (figure 10.2).[15] Studies clearly indicate that conflict is highest in the most fragmented landscapes. By feeding on cultivated crops, elephants can also obtain much higher quantities of forage, as well as plants or plant parts with superior nutritional qualities, especially protein and certain minerals such as calcium and sodium.[16] Adult male elephants also tend to raid crops much more frequently than do family groups, especially in the more intact habitats, though in the fragmented landscapes the family groups raid equally frequently.[17] The higher propensity of male elephants to enter the human domain may be a manifestation of risk-taking behaviour that has evolved in this species for obtaining better nutrition, exhibiting musth, and increasing their chances of mating (figure 10.3).[18]

10.2 Cultivated crops such as paddy and millets constitute an important component of the diet of some wild elephants. Elephant dung can be seen in this picture in a raided paddy field in Cheko village adjoining Buxa Tiger Reserve in northern West Bengal (2003).

10.3 An adult male elephant in musth walks majestically along a dry riverbed in the Motichur Sanctuary in Uttarakhand (2004). Increased nutrition from crops could potentially help a bull to maintain good body condition and express musth more succesfully.

10.4 A female elephant fitted with a collar to which is attached a Global Positioning System device that determines its location precisely every few hours. This animal collared near Dam Dim in northern West Bengal in November 2005 described a home range of over 1,000 sq. km between then and July 2006.

In order to obtain the best mix of nutritious plants, elephants thus typically move over a range of several hundred or even over a thousand square kilometres. (Sri Lanka seemed to be an exception as the early reports had hinted at much smaller home ranges.) By fitting VHF (Very High Frequency) radio-transmitters on elephants in the Nilgiris, a team from the Bombay Natural History Society found that the home ranges of three family groups were 530–800 sq. km.[19] My research team working in the moist forests and floodplains of the Duars found similar range sizes of 300–800 sq. km.[20] Even VHF telemetry may underestimate home range size to a certain extent. When we began deploying GPS (Global Positioning System) collars on elephants we found that the home range of a family group and an adult bull exceeded 1,000 sq. km (figure 10.4).[21]

Interestingly, recent telemetry studies in Sri Lanka have indicated that the elephants here do not move long distances but confine their range to about 100 sq. km.[22] Perhaps the more resource-rich habitat on the island is able to satisfy the needs of elephants within a small area. It is also possible that generations of isolation on an island in the evolutionary past resulted in overcrowding and competition, with the consequence that elephants adjusted to small-sized home ranges.

The feeding proclivities of the elephant could obviously be expected to have considerable impact on the natural vegetation, particularly the trees they debark or push over (figure 10.5). In the dry habitats of Africa this has been particularly visible at times with large stretches of woodland being transformed into savanna.[23] Biologists Dieter Mueller-Dombois and Natarajan Ishwaran working in Sri Lanka's dry forests during the 1970s, too, described how elephants could distort the crowns of various trees, damage their bark, or even push them over.[24] They however did not express any concern about the persistence of these forests or the elephants. Some researchers in southern India, on the other hand, concluded that elephants were causing irreversible declines in the populations of some trees.[25] Concerns over short-term changes in plant or even animal populations are often misplaced because of a lack of appreciation of the dynamic nature of the natural environment. Based on longer-term observations that damage to trees, their death and

10.5 A bull elephant feeding on the bark of a *Zizyphus* tree it has pushed over (1992). Such behaviour may sometimes be a social display to other elephants, with feeding being a secondary function.

10.6 Organization of elephant society can be considered as a hierarchy of increasingly complex levels of the basic family unit. This can be illustrated in this series of pictures from Kaziranga, Assam (2010), showing:
a Mother plus a single child.
b Two adult females who may be related as sisters, with their children.
c A larger elephant herd or kin group with several females and their children of various ages.

regeneration could be cyclical processes of dry ecosystems, I have cautioned against hasty judgements about overpopulation and culling of elephants.[26] In the Biligirirangans I observed heavy damage to *Acacia suma* trees during 1981–82, but this impact has tapered off since then, and the woodland still survives today. In Mudumalai I observed steep declines in the shrub *Helicteres isora* and the tree *Kydia calycina* during the 1990s, but these plants have come back strongly in recent years in spite of no appreciable change in the elephant population.

✳✳✳

The extraordinarily detailed studies of the African elephant in its savanna habitats have revealed a complex, multi-tiered society.[27] The Asian studies are only now beginning to catch up with those in Africa (figure 10.6). George McKay described what he termed as "nursing units" and "juvenile-care units" among elephant groups in Sri Lanka.[28] In the Biligirirangans I observed that the only stable unit was the family comprising one adult cow and her children; thus I preferred the term "joint family" for a group that had more than one adult cow, which could have belonged to two generations (as with grandmother-mother) or the same generation (as with sisters). More than one family group also associated with other families temporarily, while a large number of families comprising a clan came together at certain times of the year (figure 10.7). More recently, T.N.C. Vidya and I showed through genetic analyses that adult cows within a family or joint-family group are indeed sisters as they are more closely related to each other than to cows from other groups.[29] Another interesting facet of the social life of elephants we

10.7 An elephant clan comprising many related families gathers along the backwaters of the Kabini in Karnataka during March–May, prior to the onset of the monsoon (2001).

10.8 A small calf well-protected between the legs of two adult cows, one of whom is its mother and the other its aunt, within the family group at Mudumalai, Tamil Nadu (2002).

10.9 An elephant group at the Hambetta swamp at Mudumalai during the dry season (1989). The tendency of elephant families to congregate at water sources such as these gives greater opportunity for them to meet and socialize.

10.10 A full-grown tuskless bull or *makhna* in musth at Kaziranga, Assam (2009). Is it possible that tuskless bulls could be investing more resources in the expression of musth as compared to tusked bulls?

10.11 A young adult bull, aged about 25 years, sporting an exceptionally long pair of tusks that may signal superior genetic fitness through higher resistance to paraites and diseases.

found is that sub-adult bulls related to each other disperse from their family to new areas.

The size of an elephant group is dictated by a complex of several factors. Being a highly social animal, the elephant would like to associate itself with as many of its companions, especially its relatives, as possible. A large elephant group is also able to better protect its young members from predators such as tigers (figure 10.8). There are however many constraints to forming large groups. When high-quality forage is scarce, as during the dry months, it would not be very efficient for elephants to move as a large group since there would be much competition among the members while feeding. It would be better for individual families to forage by themselves. During the dry months, however, water is limited and thus many related families cluster around water sources such as rivers, streams, swamps, and ponds. In such a situation a family would have an increased chance of meeting other families and, naturally, would spend some time with each other; this would tend to increase group size during the dry period as I found in the Biligirirangans (figure 10.9).[30] With the onset of the monsoon the elephants began to disperse from their dry season range over a wider area and split into smaller groups. Nevertheless, the largest groups formed toward the end of the wet season, when forage was available in plenty, as families constituting a clan regrouped before moving to their winter range. Large groups may also form during early winter when cultivated crops are ready for harvest; our GPS-collaring in northern Bengal showed that many families totalling over 80 individuals came together for about two weeks near the border with Nepal specifically for raiding the ripening paddy crop.

Even aspects of how female and male elephants indulge in the mating game have become clearer only in recent years. Initially, it was believed that female elephants became receptive for mating about every three weeks,[31] but later studies of reproductive hormonal cycles clearly showed this to be once every 14–16 weeks.[32] A cow elephant can conceive during a narrow window of three or four days at the time of ovulation (release of egg from the ovary) when a bull gets the opportunity to sire a calf; a cow is more likely to accept a bull when it is in musth.

As in ancient times, much of our present knowledge of musth in Asian elephants comes from scientific studies of captive animals. In an early study, Sri Lankan veterinarian M.R. Jainudeen and his associates found that when a bull elephant comes into musth the levels of testosterone (male sex hormone) in the blood increase about 50-fold as compared to the non-musth period;[33] this has been confirmed by later studies in Western zoos.[34] Beginning at age 15–20 years a bull elephant typically comes into musth only once a year, though a clear annual cyclic pattern may only establish in older animals.[35] When in musth a bull elephant is reputed to become more aggressive towards competitors and become dominant in the local male hierarchy. Adult bulls in a population also come into musth at different times of the year, perhaps to avoid life-threatening conflict that has been explained within the framework of game theory for the African species.[36] Such studies are only now underway for the Asian elephant and are already revealing a very complex tale of competition or cooperation among males, and the choices exercised by females in the mating game.[37] It is possible that females could be choosing bulls with longer tusks, but that tuskless bulls could make up by growing larger and expressing musth more strongly (figures 10.10 and 10.11).[38]

Most people have heard an elephant's trumpet but the language of elephants goes much beyond this sound. Naturalists had described throbbing sounds that elephants made but had not realized the true significance of such calls. Playback experiments in Western zoos had revealed that Asian elephants are capable of hearing low-frequency

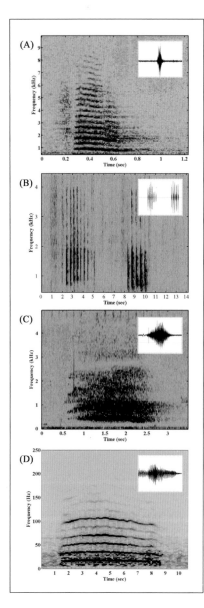

10.12 Sound spectrograms of elephant calls. The four basic call types that can be clearly recognized are (A) trumpet, (B) squeal, (C) roar, and (D) rumble. *Based on Nair et al. (2009).*

sounds (infrasound) that are not fully audible to humans.[39] In 1986 an article by Katharine Payne and her associates that characterized the infrasound made by elephants sent a ripple of excitement through the community of elephant biologists.[40] Although the study of the language of wild elephant sounds was quickly initiated in Africa,[41] it has begun only recently in Asia. With my colleagues Smita Nair and Rohini Balakrishnan I have been recording calls of wild elephants, analysing the sound spectrograms, and simultaneously videographing the animals' behaviour at Mudumalai and Kaziranga.[42] Four basic types of sounds emerge from these recordings; three of them (trumpet, roar, and squeal) are audible to us while the fourth (rumble) has low frequencies that we cannot hear (figure 10.12). There are many subtle variations in infrasound that are not easy for us to understand, though elephants presumably understand them perfectly. A bull in musth and a cow in oestrus make distinct low-frequency calls to attract each other. Elephant families communicate through infrasound that easily travels 5 kilometres or more in dense forest; with such power it is not easy for them to get lost even in unfamiliar terrain.

Elephants also communicate through chemical signals – their versatile trunk is after all a long nose with an acute sense of smell superior to that of a bloodhound. Here again our scientific knowledge of chemical communication comes mainly from studies carried out on Asian elephants in Western zoos and other captive elephant facilities. The pioneer in this field, Bets Rasmussen, along with several of her associates, has identified several important compounds in a complex array of "pheromones" that female and male elephants secrete from their temporal glands and interdigital glands (located between their toes), or excrete in urine and dung.[43] A very important finding was that female elephants, as they approach ovulation during their oestrous cycle, secrete in their urine a substance labelled (Z)-7-dodecen-1-yl acetate by chemists.[44] This finding was remarkable in that many insects such as female moths also produce an identical compound to attract their mates. A bull's interest in a cow elephant picks up when it detects this signal in the latter's urine trail or when it performs a "flehmen" to check the latter's receptivity (figure 10.13).[45]

Another interesting finding was that young bull elephants in musth secrete from their temporal glands sweet-smelling chemicals such as esters and alcohols, while older bulls secrete foul-smelling frontalins and nonanone especially during late musth, corroborating descriptions of musth in ancient Sanskrit lore.[46] Rasmussen and colleagues also identified a ketone named cyclohexanone as the chemical signal used by a musth bull to attract the attention of cows for mating.

The legendary intelligence of the elephant has not been much investigated, perhaps unsurprisingly: after all, you cannot put elephants into a laboratory maze and test them as you can do with rats. Bernhard Rensch's well-known study at Germany's Munster Zoo, reported in 1957, established that a young female Asian elephant could easily memorize at least 20 visual patterns.[47] Recently, by getting three animals to stand in front of a jumbo-sized mirror, researchers found that an elephant may be able to recognize itself among its companions.[48] Each of the three elephants began to inspect its own image in the mirror with its trunk, while one elephant also recognized a white mark placed on its forehead and began to feel the corresponding area on the mirror with its trunk. Recognition of self had previously only been known in humans, other apes, and dolphins. While more experiments need to be done on this subject, the hint that elephants may have an awareness of self indicates a high level of cognitive ability and social complexity that has otherwise only been suspected by the layman and the expert observer on elephants.[49]

Elephants share several demographic features with humans.[50] Female and male of both species typically attain sexual maturity between age 12 and 15 years; while women

10.13a and b Flehmen by a bull elephant at Minneriya, Sri Lanka (2006). The tuskless bull examines the oestrous status of a female elephant by touching the urogenital opening and then placing the tip of his trunk inside his mouth.

10.14 The Asian elephant can typically live up to 70 years of age.
a A newborn elephant is about 3 feet (90 cm) in height and weighs about 100 kg (Nagarahole 1997).
b Tara, photographed at the Mudumalai elephant camp (1984) when she was about 70 years, was about 7 feet 7 inches (230 cm) tall, and weighed about 2,800 kg.

can reproduce until about 50 years, cow elephants do so for another 10 years. The male of both species can sire children well into old age. The 20–21-month gestation in the elephant is a bit more than double that in humans. A single child is the rule in both species. Women in hunter-gatherer societies bear children every few years, depending on environmental resources, while in elephants this is typically every four to five years. Longevity in both species is the proverbial three score and ten years (figure 10.14b). Tipping the scales at 100 kilograms, a newborn elephant outweighs the average human adult by a wide margin (figure 10.14a). By the time a cow elephant is about 30 years old she weighs 3,000 kilograms while a bull of the same age is 4,500 kilograms with the possibility of gaining weight further.

The dynamics of an elephant population is of great interest from the theoretical perspective of what factors regulate change, and, at the same time, indicates its conservation status. A straightforward way of tracking change is to accurately estimate the size of an elephant population at regular intervals of time, say every few years, but there are many practical difficulties in obtaining such precise estimates. A cruder method is to deduce possible trends from the ages and gender of elephants in a population. If a population has a high proportion of young and sub-adult individuals, it is likely to be an increasing population as opposed to one that is composed of mostly older individuals. This is not foolproof as we do not know how many elephants of various ages are dying each year in the population.[51] A third approach is to estimate the birth rate of the elephant population, not a very difficult task in places where elephants are easily visible, and the death rate of the population, not an easy task in tropical forest where carcasses may go unnoticed, and use mathematical formulations to deduce trends. Using such an approach in the Biligirirangans in southern India, I concluded that Asian elephant populations are unlikely to increase at a rate greater than about 2% per year over time periods of a few decades.[52]

An elephant population is also generally resilient to a crash, unless it is targeted by poachers. The key to the stability of an elephant population is low death rates among adult females, usually not more than 2% or 3% per year. In East Africa the great drought of 1970–71 resulted in many elephants dying at Tsavo National Park but even these were not more than about 20–25% of the population; the same population was later the target of ivory poachers but has since recovered much ground. We do not understand how a severe drought or a disease epidemic (such as anthrax) could impact Asian elephant populations, though there is a record of the latter affecting wild elephants in the Chittagong hills during the mid-19th century.[53] Indications are that if we provide basic protection and space to an elephant population, it is quite capable of looking after itself!

***

The range of the wild elephant across Asia is presently only about 6% of the area it occupied about 4,000 years ago.[54] We have an estimate of between 37,000 and 51,000 Asian elephants in the wild,[55] though the figures for many populations are still guesstimates.[56] More important, the range is highly fragmented, with not more than about ten populations having over 1,000 individuals each, and dozens of lesser populations many of which are under 50 animals each.[57] This is in stark contrast to its African cousin that still enjoys an overall range ten times larger and a population size about eight times higher.[58] Indeed, northern Botswana alone has far more wild elephants than the total number, wild and captive, in Asia!

The world's human population is expected to stabilize at under 10 billion by the middle of the 21st century, not considering the effects of any major catastrophe such as a disease epidemic killing large numbers of people, or climate change creating inhospitable conditions in many densely populated regions. In a part of the Asian continent that has witnessed among the most rapid rates of economic growth globally post-World War II, the attrition of the natural habitat of the elephant has been accompanied by not just a reduction in elephant populations but also sharp increases in elephant-human conflicts. Economic growth in South and Southeast Asia has not yet peaked; among the elephant-range states even Malaysia and Indonesia, the two countries that have made the greatest progress overall, still have a lot of economic steam left. Thailand has yet to catch up with its southern neighbour. China is the fastest growing major economy in the world, although not many elephants are left in this giant Asian country. The only other country with over a billion people, India's growth story is hardly a decade old and is expected to follow the trajectory of its giant neighbour. Vietnam's economic engines are revving up, while Sri Lanka could accelerate now that its civil war has ended. The other important Asian elephant range states (Myanmar, Laos, and Cambodia), among the poorest in the world, are merely waiting in the sidelines before their people too join the race for the good life. How do we then conserve Asian elephants, hopefully for posterity, in our rapidly changing world?

The best hope for the continued survival of elephants lies in the ability of Asian countries to make available intact landscapes for these creatures. Given the high human population densities of the range countries, it is a pipe dream to attempt to completely exclude people from these landscapes. The alternative and acceptable option is to maintain the integrity of the landscape by protecting and strengthening "corridors" that can be traversed by elephants in the course of their natural movement. This requires an ecological approach in which neighbouring countries, or indeed different provinces or states within a country, have to cooperate to ensure that connectivity across an elephant landscape is maintained. For instance, landscape integrity along the Himalayan foothills requires the cooperation of India and Nepal in the west, and of India and Bhutan in the

10.15 Satellite image (1999) of the Nilgiri-Mysore-Wyanad Elephant Landscape in southern India, home to the largest population of the Asian elephant. The locations of several important "corridors" across this landscape are shown to illustrate the importance of protecting these in order to prevent fragmentation of habitat. *LANDSAT image downloaded from the Global Land Cover Facility, University of Maryland, USA.*

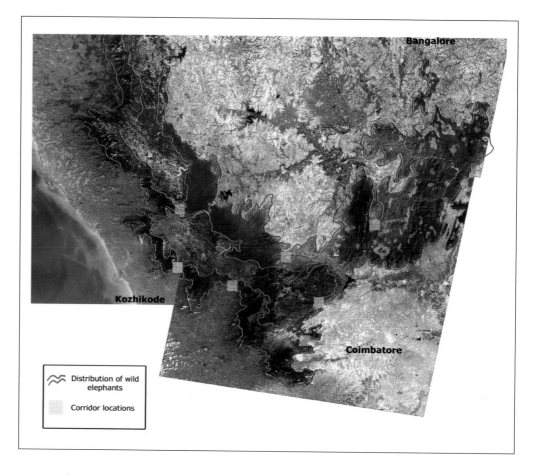

east. Within India the states of Kerala and Karnataka have to work together to ensure the movement of elephants between the Brahmagiris, Wyanad, and Kodagu regions.

Fortunately, the authorities in India now recognize the importance of maintaining corridors, and a recent compilation of such places in the country has helped raise this awareness (figure 10.15).[59] Non-government organizations have also been active in promoting the concept of corridors; two collaborating NGOs – Asian Nature Conservation Foundation[60] and Wildlife Trust of India[61] – have achieved significant success in strengthening important corridors in the south and the northeast. It is important that displacement of people is either avoided or kept to a minimum, and that those who relocate are adequately compensated; where feasible more innovative approaches such as payments (conservation easements) to local communities for maintaining their land as corridors should also be explored and implemented.

When making decisions about how large a landscape to set aside for conserving elephants we need to consider what constitutes a viable population size of the species and how many elephants a particular habitat can support.[62] The issue of what is a viable population is rather technical: in brief, the smaller the size of a population the greater the probability that it will go extinct from chance fluctuations in birth and death as well as environmental factors such as drought.[63] Managers should aim to maintain a population of 100–300 individuals, depending on factors such as male:female ratio and local ecology, within an area of 200–600 sq. km in dry forest or five times this area in rainforest, with a short-term view of conservation over the next century; a longer-term evolutionary perspective calls for a tenfold increase in these figures.

The dilemma then is what to do with small, isolated populations of elephants whose viability is highly questionable. There is no dearth of such populations, many of which are in chronic conflict with people living in their vicinity. I do not think that we can have a uniform policy on this issue. A decision on whether to give protection to such elephant populations or to do away with them would depend on regional and national circumstances. Let me illustrate this with examples of two countries, India and Vietnam, who are in very different situations as regards their elephant populations. India has about 28,000 wild elephants, including some of the largest populations in the continent, and many small populations; Vietnam has less than 100 wild elephants, all of them in very small populations. India has the luxury of not having to worry about capturing some of these small populations without compromising on the conservation of the larger ones; indeed, the costs of maintaining these isolated or dispersing groups are becoming too high in terms of their conflicts with people. There will obviously have to be some regional considerations; the state of Jharkhand in east-central India where the habitat is highly fragmented may still decide that it wants to keep some of its elephants, irrespective of viability or costs. Elephant biologists can help them select a population (or populations) that has the best chance of survival, but it is important for them to be fully aware of the efforts they have to take for managing it and nursing it back to a more viable state. During the 1980s Andhra Pradesh in southern India decided, against the grain of expert opinion, to hold on to a population of about 50 elephants that had immigrated from neighbouring states, in spite of high levels of elephant-human conflict initially. These elephants seemed to settle down in the Kaundinya Sanctuary created specifically for them, but after two decades have mostly dispersed to other areas.[64]

Although its elephants are in a desperate position, Vietnam may decide to take a shot at conserving the species at least at one place. Cat Tien National Park has not more than about 15 elephants, a vanishingly small population that would need a herculean effort to increase up to reasonably safe numbers.[65] The government has made a beginning by conferring protection upon a forestry enterprise area adjoining the national park. This would add up to a total area of over 800 sq. km that could potentially hold more than 100 elephants. Intensive management of the habitat to increase carrying capacity plus strict protection of the existing elephants would be needed if this population were to have even a glimmer of hope of surviving the coming years and decades, but it is not impossible. We have the example of the elephants of the Addo region in South Africa that were in a similar situation about a century ago but have bounced back to a population of over 400 individuals given strict protection.[66] However, the comparison is not entirely valid as African savanna elephants have the capacity to increase at higher rates than Asian elephants in tropical moist forests.[67]

An increasingly important challenge in conserving elephants during the 21st century will be to mitigate the conflicts between elephants and people. Conflicts are certainly increasing on a local scale, not just due to increasing pressures on the elephants' habitat but, ironically, also because of the success of conservation efforts resulting in increasing populations or even elephants losing their fear of people. Even if conflicts are not actually increasing, the perception of conflict is altering in tune with changing conservation paradigms and rapid economic development. Increasing wealth in society is accompanied by decreasing tolerance towards wildlife depredation. As legislated systems of conservation spread across the range of the elephant, governments are being increasingly called upon to take responsibility for containing the marauders within the confines of protected areas. Vinod Rishi, a former director of India's Project Elephant, told me an interesting story that proves this point: As a young forest officer in West Bengal nearly three decades ago he once visited a village (as he has undoubtedly done countless times) where an elephant had killed a person in the course of its nocturnal

10.16 Several approaches have been taken to mitigate elephant-human conflicts, including:
a Digging a trench along the boundary of forest and cultivation (Village Bachahalli, Bandipur National Park, Karnataka, 2009).
b Erecting an electric fence that delivers a pulsed current of millisecond duration but at a high voltage in the range of 5,000–10,000V (Village Talamalai, Satyamangalam Forest Division, Tamil Nadu, 2007).

excursion into agricultural fields. The villagers were obviously agitated over this incident but when he asked the village headman as to whether they would prefer to eliminate the offending animal he got a surprising reply. The headman told him to leave the elephant alone – after all the government imposed taxes on the people of this country; the crops they had lost was simply nature's way of imposing a tax. The mood of the people had completely changed decades later when he visited a village in the same region to inquire into another such incident of elephant-human conflict. I must interject here that crop-raiding elephants have killed about 1,000 people in northern West Bengal alone over a period of two decades. The present generation of villagers wanted the elephant to be killed. The elephant was not part of nature anymore, a nature with which their ancestors had coexisted for centuries.

Some governments have responded to their citizens' calls for relief by providing compensatory payments for loss of human lives, crops, or property, erecting barriers such as high-voltage electric fences or digging ditches along the boundary of forests and cultivation, and chasing, capturing, or eliminating elephants (figure 10.16).[68] Elephants learn how to negotiate a ditch or get past an electric fence, if they detect any weakness in its design or maintenance, and can return to their original place of capture when relocated 100–200 kilometres away. One lesson that has been learnt is that the participation of people is essential if measures to mitigate conflict are to succeed. It is also inevitable that some conflict will continue as long as elephants and humans live side by side; it is thus imperative that we promote coexistence to the extent possible.

As one in every three or four Asian elephants is presently in captivity, it is obvious that the welfare of these animals is an important consideration in the conservation of the species. At the same time, the captive population of a country or region should not merely be a sink for a declining wild population. Captive elephants are held under very different management regimes, from private or community ownership to temples, zoos, circuses, and timber or forest camps (figure 10.17). There is little or no breeding among these elephants, with the exception of the animals in timber and forest camps.[69] The real issue is not just about sufficient breeding among captive elephants but also of their physical and mental health, quality of life, and longevity.

There has been much debate in recent years about the ethics of keeping an animal such as the elephant, with superior cognitive abilities, in captivity. The animal welfare/rights movement has been particularly critical of the display of elephants in circuses and zoos, especially in the West, as well as many of the elephant husbandry practices in the Asian range countries. While this subject is too complex to be treated in detail here, I would urge the reader to refer to a recent volume that discusses the issues in sober, scientific terms.[70]

I think that one has to take a balanced approach in this matter. We cannot wish away the 15,000-odd elephants in captivity, and release them all into the wild or even into exclusive sanctuaries (as some wishful thinkers have been suggesting). More elephants from the wild are bound to be taken into captivity because their populations are small, isolated, and non-viable, or are in serious conflict with people. Trained captive elephants are also needed in managing wild populations, especially in controlling conflict. The approach should therefore be to set standards for the upkeep of captive elephants and ensure that these are enforced. Many institutions, whether it be zoos, circuses, or temples, certainly need to be circumspect about the need to keep elephants. To the extent possible elephants should be kept as social groups so as to mimic their natural behavioural inclinations. It does not do the individual elephant or the species any good if an animal is kept solitary, as in some zoos in the West and temples in the East, or as a gender-specific

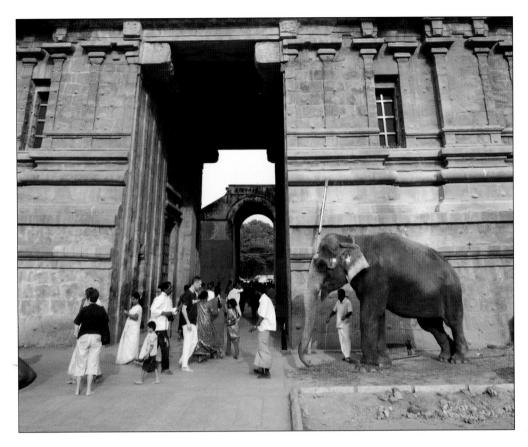

10.17 Captive elephants are kept under a variety of management situations including forest camps, zoos, temples, and private ownership. Two examples are illustrated here:
a Female elephant at the Brihadishvara temple, Thanjavur (2011).
b (following page) Elephant carrying tourists at Sunkadakatte inside Nagarahole National Park (2003).

group (all-male groups in the famous Guruvayur temple in Kerala). There are no easy solutions to these issues; you can consolidate solitary elephants into social groups, but what do you do with the 60-odd male elephants at Guruvayur? In countries such as India and Sri Lanka the sentiment of the sacred elephant has helped the species to survive. If we completely do away with elephants in captivity, would this also mean that people would begin to look upon the elephant only as a dangerous agricultural pest?

There has to be a dialogue among the various players who manage or study elephants – administrators, zoos, temples, biologists, communities who have traditionally kept elephants, and conservationists – as to how best to manage the global population of captive elephants while also ensuring this is not an unnecessary drain on the wild population.

***

In this story of the Asian elephant, I have not made a mention so far of an interesting change that proboscideans went through during the Ice Age. When we think of elephants and their ancestors, we assume that they followed only one trajectory as regards their size, namely, in the direction of becoming larger and larger until they eventually died out. Quite the opposite happened during the Ice Age when elephants were trapped on islands because of rising sea levels during warmer phases.[71] On the island of Sulawesi in the Sunda shelf of Southeast Asia, the elephant *Elephas planifrons* or an earlier form dwarfed to *Elephas celebensis*. On the Mediterranean islands of Malta and Sicily (26,000 sq. km) the elephant *Elephas namadicus* gave rise about 500,000 years ago to *Elephas falconeri* that stood only 1 metre high and is the smallest elephant known (figure 10.18). More recently, the woolly mammoth was isolated on Wrangel Island (7,600 sq. km) off the Siberian coast about 11,000 years ago, by which time its compatriots had become extinct elsewhere. Restricted by habitat and resources, these creatures began to shrink in size

10.18 A skeleton and a reconstruction of the dwarf elephant, *Elephas falconeri*, that evolved from the much larger *E. namadicus* about half a million years ago on the Mediterranean islands of Malta and Sicily.
Photographed at a travelling exhibit on the elephant at the Milwaukee County Zoo, Wisconsin, USA.

generation after generation; over a 5,000-year period or about 100 mammoth generations an adult mammoth had shrunk from 3 metres to only 1.8 metres (6 feet) at its shoulder.[72]

If I were to make a bold prediction about how *Elephas maximus* would look 10,000 years from now, assuming of course that humans have thought it fit for the species to survive, I would say that a full-grown elephant would be only half its present size and somewhat less threatening to *Homo sapiens*. We are now confining elephants to "island habitats", none of which is larger than Sicily and most being smaller than Wrangel Island. If the modern conservation ethic prevails, elephants will be maintained in high densities in these small patches of habitat. As the top predators go extinct in these habitat islands, as resources become limited for elephants and other creatures, as large elephants sporting long tusks are targeted by hunters, and as big, bad bulls in conflict with agriculture are killed, nature would select for smaller-sized individuals with the passing generations. Evolution aided by the human hand would wind the clock backward on the spectacular, 60-million-year-old proboscidean drama.

I may be hopelessly wrong. Ten thousand years is a long time in human evolution. We have come a long way from the time when humans began to domesticate plants and animals about 10,000 years ago at the end of the last Ice Age. Science and technology have equipped us to play God and tinker with the genetic basis of life, even though our understanding of the natural world is woefully inadequate. Already biologists are talking about bringing back to life the extinct woolly mammoth through genetic cloning and using the modern elephant as a surrogate mother. By the end of this century we may have radically altered the nature of Earth's biodiversity. Hopefully, we may also have found a way to preserve the elephant in all its giant glory.

notes

CHAPTER 1

1   Shoshani and Tassy 1996; also see Sukumar 2003, ch.1 for a review.

2   For long zoologists believed that a creature known as *Moeritherium* was the first animal that could be classified as a proboscidean. More recently the discovery of *Phosphatherium* (Gheerbrant et al. 1996) and *Eritherium* (Gheerbrant 2009) have pushed this ancestry back by about five million years.

3   Maglio 1973.

4   Rohland et al. 2007.

5   Vartanyan et al. 1993.

6   Vidya et al. 2009; Maglio 1973.

7   Nanda 2002.

8   DNA or deoxyribonucleic acid is the chemical that carries the genetic code of all living organisms. While most of the DNA is found in the nucleus of the cells of an animal, a small quantity of DNA is also present in the mitochondrion or powerhouse of the cell that is inherited through the mother's egg and not the father's sperm. The mitochondrial DNA is thus used to trace the matrilineal history of an animal population. The presence of two genetic clades in the Asian elephant was first shown by Hartl et al. 1996.

9   The term "haplotype" refers to a distinct sequence of the mitochondrial DNA and is used to identify all individuals in a population who can be traced in their evolutionary history to a particular ancestral mother.

10   Vidya et al. 2009.

11   The two landforms would have been connected during glacial periods when sea levels were lower because large amounts of water were locked up in ice sheets.

12   I use the term "human" to refer to any species of the genus *Homo*.

13   Gary Haynes, "Modern elephant-bone assemblages as models for interpreting Ambrona and other fossil waterside deathsites", manuscript prepared for the 2005 "Ambrona y Torralba" exhibition, Museo Arqueológico Regional, Madrid, Spain.

14   Stanford 1999, ch. 4, provides a discussion of this subject.

15   Domínguez-Rodrigo et al. 2005.

16   Howell 1966.

17   Klein 1987; Villa 1990.

18   Lister and Bahn 1994.

19   Sukumar 2003, ch. 1, and Barnosky et al. 2004 review this subject.

20   Martin 1984.

21   Surovell et al. 2005.

22   Misra 2001 is the main source for this discussion.

23   Ibid.

24   This name is used when two species, *S. insignis* and *S. ganesa* are found together and it is difficult to separate them.

25   Pappu et al. 2003, 2011.

26   Ninkovich et al. 1978.

27   Petraglia et al. 2007.

28   Williams et al. 2009.

29   Brooks and Wakankar 1976.

30   Mathpal 1984.

31   Ibid., p. 73.

32   Brooks and Wakankar 1976, p. 37 for the Kharvai image and p. 71 for the elephant hunt scene whose location has not been mentioned.

33   Ibid., p. 51.

34   Ibid., p. 35.

35   Pradhan 2001, p. 32.

36   Personal discussion with S. Pradhan on Feb. 6, 2010.

37   Nandadeva 1986.

38   Ratnagar 2001 provides a very readable account of the Indus civilization, while Lahiri 2000 brings together a collection of scholarly papers on the subject.

39   Kenoyer 1998; also see www.harappa.com.

40   Erdosy 1998; Enzel et al. 1999.

41   Sukumar et al. 1993.

42   Carrington 1959, p. 162.

43   These were pointed out to me by Prajna Chowta who has closely observed the elephant-human relationship in Karnataka. She writes (Oct. 23, 2010) that "traditionally the Jainu Kurubas... have always used a rope or ropes around the neck, where the feet are placed in position for riding and the animal knows immediately that the rider is in control when the feet are placed inside the rope. This is used in the earlier stages of training and is used continually if the rider is keen in the upkeep of the tradition (that is to always use a sack and rope around the neck, when riding an elephant)."

44   Thomas and Joglekar 1994.

45   Lahiri 1992, ch. 2.

46   Dhavalikar 1982; Singh 2009, p. 231.

47   Baker and Manwell 1983.

CHAPTER 2

1   Childe 1926.

2   Jha 1998, ch. 3; Thapar 2002, ch. 4. I have used the translation (2nd ed.)

of the *Rigveda* by R.T.H. Griffiths (1896), accessed at www.sacredtexts.com.

3   Singh 1965, p. 78.

4   *Rigveda* Book I, Hymn 64, 7.

5   *Rigveda Book* IV, Hymn 16, 14.

6   *Rigveda* Book IV, Hymn 4, 1.

7   *Rigveda* Book VIII, Hymn 33, 8.

8   Bhargava 1956, p. 100.

9   Lahiri-Choudhury 1991.

10   *Rigveda*, Book I, Hymn 140, 2.

11   *Rigveda*, Book I, Hymn 64, 7.

12   *Rigveda*, Book VIII, Hymn 33, 8; Book X, Hymn 16, 14.

13   *Rigveda*, Book X, Hymn 106, 6.

14   *Rigveda*, Book IX, Hymn 57, 3.

15   *Rigveda*, Book X, Hymn 40, 4.

16   *Rigveda*, Book X, Hymn 106, 6.

17   Singh 1965, p. 77.

18   Ibid., p. 76.

19   *Rigveda*, Book X, Hymn 92, 11.

20   *Yajurveda*, Kanda VI, Prapathaka IV, 6.4.5. R.T.H. Griffiths' (1899) translation of the *Yajurveda* has been used.

21   *Vajasaneyi Samhita* XXX, 11; *Taittiriya Samhita* III, 4.9.1.

22   *Vajasaneyi Samhita* XXIV, 11.

23   *Vajasaneyi Samhita* XXIV, 11.

24   *Atharvaveda*, Book 9, Hymn 3. R.T.H. Griffiths' (1895–96) translation of the *Atharvaveda* has been used.

25   *Atharvaveda*, Book 3, Hymn 22.

26   *Aitareya Brahmana* IV, 1; also see Lahiri-Choudhury 1991.

27   Ibid.

28   Ibid.

29   *Sama Vidhana Brahmana* III, 6, 11.

30   *Chandogya Upanishad* VII, 24, 2; cf. *Katha Upanishad* I, 1, 23, quoted by Singh 1965, p. 78.

31   Jha 1998, p. 53.

32   Lahiri-Choudhury 1991.

33   van Buitenen 1973, Book 1, Introduction.

34   Goldman 1984, Vol. 1 *Balakanda*, p. 23.

35   Thapar 1982.

36   I have used the *Ramayana* translation of Princeton University Press that is based on the critical edition of the Oriental Institute, Vadodara, under the general editorship of Robert Goldman (1984).

37   *Ramayana, Balakanda*, Sarga 6, 21–23.

38   *Ramayana, Ayodhyakanda* (henceforth AyK), Sarga 13, 10.

39   AyK, Sarga 14, 26–27.

40   AyK, Sarga 16, 26.

41   AyK, Sarga 17, 1.

42   AyK, Sarga 20, 3–4.

43   AyK, Sarga 20, 15.

44   AyK, Sarga 20, 28–31.

45   AyK, Sarga 22, 7.

46 AyK, Sarga 23, 15.
47 AyK, Sarga 24, 17.
48 AyK, Sarga 29, 9.
49 AyK, Sarga 35, 16.
50 AyK, Sarga 36, 9.
51 AyK, Sarga 35, 25.
52 AyK, Sarga 42, 5.
53 AyK, Sarga 57–58.
54 AyK, Sarga 49, 5–6; 48, 34–36.
55 AyK, Sarga 88–89.
56 AyK, Sarga 77, 1.
57 AyK, Sarga 90, 1.
58 AyK, Sarga 104, 21–23.
59 Lahiri-Choudhury 1991.
60 *Ramayana, Aranyakanda* (henceforth ArK), Sarga 10, 2–6.
61 ArK, Sarga 2.
62 ArK, Sarga 44, 18–19.
63 ArK, Sarga 54, 28.
64 *Ramayana, Kiskindhakanda*, Sarga 36, 2–9; 63, 5–7.
65 *Ramayana, Sundarakanda*, Sarga 1, 13.
66 *Ramayana, Yuddhakanda* (henceforth YuK), Sarga 3, 21–24.
67 YuK, Sarga 9, 17.
68 YuK, Sarga 28, 16.
69 YuK, Sarga 30, 14–17.
70 YuK, Sarga 31, 37-38.
71 YuK, Sarga 48, 47.
72 YuK, Sarga 58, 2–14.
73 YuK, Sarga 60, 10–11.
74 YuK, Sarga 98, 5.
75 YuK, Sarga 103, 25.
76 YuK, Sarga 116, 28.
77 AyK, Sarga 66, 30.
78 Lahiri-Choudhury 1991.
79 ArK, Sarga 22, 24.
80 Lahiri-Choudhury 1991.
81 Ibid.
82 Ibid.
83 Ibid.
84 Bakshi 2002.
85 Wakankar and Mhaiskar 2006 provide an English translation of the *Gajashastra* from a Devanagiri transcript of epigraphist V. Vijayaraghavacharya completed in 1926 through the patronage of the rajasaheb of Aundh, an erstwhile princely state in Maharashtra.
86 Edgerton 1931; Edgerton however does not believe that the *Matangalila* is necessarily a later text than the *Hastyayurveda* or the *Gajashastra*.
87 An English translation first became available for the *Matangalila* with the work of Edgerton (1931) and more recently for the *Gajashastra* under the editorship of Wakankar and Mhaiskar (2006). A full English translation of the *Hastyayurveda* is not yet available.
88 Sukumar 2003, pp. 100–01; Rasmussen et al. 2002.
89 Moorey 1994, pp. 116–25.
90 Ratnagar 2001, ch. 3.
91 The elephant tusk recovered from the Uluburun shipwreck of the 14th century BCE could have originated in northern Africa; see Lafrenz 2004.
92 Moorey 1994, p. 119.
93 Scullard 1974, ch. 1.
94 Breasted 1906, p. 233.
95 A line drawing of this scene is provided in Scullard 1974, p. 29. Painted smaller than the people leading it, the elephant with disproportionately long tusks is interpreted as being the Asian species presumably because of the small ears and the association with the Syrian contingent. The tusks are considered as "artistic license" but I think that the identity of the animal is still questionable.
96 *Inscription of Tigleth-Pileser I*, 6, 70–75, in *Records of the Past* (trans. A.H. Sayce 1888).
97 Oppenheim 1969.
98 Scullard 1974, p. 29. The Black Obelisk of Shalmaneser III that mentions the tributes of elephants and other creatures is displayed at the British Museum, London.
99 Elvin 2004, ch. 2, is an important source for China. His reconstruction is based on the work of Wen Huanran et al. 1995 (not seen in original).
100 The Shang dynasty is believed to have followed the Xia dynasty (circa 21st to 17th century BCE) of which not much is known.
101 A readable account of this subject is provided at http://www.ancientscript.com/chinese.html.
102 Elvin 2004, p. 9.
103 The elephant-shaped bronze vessel was unearthed at Shaxingshan, Lilin, and the cymbal at Shiguzhai, Ningxiang. The objects are displayed at the Hunan Provincial Museum; accessed at http://www.hnmuseum.com.
104 Yang and Capon 2000; Xu 2001.
105 J. Laing-Peach, "Sanxingdui mask relics record traces of Bronze Age", *Shanghai Star*, May 20, 2004.
106 Pit 2 dated as 12th to 11th century BCE.
107 Xu 2001.
108 *The works of Mencius* (trans. J. Legge 1895), p. 281.
109 Elvin 2004, p. 14.

CHAPTER 3

1 I have used Thapar 2002 for a general history of north and northwestern India during this period.
2 Only fragments of Ctesias' works are available from later sources. See Photius, *Indica*, 72, 7. (The *Bibliotheca* of Photius [9th century CE] that includes excerpts from Ctesias' *Persica* and *Indica* was translated by J.H. Freese 1920. Summaries of these are available at sites such as www.livius.org, and www.ccel.org.)
3 For a general history of Alexander, I have used the popular accounts by Wood 1997 and Rogers 2005; for references to elephants in Alexander's campaign I have consulted Scullard 1974, ch. 3, and checked the original Greek sources such as *Arrian's Anabasis of Alexander* (trans. E.J. Chinnock 1893).
4 Thapar 2002, p. 158.
5 *Arrian's Anabasis of Alexander*, Book 3, ch. 3, 8.
6 *Arrian's Anabasis of Alexander*, Book 3, ch. 3, 15.
7 Curtius Rufus, *Historiarum Alexandri Magni*, Book 5, ch. 2, 10. (An English translation by B. Thayer is available at http://Penelope.uchicago.edu.)
8 *Arrian's Anabasis of Alexander*, Book 4, ch. 22.
9 *Arrian's Anabasis of Alexander*, Book 4, ch. 25, 5.
10 *Arrian's Anabasis of Alexander*, Book 4, ch. 27, 9.
11 *Arrian's Anabasis of Alexander*, Book 4, ch. 30, 6.
12 *Arrian's Anabasis of Alexander*, Book 4, ch. 30, 7-8.
13 Curtius Rufus, *Historiarum Alexandri Magni*, Book 8, ch. 12, 11.
14 *Arrian's Anabasis of Alexander*, Book 5.
15 *Arrian's Anabasis of Alexander*, Book 5, ch. 11.
16 The varying figures of Puru's elephants in the Greek sources may seem puzzling. It is possible that Puru divided his force, using part to deter Craterus from crossing the Jhelum while he took another part to engage with Alexander. Thus, Puru seems to have had 200 elephants of which he may have actually used only a part in direct battle.
17 *Arrian's Anabasis of Alexander,* Book 5, ch. 15.
18 *Arrian's Anabasis of Alexander,* Book 5, ch. 15.
19 *Arrian's Anabasis of Alexander*, Book 5, ch. 18.
20 *Plutarch's Lives*, Vol. 3, *Life of Alexander*, ch. 60 (trans. A. Stewart and G. Long 1892).
21 *Arrian's Anabasis of Alexander*, Book 5, ch. 19.
22 Scullard 1974, pp. 66–67.
23 Phylarchus, *Athenaeus*: *the Deipnosophists*, Book 12, ch. 54–55 (trans. C.D. Yonge 1854).
24 Wood 1997, p. 196.
25 Diodorus Siculus, *Library of history*, Book 17, 93, 2 (trans. C.B. Welles 1963).
26 *Plutarch's Lives*, Vol. 3, *Life of Alexander*, ch. 62.
27 McCrindle 1877, pp. 32–33.
28 Diodorus Siculus, *Library of history*, Book 17, 93, 2.
29 McCrindle 1877, p. 32.
30 Scullard 1974, p. 73.

31 Trautmann 1982.

32 I have used all the three available English translations of the *Arthashastra*, the first by Shamasastry 1915, the critical edition of Kangle 1969, and the most recent by Rangarajan 1992; the last mentioned translation that groups the various chapters/sections of the *Arthashastra* according to subject is the one widely available and referred to here.

33 *Arthashastra*, Book 2, ch. 1, v. 1–20.

34 *Arthashastra*, 2.2.6.

35 *Arthashastra*, 2.2.7.

36 *Arthashastra*, 2.2.8.

37 *Arthashastra*, 7.11.3–17; Rangarajan 1992, p. 620.

38 *Arthashastra*, 2.4.3–5; Rangarajan 1992, p. 183.

39 *Arthashastra*, 2.31.17.

40 *Arthashastra*, 2.31.8–10.

41 All the translations seem to have missed the significance of the Sanskrit word, *makkana*, which has been rendered as an elephant without tusks, rather than a "tuskless male". This can also be inferred from the pointed reference to a tuskless elephant that could only mean a tuskless male as all female elephants are tuskless anyway.

42 *Arthashastra*, 2.31.16.

43 *Arthashastra*, 2.32.1; also Rangarajan 1992, pp. 813–16.

44 *Arthashastra*, 2.31.1.

45 *Arthashastra*, 2.32.16.

46 *Arthashastra*, 2.31.11–15.

47 *Arthashastra*, 2.32.22.

48 McCrindle 1877, pp. 90–93 and 218–21.

49 Lahiri-Choudhury 1991.

50 Rangarajan 1992, Appendix 13, pp. 813–16.

51 Ibid., pp. 675–742, brings together the various references in the *Arthashastra* on the subject of military organization and battle arrays.

52 McCrindle 1877, pp. 88–89.

53 *Arthashastra*, 2.2.15–16.

54 Trautmann 1982.

55 Sukumar et al. 1993.

56 Elvin 2004, p. 10, Map 2.

CHAPTER 4

1 Scullard 1974 is the main overall source for this chapter.

2 Photius, *Indica* and *Persica* in *The Bibliotheca of Photius* (trans. J.H. Freese 1920), see chapter 3, note 2.

3 *Diodorus Siculus* 2.16–18.

4 Photius, *Indica* 72.7.

5 See Scullard 1974, pp. 37–49, for a good summary of Aristotle's writings on the elephant.

6 Ibid.

7 Gröning and Saller 1998.

8 *Quintus Curtius* 10.9.18 (trans. J.C. Rolfe 1946).

9 *Diodorus Siculus* 18.34.2–6.

10 Scullard 1974, pp. 81–94.

11 *Diodorus Siculus* 18.71.6.

12 *Diodorus Siculus* 19.14.8.

13 Scullard 1974, p. 86.

14 Ibid., p. 95.

15 *Diodorus Siculus* 19.80–84.

16 See Scullard 1974, pp. 97–98, for the sources.

17 Ibid., pp. 99–100.

18 Ibid., ch. 4.

19 *Plutarch's Lives* (trans. A. Stewart and G. Long 1892), Vol. 2, *Life of Pyrrhus*, p. 15.

20 Scullard 1974, p. 103 with picture in pl. XIVa.

21 Ibid., p. 105 and pl. VIIa. Perhaps having in mind a male Indian elephant he had seen, the artist has wrongly depicted the larger elephant (presumably the mother) with tusks, without realizing that female Indian elephants are not thus endowed.

22 *Plutarch's Lives*, Vol. 2, *Life of Pyrrhus*, p. 20.

23 *Plutarch's Lives*, Vol. 2, *Life of Pyrrhus*, p. 22.

24 The two historians are Joannes Zonaras, a 12th-century Byzantine chronicler whose 18-volume *Extracts of History* covers the period from the "creation" to the year 1118 CE, and Dionysius of Halicarnassus (circa 60 BCE to later than 7 BCE), a Greek historian whose *Roman Antiquities* covers the period from the mythical origin of Rome to the mid-3rd century BCE. Scullard 1974, ch. 4, discusses these accounts in more detail.

25 The Capena plate referred to above (see note 21), perhaps refers to this mother-calf pair.

26 Scullard 1974, pp. 113–15.

27 *Pliny the Elder: the natural history* (trans. J. Bostock and H.T. Riley 1855) 8.9.

28 Scullard 1974, p. 114.

29 Ibid., ch. 5.

30 Lucian, *Zeuxis and Antiochus*, trans. H.W. Fowler and F.G. Fowler 1905.

31 Scullard 1974, pp. 124–25. There seems to be some confusion as to how many elephants were displayed at the procession because the term "real elephants" has been used for those drawing the chariot with Alexander's statue, implying that the other elephants were dummies. Scullard however argues that all were live elephants, totalling perhaps 28 elephants. If four elephants each also drew every chariot, the number of elephants used in the procession goes up to 100 (four elephants drawing the chariot with Alexander's statue and 96 elephants drawing the other chariots), but this many elephants is unlikely.

32 Scullard 1974, p. 134.

33 None of the elephants brought from India by Seleucus Nikator would have survived by 217 BCE. In a battle that Antiochus III fought in 221 BCE against his rebellious governor Molon of Media, the former fielded only 10 elephants (see *Polybius: the histories* [trans. W.R. Paton 1923] 5.53). It is obvious that, between 221 and 217 BCE, Antiochus III obtained many more elephants from the east.

34 *Polybius: the histories* 5.79–86.

35 Scullard 1974, p. 143.

36 Sukumar 2003, pp. 86–87.

37 *Polybius: the histories* 5.84.5–7.

38 *Pliny the Elder: the natural history* 8.9.

39 Adult African forest elephants *Loxodonta africana cyclotis* (or a separate species *Loxodonta cyclotis* as suggested by more recent genetic evidence) are indeed smaller than adult Asian elephants.

40 The identity of Sophagasenus has not been resolved. Various possibilities have been proposed including that he was Subhagasena who ruled in the northwest or was a Mauryan king.

41 *Polybius: the histories* 11.34.11–12.

42 Scullard 1974, p. 145.

43 Sukumar 2003, ch. 2 reviews this aspect.

44 Scullard 1974, ch. 6, is the best source to begin exploring this topic.

45 *Polybius: the histories* 3.45.11–12.

46 Titus Livius (circa 59 BCE –17 CE), also known as Livy, wrote a comprehensive history of Rome *Ab urbe condita* or "From the founding of the city".

47 *Livy: the history of Rome* (trans. B.O. Foster 1929) 21.56.

48 *Livy: the history of Rome* 21:58.

49 *Livy: the history of Rome* 22:2.

50 de Beer 1969, p. 191; Scullard 1974, pp. 170–73; Chandler 1987.

51 Scullard 1974, p. 170. He reproduces these coins and describes the features of the elephant – convexity of the back, sharply sloping hindquarters, low head carriage, and a convex head profile – to argue for it being Indian. The ears seem a bit large but not beyond what a full-grown Asian elephant would possess.

52 *Pliny the Elder: the natural history* 8.5.

53 Scullard also argues (pp. 174–75) that in Latin the term *surus* came to have the same meaning as the English "stake", implying a pun whereby the one-tusked elephant was described as carrying a stake that it used effectively in battle.

54 Ibid., ch. 7.

55 *I Maccabees* 6: 34–46.

56 Scullard 1974, pp. 178 and 185.

57 Shelton 2001.

58 Ibid.

59 *Pliny the Elder: the natural history* 8.6.

60 *Pliny the Elder: the natural history* 8.7.

61 *Plutarch's Lives*, Vol. 3, *Life of Pompeius*, p. 52.

62 *Pliny the Elder: the natural history* 8.7.

63 Cicero, *ad Familiares* 7.1 (*Letters of Cicero*, trans. E.S. Shuckburgh 1899).

64 *Historia Augusta* (trans. D. Magie 1921–24): *The Life of Aurelian* 1.5.6.

65 Presentation by Jo-Ann Shelton at a workshop "Elephants: cultural, behavioural, and ecological perspectives" held at the University of California, Davis, October 2000.

66 Scullard 1974, pp. 198–207 covers some of this history.

67 *Historia Augusta*: *Severus Alexander*, 3.55–57.

68 Herodian, *History of the Roman Empire*, Book 6, *Severus Alexander* (trans. E.C. Echols 1961).

69 The piece is at the Metropolitan Museum of Art, New York, Acc. No. 48.154.8. The two-domed head and the front folding of the top edge of the ear clearly indicate this to be the Asian elephant. The tusk portion of the sculpture has been damaged; thus this is also a bull elephant.

70 Druce 1919.

71 The earliest Latin account comes from Manuscript 10074 at the Bibliotheque Royale, Brussels, dating to the later part of the 10th century CE. A 13th-century translation of this text is available in English (MS. Harl. 3244) at the British Museum, London.

72 Gröning and Saller 1998, p. 242.

73 Ibid., p. 246.

74 Matthaeus Parisiensis (or Matthew Paris) illustrated this elephant in his *Chronica Majora* (1255 CE), now at Corpus Christi College, Cambridge, England. This has been reproduced in Gröning and Saller 1998, p. 248.

75 Bedini 1997.

76 Ibid., pp. 30–31.

77 Ibid., pp. 80–81.

78 This cause is mentioned in Gröning and Saller 1998, p. 249. However, the definitive history of Hanno by Bedini (ch. 6) merely mentions that the elephant was constipated and suffocating. A purgative of gold was given to the animal to clear its constipation, but this was of no avail.

79 Sereno is quoted in Bedini 1997, p. 60.

80 Part of Leo X's epitaph quoted in Bedini 1997, p. 145.

CHAPTER 5

1 *Jaccandha*, ch. 6 in *Minor anthologies of the Pali canon* (trans. F.L. Woodward 1935).

2 *Jaccandha*, ch. 6, p. 83.

3 Thomas 1927 provides a history of the Buddha's life and teachings.

4 The Pali *Jataka*s translated into English under the editorship of E.B. Cowell (1895–1907) are the most commonly referred to sources for these folk tales.

5 *Silavananga Jataka* 72, *Dummedha Jataka* 50.

6 *Kasava Jataka* 22.

7 *Kakkata Jataka* 267.

8 *Upahana Jataka* 231, *Sagamavacara Jataka* 182.

9 *Tayodhamma Jataka* 58, *Vanarinda Jataka* 57.

10 *Dubbalakattha Jataka* 105.

11 *Susima Jataka* 163.

12 *Mahasupina Jataka* 77.

13 *Palayi Jataka* 229, *Kamanita Jataka* 228.

14 *Mahasilava Jataka* 51.

15 *Kulavaka Jataka* 31.

16 *Mahisa Jataka* 278.

17 *Abhinha Jataka* 27.

18 *Guthapana Jataka* 227, *Dubbalakattha Jataka* 105.

19 *Kurudhamma Jataka* 276.

20 Marshall 1939.

21 Dhavalikar 2003.

22 Gupta 1983, p. 33.

23 *Chhaddanta Jataka* 514.

24 Thapar 2002, p. 181.

25 Dhammika 1993.

26 Ibid.

27 Art Historian S.K. Gupta is of the opinion that the "prominence given to figures of elephants and other animals in this [i.e. Ashokan] period cannot be said to be a matter of chance. Perhaps it was a continuation of that old [non-Vedic] tradition of animal worship." Gupta 1983, p. 13.

28 Gupta 1983, p. 15.

29 Thapar 2002, p. 287.

30 Comaraswamy 1994, pp. 6–15, pls. 16–17.

31 Pal 1994, Cat. 86B, 107.

32 Pal 1994, Cat. 93.

33 Pal 1994, Cat. 72B.

34 Pal 1994, Cat. 73; Cort 1995.

35 Mitra 1942, pp. 27–28.

36 Ibid., pp. 41–42.

37 Ibid., p. 18.

38 Ibid., p. 16.

39 Vallely 2002.

40 Dundas 2002.

41 Ibid.

42 Dhavalikar 2003.

43 Lahiri-Choudhury 1991.

44 Nicholas 1954a.

45 McCrindle 1877, p. 61.

46 Ibid., pp. 174–75.

47 *Mahavamsa* 7, 56. The *Mahavamsa* was translated from Pali into German by W. Geiger, from German into English by M.H. Bode, and then revised by W. Geiger; see Geiger and Bode 1912.

48 *Mahavamsa*, ch. 14.

49 *Mahavamsa*, ch. 15.

50 Wisumperuma 2004.

51 Paranavitana 1959a.

52 Wisumperuma 2004.

53 Peris 2005 is a delightful account of the war elephant Kandula, as well as more generally of the use of elephants in war.

54 *Mahavamsa*, ch. 22, 61–63; Peris 2005, ch. 3.

55 *Mahavamsa*, ch. 24, 1.

56 *Mahavamsa*, ch. 25, 22.

57 *Mahavamsa*, ch. 24.

58 Peris 2005, p. 66.

59 *Mahavamsa* 25, 29–31.

60 *Mahavamsa*, 25, 32. Sura is an intoxicating drink. The elephant is being reminded that he has not come here for pleasure's sake.

61 *Mahavamsa*, 25, 35.

62 *Mahavamsa*, 25, 38.

63 Peris 2005, ch. 8.

64 *Mahavamsa* 25, 69–70.

65 Peris 2005, p. 106; *Mahavamsa*, ch. 25, 84–85.

66 *Mahavamsa*, ch. 25, 86–87.

67 Paranavitana 1959b.

68 *Mahavamsa* 29, 4.

69 *Mahavamsa*, 33, 36–44.

70 Kurt and Garai 2007, p. 11.

71 Wisumperuma 2004.

72 Ibid., quoting other authorities.

73 Nicholas 1954a.

74 A photograph of the original *hatthipakara* or elephant wall is available in Attygalle et al. 1959, pl. XV.

75 Kurt et al. 1995.

76 McCrindle 1901, section VIII, translation of Cosmas Indicopleustes. The name Indicopleustes means the Indian navigator but some authorities such as McCrindle are not convinced that he actually travelled to India.

77 Cosmas actually states that the "tusks of the Indian elephants are not large, though on occasion they do elongate and have to be trimmed". This could be generally referring to the absence of full-blown tusks in female Asian elephants and only some males having tusks. As this passage is found in his description of Taprobane, Nicholas (1954a) has taken this to specifically refer to the elephants of Sri Lanka, and to the fact that most male elephants too did not possess tusks on the island.

78 This perceived difference between tuskless bulls (*makhnas*) and tuskers has not been corroborated through morphological measurements but remains anecdotal.

79 Nicholas 1954a.

80 Wisumperuma 2004.

81 See Sukumar 2003, pp. 295–97 for details of this model.

82 Livy, *History of Rome* (trans. G. Baker 1823), 27.14. The term *genus anceps* is taken from *Ab Urbe Condita Libri* (Books from the Foundation of the City), the original Latin version of Livy's history.

83 Peris 2005, pp. 52–53.

84 *Culavamsa* 39, 24–28 (trans. W. Geiger and C.M. Rickmers 1929–30).

85 *Culavamsa* 50, 21–24.

86 Nicholas 1959.

87 Seneviratne 1973 quoted in Jayewardene 1994, p. 6.

88 *Culavamsa*, ch. 76.

89 Nicholas 1954a.

90 Vidya et al. 2009.

91 Codrington 1934.

92 Davidson 1975.

93 Kan 1954.

94 Collection of the Freer Gallery of Art, Smithsonian Institution, Washington DC.

95 Collection of the Freer Gallery of Art, Smithsonian Institution, Washington DC.

96 Elvin 2004, p. 10, Map 2; also see Olivier 1978a.

97 Elvin 2004, p. 15.

98 Ibid., p. 14.

99 Ibid., p. 15.

100 Ka 1958.

101 Duroiselle 1913–14.

102 R.M. Cooler, "The Art and Culture of Burma", accessed at: http://www.seasite.niu.edu/burmese/cooler.

103 Ka 1958.

104 *The travels of Marco Polo* (trans. H. Yule 1903).

105 Yule 1903, vol. 1, ch. 4.

106 Ibid., vol. 2, ch. 51.

107 Ibid., vol. 2, ch. 52.

108 Ringis 1996, ch. 4, provides references to the elephant in the Ramkhamhaeng stele.

109 Ibid., p. 62.

110 Ringis 1996, ch. 5 provides an excellent overview of the white elephant in Thailand; McNeely and Wachtel 1988, ch. 10, provide a popular account of this subject.

111 McNeely and Wachtel 1988, pp. 105–07.

112 A reference to *Suvarnadipa* is made in the *Ramayana* and refers to the island of Sumatra or the Malay Peninsula; see Lamb 1975.

113 Miksic 1990, p. 39.

114 Lamb 1975.

CHAPTER 6

1 Sastri 1975, p. 71. K.A. Nilakanta Sastri's history of south India, first published in 1955, is still the most comprehensive work on this region. I have used the 4th edition published in 1975.

2 Old Testament, I Kings 9,28; 10,22; 10,18.

3 Sastri 1975, p. 71. Also see Thundy 1993, p. 213 for a more detailed argument on this topic. The Old Testament words for peacock (*tuki*), ivory (*shen habbin*), and ape (*kof*), seem to be derived from the Indian counterparts *tokei*, *ab*, and *kapi*, respectively. Sandalwood (*almug*), also mentioned as one of the products, could only have come from southern India. Sastri points out that silver was not an Indian product, though the ivory could certainly have come from India, especially since the Hebrew, Egyptian, and Greek names for the elephant are ultimately derived from the Sanskrit *ibha*, see Chapter 2.

4 Thapar 2002, p. 229. While the Cholas, Pandyas, and Cheras are well recognized in south Indian history, the Satiyaputras seem to have a more limited history.

5 Sastri 1975, p. 104; Thapar 2002, pp. 212–13 reproduce this inscription.

6 Hart 1975, ch. 1.

7 Sastri 1975, p. 104.

8 Varadarajaiyer 1945 provides a good compilation of references to the elephant in the Sangam texts.

9 Visvanathan 2009.

10 Varadarajaiyer 1945, p. 21: *Agam* 205.

11 Ibid., p. 24: *Agam* 91.

12 Ibid., p. 10: *Puram* 140.

13 Ibid., pp. 22–23: *Narrinai* 114.

14 Ibid., p. 77: *Kalithogai* 42.

15 Ibid., pp. 2–3.

16 Ibid., pp. 14–21.

17 Ravana makes a similar comparison when he woos Sita, see Chapter 2.

18 Ibid., pp. 18–19: *Karnarpadu* 12.

19 Ibid., pp. 11, 36; Hart 1975, pp. 250–51.

20 Varadarajaiyer 1945; Hart 1975.

21 Several objects I have examined at the Wildlife Forensics Laboratory of the Wildlife Institute of India, Dehra Dun, have been determined as sculpted bone. Dr J.V. Cheeran however opines that *gajamuktas* do exist.

22 Varadarajaiyer 1945, pp. 20–21.

23 Ibid., p. 20: *Malapadukadam* 9.

24 Sukumar 1994b, p. 72.

25 Varadarajaiyer 1945, p. 21: *Puram* 81.

26 Ibid., pp. 26-32. The plants mentioned in the Sangam texts cannot be identified with certainty in some cases; for instance, *omai* is given as tooth-brush tree (*Salvadora persica*) by Varadarajaiyer but several other sources (e.g. Rao and Krishnaswamy 1941) identify this as the charcoal tree (*Trema orientalis*). *Maramaram* is not identified by Varadarajaiyer; this is usually listed as the common name in Malayalam and sometimes Tamil for the sal tree (*Shorea robusta*) – which is highly unlikely for the Sangam period as sal is found naturally only in northern India. However, *Shorea roxburghii* is a common tree in the dry hill forests of the south.

27 Ibid., pp. 25, 40: *Kuruntokai* 116, *Narrinai* 116.

28 The production of so-called "secondary compounds" by plants to protect themselves from being eaten is well known in the biological literature. See Sukumar 2003, ch. 6, for more details.

29 Varadarajaiyer 1945, p. 30: *Narrinai* 186.

30 Sukumar 2003, ch. 6 discusses this possibility.

31 Varadarajaiyer 1945, p. 31: *Kuruntokai* 37. It has not been possible to identify the tree referred to as *ya*.

32 *Kuruntokai* 307 (trans. G. Hart 1975), pp. 166–67.

33 Hart 1975, p. 167.

34 Varadarajaiyer 1945, p. 33.

35 Ibid., pp. 30–33: *Narrinai* 186, *Kuruntokai* 307, *Aindhinayam* 32.

36 Shoshani and Marchant 2001.

37 Varadarajaiyer 1945, p. 38: *Agam* 295.

38 Ibid., p. 39: *Agam* 298.

39 *Purananuru* 94 (trans. G.L. Hart and H. Heifetz 1999), p. 66

40 Varadarajaiyer 1945, pp. 39–40: *Agam* 332.

41 See Chapter 10 for more details of musth and temporal gland secretion in bull elephants.

42 Varadarajaiyer 1945, pp. 46–47: *Purananuru* 104, *Malaipadu* 211, *Tirukkural* 495.

43 Ibid., pp. 39, 55–56.

44 Ibid., p. 55: *Kalittokai* 20.

45 Ibid., pp. 27, 36, 48, 57.

46 Ibid., pp. 48–49: *Narrinai* 108.

47 Sukumar and Gadgil 1988; Sukumar 2003, ch. 8.

48 Varadarajaiyer 1945, p. 36: *Narrinai* 351.

49 Ibid., pp. 26–27: *Agam* 348.

50 Ibid., pp. 49–50, 59–69.

51 *Tirukkural* 678. The dating of the *Tirukkural* is problematic; some scholars believe it was composed in the second half of the 1st century CE (e.g. Chakravarti 1953, Introduction), while other authorities place it in the late 5th century or even later (e.g. Sastri 1975, p. 332).

52 Varadarajaiyer 1945, pp. 6–7, 10–11.

53 Ibid., pp. 64, 67.

54 Ibid., pp. 68–69, 76: *Puram* 3, 4, 6, 31, 97.

55 Ibid., p. 60: *Purananuru* 55.

56 Behl 2008.

57 British Museum, London. Accession No. 783624001.

58 British Museum, London. Accession No. 783701001.

59 *Manu Smriti*, ch. 7, 192; see *The Laws of Manu* (trans. Bühler 1886).

60 Flood 1996, p. 56; as Flood himself states on p. 61, an earlier rather than a later date is likely for the *Manu Smriti*.

61 Thapar 2002, p. 279.

62 Sharma 2005, p. 232.

63 For a contrary view see Jha 1998, ch. 8

64 Sharma 2005, p. 233. The Buddhist temple at Gaya was built on land granted by Samudragupta.

65 Sharma 2005, p. 240.

66 Jha 1998, p. 152; also see Legge 1886.

67 Kalidasa's *Meghaduta*, v. II (trans. Arthur W. Ryder 1912).

68 Kalidasa's *Ritusamhara*, The Rains (trans. A.W. Ryder 1912).

69 Kalidasa's *Abhijnanasakuntalam*, Act I (trans. A.W. Ryder 1912).

70 Ibid., Act V.

71 *The Kama Sutra of Vatsyayana* (trans. Richard Burton 1883).

72 *Kama Sutra*, ch. 6.

73 Bhat 1987, pp. 595–97.

74 Ibid., p. 598.

75 Ibid., p. 825.

76 Ibid., p. 742.

77 Ibid., p. 747.

78 Behl 2007.

79 Naravane 1965.

80 Ram 2007, p. 12.

81 The earliest monograph on Ganesha is that of Alice Getty (1936), while Paul Courtright (1985) is a more recent study of the legend of Ganesha. Scholarly papers on Ganesha are available in the edited volume of Robert Brown (1991a). For more popular accounts of this god, I would recommend Shakuntala Jagannathan and Nandita Krishna (1992) and the volume edited by Pratapaditya Pal (1995).

82 Foreword by W. O'Flaherty in Courtright, 1985.

83 Apart from the earlier references mentioned, also see Sukumar 2003, ch. 2, for a discussion of the origins and significance of Ganesha.

84 Narain 1991.

85 Dhavalikar 1991. The connection is made through texts such as the *Baudhyayana Grihyaparisheshasutra* and *Baudhyayana Dharmasutra* (2nd–3rd century CE) that mention *Hastimukha* and epithets such as Vighna and Vinayaka eventually used in defining Ganesha.

86 Dhavalikar 1991.

87 Narain 1991.

88 Dhavalikar 1991.

89 Ibid.; also personal communication with R. Balasubramanian, Curator, Government Museum, Chennai.

90 Getty 1936, p. 25.

91 Dhavalikar 1991.

92 Shetti 1995.

93 Brown 1991a, p. 216.

94 Ghurye 1962, p. 70.

95 Brown 1991b.

96 Ghurye 1962, p. 58.

97 Dhavalikar 1991.

98 Ghurye 1962, p. 61.

99 Sukumar 2003, pp. 70–75.

100 Ghurye 1962, p. 91.

101 Harris 1977, ch. 12; also see Sukumar 2003, pp. 70–75 for a more complete discussion.

102 Sachau 1888, p. 560; also see Chapter 7.

103 The *purana*s are rather difficult to date precisely. While the earliest are from about 400 CE, the legends relating to Ganesha are mostly from works of the 6th to 13th century.

104 See Courtright 1985, ch. 2, for an account of these legends.

105 Sastri 1975, p. 91.

106 Annual Report of Archaeological Survey of India, 1906–07, p. 221; Minakshi 1977, p. 4. Pallavamalla was enthroned around 732.

107 Nagaswamy 2008 is a concise and up-to-date account of the monuments at Mamallapuram.

108 Ibid., Introduction.

109 Ibid., p. 4. The theory that all the monuments at Mamallapuram were the creation of a single ruler, Rajasimha, is based on the evidence from inscriptions, and contradicts earlier theories that they were created over the successive reigns of various kings beginning with Mahendra. Thus, the dates of the Mamallapuram monuments are at least half a century later than those given in most volumes on Indian art history; see Nagaswamy 2008, pp. 18–19.

110 *Life of Hiuen-Tsang* (transl. S. Beal 1911), pp. 145–46.

111 Naravane 1965; Gupta 1983; Dhavalikar 2003, pp. 41–71.

112 Naravane 1965; Gupta 1983; Dhavalikar 2003, pp. 41–71.

113 Stierlin 2002, pp. 127–66.

114 Ram 2007, p. 25.

115 As one faces the entrance the elephant on the left is still standing while the one on the right is missing.

116 Chandra 2004, p. 20.

117 Stierlin 2002, pp. 94, 98.

118 Stierlin 2002, pp. 169–87; also see Settar 1992 for an encyclopaedic treatment of the Hoysala temples.

119 Settar 1992, vol. 1, pp. 323–24.

120 Stierlin 2002, pp. 105–25.

121 The remark is attributed to James Fergusson and is quoted in Mitra 2003, p. 7, and Donaldson 2003, p. 1.

122 This slab is now at the Orissa State Museum, Bhubaneswar.

123 These *gaja-kranta*s were placed here during restoration in the 20th century. It would be pertinent to add here that an elephant cannot survive for more than about 30 minutes if recumbent in the sternal position as depicted in this sculpture.

124 Swain 2008.

125 Das 1982, p. 32.

126 The sources for this account are Major 1857; Sewell 1900; Longhurst 1917; Sarkar 1960; Sastri 1975; Devakunjari 1998; Verghese 2002.

127 Longhurst 1917; Devakunjari 1998.

128 Longhurst 1917, p. 124.

129 Ibid., p. 86.

130 *Journey of Abd-er-Razzak* (trans. R.H. Major 1857, p. 27.

131 Ibid., p. 87.

132 Ibid., p. 27.

133 Sastri 1975, p. 278.

134 *Chronicles of Paez and Nuniz* in Sewell 1900, pp. 326–41.

135 Sastri 1975, p. 267. The figure of 1,550 elephants seems excessive but it implies that most of Vijayanagara's elephants did not fall into the hands of the enemy.

The account by Sarkar 1960, ch. 14, does not mention this event but merely states (p. 100) that a wounded Tirumala and his gallant son pass out of history after this battle.

136 Sarkar 1960, ch. 21.

137 Ibid., pp. 155–62.

138 Duff 1826, vol. 1, p. 360.

139 Ibid., vol. 2, pp. 139–40.

140 Ibid., pp. 153–55.

141 Sadhale and Nene 2004a, b, c, provide an exhaustive account of the references to elephants in the *Manasollasa* in a series of three papers.

142 *Manasollasa*, v. 171 (Sadhale and Nene 2004a).

143 *Manasollasa*, v. 183–221 (Sadhale and Nene 2004a).

144 *Manasollasa*, v. 622 (Sadhale and Nene 2004b).

145 *Manasollasa*, v. 172–79 (Sadhale and Nene 2004a).

146 The *Gajagrahananaprakara* attributed to Narayana Dikshitar and the *Gajashiksha* by Naradamuni with English summaries by E.R. Sreekrishna Sarma have been brought out in 1968 and 1975, respectively, by Sri Venkateswara University. These manuscripts seem to be from a later date than the *Manasollasa*.

147 *Hastividyarnava* (ed. P.C. Choudhury 1976).

148 Thapar 2002, p. 325.

149 I have used Lamb 1975 for the basic history of Indian influence in Southeast Asia.

150 This may be a Chinese rendition of an ancient Khmer word, *bnam*, meaning mountain, see Rooney 1999, p. 21.

151 See Mabbett and Chandler 1995, p. 74 for sources.

152 Ibid.

153 The Chinese version is different in that Kaundinya kidnapped the local queen and married her, thereby wresting the *naga* kingdom.

154 While the dates of the Angkor period are commonly accepted as 802–1432, some scholars suggest an even earlier beginning, see Mabbett and Chandler 1995, p. 91.

155 Rooney 1999, p. 14.

156 Ibid., pp. 138–46 for fuller descriptions of the bas-reliefs.

157 Mabbett and Chandler 1995, ch. 12.

158 Ibid., pp. 156–57.

159 Chou Ta-kuan's account, available in a French publication by P. Pelliot 1951, is reproduced in English by Mabbett and Chandler 1995, p. 211.

160 Getty 1936, chs. 5 and 6; Brown 1991b.

161 These squatting Ganeshas can be seen at the National Museum, Phnom Penh, and some are also illustrated in the above references.

162 Brown 1991b.

163 Two inscriptions, one at Angkor Borei, dated as 611 CE, and the other from the reign of Jayavarman I (656–681 CE) mention sanctuaries dedicated to "Mahaganapati" and "Sri-Ganapati", respectively; see Brown 1991b, p. 180, for sources.

164 Brown 1991b.

165 Ibid.

166 Ibid.

167 Getty 1936, chs. 7 and 8; Lancaster 1991; Sanford 1991.

168 Bhattacharya 1995.

169 Getty 1936, p. 69.

170 Bartholomew 1995, pp. 120–21.

CHAPTER 7

1 *Sura* 105.

2 I have used Rizvi 1975a and 1975b for the general Islamic history of the subcontinent. A good overall source for the military history of the elephant during the Islamic period is Sarkar 1960.

3 *Ferishta* (trans. Briggs 1829), vol. 1, ch. 1, p. 47.

4 Sachau 1888.

5 Ibid., p. 118.

6 Ibid., p. 402.

7 Ibid., p. 658.

8 Ibid., p. 191.

9 Ibid., pp. 559–61.

10 Digby 1971, pp. 55–56.

11 *Ferishta*, vol. 1, ch. 2, pp. 172–73; Sarkar 1960, ch. 5.

12 *Ferishta*, vol. 1, ch. 2, pp. 175–76.

13 Ibid., pp. 176–77.

14 Digby 1971.

15 Ibid., p. 52, draws upon the description of Al-Umari.

16 From the *Tughlaq-nama* as quoted by Digby 1971, p. 53.

17 This account mentions seven male elephants and one old aggressive female elephant; it is entirely possible that this "female" was actually a tuskless male mistakenly identified; see *Tarikh-i-Firoz Shahi* of Shams-i Siraj, Afif in Elliot 1871, vol. 3, pp. 313–14.

18 See Digby 1971, pp. 55–73, for sources.

19 *Tarikh-i-Alai* by Amir Khusru in Elliot 1871, vol. 3, pp. 90–92.

20 *Tarikh-i-Firoz Shahi* by Ziaud din Barni in Elliot 1871, vol. 3; also see Digby 1971, p. 58.

21 *Tarikh-i-Firoz Shahi* by Ziaud din Barni, vol. 3, pp. 150-51.

22 *Tarikh-i-Firoz Shahi* by Ziaud din Barni, vol. 3, p. 235.

23 *Zafarnama* of Sharaf ud din Yazdi in Elliot 1871, vol. 3, p. 499.

24 Quoted in Digby 1971, p. 80.

25 *Zafarnama*, vol. 3, p. 499.

26 *Baburnama*, vol. 2 (trans. A.S. Beveridge 1922), p. 470; Spear 1965, p. 22.

27 *Baburnama*, vol. 2, p. 488.

28 Ibid., p. 489.

29 Spear 1965, p. 26.

30 The *Akbarnama* (trans. H. Beveridge 1897–1939) and the *Ain-i-Akbari* (trans. H. Blochmann and H.S. Jarrett 1873–1907) are the main sources for Akbar's relationship with the elephant.

31 *Akbarnama* vol. 2, ch. 18.

32 *Akbarnama*, vol. 1, ch. 9.

33 Sarkar 1960, p. 67.

34 Ibid., ch. 10.

35 *Akbarnama* vol. 1, ch. 11.

36 Das 1999.

37 *Akbarnama*, vol. 2, ch. 37.

38 *Akbarnama*, vol. 2, ch. 18.

39 *Akbarnama*, vol. 2, ch. 37.

40 *Ain-i-Akbari*, vol. 1, chs. 41–48 describe Akbar's elephant establishment.

41 *Ain-i-Akbari*, vol. 1, ch. 42.

42 *Ain-i-Akbari*, vol. 1, ch. 43.

43 *Ain-i-Akbari*, vol. 1, ch. 44.

44 *Ain-i-Akbari*, vol. 1, ch. 48.

45 *Ain-i-Akbari* vol. 1, ch. 45.

46 *Ain-i-Akbari*, vol. 1, ch. 41.

47 *Ain-i-Akbari*, vol. 1, ch. 41.

48 Poole 1989.

49 *Akbarnama*, vol. 2, ch. 54.

50 Sarkar 1960, ch. 11.

51 Ibid., ch. 12.

52 *Akbarnama*, vol. 3, ch. 68.

53 S. Moosvi, "Elephants in Medieval India". Presentation at the seminar "Call of the Elephant" held at the Indian Museum, Kolkata, August 2001.

54 Alvi and Rahman 1968.

55 Note by Sálim Ali in Alvi and Rahman 1968.

56 *Jahangirnama* (trans. W.H. Thackston 1999), p. 160.

57 *Jahangirnama*, p. 193.

58 *Jahangirnama*, p. 270.

59 A shaded drawing of Pawan Gaj by a painter named Nanha was found in a private collection at Kuwait; see Das 1999.

60 Ibid.

61 Lahiri-Choudhury 1991.

62 Das 1999; also see *Tuzuk-i-Jahangiri*, trans. A. Rogers and H. Beveridge 1909–14, vol. 1, p. 140 and vol. 2, p. 260.

63 Das 1999.

64 Bernier 1891, p. 154.

65 Sarkar 1917, pp. 34–36. The account of the elephant fight is taken from the *Padshahnamah* of Abdul Hamid. The name of the tusked elephant is mentioned several times as Sudhakar in this account. After Shahjahan presented the elephant to young Aurangzeb it is possible that its name was changed to Sidhkar.

66 Sarkar 1960, ch. 16; also see Bernier 1891, pp. 49–54.

67 Sarkar 1917, p. 12.

68 Ibid.

69 Ibid., p. 64.

70 *Baburnama*, vol. 2, p. 488.

71 *Ain-i-Akbari*, vol. 1, ch. 41. While most of the place names mentioned here can be identified, others are not easily recognized. The places clearly recognizable are: Uttar Pradesh state (Agra); Madhya Pradesh (Ratanpur, Nandanpur, Malwa, Handiah, Uchhod, Chanderi, Satwas, Bijagarh, Raisen, Hoshangabad, Garh, Haryagarh); Chhattisgarh (Bastar); Bihar/Jharkhand (Rohtas). Dr Raziuddin Aquil (in litt.) identifies Pattah as Bhatta or Rewa in Baghelkhand (Madhya Pradesh), Sargachh as Sarguja (Chattisgarh), and Bayawan and Narwar as regions in Madhya Pradesh.

72 S. Moosvi, op. cit. (see note 53).

73 *Chronicles of Paez and Nuniz* in Sewell 1900, p. 381.

74 *The voyage of Francois Pyrard de Laval* (trans. A. Gray and H.C.P. Bell 1887), vol. 2, part 2, p. 346. These figures seem to be the basis for the figure of 40,000 elephants possessed by Jahangir given by W. Jardine 1836 that is quoted in Olivier 1978a.

75 Basham 1967, pp. 129–30.

76 Digby 1971.

CHAPTER 8

1 Tennent 1859, vol. 2, ch. 1; Codrington 1926, ch. 6.

2 Nicolas 1954b.

3 Ibid.

4 De Barro's account of the history of India is quoted in Nicholas 1954b.

5 *The book of Duarte Barbosa* (trans. Dames 1918–21), vol. 1, p. 118.

6 Nicholas 1954b.

7 Ibid.

8 Wisumperuma 2003.

9 Nicholas (1954b) mentions that Rajasinha I used 2,200 elephants at the siege of Colombo in 1587–88 but this number is unlikely given the much smaller number of 200 elephants used at Mulleriyawa; see Wisumperuma 2004.

10 Nicholas 1954b.

11 Wisumperuma 2004.

12 de Silva 1990.

13 Ibid.

14 Nicholas 1954b.

15 de Silva 1990

16 Nicholas 1954b, p. 105.

17 de Silva 1990.

18 Nicholas 1954b; de Silva 1990.

19 de Silva 1990 mistakenly takes the weight of an adult elephant to be 8–10 tonnes. In fact, the weight of a full-grown bull would only be about half this figure. The average weight of an elephant would be much less assuming that adult female elephants as well as young elephants would have been exported.

20 Codrington 1926, ch. 8.

21 Nicholas 1954b.

22 This story is mentioned in Nicholas 1954b. Otherwise a very reliable observer, C.W. Nicholas may have accepted this story uncritically because until recently it was generally believed that elephants could live well beyond 100 years. It is impossible for Hortala, already an adult in 1655–56, to have lived up to 1796 when the Dutch yielded Colombo to the British.

23 Tennent 1859, p. 52.

24 This directive dated November 20, 1667, is quoted in detail by Nicholas 1954b, p. 107.

25 The memoirs of Ryclof van Goens, the Dutch Governor of Ceylon during 1675–79, were left to his successor Laurens Pyl. The account on elephant trade given in Jurriaanse (1940) has been reproduced by Jayewardene (1994), p. 10.

26 Nicholas 1954b.

27 Deraniyagala 1955, p. 93.

28 Jayewardene 1994, p. 10.

29 Ibid., p. 10, quoting Jurriaanse 1940.

30 Nicholas 1954b.

31 Ibid. The Dutch elephant establishment included a Sinhalese chief of the whole group, chiefs of various divisions, informants of elephant presence, veterinarians, mahouts, trainers, grass-cutters, and those involved in networking among these categories.

32 Nicholas 1954b. Of the 97 elephants only seven were tusked males, 37 were tuskless males, while the rest were females.

33 Nicholas 1954b.

34 Jayewardene 1994, p. 11.

35 Nicholas 1954b.

36 Ibid.; Jayewardene 1994 gives the year of the order as 1761 but this is a typographical error.

37 Nicholas 1954b.

38 A stock of 300 tusked male elephants would also imply a much larger stock of elephants overall, perhaps up to 1,000 animals. Considering that in 1697 the stalls at Matara had only seven tuskers out of 44 males and 97 elephants overall, the figure of 300 tuskers at Kandy could either be an error or imply large imports from India and Burma. It would be interesting to look for such records.

39 *Culavamsa* (trans. W. Geiger and C.M. Rickmers 1929–30), ch. 76.

40 *The book of Duarte Barbosa*, vol. 2, pp. 154–56.

41 Ralph Fitch's narrative is available in Ryley 1899; see p. 159 for this quote.

42 Ibid., p. 184. I must add that the present-day captive elephants of Pegu are no larger than either the elephants of Sri Lanka or India.

43 Cranbrook et al. 2007.

44 Olivier 1978a.

45 Ibid.

46 Cranbrook et al. 2007.

47 Ibid.

48 Santiapillai and Jackson 1990.

49 Fernando et al. 2003; Cranbrook et al. 2007.

50 Cranbrook et al. 2007 provides a number of historical references for the presence of elephants in Sulu.

51 Hunt is quoted in Cranbrook et al. 2007.

52 Cranbrook et al. 2007 cites various sources; also see Olivier 1978a. The year 1750 is usually mentioned for the release in Sabah of the elephants that had been gifted to the sultan.

53 Hooijer 1972 ; Cranbrook et al. 2007.

54 Fernando et al. 2003.

55 Shim 2003.

56 Deraniyagala 1955, p. 124.

57 Shim 2003; also see Cranbrook et al. 2007.

58 Sivasundaram 2005.

59 Ibid., pp. 32-33.

60 Hunter 1897, pp. 86-91; Sivasundaram 2005.

61 Bowring 1893, pp. 112–13.

62 Gopal 1971, p. 51.

63 Bowring 1893, p. 222.

64 Moon 1989, p. 256.

65 Sanderson 1878, p. 56, records that Captain Sandys commanded 150 elephants in the war with Tipu.

66 Sivasundaram 2005, quoting archived correspondence of R. Barclay in 1800.

67 Sivasundaram 2005, p. 35 quoting archived correspondence of 1803.

68 Keay 2000, p. 5.

69 Krishnamurthy and Wemmer 1995a.

70 Sivasundaram 2005, p. 33, quoting the adjutant-general to John Adams in 1809.

71 Ibid., p. 34, quoting J. Paton in 1811.

72 Ibid., p. 35, quoting J. Sullivan in 1824.

73 Ibid., p. 35 quoting R. Peter in 1825.

74 Ibid., pp. 35–36.

75 Gadgil and Guha 1992, ch. 4.

76 The scientific name for teak is *Tectona grandis*, for sal *Shorea robusta*, and for deodar *Cedrus deodara*.

77 Ribbentrop 1900, pp. 69–70.

78 Skaria 1998.

79 Krishnamurthy and Wemmer 1995b.

80 Ibid.

81 Sanderson 1878, ch. 11; Barua and Bist 1995.

82 Sanderson 1878, p. 125.

83 Ibid., p. 126.

84 Sukumar 1989, p. 9.

85 Balfour 1885.

86 *Imperial Gazetteer of India* 1907.

87 Stracey 1963, ch. 2.

88 Ibid.

89 Deraniyagala 1955, p. 119, quotes figures supplied to him by naturalist and tea planter E.P. Gee.

90 Sukumar 1989, pp. 8–9. The pit captures in Mysore pertain to the period 1878–98 by the prince and the forest department.

91 Ibid., p. 9; also see Neginhal 1974.

92 Sanderson 1878, ch. 10.

93 Neginhal 1974, Appendix 5.

94 Ibid. This period includes the post-independence years of 1947–71. The total number of elephants captured as per available records is 1,977 individuals but of this only 1,837 elephants were retained, the rest being "released" presumably back into the forest. Even this figure is likely to be incomplete, especially for the late 19th century.

95 The nature of the understanding between the British and the Kandyan chiefs for capturing elephants is not clear; see Nicholas 1954b, and Jayewardene 1994, p. 12.

96 Nicholas 1954b.

97 Jayewardene 1994, p. 17, based on J.W. Bennett 1843 not seen in original.

98 Tennent 1859, pp. 393–94 provides figures showing that 86 out of 138 deaths for which time of death was recorded happened within two years of their capture.

99 Nicholas 1954b.

100 Jayewardene 1994, p. 14.

101 Ibid., p. 16.

102 Evans 1910, p. 5.

103 Williams 1950, p. 49.

104 Lair 1997, p. 103.

105 Olivier 1978a; Blower 1985; Sukumar 1989, p. 9.

106 Neginhal 1974, Appendix 5.

107 Sanderson 1878, pp. 174–75. This death rate among captive elephants is quite high relative to average death rates in the wild or among well-managed captive populations.

108 Krishnamurthy and Wemmer 1995b.

109 W. Gilchrist's "A memoir on the history and treatment of the elephant, with instructions for preserving its efficiency as an animal of transport and a general outline of its anatomy; also an account of the medicines used in the cure of its diseases", Board's Military Collection, L/MIL/5/482, EICR. Although this work was published in 1841 at Calcutta, the November 20, 1816 date of this record at National Archives of UK suggests a much earlier compilation.

110 Quoted in Krishnamurthy and Wemmer 1995b.

111 Evans 1910. The first edition of this publication came out in 1901, but the revised edition in 1910 is the one widely available today.

112 Wemmer 1995; Milroy 1922. A new edition of Milroy's original work has been recently published; see Bist 2002a.

113 Wemmer 1995.

114 Krishnamurthy and Wemmer 1995b.

115 Sukumar et al. 1997.

116 Stracey 1963, p. 73

117 Williams 1950, p. 25.

118 Ibid., p. 49.
119 MacKenzie 1987.
120 Ibid., p. 42.
121 Ibid., p. 50.
122 Lahiri-Choudhury 1999; see Introduction.
123 Tennent 1859, vol. 2, p. 324. The quantity of ivory would still have been rather small considering that only some bull elephants in Ceylon possessed full-grown tusks while the rest, including females, would have only yielded tushes.
124 Ibid., p. 332.
125 Rangarajan 2001.
126 Lahiri-Choudhury 1999, p. xxvi of Introduction.
127 Ibid.
128 Tennent, 1859, vol. 2, p. 332.
129 Ibid., pp. 323–24.
130 Letter from Hudleston to his mother, dated February 16, 1816; reference D HUD 13/6/9 held by the Cumbria Record Office, Carlisle Headquarters.
131 Sivasundaram 2005.
132 Peacock 1933, p. 88.
133 Olivier 1978a, p. 397, based on several sources.
134 MacKenzie 1987, p. 42.
135 Ibid., p. 50. Social Darwinism refers to the ideology that only humans with "superior" qualities or genes should increase, while eugenics refers to the selective breeding of such humans.
136 George Orwell 1936, "Shooting an Elephant", New Writing, London.
137 Baker 1854, ch. 1.
138 Poole 1989.
139 Watve and Sukumar 1997.
140 Harris et al. 2002.
141 Tennent 1859, vol. 2, p. 323. The quote about sportsmen being tender-hearted is from Baker 1854.
142 Stracey 1963, pp. 55–57.
143 Pollock 1894, p. 154.
144 Lahiri-Choudhury, 1999, p. xxiv of Introduction.
145 Jayewardene 1994, p. 62.
146 Many studies have shown that secondary vegetation in tropical moist forests are preferred over primary forests by elephants and other large mammalian herbivores; see Sukumar 1989, ch. 9; Sukumar 2003, pp. 326–30.
147 Ibid.
148 Report in The New York Times, March 23, 1862.
149 Heiss and Heiss 2007, ch. 1.
150 Gröning and Saller 1998, p. 258.
151 Ibid., p. 266.
152 Ibid.
153 Ibid., pp. 270–73.
154 Ibid.
155 Ibid., p. 275.
156 Scigliano 2002, pp. 197–98.
157 Altick 1978, p. 310; Sivasundaram 2005.
158 Altick 1978, ch. 22, gives a full account of Chuny.

159 Ibid., p. 311.
160 Anon. 1843, The Menageries, vol. 2, p. 20.
161 Altick 1978, p. 313.
162 Gröning and Saller 1998, p. 275.
163 Sivasundaram 2005.
164 Altick 1978.
165 Ibid., p. 57.
166 Ibid., p. 313.
167 Scigliano 2002, ch. 14 and 15.
168 Ibid., p. 181 from accounts in various newspapers.
169 Sivasundaram, 2005.
170 Ibid., p. 63.
171 Ibid.
172 Ibid., p. 246.
173 Williams 1950, pp. 247–50; Lair 1997, pp. 103–04.
174 Williams 1950, p. 229.
175 Gale 1974, ch. 7.
176 Ghurye 1962; also see Kaur 2003 for a more detailed history of the Ganapati cult.
177 Underhill 1921, p. 50.
178 This quote from Stanley Wolpert 1962 is reproduced in Courtright 1985, p. 227.

CHAPTER 9
1 Guha 2007, p. 5.
2 Sri Adhiati and Bobsien, "Indonesia's transmigration programme – an update", 2001. Accessed at http://www.dte.gn.apc.org.
3 FWI/GFW 2002, ch. 2.
4 Data from the Indonesian Palm Oil Association quoted in a Commodity Intelligence Report of the US Department of Agriculture, dated December 31, 2007.
5 U. Scholze 1983 quoted in Santiapillai and Jackson 1990, p. 38.
6 Santiapillai and Ramono 1990, on the basis of surveys carried out earlier by Blouch, Haryanto, and Simbolon.
7 UNDP/FAO 1982 pertains to a report National conservation plan for Indonesia, Vol. 2, Sumatra (Bogor), quoted in Santiapillai and Jackson 1990, p. 39. The later surveys were carried out by Blouch and Simbolon 1985.
8 A report of World Wide Fund for Nature dated April 4, 2006 entitled "Urgent action needed to protect Sumatran elephants" estimated that elephants had declined by 75% during 1995–2006. Accessed at http://www.wwf.org.uk.
9 Hedges et al. 2005.
10 Santiapillai and Ramono 1993; Nyhus et al. 2000.
11 Report of working group on Elephant Training Centres, pp. 47–51 in Tilson et al. 1994.
12 Suprayogi et al. 2002.
13 Mikota et al. 2008 provide a comprehensive overview of this topic.
14 Krishnamurthy 1992.
15 Suprayogi et al. 2002; Mikota et al. 2008.
16 Suprayogi et al. 2002.

17 Hedges et al. 2006.
18 The Jakarta Post, Surabaya, September 5, 2006.
19 Letter dated March 4, 2001 from Susan Mikota and Hank Hammatt to Koes Saparjadi, Director-General of Forest Protection and Nature Conservation, Jakarta.
20 Santiapillai and Jackson 1990, ch. 8.
21 An undated report circa 1991, "The Malayan Elephant: A Species Plan for Its Conservation" by M. Mohammad Khan, Department of Wildlife and National Parks, Kuala Lumpur, is the basis for much of the information for Peninsular Malaysia; see Khan 1991.
22 Ibid., p. 58.
23 Ibid., p. 16.
24 Khan 1991, p. VII; Shariff Daim 2002. In hindsight this may have been an underestimate.
25 Shariff Daim 2002.
26 Khan 1991, p. 61.
27 Shariff Daim 2002.
28 Blair et al. 1979.
29 Ibid., p. 38.
30 Ibid., pp. 48–55. The high-voltage electric fence uses an energizer to boost the voltage from a car battery (12-volt) to between 5,000 and 10,000 volts but the output is a pulsed current of about 1/3,000 second duration. This fence is not fatal to an animal coming in contact with it.
31 Khan 1991, p. 60.
32 Ibid., pp. 61–65.
33 Ibid., p. 64.
34 Abdul and Othman 2004.
35 Stibig and Malingreau 2003.
36 Abdul and Othman 2004.
37 The earlier estimates were mostly guesses and possibly underestimates; it is unlikely that the elephant population had actually increased in recent decades.
38 A news item "Jumbo-sized discovery made in Malaysia" dated January 14, 2009 accessed at http://www.newswise.com/articles/view/548103) suggests that consolidation has worked favourably in the Peninsula.
39 Ambu et al. 2004.
40 Report on "State, communities and forests in contemporary Borneo," 2005, table 1.1, ch. 1 in "Recent development and conservation interventions in Borneo" by F.M. Cooke. Accessed at http://epress.anu.edu.au/apem/borneo.
41 Ambu et al. 2004.
42 Ibid.
43 Abdul and Othman 2004.
44 Ambu et al. 2004.
45 Several papers in Osborn and Vinton 1999; Duckworth and Hedges 1998.
46 Stellman et al. 2003. Agent Orange contained 2,4,5-Erichlorophenoxyacetic acid.

47 Westing 1971.

48 Sukumar et al. 2002.

49 Presentation made by L.V. Khoi and D. Tuoc at the meeting of the IUCN/SSC Asian Elephant Specialist Group meeting held at Bogor, Indonesia, May 20–22, 1992.

50 Based on a presentation "Dynamics of forest resources and tentative Vietnam REDD strategy" by Pham Manh Cuong, National REDD Focal Point, Ministry of Agriculture and Rural Development, Hanoi.

51 P. Pfeffer's personal communication in 1975 to R.C.D. Olivier 1978a.

52 A *New York Times* dispatch from Saigon, dated June 21, 1966. For a scientific perspective see Dudley et al. 2002.

53 Bazé 1955, ch. 3.

54 L.V. Khoi, "Some biological characteristics of elephant and elephant domestication in Vietnam", presentation at the IUCN/SSC Asian Specialist Group meeting held at Chiang Mai, Thailand, January 1988.

55 Dawson et al. 1993.

56 Duckworth and Hedges 1998.

57 Osborn and Vinton 1999.

58 Based on information received from wildlife officials and newspaper reports in 2001 when I was carrying out field research in the region.

59 Cuong et al. 2002.

60 Ibid.; Stiles 2008, Executive Summary. The decrees and laws include the Prime Minister's directive 134/TTg, dated June 21, 1960, specifically prohibiting elephant hunting, and several similar decrees passed in 1963, 1991, 1992, 1993, and 1996 for protection of forests and wildlife. The Revised Criminal Law of Vietnam came into effect on July 1, 2000.

61 Convention on International Trade in Endangered Species of Wild Fauna and Flora.

62 Stiles 2008.

63 Heffernan and Cuong 2004.

64 Sukumar et al. 2002; Varma et al. 2008; Vidya et al. 2009.

65 Cuong et al. 2002.

66 A figure of 73% forest cover has been quoted in several publications for the years 1965–70.

67 National forest products statistics, Cambodia, see Ma and Broadhead 2002.

68 Barney 2005.

69 "Forest cover changes in Cambodia 2002–2006". Paper prepared by the TWG, Forestry and Environment for the Cambodia Development Cooperation Forum, June 19–20, 2007, accessed at http://www.phnompenh.um.dk/NR/rdonlyres.

70 Table 2, Annex 3 in State of the World's Forests, 1997. FAO, Rome, Italy.

71 Barney 2005.

72 Biological survey of the Cardamom mountains, southwestern Cambodia, Interim Report, April 2000. Fauna and Flora International, Cambridge, UK.

73 Desai et al. 2002.

74 P.L. Cheav is quoted in Olivier 1978a, p. 401. In hindsight a figure of 10,000 elephants in Cambodia is highly unlikely for 1969. Chan Sarun of the Cambodian government mentioned a figure of only 1,000–1,500 elephants during the 1960s at a meeting of the IUCN/SSC Asian Elephant Specialist Group held at Bogor, Indonesia, May 20–22, 1992.

75 Weiler and Soriyun 1999.

76 Ibid., p. 52.

77 Vuthy et al. 2004.

78 J. McNeely, Draft report on wildlife and national parks in the Lower Mekong basin, Mekong Committee, 1975.

79 Lair 1997, p. 46.

80 Weiler et al. 2001.

81 Vuthy et al. 2004.

82 Global Forest Resources Assessment 2000. Food and Agriculture Organization of the United Nations, Rome, Italy. Accessed at http://www.fao.org/docrep/004.

83 The figure of 42% forest cover comes from the Ministry of Agriculture and Forestry's 2005 report, "Forestry strategy to the year 2020 of the Lao PDR", Vientiane.

84 Venevongphet's presentation was made at the meeting of the IUCN/SSC Asian Elephant Specialist Group held at Chiangmai, Thailand, in January 1988.

85 Khounboline 1999.

86 Khounboline 2004.

87 Lair 1997, p. 97.

88 Ibid., p. 94 quoting figures from B. Souvannaphanh.

89 Khounboline 1999.

90 Ibid., quoting R. Salter 1993.

91 Khounboline 2004.

92 Ibid. Decree No. 185 of the Council of Ministers made all wildlife, with the exception of captive elephants, the property of the state since 1986. This may have provided a loophole for illegal captures of elephants. The hunting or even wounding of wild elephants is prohibited.

93 Summary environmental and social impact assessment: Nam Theun II hydroelectric project in the Lao PDR, November 2004. Asian Development Bank, Bangkok.

94 Ringis 1996, ch. 5.

95 Lorsirirat 2007 gives a figure of 57% of the land area but other sources place the figure at 53%.

96 FAO 2007, Annex.

97 Lair 1997, ch. on Thailand, pp. 165–218.

98 Ibid., p. 199, quoting a report by A. Achakulwisut in *Bangkok Post*, dated March 25, 1992.

99 Lair 1997, p. 196, citing Lekagul and McNeely 1977, and p. 168 giving government data.

100 Lekagul and McNeely 1977.

101 Srikrachang and Srikosamatara 2004.

102 Lekagul and McNeely 1977; also statistics of Ministry of Agriculture, Thailand, quoted by Lair 1997, p. 169.

103 Statistics of Ministry of Interior, Thailand, quoted by Lair 1997, pp. 170–71. Lair believes there could have been more captive elephants.

104 Ringis 1996, ch. 2.

105 Ibid., p. 27.

106 Srikrachang and Srikosamatara 2004.

107 Storer 1981.

108 Martin and Stiles 2002.

109 Uga 2004. FAO however estimates that about 50% of Myanmar was under forests in 2000.

110 Sukumar 1989, p. 20; Santiapillai and Jackson 1990, p. 17.

111 Presentation made by Ye Htut at the meeting of the IUCN/SSC Asian Elephant Specialist Group at Bangkok, Thailand, in March 1996.

112 Uga 2004.

113 Sukumar 1989, p. 9, based on figures provided in Blower in WWF Report Dec. 1985, and Olivier 1978a.

114 Lair 1997, p. 117 using data provided by K.U. Mar.

115 Uga 2004.

116 This delegation in 1994 of the IUCN/SSC Asian Elephant Specialist Group was led by its chair, Lyn de Alwis, and included Charles Santiapillai and this author.

117 Uga 2004.

118 Shepherd and Nijman 2008.

119 Caughley 1980.

120 K.U. Mar's data from her 1995 report *Research on reproduction of captive Asian elephants of Myanmar* is provided in Lair 1997, p. 117.

121 Mar 2002; also see Lair 1997, pp. 118–19.

122 Uga 2004.

123 Report on Rakhine Yoma, AERCC, Bangalore.

124 Li et al. 2009.

125 Pan et al. 2009.

126 Zhang 2004.

127 Zhang et al. 2008.

128 Report in *The Independent*, London, June 2, 2007.

129 See Santiapillai et al. 2004 for sources.

130 Fernando 2000.

131 Olivier 1978a.

132 The first discussion on establishing corridors for elephants was held by the Central Board of Agriculture in 1956 and a plan developed in 1959 by the Committee for the Protection of Wildlife; see Jayewardene 1994, p. 96.

133 Fernando and Lande 2000; Santiapillai et al. 2004.

134 Sukumar 1989, pp. 162–63; Santiapillai et al. 2004; Werellagama et al. 2004.

135 Santiapillai et al. 2004.

136 Jayewardene 1994, p. 88 and Appendix IV. The largest of the plantations raised by Pelawatte Sugar Company alone covered 8,000 hectares.

137 Jayewardene 1994, pp. 81–85.

138 Ibid, p. 85.

139 Santiapillai et al. 2004.

140 Ibid. The most recent survey in August 2011 suggests much higher numbers of wild elephants on the island.

141 Martin and Stiles 2002.

142 Santiapillai et al. 2004.

143 *Mahavamsa* (trans. W. Geiger and M.H. Bode 1912), 99, 55.

144 Islam 2004.

145 A. Rivkin, "A new measure of well-being from a happy little kingdom", *The New York Times*, October 4, 2005.

146 FAO gives the forest cover as 58.6% in 1995.

147 Wangchuk 2007.

148 Santiapillai and Jackson 1990, pp. 13–15.

149 Mishra 1980, p. 59.

150 Bhatta 2004.

151 Ibid.

152 We only have an older estimate of 80 elephants in captivity in 1985; see Santiapillai and Jackson 1990, p. 57.

153 Menon and Kumar 1998, pp. 22–23.

154 Guha 2007, ch. 10.

155 Ibid.

156 A figure of about 30 million hectares may perhaps not be an unreasonable estimate.

157 Gadgil and Guha 1992, p. 196.

158 Cutler et al. 2007. Another ecological impact of the anti-malaria campaign resulted from the extensive spraying of the chemical pesticide DDT, dichloro-diphenyl-trichloroethane.

159 A contiguous distribution along the Himalayan foothills is most likely prior to Indian independence. A few elephants may also have been present in northern Bihar bordering Nepal.

160 Most of the elephant range today lies in the state of Uttarakhand carved out of Uttar Pradesh in 2000.

161 Singh 1969.

162 Ibid., p. 245.

163 Ibid.

164 Singh 1978.

165 Singh 1995.

166 Bist 2002b; Johnsingh et al. 2004.

167 Lahiri-Choudhury 1980.

168 Quoted in Barua and Bist, 1995.

169 Ibid.

170 Ibid.

171 Barua and Bist 1995. Parbati Barua is incidentally the first female mahout in recent recorded history, and has first-hand experience in catching elephants. She learnt her skill from her father, Prakritish Barua, whose expertise on Asian elephants was well known.

172 Ibid.

173 A number of film documentaries have been made on this subject and broadcast in international channels such as National Geographic and Discovery. One documentary named *The dark side of elephants* even portrayed the bull elephant of northern Bengal as a psychopathic killer taking revenge on humans.

174 Sukumar et al. 2003; Venkataraman et al. 2005.

175 Barua and Bist 1995.

176 Sukumar et al. 2003.

177 Barua and Bist 1995.

178 Unpublished data.

179 Meghalaya was carved out of Assam in 1972.

180 Lahiri-Choudhury 1986.

181 Ibid.

182 Ramakrishnan 1992.

183 Sukumar 1989, ch. 9.

184 Lahiri-Choudhury 1980; Williams and Johnsingh 1996.

185 Marcot et al. 2002.

186 Srivastava et al. 2002; Kushwaha and Hazarika 2004; A. Saikia et al., "No living space? Shrinking habitat and human elephant conflict in Assam, India", Report submitted to the Rufford Small Grants Foundation, London, UK, 2007.

187 Kushwaha and Hazarika 2004.

188 Article by J. Benn and J. Vertefenille, "Lines of defense: elephant protection in India's North Bank landscape", posted on September 26, 2006 at www.panda.org.

189 Lahiri-Choudhury 1986.

190 Menon et al. 1997; Menon 2002.

191 Menon 2002, p. 111.

192 Nearly half the 1,313 bulls captured were tuskless according to figures reported by Deraniyagala 1955; there would of course be some bias towards tuskers in capture operations.

193 The data pertain to bulls older than 20 years and are based on studies during 2005–10 by my research team, including C. Arivazhagan and K. Chelliah, at Kaziranga.

194 Menon et al. 1997; Menon 2002, ch. 6.

195 Choudhury and Menon 2004.

196 Choudhury 1999; Choudhury and Menon 2004.

197 The northern West Bengal elephant population is genetically contiguous with western Assam, Bhutan, and Arunachal and should thus be treated as a single population.

198 Tiwari et al. 2005.

199 Choudhury 1995.

200 Shahi and Chowdhury 1985.

201 Singh and Chowdhury 1999.

202 Shahi and Chowdhury 1985.

203 Datye and Bhagwat 1995.

204 Sukumar 1994a.

205 Ibid.

206 El Niño Southern Oscillation refers to a greater than average warming of the surface waters of the eastern Pacific Ocean. This event causes global climatic anomalies.

207 Sukumar 1995; Sukumar 2003, pp. 320–21.

208 See Mike Pandey's film on this operation, *The last migration: wild elephant capture in Sarguja*, 1994.

209 Singh 2002; Chhattisgarh was carved out of Madhya Pradesh in 2000.

210 Personal communication with D.S. Srivastava, Daltonganj, Jharkhand.

211 Swain and Patnaik 2002; Sar et al. 2008.

212 Unpublished study during 2009 by my research team.

213 Sukumar et al. 2004; Venkataraman et al. 2002.

214 Nair and Gadgil 1980.

215 Ibid.

216 Nair et al. 1977.

217 Ibid.

218 The Nilgiri Biosphere Reserve, the country's first such reserve declared in 1986, encompassed a 5,520 sq. km tract of forest. See Sukumar 1987.

219 Baskaran et al. 1995.

220 Gadgil and Guha 1995, p. 73.

221 Vidya et al. 2005.

222 Sukumar 1989, pp. 160–62; Baskaran et al. 2007. The estimates of the wild elephant population for this landscape are not very robust, but a conservative figure of 2,500 individuals may be taken for the present based on censuses by the forest department and other studies.

223 Kumar et al. 2010; Baskaran et al. 2007.

224 The estimates are based on unpublished reports of elephant census during 2005 in this landscape by forest departments of Kerala and Tamil Nadu; also see Sukumar et al. 2004 and Ramakrishnan et al. 1998.

225 Sukumar et al. 2004 ; Varma 2008.

226 K.S. Sudhi, "Lilliput jumbos – a subject of debate", *The Hindu*, April 12, 2010.

227 Sivaganesan and Kumar 1995.

228 The estimate of 70 elephants in 1993 on the basis of dung counts by Sivaganesan and Kumar (1995) is unlikely; a later study by S. Krishnan and R. Ali in 2001 found not more than half this number (unpublished report), but see Ali 2004.

229 A report by this author and E.A. Jayson after a short field visit in April 2009 made these recommendations after taking into consideration the logistical issues, including resources needed, to capture and transport these elephants to the mainland.

230 Saberwal et al. 2000, ch. 4.

231 Divyabhanusinh 2005, ch. 3.

232 Ibid. Interestingly, the Reserve Bank of India recognized this gaffe and selected the tiger as its emblem.

233 M. Krishnan, "A bird emblem for India" (1961) in Guha 2000, pp. 44–47.

234 Sukumar 1989, pp. 170–73.

235 Martin and Vigne 1989.

236 Sukumar 1989, pp. 170–73.

237 Martin 1980.

238 Sukumar 1989, pp. 170–73.

239 Douglas-Hamilton 1987; Douglas-Hamilton and Douglas-Hamilton 1992; Sukumar 2003, ch. 8.

240 Menon 2002, chs. 12 and 13.

241 Ibid., ch. 18.

242 Sukumar 1989, ch. 10.

243 Martin and Vigne 1989.

244 Ramakrishnan et al. 1998.

245 Arivazhagan and Sukumar 2005.

246 Ibid.

247 Ibid.

248 Menon 2002.

249 Ibid., ch. 8.

250 In an article "Understanding Elephants" published in *Sanctuary Asia* magazine (1985, vol. 5, pp. 232–41 and 286–90), this author had called for the launch of Project Elephant. This author was a member of the task force set up in 1990 and headed by S. Deb Roy, Additional Inspector-General of Forests (Wildlife) at the Ministry of Environment and Forests, New Delhi, to prepare the plan for the project.

251 See the document "Project Elephant" issued by Ministry of Environment and Forests, New Delhi, in February 1993; also see Sukumar 1996.

252 The original term "Elephant Reserve" was used for a landscape entity that covered the elephant habitat in one or more states of the country. Later, this term was restricted to the portion of the landscape falling within a given state and a new term "Elephant Range" substituted for the landscape; see Bist 2002b. In 2010 the appellation was again changed to "Elephant Landscape" (see note 257).

253 Bist 2002b.

254 To give two examples, a proposed highway expansion in northern West Bengal was diverted through a non-forested route, while a proposed railway line cutting through the landscape of the Nilgiris and the Biligirirangans in the south has been shelved for the present.

255 Bist 2002.

256 Ghosh 2005.

257 Rangarajan et al. 2010.

CHAPTER 10

1 Sanderson 1878. Sanderson observed accurately that an elephant "herd is invariably led by a female, never a male" (ch. 6), contrary to the accounts of shikaris.

2 Benedict 1936.

3 Krishnan 1972.

4 Eisenberg and Lockhart 1972; McKay 1973; Kurt 1974.

5 Ishwaran 1981, 1993; Santiapillai et al. 1984.

6 Nair et al. 1977; Nair and Gadgil 1980; also papers in J.C. Daniel (ed.), "The Asian elephant in the Indian subcontinent", Report of the IUCN/SSC Asian Elephant Specialist Group, 1980.

7 Sukumar 1985, 1989, 1994b.

8 Baskaran et al. 1995; Williams et al. 2001; Fernando and Lande 2000; Fernando et al. 2008.

9 Olivier 1978b provided a basic account of feeding ecology of elephants in Peninsular Malaysia.

10 Sukumar 2003, ch. 5, provides a detailed discussion of feeding by elephants.

11 Sukumar 1989, 2003.

12 Vancuylenberg 1977; also see Wing and Buss 1970 for similar conclusions from Uganda.

13 Sukumar et al. 1987, Sukumar and Ramesh 1992.

14 Bamboo belongs to the grass family but the mode of feeding and the isotopic signature resemble those of browse.

15 Sukumar 2003, ch. 8, provides a more complete discussion.

16 Sukumar 1989, ch. 7.

17 Ibid.; de Silva 1998; Sukumar 2003, ch. 8.

18 Sukumar and Gadgil 1988.

19 Baskaran et al. 1995.

20 Sukumar et al. 2003.

21 R. Sukumar and team, unpublished data for 2005–06.

22 Fernando et al. 2008.

23 Laws 1970; also see Sukumar 2003, ch. 6, for a detailed discussion of this topic.

24 Mueller-Dombois 1972; Ishwaran 1983.

25 Daniel et al. 1995.

26 Sukumar 2003, ch. 6.

27 Douglas-Hamilton and Douglas-Hamilton 1975; Moss and Poole 1983.

28 McKay 1973, p. 72.

29 Vidya and Sukumar 2005.

30 Sukumar 1985, vol. 1, ch. 4.

31 Eisenberg et al. 1971.

32 Hess et al. 1983; Brown 2000.

33 Jainudeen et al. 1972.

34 Rasmussen et al. 1984; Niemuller and Liptrap 1991.

35 Lincoln and Ratnasooriya 1996.

36 Poole 1989.

37 This study is being carried out by Karpagam Chelliah at Kaziranga in Assam.

38 Watve and Sukumar 1997 discuss the possibility that longer tusks in a bull could indicate superior genes for better resistance to parasites and diseases; also see Sukumar 2003, ch. 3.

39 Heffner and Heffner 1980.

40 Payne et al. 1986.

41 Poole et al. 1988; Garstang et al. 1995.

42 Nair et al. 2009.

43 Rasmussen 1998, Rasmussen and Krishnamurthy 2000; the term pheromone refers to a volatile chemical that acts as a signal.

44 Rasmussen and Munger 1996.

45 The term flehmen refers to a bull placing the tip of its trunk in the urogenital opening of a female elephant, and inserting its trunk into the roof of its mouth, where a pair of vomeronasal organs provides the identity of the chemical substance that signals the female's reproductive state.

46 Rasmussen et al. 2002; ancient descriptions of musth are given in Nilakantha's *Matangalila*, see Edgerton 1931 for translation.

47 Rensch 1957.

48 Plotnik et al. 2006.

49 Bates et al. 2008.

50 Sukumar 2003, pp. 257–71.

51 Sukumar 1989, ch. 11.

52 Ibid.

53 Sanderson 1878, p. 59.

54 Sukumar 2003, p. 45.

55 Santiapillai and Sukumar 2004, Table 1.1.

56 Blake and Hedges 2004.

57 Santiapillai and Jackson 1990; Santiapillai and Sukumar 2004.

58 Database of the IUCN/SSC African Elephant Specialist Group; www.african-elephant.org.

59 Menon et al. 2005.

60 www.asiannature.org.

61 www.wti.org.

62 Sukumar 2003, pp. 355–63.

63 Sukumar 1995.

64 Discussions with officials of Andhra Pradesh Forest Department.

65 Varma et al. 2008.

66 Whitehouse and Harley 2001.

67 Sukumar 2003, ch. 7.

68 See Sukumar 2003, ch. 8 for a more detailed discussion.

69 Sukumar et al. 1997; Taylor and Poole 1998; Kurt et al. 2008.

70 The papers in Wemmer and Christen 2008 provide excellent discussions of the ethics of coexistence between humans and elephants. The following articles are especially relevant to the discussion on captive elephants: Brown et al. 2008, Lehnhardt and Galloway 2008, Kreger 2008, Alward 2008, Schmitt 2008, Garrison 2008, Hancocks 2008, Hutchins et al. 2008, Mellen et al. 2008, Kurt et al. 2008; also see Ghosh 2005 for an account of the problems that captive elephants face in India.

71 See Sukumar 2003, ch. 1 for a summary.

72 Vartanyan et al. 1993.

APPENDIX

Status and Distribution of the Asian Elephant

The Asian elephant is distributed across 13 countries in South and Southeast Asia, the overall range of its distribution covering about 500,000 sq. km of habitat. Figures for the wild elephant population are approximate and for some countries little more than educated guesses. I have provided the minimum and maximum numbers based on several sources described in the text (Chapter 9) as well as the website of the IUCN/SSC Asian Elephant Specialist Group (www.asesg.org); even these are under constant review as in the case of Sri Lanka that is now likely to be greater than 5,800 (based on a survey in August 2011) wild elephants rather than the range of 2,500–4,000 elephants reported earlier.

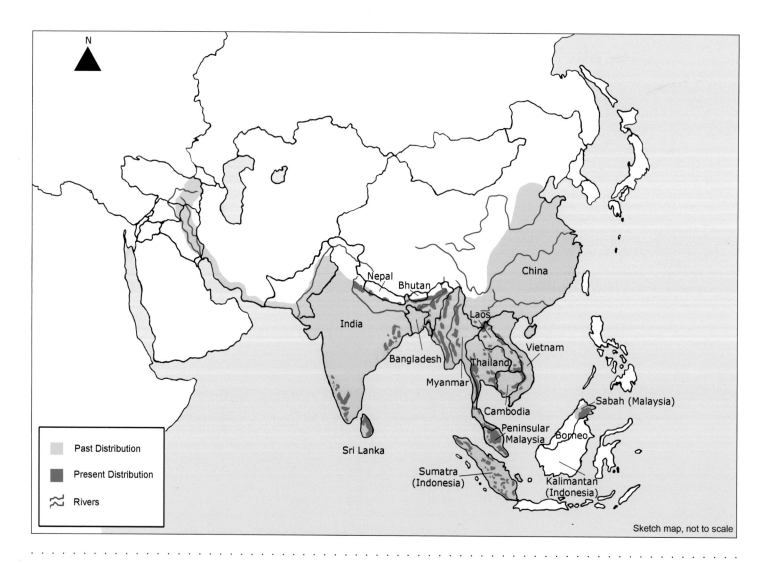

				TABLE:STATUS OF ASIAN ELEPHANT POPULATIONS	
S. No.	**Country**	**Area of range country (km²)**	**Area of elephant range (km²)**	**Population estimates**	
				Minimum	Maximum
1.	India South Central Northwest Northeast Islands	3,287,590	110,000 (39,500) (23,500) (5,500) (41,000) (500)	26,390 (13,000) (2,400) (750) (10,200) (40)	30,770 (15,000) (2,700) (1,000) (12,000) (70)
2.	Nepal	141,400	> 2,500	100	125
3.	Bhutan	46,600	1,500	250	500
4.	Bangladesh	147,570	1,800	150	250
5.	China	9,579,000	2,500	200	250
6.	Myanmar	678,000	115,000	4,000	5,000
7.	Thailand	513,115	25,500	2,500	3,200
8.	Lao PDR	236,800	> 20,000	500	1,000
9.	Cambodia	181,035	> 40,000	250	600
10.	Vietnam	340,000	> 3,000	70	150
11.	Malaysia Peninsular Sabah	329,750 (131,598) (80,520)	45,000 (> 20,000) (> 25,000)	2,100 (1,000) (1,100)	3,100 (1,500) (1,600)
12.	Indonesia Sumatra Kalimantan	1,919,440 (524,100) (550,200)	105,000 (> 100,000) (< 5,000)	2,400 (2,400) (?)	3,400 (3,400) (?)
13.	Sri Lanka *see text opposite	65,610	> 15,000	2,500*	4,000*
	TOTAL	17,465,910	> 486,800	41,410	52,345

The figures for the country (in the case of India, Malaysia, and Indonesia) are inclusive of the regional figures in brackets.

bibliography

A

Abdul, J. bin and N. Othman. 2004. Malaysia: Peninsular Malaysia. Ch. 15 in Santiapillai and Sukumar (2004).

Ali, R. 2004. The effect of introduced herbivores on vegetation in the Andaman islands. *Current Science* 86: 1103–12.

Altick, R.D. 1978. *The shows of London.* Harvard University Press, Cambridge, Massachusetts.

Alvi, M.A. and A. Rahman. 1968. *Jahangir: the naturalist.* Indian National Science Academy, New Delhi.

Alward, L. 2008. Why circuses are unsuited to elephants. Pp. 205–26 in Wemmer and Christen (2008).

Ambu, L.N., P.M. Andau, S. Nathan, A. Tunga, S.M. Jensen, R. Cox, R. Alfred, and J. Payne. 2004. Malaysia: Sabah. Ch. 16 in Santiapillai and Sukumar (2004).

Anon. 1843. *The Menageries: Quadrupeds described and drawn from living subjects*, Vol. 2. Charles Knight, London.

Arivazhagan, C. and R. Sukumar. 2005. Comparative demography of Asian elephant populations (*Elephas maximus*) in southern India. Technical Report No. 106, Centre for Ecological Sciences, Indian Institute of Science, Bangalore.

Attygalle, N., W.J.F. LaBrooy, S. Natesan, C.W. Nicholas, and S. Paranavitana (eds.) 1959. *History of Ceylon, Vol. 1: from the earliest times to 1505.* Ceylon University Press, Colombo.

B

Baker, C.M.A. and C. Manwell. 1983. Man and elephant: the "dare theory" of domestication and origin of breeds. *Zeitschrift für Tierzüchtung und Zuchtüngsbiologie* 100: 55–75.

Baker, G. (trans.) 1823. *Titus Livius (Livy), History of Rome*, Vol. 3. Peter A. Meiser, New York.

Baker, I. and M. Kashio (eds.) 2002. *Giants on our hands: proceedings of an international workshop on the domesticated Asian elephant.* Food and Agriculture Organization, Bangkok, Thailand.

Baker, S.W. 1854. *The rifle and hound in Ceylon.* Longman, Brown, Green and Longman, London.

Bakshi, G.D. 2002. *The Indian art of war: the Mahabharata paradigm.* Sharada Publishing House, New Delhi.

Balfour, E. 1885. *The cyclopaedia of India*, Vol. 1. Bernard Quaritch, London.

Barney, K. 2005. *Customs, concessionaires and conflict: tracking Cambodia's forestry commodity chains and export links to China.* Forest Trends, Washington DC.

Barnosky, A.D., P.L. Koch, R.S. Feranec, S.L. Wing, and A.B. Shabel. 2004. Assessing the causes of Late Pleistocene extinctions on the continents. *Science* 306: 70–76.

Bartholomew, T.T. 1995. Spirit king, demon, and god of wealth: Ganesh in East Asia. Pp. 115–32 in Pal (1995).

Barua, P. and S.S. Bist. 1995. Changing patterns in the distribution and movement of wild elephants in north Bengal. Pp. 66–84 in Daniel and Datye (1995).

Basham, A.L. 1967. *The wonder that was India.* 3rd edn. Macmillan Publishers, London.

Basham, A.L. (ed.) 1975. *A cultural history of India.* Oxford University Press, New Delhi.

Baskaran, N., M. Balasubramanian, S. Swaminathan, and A.A. Desai. 1995. Home range of elephants in the Nilgiri Biosphere Reserve. Pp. 296–313 in Daniel and Datye (1995).

Baskaran, N., G. Kannan, U. Anbarasan, and R. Sukumar, 2007. *Conservation of the elephant population in the Anamalais – Nelliyampathis and Palani hills (Project Elephant Range 9), southern India.* Final report to USFWS. Asian Nature Conservation Foundation, Bangalore.

Bates, L.A., P.C. Lee, N. Njiraini, J.H. Poole, K. Sayialel, S. Sayialel, C.J. Moss, and R.W. Byrne. 2008. Do elephants show empathy? *Journal of Consciousness Studies* 15: 204–25.

Bazé, W. 1955. *Just elephants* (translated from the French by H.M. Burton). Elek Books, London.

Beal, S. (trans.) 1911. *Life of Hiuen-Tsang.* Kegan Paul, Trench Trübner and Co., London. Reprinted by Asian Educational Services, New Delhi, 1998.

Bedini, S.A. 1997. *The pope's elephant: an elephant's journey from deep in India to the heart of Rome.* Penguin Books, New York.

Behl, B.K. 2007. Grandeur in caves. *Frontline* Sept. 22.

Behl, B.K. 2008. Culture of peace. *Frontline* Aug. 30.

Benedict, F.G. 1936. *The physiology of the elephant.* Carnegie Institute, Washington DC.

Bernier, F. 1891. *Travels in the Mogul empire AD 1656–1668.* English translation based on Irving Brock. Archibald Constable, London.

Beveridge, H. (trans.) 1897–1939. *The Akbarnama of Abu'l Fazl*, 3 vols. Asiatic Society of Bengal, Calcutta.

Beveridge, A.S. (trans.) 1922. *The Baburnama in English*, 2 vols. Luzac and Co., London.

Bhargava, P.L. 1956. *India in the Vedic age.* 3rd revised edn. published by D.K. Printworld, New Delhi, 2001.

Bhat, M.R. (trans.) 1987. *Varahamihira's Brihat Samhita*, Part 2. Motilal Banarsidass, New Delhi.

Bhatta, S.R. 2004. Nepal. Ch. 18 in Santiapillai and Sukumar (2004). Also published in *Gajah* 25: 87–90 (2006).

Bhattacharya, G. 1995. The dual role of Ganesh in the Buddhist art of South Asia. Pp. 65–80 in Pal (2005).

Bist, S.S. (ed.) 2002a. *A.J.W. Milroy's Management of elephants in captivity.* Natraj Publishers, Dehra Dun.

Bist, S.S. 2002b. An overview of elephant conservation in India. *The Indian Forester* 128: 121–36.

Blair, J.A.S., G.G. Boon, and N.M. Noor. 1979. Conservation or cultivation: the confrontation between the Asian elephant and land development in peninsular Malaysia. *Land Development Digest*, 2: 27–59.

Blake, S. and S. Hedges. 2004. Sinking the flagship: the case of forest elephants in Asia and Africa. *Conservation Biology* 18: 1191–1202.

Blochmann, H. and H.S. Jarrett. (trans.) 1873–1907. *The Ain-i-Akbari of Abul Fazl Allami*, 3 vols. Asiatic Society of Bengal, Calcutta.

Blouch, R.A. and Haryanto 1984. Elephants in

southern Sumatra. IUCN/WWF Report No. 3, Project 3033, Bogor, Indonesia.

Blouch, R.A. and K. Simbolon. 1985. Elephants in northern Sumatra. IUCN/WWF Report No. 9, Project 3033, Bogor, Indonesia.

Blower, J. 1985. Elephants in Burma. WWF Monthly Report, December 1985, pp. 279–85. World Wildlife Fund, Gland, Switzerland.

Bostock, J. and H.T. Riley (trans.) 1855. *Pliny the Elder: the natural history.* Taylor and Francis, London.

Bowring, L.B. 1893. *Rulers of India: Haidar Ali and Tipu Sultan and the struggle with the Musalman powers of the south.* Henry Frowde, London.

Breasted, J.H. (trans.) 1906. *Ancient records of Egypt, Vol. 2: The eighteenth dynasty.* The University of Chicago Press, Chicago.

Briggs, J. (trans.) 1829. *History of the rise of the Mohamedan power in India, till the year* AD *1612: translated from the original Persian of Mahomed Kasim Ferishta,* 4 vols. Longman, Rees, Orme, Browne, and Green, London.

Brooks, R.R.R. and V.S. Wakankar. 1976. *Stone age painting in India.* Yale University Press, New Haven.

Brown, J.L. 2000. Reproductive endocrine monitoring of elephants: an essential tool for assisting captive management. *Zoo Biology* 19: 347–67.

Brown, J.L., N. Wielebnaoski, and J.V. Cheeran (eds.) 2008. Pain, stress, and suffering in elephants. Pp. 121–48 in Wemmer and Christen (2008).

Brown, R.L. (ed.) 1991a. *Ganesh: studies of an Asian god.* State University of New York Press, Albany.

Brown, R.L. 1991b. Ganesa in southeast Asian art: Indian connections and indigenous developments. Pp. 171–234 in Brown 1991a.

Bühler, G. (trans.) 1886. *Sacred books of the East: The laws of Manu,* Vol. 25. Oxford.

Burton, R. (trans.) 1883. *The Kama Sutra of Vatsyayana.* London.

C

Carrington, R. 1959. *Elephants: their natural history, evolution and influence on mankind.* Basic Books, Inc., New York.

Caughley, G. 1980. Comments on elephants in Burma. FAO, Bangkok. Reprinted in *Gajah* 14: 1–9, 1995.

Chakravarti, A. 1953. *Tirukkural.* Diocesan Press, Madras.

Chandler, W.B. 1987. Hannibal: nemesis of Rome. Pp. 282–321 in *Great black leaders: ancient and modern* (ed. I.V. Sertima). Incorporating the *Journal of African Civilizations.* Transaction Publishers, New Brunswick, NJ.

Chandra, S. 2004. *Medieval India: from Sultanat to the Mughals, Part 1, Delhi Sultanat (1206–1526).* 3rd edn. Har-Anand Publications, New Delhi.

Chapple, C.K. (ed.) 2002. *Jainism and ecology.* Harvard University Press, Cambridge, Massachusetts.

Childe, V.G. 1926. *The Aryans: a study of Indo-European origins.* London.

Chinnock, E.J. (trans.) 1893. *Arrian's Anabasis of Alexander and Indica.* George Bell and Sons, London.

Choudhury, A. 1995. Status of elephant in Dibang valley of Arunachal Pradesh. *Journal of the Bombay Natural History Society* 92: 417.

Choudhury, A. and V. Menon. 2004. North-East India. Ch. 9 in Santiapillai and Sukumar (2004). Reprinted in *Gajah* 25: 47–60, 2006.

Choudhury, A.U. 1999. Status and conservation of the Asian elephant *Elephas maximus* in north-eastern India. *Mammal Review* 29: 141–73.

Choudhury, P.C. (ed.) 1976. *Hastividyarnava.* Publication Board, Gauhati, Assam.

Codrington, H.W. 1926. *A short history of Lanka.* Macmillan and Co., London.

Codrington, H.W. 1934. The Gadaladeniya inscription of Senasammata Vikrama Bahu. Pp. 8–15 in *Epigraphia Zeylanica,* Vol. IV (eds. H.W. Codrington and S. Paranavitana). London.

Coomaraswamy, A.K. 1994. *Jaina art.* Munshiram Manoharlal, New Delhi.

Cort, J.E. 1995. Absences and transformations: Ganesh in the Shvetambar Jain tradition. Pp. 81–94 in Pal (1995).

Courtwright, P.B. 1985. *Ganeśa: Lord of obstacles, lord of beginnings.* Oxford University Press, New York.

Cowell, E.B. (ed.) 1895–1907. *The Jataka or stories of the Buddha's former births.* 6 volumes. University Press, Cambridge, UK. Vol. 1 trans. R. Chambers (1895); Vol. 2 trans. W.H.D. Rouse (1895); Vol. 3 trans. H.T. Francis and R.A. Neil (1897); Vol. 4 trans. W.H.D. Rouse (1901); Vol. 5 trans. H.T. Francis (1905); Vol. 6 trans. E.B. Cowell and W.H.D. Rouse (1907).

Cranbrook, Earl of, J. Payne, and C.M.U. Leh. 2007. Origin of the elephants *Elephas maximus*

L. of Borneo. *Sarawak Museum Journal* 63: 95–125.

Cutler, D., W. Fung, M. Kremer, M. Singhal, and T. Vogl. 2007. Mosquitoes: the long-term effects of malaria eradication in India. National Bureau of Economic Research, Cambridge, Massachusetts.

Cuong, T.V., T.T. Lien, and P.M. Giao, 2002. The present status and management of domesticated Asian elephants in Vietnam. Pp. 111–28 in Baker and Kashio (2002).

D

Dames, M.L. (trans.) 1918–21. *The book of Duarte Barbosa: an account of the countries bordering on the Indian Ocean and their inhabitants* (orig. 1518). Reprinted by Asian Educational Services, New Delhi, 1989.

Daniel, J.C. (ed.) 1980. *The status of the Asian elephant in the Indian subcontinent.* Asian Elephant Specialist Group, c/o Bombay Natural History Society, Bombay.

Daniel, J.C. and H. Datye (eds.) 1995. *A week with elephants.* Bombay Natural History Society, Bombay, and Oxford University Press, New Delhi.

Daniel, J.C., V. Krishnamurthy, A.A. Desai, N. Sivaganesan, H.S. Datye, R. Kumar, N. Baskaran, M. Balasubramanian, and S. Swaminathan. 1995. Ecology of the Asian elephant. Final report (1987–92). Bombay Natural History Society, Mumbai.

Das, A.K. 1999. The elephant in Mughal painting. Pp. 36–54 in *Flora and fauna in Mughal art* (ed. S.P. Verma). Marg Publications, Mumbai.

Das, J.P. 1982. *Puri paintings: the chitrakāra and his work.* Arnold-Heinemann Publishers (India), New Delhi.

Datye, H.S. and A.M. Bhagwat. 1995. Home range of elephants in fragmented habitats of central India. *Journal of the Bombay Natural History Society* 92: 1–10.

Davidson, J.L. 1975. Indian influences on China. Pp. 455–60 in Basham (1975).

Dawson, S., D. Tuoc, L.V. Khoi, and T.V. Cuong. 1993. *Elephant surveys in Vietnam.* WWF-Indochina Programme, Hanoi.

de Beer, G. 1969. *Hannibal: challenging Rome's supremacy.* The Viking Press, New York.

Deraniyagala, P.E.P. 1955. *Some extinct elephants, their relatives and the two living species.* Ceylon National Museum Publication, Colombo.

Desai, A.A., C. Sokhavicheaboth, O. Ratanak, L. Vuthy, and A. Maxwell. 2002. *Initial surveys to determine the distribution of wild*

Asian elephant populations in selected areas of northeastern Cambodia, 2000–01. WWF Indochina Programme Office, Phnom Penh.

de Silva, C.R. 1990. Peddling trade, elephants and gems: some aspects of Sri Lanka's trading connections in the Indian Ocean in the 16th and early 17th centuries. Pp. 287–302 in *Asian Panorama Essays in Asian History, Past and Present* (eds. K.M. de Silva, S. Kiribamune, and C.R. de Silva). Vikas Publishing House, New Delhi.

de Silva, M. 1998. Status and conservation of the elephant (*Elephas maximus*) and the alleviation of man-elephant conflict in Sri Lanka. *Gajah* 19: 1–68.

Devakunjari, D. 1998. *Hampi.* Archaeological Survey of India, New Delhi.

Dhammika, V.S. 1993. *The edicts of King Ashoka.* Buddhist Publication Society, Kandy.

Dhavalikar, M.K. 2003. *Ellora.* Oxford University Press, New Delhi.

Dhavalikar, R. 1982. Daimabad bronzes. Pp. 362–66 in *Harappan civilization: a contemporary perspective* (ed. G.L. Possehl). Aris and Phillips Ltd., Warminster, England.

Dhavalikar, R. 1991. Ganeśa: myth and reality. Pp. 49–68 in Brown (1991a).

Digby, S. 1971. *War horse and elephant in the Dehli Sultanate: a study of military supplies.* Orient Monographs, Oxford, UK.

Divyabhanusinh. 2005. *The story of Asia's lions.* Marg Publications, Mumbai.

Dominguez-Rodrigo, M., T.R. Pickering, S. Semav, and M.J. Rogers. 2005. Cutmarked bones from Pliocene archaeological sites at Gona, Afar, Ethiopia: implications for the function of the world's oldest stone tools. *Journal of Human Evolution* 48: 109–21.

Donaldson, T. 2003. *Konarak.* Oxford University Press, New Delhi.

Douglas-Hamilton, I. 1987. African elephants: population trends and their causes. *Oryx* 21: 11–14.

Douglas-Hamilton, I. and O. Douglas-Hamilton. 1975. *Among the elephants.* The Viking Press, New York.

Douglas-Hamilton, I. and O. Douglas-Hamilton. 1992. *Battle for the elephants.* Doubleday, London.

Druce, G.C. 1919. The elephant in medieval legend and art. *Journal of the Royal Archaeological Insitute, London,* Vol. 70.

Duckworth, J.W. and S. Hedges. 1998. *A review of the status of tiger, Asian elephant, gaur and banteng in Vietnam, Lao PDR, Cambodia and Yunnan Province (China), with recommendations for future conservation action.* WWF Indochina Programme, Hanoi.

Dudley, J.P., J.R. Ginsberg, A.J. Plumptre, J.A. Hart, and L.C. Campos. 2002. Effects of war and civil strife on wildlife and wildlife habitats. *Conservation Biology* 16: 319–29.

Duff, J.G. 1826. *A history of the Mahrattas,* 3 vols. Longmans, Rees, Orme, Brown, and Green, London.

Dundas, P. 2002. The limits of a Jain environmental ethic. Pp. 95–117 in Chapple (2002).

Duroiselle, C. 1913–14. Stone sculptures in the Ananda temple at Pagan. *Archaeological Survey of India, Annual Report 1913–14*, Delhi, pp. 63–67.

E

Echols, E.C. (trans.) 1961. *Herodian of Antioch's history of the Roman empire.* University of California Press, Berkeley.

Edgerton, F. 1931. *The elephant-lore of the Hindus: the elephant-sport (Matanga-lila) of Nilakantha.* Yale University, New Haven, Connecticut. Reprinted by Motilal Banarsidass, New Delhi, 1985.

Eisenberg, J. and M. Lockhart. 1972. An ecological reconnaissance of the Wilpattu National Park, Ceylon. *Smithsonian Contributions to Zoology* 101: 1–118.

Eisenberg, J., G.M. McKay, and M.R. Jainudeen. 1971. Reproductive behaviour of the Asiatic elephant (*Elephas maximus maximus* L.). *Behaviour* 38: 193–225.

Elliot, H.M. 1871. *The history of India as told by its own historians: the Muhammadan period* (ed. J. Dowson), Vol. 3. Trübner and Co., London.

Elvin, M. 2004. *The retreat of the elephants: an environmental history of China.* Yale University Press, New Haven, Connecticut.

Enzel, Y., L.L. Ely, S. Mishra, R. Ramesh, R. Amit, B. Lazar, S.N. Rajaguru, V.R. Baker, and A. Sandler. 1999. High resolution Holocene environmental changes in the Thar desert, northwestern India. *Science* 284: 125–28.

Erdosy, G. 1998. Deforestation in pre- and protohistoric south Asia. Pp. 51–69 in Grove et al. (1998).

Evans, G.H. 1910. *Elephants and their diseases.* Government Press, Rangoon.

F

FAO. 2007. *State of the world's forests 2007.* Food and Agriculture Organization of the United Nations, Rome, Italy.

Fernando, P. 2000. Elephants in Sri Lanka: past, present and future. *Loris* 22: 38–44.

Fernando, P. and R. Lande. 2000. Molecular genetic and behavioral analysis of social organization in the Asian elephant (*Elephas maximus*). *Behavioural Ecology and Sociobiology* 48: 84–91.

Fernando, P., T.N.C. Vidya, J. Payne, M. Stuewe, G. Davison, R.J. Alfred, P. Andau, E. Bosi, A. Kilbourn, and D.J. Melnick. 2003. DNA analysis indicates that Asian elephants are native to Borneo and are therefore a high priority for conservation. *PLoS Biology* 1: 110–15.

Fernando, P., E.D. Wikramanayake, H.K. Janaka, L.K.A. Jayasinghe, M. Gunawardena, S.W. Kotagama, D. Weerakoon, and J. Pastorini. 2008. Ranging behavior of the Asian elephant in Sri Lanka. *Zeitschrift für Säugetierkunde* 73: 2–13.

Flood, G. 1996. *An introduction to Hinduism.* Cambridge University Press, Cambridge, UK.

Foster, B. (trans.) 1929. *Livy: the history of Rome,* Vol. 5, Books 21–22. Loeb Classical Library, Harvard University Press, Cambridge, Massachusetts.

Fowler, H.W. and F.G. Fowler (trans.) 1905. *The works of Lucian, Vol. 2: Zeuxis and Antiochus.* Clarendon Press, Oxford.

FWI/GFW. 2002. *The State of Forest: Indonesia.* Forest Watch Institute, Bogor, Indonesia, and Global Forest Watch, Washington DC.

G

Gadgil, M. and R. Guha. 1992. *This fissured land: an ecological history of India.* Oxford University Press, New Delhi.

Gadgil, M. and R. Guha. 1995. *Ecology and equity: the use and abuse of nature in contemporary India.* Routledge, London.

Gale, U.T. 1974. *Burmese timber elephant.* Trade Corporation, Rangoon.

Garrison, J. 2008. The challenges of meeting the needs of captive elephants. Pp. 237–58 in Wemmer and Christen (2008).

Garstang, M., D. Larom, R. Raspet, and M. Lindeque. 1995. Atmospheric controls on elephant communication. *The Journal of Experimental Biology* 198: 939–51.

Geiger, W. and M.H. Bode (trans.) 1912. *The Mahavamsa (or the great chronicle of Ceylon).* Oxford University Press, London on behalf of the Pali Text Society. Reprinted by Asian

Educational Services, New Delhi, 1986.

Geiger, W. and C.M. Rickmers. (trans.) 1929–30. *The Culavamsa (being the more recent part of the Mahavamsa)*, 2 vols. Pali Text Society, London. Reprinted by Asian Educational Services, New Delhi, 1992.

Getty, A. 1936. *Ganeša: a monograph on the elephant-faced god.* Clarendon Press, Oxford.

Gheerbrant, E. 2009. Paleocene emergence of elephant relatives and the rapid evolution of African ungulates. *Proceedings of the National Academy of Sciences* (USA) 106: 10717–21.

Gheerbrant, E., J. Sudre, and H. Cappetta, 1996. A Palaeocene proboscidean from Morocco. *Nature* 383: 68–70.

Ghosh, R. 2005. *Gods in chains.* Foundation Books, New Delhi.

Ghurye, G.S. 1962. *Gods and men.* Popular Book Depot, Bombay.

Goldman, R.P. (ed.) 1984. *The Ramayana of Valmiki*, 6 vols. Vol. 1 (*Balakanda*) by R.P. Goldman (1984); Vol. 2 (*Ayodhyakanda*) by S.I. Pollock (1984); Vol. 3 (*Aranyakanda*) by S.I. Pollock (1984); Vol. 4 (*Kiskindakanda*) by R. Lefeber (1994); Vol. 5 (*Sundarakanda*) by R.P. Goldman (1996); Vol. 6 (*Yuddhakanda*) by R.P. Goldman, S.J.S. Goldman, and B.A. van Nooten (2009). Princeton University Press, Princeton, NJ.

Gopal, M.H. 1971. *Tipu Sultan's Mysore: an economic study.* Popular Prakashan, Bombay.

Gray, A. and H.C.P. Bell. (trans.) 1887. *The voyage of Francois Pyrard de Laval to the East Indies, the Maldives, the Moluccas and Brazil*, 2 vols. Haklyut Society, London.

Griffiths, R.T.H. (trans.) 1896: *The hymns of the Rigveda.* 1899: *The texts of the white Yajurveda.* 1895–96: *The hymns of the Atharvaveda.* 1895: *The hymns of the Samaveda.* E.J. Lazarus, Benaras.

Gröning, K. and M. Saller. 1998. *Elephants: a cultural and natural history.* Könemann, Cologne.

Grove, R.H., V. Damodaran, and S. Sangwan (eds.) 1998. *Nature and the Orient: the environmental history of south and southeast Asia.* Oxford University Press, New Delhi.

Guha, R. (ed.) 2000. *Nature's spokesman: M. Krishnan and Indian wildlife.* Oxford University Press, New Delhi.

Guha, R. 2007. *India after Gandhi: the history of the world's largest democracy.* Picador, New Delhi.

Gupta, S.K. 1983. *Elephant in Indian art and mythology.* Abhinav Publications, New Delhi.

H

Hancocks, D. 2008. Most zoos do not deserve elephants. Pp. 259–84 in Wemmer and Christen (2008).

Harris, M. 1977. *Cannibals and kings: the origins of cultures.* Random House, New York.

Harris, R.B., W.A. Wall, and F.W. Allendorf. 2002. Genetic consequences of hunting: what do we know and what should we do? *Wildlife Society Bulletin* 30: 634–43.

Hart, G. 1975. *The poems of ancient Tamil: their milieu and their Sanskrit counterparts.* Oxford University Press, New Delhi. Reprinted with a new Preface, 1999.

Hart, G.L. and H. Heifetz. 1999. *The Purananuru: four hundred songs of war and wisdom.* Columbia University Press, New York.

Hartl, G.B., F. Kurt, R. Tiedemann, C. Gmeiner, K. Nadlinger, K.U. Mar, and A. Rubel. 1996. Population genetics and systematic of Asian elephant (*Elephas maximus*): a study based on sequence variation at the Cyt b gene of PCR-amplified mitochondrial DNA from hair bulbs. *Zeitschrift für Säugetierkunde* 61: 285–94.

Hedges, S., M.J. Tyson, A. Sitompul, M. Kinnaird, D. Gunaryadi, and Aslan. 2005. Distribution, status, and conservation needs of Asian elephants (*Elephas maximus*) in Lampung province, Sumatra, Indonesia. *Biological Conservation* 124: 35–48.

Hedges, S., M.J. Tyson, and A. Sitompul. 2006. Why inter-country loans will not help Sumatra's elephants. *Zoo Biology* 25: 235–46.

Heffernan, J. and T.V. Cuong. 2004. *A review of the conservation status of the Asian elephant in Vietnam.* Indochina Asian Elephant Programme. Fauna and Flora International, Cambridge, UK.

Heffner, R. and H. Heffner. 1980. Hearing in the elephant (*Elephas maximus*). *Science* 208: 518–20.

Heiss, M.L. and R.J. Heiss. 2007. *The story of tea: a cultural history and drinking guide.* Ten Speed Press, Berkeley, California.

Hess, D.L., A.M. Schmidt, and M.J. Schmidt. 1983. Reproductive cycle of the Asian elephant (*Elephas maximus*) in captivity. *Biology of Reproduction* 28: 767–73.

Hooijer, D.A. 1972. Prehistoric evidence for *Elephas maximus* L. in Borneo. *Nature* 239: 238.

Howell, F.C. 1966. Observations on the earliest phases of the European Lower Paleolithic. *American Anthropologist* 68: 88–201.

Hunter, W.W. 1897. *The Thackerays in India and some Calcutta graves.* Henry Frowde, London.

Hutchins, M., B. Smith, and M. Keele. 2008. Zoos as responsible stewards of elephants. Pp. 285–306 in Wemmer and Christen (2008).

I

Ishwaran, N. 1981. Comparative study of Asiatic elephant *Elephas maximus* populations in Gal Oya, Sri Lanka. *Biological Conservation* 21: 303–13.

Ishwaran, N. 1983. Elephant and woody-plant relationships in Gal Oya, Sri Lanka. *Biological Conservation* 26: 255–70.

Ishwaran, N. 1993. Ecology of the Asian elephant in lowland dry zone habitat of the Mahaweli River Basin, Sri Lanka. *Journal of Tropical Ecology* 9: 169–82.

Islam, M.A. 2004. Bangladesh. Ch. 3 in Santiapillai and Sukumar (2004). Reprinted in *Gajah* 25: 21–26, 2006.

J

Jagannathan, S. and N. Krishna. 1992. *Ganesha the auspicious ... the beginning.* Vakils, Feffer & Simons, Bombay.

Jainudeen, M.R., C.B. Katongole, and R.V. Short. 1972. Plasma testosterone levels in relation to musth and sexual activity in the male Asiatic elephant, *Elephas maximus. Journal of Reproduction and Fertility* 29: 99–103.

Jayewardene, J. 1994. *The elephant in Sri Lanka.* The Wildlife Heritage Trust of Sri Lanka, Colombo.

Jha, D.N. 1998. *Ancient India: in historical outline.* Manohar, Delhi. Reprinted 2007.

Johnsingh, A.J.T., Q. Qureshi, D. Mohan, and C.A. Williams. 2004. North-west India. Ch. 10 in Santiapillai and Sukumar (2004). Reprinted in *Gajah* 25: 61–70, 2006.

Jurriaanse, M.W. 1940. The Ceylon elephant in Dutch times. *Loris* Vol. 2, No. 3.

K

Ka, T. 1958. The early art of Burma. *The Atlantic Magazine*, February 1958.

Kan, L. 1954. Six-tusked elephants on a Han bas-relief. *Harvard Journal of Asiatic Studies* 17: 366–69.

Kangle, R.P. (trans.) 1969. *The Kautiliya Arthasastra*, 3 vols. 2nd edn. Motilal Banarsidass, Delhi.

Kaur, R. 2003. *Performative politics and the cultures of Hinduism: public uses of religion in western India.* Permanent Black, New Delhi.

Keay, J. 2000. *The great arc: the dramatic tale of how India was mapped and Everest was named*. HarperCollins, New York.

Kenoyer, J. 1998. *Ancient cities of the Indus valley civilization*. Oxford University Press, Karachi.

Khan, M.M. 1991. *The Malayan elephant: a species plan for its conservation*. Department of Wildlife and National Parks, Kuala Lumpur.

Khounboline, K. 1999. The status of the Asian elephant (*Elephas maximus*) in Lao PDR. Pp. 47–50 in Osborn and Vinton (1999).

Khounboline, K. 2004. Lao PDR. Ch. 14 in Santiapillai and Sukumar (2004).

Klein, R.G. 1987. Reconstructing how early people exploited animals: Problems and prospects. Pp. 11–45 in *Evolution of human hunting* (eds. M.H. Nitecki and D.V. Nitecki). Plenum Press, New York.

Kreger, M.D. 2008. Canvas to concrete. Pp. 185–204 in Wemmer and Christen (2008).

Krishnamurthy, V. 1992. Recommendations for improving the management of captive elephants in Way Kambas National Park, Lampung, Sumatra, Indonesia. *Gajah* 9: 4–13.

Krishnamurthy, V. and C. Wemmer. 1995a. Veterinary care of Asian timber elephants in India: historical accounts and current observations. *Zoo Biology* 14: 12–133.

Krishnamurthy, V. and C. Wemmer. 1995b. Timber elephant management in the Madras Presidency of India (1844–1947). Pp. 456–72 in Daniel and Datye (1995).

Krishnan, M. 1972. An ecological survey of the larger mammals of peninsular India: the Indian elephant. *Journal of the Bombay Natural History Society* 69: 297–315.

Kumar, M.A., D. Mudappa, and T.R.S. Raman. 2010. Asian elephant *Elephas maximus* habitat use and ranging in fragmented rainforest and plantations in the Anamalai hills, India. *Tropical Conservation Science* 3: 143–58.

Kurt, F. 1974. Remarks on the social structure and ecology of the Ceylon elephant in the Yala National Park. Pp. 618–24 in *The behaviour of ungulates and its relation to management*, Vol. 2 (eds. V. Geist and F. Walther). International Union for Conservation of Nature and Natural Resources, Morges, Switzerland.

Kurt, F., G. Hartl, and R. Tiedemann. 1995. Tuskless bulls in Asian elephant *Elephas maximus*: history and population genetics of a man-made phenomenon. *Acta Theriologica* 3 (Suppl.): 125–43.

Kurt, F. and M.E. Garai. 2007. *The Sri Lankan elephant in captivity*. Foundation Books, New Delhi.

Kurt, F., K.U. Mar, and M.E. Garai. 2008. Giants in chains. Pp. 327–48 in Wemmer and Christen (2008).

Kushwaha, S.P.S. and R. Hazarika. 2004. Assessment of habitat loss in Kameng and Sonitpur Elephant Reserves. *Current Science* 87: 1447–53.

L

Lafrenz, K.A. 2004. Tracing the source of the elephant and hippopotamus ivory from the 14th century BC Uluburun shipwreck. M.S. dissertation, University of South Florida.

Lahiri-Choudhury, D.K. 1980. An interim report on the status and distribution of elephants in northeast India. Pp. 43–58 in Daniel (1980).

Lahiri-Choudhury, D.K. 1986. Elephants in northeast India. WWF Monthly Report. World Wildlife Fund, Gland, Switzerland, pp. 7–17, January 1986.

Lahiri-Choudhury, D.K. 1991. Indian myths and history. Pp. 130–47 in *The illustrated encyclopaedia of elephants* (ed. S.K. Eltringham). Salamander Books, London.

Lahiri-Choudhury, D.K. 1999. *The great Indian elephant book: an anthology of writings on elephants in the Raj*. Oxford University Press, New Delhi.

Lahiri, N. 1992. *The archaeology of Indian trade routes (up to c. 200 BC)*. Oxford University Press, New Delhi.

Lahiri, N. (ed.) 2000. *The decline and fall of the Indus civilization*. Permanent Black, Delhi.

Lair, R.C. 1997. *Gone astray: the care and management of Asian elephants in domesticity*. Food and Agriculture Organization, Rome and Bangkok.

Lamb, A. 1975. Indian influence in ancient south-east Asia. Ch. 31 in Basham (1975).

Lancaster, L.R. 1991. Ganesa in China: methods of transforming the demonic. Pp. 277–86 in Brown (1991a).

Laws, R.M. 1970. Elephants as agents of habitat and landscape change in East Africa. *Oikos* 21: 1–15.

Legge, J. (trans.) 1886. *A record of Buddhistic kingdoms, being an account by the Chinese monk Fa-hien of his travels in India and Ceylon (AD 399–412)*. Clarendon Press, Oxford.

Legge, J. (trans.) 1895. *The works of Mencius*, Vol. II of *The Chinese Classics* series. Clarendon Press, Oxford.

Lehnhardt, J. and M. Galloway. 2008. Carrots and sticks, people and elephants. Pp.167–84 in Wemmer and Christen (2008).

Lekagul B. and J. McNeely. 1977. Elephants in Thailand: importance, status and conservation. *Tigerpaper* 1: 22–25.

Li, H., Y. Ma, W. Liu, and W. Liu. 2009. Clearance and fragmentation of tropical rain forest in Xishuanghanna, S.W. China. *Biodiversity and Conservation*, published online May 24, 2009.

Lincoln, G.A. and W.D. Ratnasooriya. 1996. Testosterone secretion, musth behavior and social dominance in captive male elephants living near the equator. *Journal of Reproduction and Fertility* 108: 107–13.

Lister, A.M. and P. Bahn. 1994. *Mammoths*. Boxtree, London.

Longhurst, A.H. 1917. *Hampi ruins: described and illustrated*. Government Press, Madras.

Lorsirirat, K. 2007. Effect of forest cover change on sedimentation in Lam Phra Phloeng Reservoir, northeastern Thailand. Pp. 168–77 in *Forest environments in the Mekong river basin* (eds. H. Sawada, M. Araki, N.A. Chappell, J.V. La Frankie, and A. Shimizu). Springer, New York.

M

Ma, Q. and J.S. Broadhead. (eds.). 2002. *An overview of forest products statistics in south and southeast Asia*. FAO Regional Office for Asia and the Pacific, Bangkok.

Mabbett, I. and D. Chandler. 1995. *The Khmers*. Blackwell, Oxford, UK.

MacKenzie, J.M. 1987. Chivalry, social Darwinism and ritualized killing: the hunting ethos in Central Africa up to 1914. Pp. 41–61 in *Conservation in Africa: People, Policies and Practice* (eds. D. Anderson and R. Grove). Cambridge University Press, Cambridge, UK.

Magie, D. (trans.) 1921–24. *Historia Augusta*, 2 vols. Loeb Classical Library, Harvard University Press, Cambridge, Massachusetts.

Maglio, V.J. 1973. Origin and evolution of the Elephantidae. *Transactions of the American Philosophical Society of Philadelphia* 63: 1–149.

Major, R.H. (ed.) 1857. *India in the fifteenth century*. Hakluyt Society, London.

Mar, K.U. 2002. The studbook of timber elephants of Myanmar with special reference to survivorship analysis. Pp. 195–212 in Baker and Kashio (2002).

Marcot, B.G., A. Kumar, P.S. Roy, V.B. Sawarkar, A. Gupta, and S.N. Sangma. 2002. Assessment of large-scale deforestation in Sonitpur district of Assam. *Current Science* 95: 1458–63.

Marshall, J. 1939. *Monuments of Sanchi, Bhopal State*, Vol. I, p. 183. Calcutta and London.

Martin, E. and D. Stiles. 2002. *The south and southeast Asian ivory markets*. Save the Elephants, Nairobi.

Martin, E.B. 1980. The craft, the trade and the elephants. *Oryx* 15: 363–66.

Martin, E.B. and L. Vigne. 1989. The rise and fall of India's ivory industry. *Pachyderm* 12: 4–21.

Martin, P.S. 1984. Prehistoric overkill: the global model. Pp. 354–403 in *Quaternary extinctions: a prehistoric revolution* (eds. P.S. Martin and R.G. Klein). University of Arizona Press, Tucson.

Mathpal, Y. 1984. *Prehistoric rock paintings of Bhimbetka*. Abhinav Publications, Delhi.

McCrindle, J.W. 1877, reprinted 1926. *Ancient India as described by Megasthenes and Arrian*. Calcutta. Reprinted by Munshiram Manoharlal Publishers, New Delhi, 2000.

McCrindle, J.W. 1901. *Ancient India as described in classical literature*. Westminster. Reprinted by Oriental Books Reprint Corp., New Delhi, 1979.

McKay, G.M. 1973. Behavior and ecology of the Asiatic elephant in southeastern Ceylon. *Smithsonian Contributions to Zoology* 125: 1–113.

McNeely, J.A. and P.S. Wachtel. 1988. *The soul of the tiger: searching for nature's answers in exotic Southeast Asia*. Doubleday, New York.

Mellen, J.D., J.C.E. Barber, and G.W. Miller. 2008. Can we assess the needs of elephants in zoos? Can we meet the needs of elephants in zoos? Pp. 307–26 in Wemmer and Christen (2008).

Menon, V. 2002. *Tusker: the story of the Asian elephant*. Penguin, New Delhi.

Menon, V. and A. Kumar. 1998. *Signed and sealed: the fate of the Asian elephant*. Asian Elephant Research and Conservation Centre, Bangalore, and Wildlife Protection Society of India, New Delhi.

Menon, V., R. Sukumar, and A. Kumar. 1997. *A god in distress: threats of poaching and the ivory trade to the Asian elephant in India*. Asian Elephant Conservation Centre, Bangalore, and Wildlife Protection Society of India, New Delhi.

Menon, V., S.K. Tiwari, P.S. Easa, and R. Sukumar. (eds.) 2005. *Right of passage: elephant corridors of India*. Wildlife Trust of India, New Delhi.

Mikota, S.K., H. Hammatt, and Y. Fahrimal.

2008. Sumatran elephants in crisis: time for change. Pp. 361–80 in Wemmer and Christen (2008).

Miksic, J. 1990. *Borobudur: golden tales of the Buddha*. Periplus Editions, Hong Kong.

Milroy, A.J.W. 1922. *A short treatise on the management of elephants*. Shillong.

Minakshi, C. 1977. *Administration and social life under the Pallavas*. University of Madras, Madras.

Mishra, H.R. 1980. Status of the Asian elephant in Nepal. Pp. 73–74 in Daniel (1980).

Misra, V.N. 2001. Prehistoric human colonization of India. *Journal of Biosciences* 26: 491–531.

Mitra, D. 1942. *Udayagiri and Khandagiri*. Archaeological Survey of India, New Delhi.

Mitra, D. 2003. *Konarak*. Archaeological Survey of India, New Delhi.

Moon, P. 1989. *The British conquest and dominion of India*. Duckworth, London.

Moorey, P.R.S. 1994. *Ancient Mesopotamian materials and industries: the archeological evidence*. Clarendon Press, Oxford.

Moss, C.J. and J.H. Poole. 1983. Relationships and social structure of African elephants. Pp. 315–25 in *Primate social relationships: an integrated approach* (ed. R.A. Hinde). Blackwell, Oxford.

Mueller-Dombois, D. 1972. Crown distortion and elephant distribution in the woody vegetations of Ruhuna National Park, Ceylon. *Ecology* 53: 208–26.

Mukherjee, S.N. (ed.) 1982. *India: history and thought – Essays in honour of A.L. Basham*. Subarnarekha, Calcutta.

N

Nagaswamy, R. 2008. *Mahabalipuram*. Oxford University Press, New Delhi.

Nair, P.V. and M. Gadgil. 1980. The status and distribution of elephant populations of Karnataka. *Journal of the Bombay Natural History Society* 75 (Suppl.): 1000–16.

Nair, S.S.C., P.V. Nair, H.C. Sharatchandra, and M. Gadgil. 1977. An ecological reconnaissance of the proposed Jawahar National Park. *Journal of the Bombay Natural History Society* 74: 401–35.

Nair, S., R. Balakrishnan, C.S. Seelamantula, and R. Sukumar. 2009. Vocalizations of wild Asian elephants (*Elephas maximus*): Structural classification and social context. *The Journal of the Acoustical Society of America* 126: 2768–78.

Nanda, A.C. 2002. Upper Siwalik mammalian fauna of India and associated events. *Journal of Asian Earth Sciences* 21: 47–58.

Nandadeva, B.D. 1986. Rock art sites of Sri Lanka: a catalogue. *Ancient Ceylon* 6: 173–208.

Narain, A.K. 1991. Ganeśa: a protohistory of the idea and the icon. Pp. 19–48 in Brown (1991a).

Naravane, V.S. 1965. The elephant and the lotus. Ch. 5, pp. 51–62 in *The elephant and the lotus: essays in philosophy and culture*. Asia Publishing House, Bombay.

Neginhal, S.G. 1974. *Project Tiger: management plan of the Bandipur Tiger Reserve*. Karnataka Forest Department, Bangalore.

Nicholas, C.W. 1954a. The Ceylon elephant in antiquity. (i) The Sinhalese Period. *The Ceylon Forester* 1: 52–58.

Nicholas, C.W. 1954b. The Ceylon elephant in antiquity. (ii) The Portuguese, Dutch and British Periods. *The Ceylon Forester* 1: 103–11.

Nicholas, C.W. 1959. Irrigation. Ch. 6, Book 3, pp. 352–59 in Attygalle et al. (1959).

Niemuller, C. and R.M. Liptrap. 1991. Altered androstenedione to testosterone ratios and LH concentrations during musth in the captive male Asian elephant (*Elephas maximus*). *Journal of Reproduction and Fertility* 91: 139–46.

Ninkovich, D., R.S.J. Sparks, and M.T. Ledbetter. 1978. The exceptional magnitude and intensity of the Toba eruption, Sumatra: an example of the use of deep-sea tephra layers as a geological tool. *Bulletin Volcanologique* 41: 1–13.

Nyhus, P.J., R. Tilson, and Sumianto. 2000. Crop-raiding elephants and conservation implications at Way Kambas National Park, Sumatra, Indonesia. *Oryx* 34: 262–74.

O

Olivier, R. 1978a. Distribution and status of the Asian elephant. *Oryx* 14: 379–424.

Olivier, R.C.D. 1978b. On the ecology of the Asian elephant. PhD thesis, University of Cambridge, UK.

Oppenheim, A.L. 1969. The banquet of Ashurnasirpal II. Pp. 558–61 in *Ancient Near Eastern texts pertaining to the Old Testament* (ed. J.B. Pritchard). 3rd edn. Princeton University Press, Princeton, NJ.

Osborn, F.V. and M.D. Vinton (eds.). 1999. *Proceedings of the conference: conservation of the Asian elephant in Indochina, Hanoi, Vietnam, 24–27 November 1999*. Fauna and Flora International, Hanoi.

Osborn, H.F. 1936 and 1942. *Proboscidea: A monograph of the discovery, evolution, migration and extinction of the mastodonts and elephants of the world*, 2 vols. American Museum Press, New York.

P

Pal, P. 1994. *The peaceful liberators: Jain art from India*. Los Angeles County Museum of Art, Los Angeles.

Pal, P. (ed.) 1995. *Ganesh the benevolent*. Marg Publications, Mumbai.

Pan, W., L. Lin, A. Luo, and Li. Zhang. 2009. Corridor use by Asian elephants. *Integrative Zoology* 4: 200–31.

Pappu, S., Y. Gunnell, M. Taieb, J.P. Brugal, K. Anupama, R. Sukumar, and A. Kumar. 2003. Excavations at the Palaeolithic site of Attirampakkam, south India. *Antiquity* 77 (297), Sept. 2003 (online).

Pappu, S., Y. Gunnell, K. Akhilesh, R. Braucher, M. Taieb, F. Demory, and N. Thouveny. 2011. Early Pleistocene presence of Acheulian homonyms in south India. *Science* 331: 1596–98.

Paranavitana S. 1959a. The introduction of Buddhism. Pp. 125–43 in Attygalle et al. (1959).

Paranavitana, S. 1959b. Triumph of Dutthagamani. Ch. 3, Book 2. Pp. 144–63 in Attygalle et al. (1959).

Paton, W.R. (trans.) 1923. *Polybius: the histories*, Vol. 3, Books 5–8. Loeb Classical Library, Harvard University Press, Cambridge Massachusetts.

Payne, K.B., W.R. Langbauer, Jr., and E.M. Thomas. 1986. Infrasonic calls of the Asian elephant (*Elephas maximus*). *Behavioural Ecology and Sociobiology* 18: 297–301.

Peacock, E.H. 1933. *A game book for Burma and adjoining territories*. H.F. and G. Witherby, London.

Peris, M. 2005. *Kandula: the elephant at war*. Godage International Publishers, Colombo.

Petraglia, M., R. Korisettar, N. Boivin, C. Clarkson, P. Ditchfield, S. Jones, J. Koshy, M.M. Lahr, C. Oppenheimer, D. Pyle, R. Roberts, J.C. Schwenniger, L. Arnold, and K. White. 2007. Middle Pleistocene assemblages from the Indian subcontinent before and after the Toba super-eruption. *Science* 317: 114–16.

Plotnik, J.M., F.B.M. de Waal, and D. Reiss. 2006. Self-recognition in an Asian elephant. *Proceedings of the National Academy of Sciences* (USA) 103: 17053–57.

Pollock, A.J.O. 1894. *Sporting days in southern India*. Horace Cox, London.

Poole, J.H. 1989. Announcing intent: the aggressive state of musth in African elephants. *Animal Behaviour* 37: 140–52.

Poole, J.H., K. Payne, W.R. Langbauer, and C.J. Moss. 1988. The social context of some very low frequency calls of African elephants. *Behavioural Ecology and Sociobiology* 22: 385–92.

Pradhan, S. 2001. *Rock art in Orissa*. Aryan Books International, New Delhi.

R

Ram, V. 2007. *Elephant kingdom: sculptures from Indian architecture*. Mapin Publishing, Ahmedabad.

Ramakrishnan, P.S. 1992. *Shifting agriculture and sustainable development: an interdisciplinary study from northeastern India*. MAB Series, Vol. 10, UNESCO, Paris.

Ramakrishnan, U., J.A. Santosh, U. Ramakrishnan, and R. Sukumar. 1998. The population and conservation status of Asian elephants in the Periyar Tiger Reserve, southern India. *Current Science* 74: 110–13.

Rangarajan, L.N. (ed. and trans.) 1992. *Kautilya: the Arthashastra*. Penguin, New Delhi.

Rangarajan, M. 2001. *India's wildlife history: an introduction*. Permanent Black, New Delhi.

Rangarajan, M., A. Desai, R. Sukumar, P.S. Easa, V. Menon, S. Vincent, S. Ganguly, B.K. Talukdar, B. Singh, D. Mudappa, S. Chowdhary, and A.N. Prasad. 2010. *Gajah: securing the future for elephants in India*. The report of the Elephant Task Force, Ministry of Environment and Forests, New Delhi.

Rao, V.N.S. and M.H. Krishnaswamy. 1941. *List of the more important trees, shrubs, climbers and herbs occurring in the forests of the Madras Presidency with their local names*. Government Press, Madras.

Rasmussen, L.E.L. 1998. Chemical communication: an integral part of functional Asian elephant (*Elephas maximus*) society. *Ecoscience* 5: 410–26.

Rasmussen, L.E., I.O. Buss, D.L. Hess, and M.J. Schmidt. 1984. Testosterone and dihydrotestosterone concentrations in elephant serum and temporal gland secretions. *Biology of Reproduction* 30: 352–62.

Rasmussen, L.E.L. and B.L. Munger. 1996. The sensorineural specializations of the trunk tip (finger) of the Asian elephant, *Elephas maximus*. *The Anatomical Record* 246: 127–34.

Rasmussen, L.E.L. and V. Krishnamurthy. 2000. How chemical signals integrate Asian elephant society: the known and the unknown. *Zoo Biology* 19: 405–23.

Rasmussen, L.E.L., H.S. Riddle, and V. Krishnamurthy. 2002. Mellifluous matures to malodorous in musth. *Nature* 415: 975–76.

Ratnagar, S. 2001. *Understanding Harappa: civilization in the Greater Indus Valley*. Tulika, New Delhi.

Rensch, B. 1957. The intelligence of elephants. *Scientific American* (February): 44–49.

Ribbentrop, B. 1900. *Forestry in British India*. Government Printing, Calcutta.

Ringis, R. 1996. *Elephants of Thailand in myth, art and reality*. Oxford University Press, New York.

Rizvi, S.A.A. 1975a. The Muslim ruling dynasties. Pp. 245–65 in Basham (1975).

Rizvi, S.A.A. 1975b. Islam in medieval India. Pp. 281–93 in Basham (1975).

Rogers, A. and H. Beveridge (trans.) 1909–14. *The Tuzuk-i-Jahangiri or memoirs of Jahangir*, 2 vols. Royal Asiatic Society, London.

Rogers, G.M. 2005. *Alexander: the ambiguity of greatness*. Random House, New York.

Rohland, N., A. Malaspinas, J.L. Pollack, M. Slatkin, P. Matheus, and M. Hofreiter. 2007. Proboscidean mitogenomics: chronology and mode of elephant evolution using mastodon as outgroup. *PLoS Biology* 5: 1663–71.

Rolfe, J.C. (trans.) 1946. *Quintus Curtius: history of Alexander*. Harvard University Press, Cambridge, Massachusetts.

Rooney, D. 1999. *Angkor*. Odyssey Publications, Hong Kong.

Ryder, A.W. 1912. *Kalidasa: translations of Shakuntala and other works*. J.M. Dent and Sons, London.

Ryley, J.H. (ed.) 1899. *Ralph Fitch: England's pioneer to India and Burma*. T. Fisher Unwin, London.

S

Saberwal, V., M. Rangarajan, and A. Kothari. 2000. *People, parks and wildlife: towards coexistence*. Orient Longman, New Delhi.

Sachau, E.C. (trans.) 1888. *Alberuni's India*. Trübner and Co., London. Reprinted by Rupa and Co., New Delhi, 2002.

Sadhale, N. and Y.L. Nene. 2004a. On elephants in Manasollasa: 1. Characteristics, habitat, methods of capturing and training. *Asian Agri-history* 8: 5–25.

Sadhale, N. and Y.L. Nene. 2004b. On elephants in Manasollasa: 2. Diseases and treatment. *Asian Agri-history* 8: 115–27.

Sadhale, N. and Y.L. Nene. 2004c. On elephants in Manasollasa: 3. *Gajavahyali*: sports with elephants in the arena. *Asian Agri-history* 8: 189–213.

Sanderson, G.P. 1878. *Thirteen years among the wild beasts of India*. W.H. Allen, London.

Sanford, J.H. 1991. Literary aspects of Japan's dual-Ganesa cult. Pp. 287–335 in Brown (1991a).

Santiapillai, C. and P. Jackson. 1990. *The Asian elephant: an action plan for its conservation*. IUCN – The World Conservation Union, Gland, Switzerland.

Santiapillai, C. and W.S. Ramono. 1990. Sumatran Elephant Database. IUCN/SSC Asian Elephant Specialist Group Newsletter No. 5, Special Issue, Summer.

Santiapillai, C. and W.S. Ramono. 1993. Why do elephants raid crops in Sumatra? *Gajah* 11: 59–63.

Santiapillai, C. and R. Sukumar. (eds.) 2004. *The Asian elephant: status and conservation action plan*. Final report to USFWS. IUCN/SSC Asian Elephant Specialist Group. Accessed at URL http://www.asiannature.org.

Santiapillai, C., M.R. Chambers, and I. Ishwaran. 1984. Aspects of the ecology of the Asian elephant *Elephas maximus* L. in the Ruhuna National Park, Sri Lanka. *Biological Conservation* 29: 47–61.

Santiapillai, C., P. Fernando, and M. Gunewardene. 2004. Sri Lanka. Ch. 19 in Santiapillai and Sukumar (2004). Reprinted in *Gajah* 25: 91–102, 2006.

Sar, C.K., S. Varma, and R. Sukumar. 2008. The Asian elephants in Orissa, India. Asian Nature Conservation Foundation, Bangalore.

Saravana, V. 2008. Economic exploitation of forest resources in south India during the pre-Forest Act colonial era, 1793–1882. *International Forestry Review* 10: 65–73.

Sarkar, J. 1917. *Anecdotes of Aurangzib and historical essays*. M.C. Sarkar and Sons, Calcutta.

Sarkar, J. 1960. *Military history of India*. Orient Longmans, New Delhi.

Sastri, K.A.N. 1975. *A history of south India: from prehistoric times to the fall of Vijayanagar*. 4th edn. Oxford University Press, New Delhi.

Sayce, A.H. (trans.) 1888. *Records of the past: ancient monuments of Egypt and western Asia*, Vol. 1. Samuel Bagster and Sons, London.

Schmitt, D. 2008. View from the big top. Pp. 227–36 in Wemmer and Christen (2008).

Scigliano, E. 2002. *Love, war and circuses: the age-old relationship between elephants and humans*. Houghton-Mifflin, Boston and New York.

Scullard, H.H. 1974. *The elephant in the Greek and Roman world*. Cornell University Press, Ithaca, NY.

Settar, S. 1992. *The Hoysala temples*, 2 vols. Kala Yatra Publications, Bangalore.

Sewell, R. 1900. *A forgotten empire (Vijayanagar)*. London. Reprinted with the title *Chronicles of Paes and Nuniz* by Asian Educational Services, New Delhi, 2003.

Shahi, S.P. and S. Chowdhury. 1985. Report of the Central India Task Force (Bihar and Orissa). IUCN/SSC Asian Elephant Specialist Group.

Shamasastry, R. (trans.) 1915. *Kautilya's Arthasastra*. 6th edn. published by Mysore Printing and Publishing House, Mysore, 1960.

Shariff Daim, M. 2002. The care and management of domesticated elephants in Malaysia. Pp. 149–56 in Baker and Kashio (2002).

Sharma, R.S. 2005. *India's ancient past*. Oxford University Press, New Delhi.

Shelton, J.A. 2001. The display of elephants in ancient Roman arenas. ISAZ Newsletter, May 2001, pp. 2–6. Accessed at URL http://www.vetmed.ucdavis.edu.

Shepherd, C.R. and V. Nijman. 2008. Elephant and ivory trade in Myanmar. TRAFFIC Southeast Asia, Petaling Jaya, Selangor, Malaysia.

Shetti, B.V. 1995. Aspects of Ganesha worship in Maharashtra. Pp.13–26 in Pal (1995).

Shim, P.S. 2003. Another look at the Borneo elephant. *Sabah Society Journal* 20: 7–14.

Shoshani, J. and G.H. Marchant. 2001. Hyoid apparatus: a little known complex of bones and its "contribution" to proboscidean evolution. The World of Elephants – International Congress, Rome 2001.

Shoshani, J. and P. Tassy (eds.) 1996. *The Proboscidea: evolution and palaeoecology of elephants and their relatives*. Oxford University Press, New York.

Shuckburg, E.S. (trans.) 1899. *The letters of Cicero*, Vol. 1. George Bell and Sons, London.

Singh, K.N. 1995. Asiatic elephants in U.P. (India): status and strategy for conservation. Pp. 32–48 in Daniel and Datye (1995).

Singh, R.K. 2002. *Elephants in exile: a rapid assessment of the human-elephant conflict in Chhattisgarh*. Wildlife Trust of India, New Delhi.

Singh, R.K. and S. Chowdhury. 1999. Effect of mine discharge on the pattern of riverine habitat use of elephants *Elephas maximus* and other mammals in Singhbum forests, Bihar, India. *Journal of Environmental Management* 57: 177–92.

Singh, S.D. 1965. *Ancient Indian warfare*. Leiden. Reprinted by Motilal Banarsidass, New Delhi, 1989.

Singh, U. 2009. *A history of ancient and early mediaeval India: from the Stone Age to the 12th century*. Pearson Education, New Delhi.

Singh, V.B. 1969. The elephant (*Elephas maximus* Linn.) in Uttar Pradesh, India. *Journal of the Bombay Natural History Society* 66: 239–50.

Singh, V.B. 1978. The elephant in U.P. (India): a resurvey of its status after 10 years. *Journal of the Bombay Natural History Society* 75: 71–82.

Sivaganesan, N. and A. Kumar. 1995. Status of feral elephants in Andamans. Pp. 97–119 in Daniel and Datye (1995).

Sivasundaram, S. 2005. Treading knowledge: the East India Company's elephants in India and Britain. *The Historical Journal* 48: 27–63.

Skaria, A. 1998. Timber conservancy, desiccationism and scientific forestry: the Dangs 1840s–1920s. Pp. 596–635 in Grove et al. (1998).

Spear, P. 1965. *A history of India, Vol. 2: from the sixteenth century to the twentieth century*. Penguin, New Delhi.

Srikrachang, M. and S. Srikosamatara. 2004. Thailand. Ch. 20 in Santiapillai and Sukumar (2004).

Srivastava, S., T.P. Singh, H. Singh, S.P.S. Kushwaha, and P.S. Roy. 2002. Assessment of large-scale deforestation in Sonitpur district of Assam. *Current Science* 82: 1479–84.

Stanford, C.B. 1999. *The hunting apes: meat eating and the origins of human behavior*. Princeton University Press, Princeton, NJ.

Stellman, J.M., S.D. Stellman, R. Christian, T. Weber, and C. Tomasallo. 2003. The extent and patterns of usage of Agent Orange and other herbicides in Vietnam. *Nature* 422, 681–87.

Stewart, A. and G. Long (trans.) 1892. *Plutarch's Lives*, 4 vols. George Bell and Sons, London.

Stibig, H.J. and J.P. Malingreau. 2003. Forest cover of insular southeast Asia mapped from recent satellite images of coarse spatial resolution. *Ambio* 32: 469–75.

Stierlin, H. 2002. *Hindu India: from Khajuraho to the temple city of Madurai.* Taschen, Köln.

Stiles, D. 2008. *An assessment of the illegal ivory trade in Viet Nam.* TRAFFIC Southeast Asia, Petaling Jaya, Selangor, Malaysia.

Stracey, P.D. 1963. *Elephant Gold.* Weidenfeld and Nicolson, London.

Storer, P. 1981. Elephant populations in Thailand. *Natural History Bulletin of the Siam Society* 29: 1–30.

Sukumar, R. 1985. Ecology of the Asian elephant (*Elephas maximus*) and its interaction with man in south India. PhD thesis, Indian Institute of Science, Bangalore.

Sukumar, R. 1987. Conserving the Nilgiris. *Frontline* July 25, pp. 76–81.

Sukumar, R. 1989. *The Asian elephant: ecology and management.* Cambridge University Press, Cambridge, UK.

Sukumar, R. 1994a. Wayward elephants: issues of habitat conservation. *Frontline* Feb. 25, pp. 80–82.

Sukumar, R. 1994b. *Elephant days and nights: ten years with the Indian elephant.* Oxford University Press, New Delhi.

Sukumar, R. 1995. Elephant raiders and rogues. *Natural History* 104: 52–60.

Sukumar, R. 1996. Project Elephant: answering a distress call. *The Hindu Survey of the Environment*, pp. 159–63.

Sukumar, R. 2003. *The living elephants: evolutionary ecology, behavior and conservation.* Oxford University Press, New York.

Sukumar, R., S.K. Bhattacharya, and R.V. Krishnamurthy. 1987. Carbon isotopic evidence for different feeding patterns in an Asian elephant population. *Current Science* 56: 11–14.

Sukumar, R. and M. Gadgil. 1988. Male-female differences in foraging on crops by Asian elephants. *Animal Behaviour* 36: 1233–35.

Sukumar, R. and R. Ramesh. 1992. Stable carbon isotope ratios in Asian elephant collagen: implications for dietary studies. *Oecologia* 91: 536–39.

Sukumar, R., R. Ramesh, R.K. Pant, and G. Rajagopalan. 1993. A d^{13}C record of late Quaternary climate change from tropical peats in southern India. *Nature* 364: 703–06.

Sukumar, R., V. Krishnamurthy, C. Wemmer, and M. Rodden. 1997. Demography of captive Asian elephants (*Elephas maximus*) in southern India. *Zoo Biology* 16: 263–72.

Sukumar, R., S. Varma, N.X. Dang, and T. Van Thanh. 2002. *The status and conservation of Asian elephants in Cat Tien National Park, Vietnam.* Technical Report, WWF – Cat Tien National Park Conservation Project, Vietnam.

Sukumar, R., A.B. Venkataraman, J.V. Cheeran, P.P. Mujumdar, N. Baskaran, G. Dharmarajan, M. Roy, H.S. Suresh, and K. Narendran. 2003. *Study of elephants in Buxa Tiger Reserve and adjoining areas in northern West Bengal and preparation of conservation action plan.* Report submitted to West Bengal Forest Department. Centre for Ecological Sciences, Indian Institute of Science, Bangalore.

Sukumar, R., P.S. Easa, S. Varma, A. Venkataraman, N. Baskaran, and N. Sivaganesan. 2004. South India. Ch. 11 in Santiapillai and Sukumar (2004). Reprinted in *Gajah* 25: 71–86, 2006.

Suprayogi, B, J. Sugardjito, and R.P.H. Lilley. 2002. Management of Sumatran elephants in Indonesia: problems and challenges. Pp. 183–94 in Baker and Kashio (2002).

Surovell, T., N. Waguespack, and P.J. Brantingham. 2005. Global archaeological evidence for proboscidean overkill. *Proceedings of the National Academy of Sciences* (USA) 102: 6231–6236.

Swain, D. 2008. Elephants in art, architecture and history of Orissa. *Orissa Review*, June 2008, pp. 36–49.

Swain, D. and S.K. Patnaik. 2002. Elephants of Orissa: conservation issues and management options. *The Indian Forester* 128: 145–54.

T

Taylor, V.J. and T.B. Poole. 1998. Captive breeding and infant mortality in Asian elephants: a comparison between twenty western zoos and three eastern elephant centers. *Zoo Biology* 17: 311–32.

Tennent, J.E. 1859. *Ceylon: an account of the island*, 2 vols. Longman Green, Longman and Roberts, London. Reprinted by Asian Educational Services, New Delhi, 1999.

Thackston, W.H. (trans.) 1999. *The Jahangirnama.* Freer Gallery of Art and Arthur M. Sackler Gallery, Smithsonian Institution, Washington DC and Oxford University Press, New York.

Thapar, R. 1982. The *Rāmāyana*: theme and variation. Pp. 221–53 in Mukherjee (1982).

Thapar R. 2002. *Early India: from the origins to AD 1300.* Allen Lane, Penguin, London.

Thomas, E.J. 1927. *The life of Buddha as legend and history.* Kegan Paul, Trench, Trübner and Co., London.

Thomas, P.K. and P.P. Joglekar. 1994. Holocene faunal studies in India. *Man and Environment* 19: 179–203.

Thundy, Z.P. 1993. *Buddha and Christ: nativity stories and Indian traditions.* E.J. Brill, Leiden.

Tilson, R., K. Soemarna, W. Ramono, R. Sukumar, U. Seal, K. Traylor-Holzer, and C. Santiapillai. 1994. *Asian elephant in Sumatra: population and habitat viability analysis.* IUCN/SSC Captive Breeding Specialist Group.

Tiwari, S.K., S.K. Karyong, P. Sarkar, A. Choudhury, and A.C. Williams. 2005. Elephant corridors of north-eastern India. Ch. 7 in Menon et al. (2005).

Trautmann, T.R. 1982. Elephants and the Mauryas. Pp. 254–81 in Mukherjee (1982).

U

Uga, U. 2004. Myanmar. Ch. 17 in Santiapillai and Sukumar (2004).

Underhill, M.M. 1921. *The Hindu religious year.* Oxford University Press, London. Reprinted by Asian Educational Services, New Delhi, 1998.

V

Vallely, A. 2002. From liberation to ecology: ethical discourses among orthodox and diaspora Jains. Pp. 209–10 in Chapple (2002).

van Buitenen, J.A.B. (trans.). 1973. *The Mahabharata, 1. Book of the Beginning.* University of Chicago Press, Chicago.

Vancuylenberg, B.W.B. 1977. Feeding behaviour of the Asiatic elephant in southeast Sri Lanka in relation to conservation. *Biological Conservation* 12: 33–54.

Varadarajaiyer, E.S. 1945. *The elephant in the Tamil land.* Annamalai University, Annamalainagar.

Varma, S. 2008. Spatial distribution of Asian elephant (*Elephas maximus*) and its habitat usage pattern in Kalakad-Mundanthurai Tiger Reserve, Western Ghats, southern India. *Current Science* 94: 501–06.

Varma, S., N.X. Dang, T.V. Thanh, and R. Sukumar. 2008. The elephants (*Elephas maximus*) of Cat Tien National Park, Vietnam: status and conservation of a vanishing population. *Oryx* 42: 92–99.

Vartanyan, S.L., V.E. Garutt, and A.V. Sher, 1993. Holocene dwarf mammoths from Wrangel island in the Siberian Arctic. *Nature* 362: 337–40.

Venkataraman, A.B., N. Venkatesa Kumar, S. Varma, and R. Sukumar. 2002. Conservation of a flagship species: prioritizing Asian elephant

(*Elephas maximus*) conservation units in southern India. *Current Science* 82: 1022–32.

Venkataraman, A.B., R. Saandeep, N. Baskaran, M. Roy, A. Madhivanan, and R. Sukumar. 2005. Using satellite telemetry to mitigate elephant-human conflict: an experiment in northern West Bengal, India. *Current Science* 88: 1827–1831.

Verghese, A. 2002. *Hampi*. Oxford University Press, New Delhi.

Vidya T.N.C., P. Fernando, D.J. Melnick, and R. Sukumar. 2005. Population genetic structure of the Asian elephant (*Elephas maximus*) in southern India based on mitochondrial and microsatellite DNA. *Heredity* 94: 71–80.

Vidya, T.N.C. and R. Sukumar. 2005. Social organization of the Asian elephant (*Elephas maximus*) in southern India inferred from microsatellite DNA. *Journal of Ethology* 23: 205–10.

Vidya, T.N.C., S. Varma, N.X. Dang, T.V. Thanh, and R. Sukumar. 2007. Minimum population size, genetic diversity, and social structure of the Asian elephant in Cat Tien National Park and its adjoining areas, Vietnam, based on molecular genetic analyses. *Conservation Genetics* 8: 1471–78.

Vidya, T.N.C., R. Sukumar, and D.J. Melnick. 2009. Range-wide mtDNA phylogeography yields insights into the origins of Asian elephants. *Proceedings of the Royal Society B* 276: 893–902.

Villa, P. 1990. Torralba and Aridos: elephant exploitation in middle Pleistocene Spain. *Journal of Human Evolution* 19: 299–309.

Visvanathan, M. 2009. Of death and fertility: landscapes of heroism in ancient south India. Pp. 174–204 in U. Singh and N. Lahiri (eds.), *Ancient India: new research*. Oxford University Press, New Delhi.

Vuthy, L., M. Soriyun, and C. Dany. 2004. Cambodia. Ch. 5 in Santiapillai and Sukumar (2004).

W

Wakankar, S.Y. and V.B. Mhaiskar (eds.) 2006. *Maharsi Palakapya's Gajasastram*. Bharatiya Kala Prakashan, Delhi.

Wangchuk, S. 2007. Maintaining ecological resilience by linking protected areas through biological corridors in Bhutan. *Tropical Ecology* 48: 176–87.

Watve, M.G. and R. Sukumar. 1997. Asian elephants with longer tusks have lower parasite loads. *Current Science* 72: 885–89.

Weiler, H. and M. Soriyun. 1999. The updated status of the wild Asian elephant (*Elephas maximus*) in Cambodia. Pp. 51–53 in Osborn and Vinton (1999).

Weiler, H., C. Dang, K. Tong, and S. Han. 2001. *Chaw o lebess: a report on the status, distribution and issues surrounding the domesticated elephant in Cambodia*. Fauna and Flora International, Indochina Programme, Hanoi.

Welles, C.B. (trans.) 1963. *Didorus Siculus: the library of history*, Vol. 8. Loeb Classical Library, Harvard University Press, Cambridge, Massachusetts.

Wemmer, C. 1995. Gaonbura Sahib – A.J.W. Milroy of Assam. Pp. 483–96 in Daniel and Datye (1995).

Wemmer, C. and C.A. Christen. eds. 2008. *Elephants and ethics: toward a morality of coexistence*. The Johns Hopkins University Press, Baltimore.

Werellagama, D.R.I.B., V. Jeyavijitha, J. Manatunga, and M. Nakayama. 2004. Lessons learned from communities displaced by the Mahaweli multipurpose development project, Sri Lanka. Accessed at URL http://www.wrrc.dpri.kyoto-u.ac.japan.

Westing, A.H. 1971. Ecological effects of military defoliation on the forests of South Vietnam. *BioScience* 21: 893–98.

Whitehouse, A.M. and E.R. Harley. 2001. Post-bottleneck genetic diversity of elephant populations in South Africa, revealed using microsatellite analysis. *Molecular Ecology* 10: 2139–49.

Williams, A.C. and A.J.T. Johnsingh, 1996. *Status survey of elephants (Elephas maximus), their habitats and an assessment of elephant-human conflict in Garo Hills, Meghalaya*. Wildlife Institute of India, Dehra Dun.

Williams, A.C., A.J.T. Johnsingh, and P.R. Krausman. 2001. Elephant-human conflicts in Rajaji National Park, northwestern India. *Wildlife Society Bulletin* 29: 1097–1104.

Williams, J.H. 1950. *Elephant Bill*. Doubleday, Garden City, New York.

Williams, M.A.J., S.H. Ambrose, S. van der Kaars, C. Ruehlemann, U. Chattopadhyaya, J. Pal, and P. Chauhan. 2009. Environmental impact of the 73 ka Toba super-eruption in South Asia. *Palaeogeography, Palaeoclimatology, Palaeoecology* 284: 295–314.

Wing, L.D. and I.O. Buss. 1970. Elephants and forests. *Wildlife Monographs* 19: 1–92.

Wisumperuma, D. 2004. Human–elephant relationships in Sri Lanka: an historical and archaeological perspective. Pp. 6–12 in J. Jayewardene (ed.), *Endangered Elephants:*

Past, Present and Future. Biodiversity and Elephant Conservation Trust, Rajagiriya, Sri Lanka.

Wood, M. 1997. *In the footsteps of Alexander the Great: a journey from Greece to Asia*. BBC Books, London.

Woodward, F.L. (trans.) 1935. *Minor anthologies of the Pali canon*. Part 2: *Udāna and Itivuthakka*. Oxford University Press, London.

X

Xu, J. 2001. The enigmatic art of Sanxingdui: bronze trees and masks evoke the spirit worlds of a lost civilization in China. *Natural History Magazine*, Nov. 2001.

Y

Yang, L. and E. Capon. 2000. *Masks of mystery: ancient Chinese bronzes from Sanxingdui*. Art Gallery of New South Wales, Sydney.

Yonge, C.D. (trans.) 1854. *The Deipnosophists or banquet of the learned of Athenaeus* (3 vols.). Henry G. Bohn, London.

Yule, H. (trans.) 1903. *The travels of Marco Polo*, 2 vols. 3rd revised edn. published by H. Cordier, Paris, 1920.

Z

Zhang, L. 2004. China. Ch. 6 in Santiapillai and Sukumar (2004).

Zhang, L., N. Hua, and S. Sun, 2008. Wildlife trade, consumption and conservation awareness in southwest China. *Biodiversity and Conservation* 17: 1493–1516.

index

About the Author

Raman Sukumar is Professor and Chair of the Centre for Ecological Sciences, Indian Institute of Science, Bangalore. Born at Chennai in 1955, Sukumar's early interests in natural history developed here; he documented the flora and fauna of Guindy National Park during the 1970s. Moving to Bangalore in 1979, he obtained his PhD in Ecology in 1985 from the Indian Institute of Science. His thesis on the ecology of elephant-human interactions, considered a landmark in this field, was published by Cambridge University Press.

Sukumar's research on the elephant includes its movement patterns, genetics, reproductive biology, communication, and cultural history. In 1992 he helped the Indian government set up Project Elephant, and during 1997–2004 he was Chair of the World Conservation Union's Asian Elephant Specialist Group and initiated conservation programmes in countries such as Burma, Cambodia, and Vietnam. In 1997, Sukumar set up the Asian Nature Conservation Foundation that has carried out several field projects in India and other Asian countries. He has also been a member of the Indian Board for Wildlife (chaired by the Prime Minister).

Sukumar has travelled and lectured extensively around the world and is Adjunct Professor at Columbia University, New York (since 2001). He is the recipient of several awards including the Presidential Award of the Chicago Zoological Society (1992), Order of the Golden Ark (The Netherlands, 1997), Whitley Gold Award for International Nature Conservation, UK (2003), International Cosmos Prize, Japan (2006), J.C. Bose National Fellowship (2010), and Taru Lalvani Award of Rotary Club of Bombay (2011). In 2007 he received a commendation from the Prime Minister for his contribution to the Intergovernmental Panel on Climate Change that shared the Nobel Peace Prize. His publications include three books and over a hundred scholarly papers in the area of elephant biology, tropical forest ecology, climate change, and nature conservation.

An adult male elephant in musth walks majestically along a dry riverbed in the Motichur Sanctuary in Uttarakhand (2004).